HIMSS Dictionary of Healthcare Information Technology Terms, Acronyms and Organizations

Third Edition

- Authoritative, Timely Definitions
- Comprehensive Acronym Listings
- Organizations and Associations Linked to Health IT
- Healthcare Credentials
- Evolution of Health IT Terms

D0208914

About HIMSS

HIMSS is a cause-based, not-for-profit organization exclusively focused on providing global leadership for the optimal use of information technology (IT) and management systems for the betterment of health and healthcare. Founded 52 years ago, HIMSS and its related organizations are headquartered in Chicago with additional offices in the United States, Europe and Asia. HIMSS represents more than 52,000 individual members, of which more than two thirds work in healthcare provider, governmental and not-for-profit organizations. HIMSS also includes over 600 corporate members and more than 225 not-for-profit partner organizations that share our mission of transforming healthcare through the best use of information technology and management systems. HIMSS frames and leads healthcare practices and public policy through its content expertise, professional development, research initiatives, and media vehicles designed to promote information and management systems' contributions to improving the quality, safety, access, and cost-effectiveness of patient care. To learn more about HIMSS and to find out how to join us and our members in advancing our cause, please visit our website at www.himss.org.

HIMSS Vision

Advancing the best use of information and management systems for the betterment of healthcare.

HIMSS Mission

To lead healthcare transformation through the effective use of health information technology.

© 2013 by the Healthcare Information and Management Systems Society.

All rights reserved. No part of this publication may be reproduced, adapted, translated, stored in a retrieval system, or transmitted in any form or by any means, electronic, mechanical, photocopying, recording, or otherwise, without the prior written permission of the publisher.

Printed in the U.S.A. 5 4 3 2 1

Requests for permission to reproduce any part of this work should be sent to:

Permissions Editor
HIMSS
33 W. Monroe, Suite 1700
Chicago, IL 60603
mschlossberg@himss.org

ISBN: 978-1-938904-28-8

The inclusion of an organization name, product or service in this publication should not be considered as an endorsement of such organization, product, or service, nor is the failure to include an organization name, product or service to be construed as disapproval.

For more information about HIMSS, please visit www.himss.org

Contents

Foreword

By J. Michael Fitzmaurice, PhD, FACMI

After reading 10 years of bi-weekly summaries of my health information technology activities, my boss told me, 'I am starting the get the hang of some of these acronyms.' It may have helped that at one time I started a list of acronyms. The pressure of a growing number of health IT events, plus keeping up with my assigned duties, kept me from continuing the glossary. Also, by the time readers of my summaries reached the glossary at the end, they had already figured out or read in my summary what the acronym meant. Many workers in health IT probably write summaries for their bosses, too, and use many of the same acronyms. It is my pleasure to let you know that you don't have to invent a glossary for your boss; this dictionary contains most of the acronyms you will need and explains them well.

With my glossary work behind me, I quickly saw the value of joining a team to produce the first HIMSS health informatics dictionary. With talented contributors outpacing together what any of us alone could have done, the resulting work become an accepted reference. Now, in its third edition its usefulness is established for informatics practitioners, our bosses, and our colleagues in other fields who want to know more about what we do.

You may ask, 'Why three editions in six years?' Well, every week a new committee, organization, or project springs forth with an ambitions scope of work and a three-letter acronym. That is a generalization, of course; sometimes they are four-, five-, and six-letter acronyms. Indeed, sometimes they are three letters when logic says they should be four—CMS, anyone? My favorite acronym is DAWG. Within the Department of Health & Human Services (HHS), it stood at first for Data Analysis Working Group. (Those of you who remember anything from the cartoons of the 1960s may understand why I never volunteered to be the Deputy to the DAWG leader.) Then the group morphed into the HHS Data Council.

Never fear, several years later the Data Architecture Work Group sprang forth from the HHS Office of the Chief Information Officer, adopting the DAWG acronym. Alas, that group has now morphed into the HHS Data Architecture Committee. Nevertheless, I have hopes the acronym will rise again and perhaps deserve a place in the HIMSS Data Dictionary Hall of Fame. It has my vote.

In addition to keeping up with a growing number of health informatics activities, there is another reason to consult this dictionary—to test yourself. Some people at some point in their lives began 'reading' a word dictionary to build their vocabularies and to assess of how many words they knew the meaning of. In a similar manner, as I initially read through this informatics dictionary, I began challenging myself to see how many terms I knew and could accurately relate to other terms. Can any reader of this dictionary avoid challenging himself or herself?

Dr. Fitzmaurice is Senior Science Advisor for Information Technology at the Agency for Healthcare Research and Quality (AHRQ), a federal agency within the Department of Health & Human Services. He can be reached at michael.fitzmaurice@ahrq.hhs.gov.

Foreword

by Raymond D. Aller, MD, FHIMSS

I am honored to have contributed the Foreword to the first three editions of this dictionary. This volume has come to occupy an important niche within healthcare informatics.

My first contact with clinical informatics and pathology informatics was via a healthcare word book—I contributed to the first edition of SNOMED, which has now become the standard international nomenclature for medical diagnoses, findings and more. I was also fortunate to be involved in the evolution of the LOINC code—for defining the diagnostic and therapeutic procedures used throughout healthcare. The *HIMSS Dictionary* occupies a different niche: words defining the systems, devices and procedures we use to manage medical information.

My colleagues tell me that one of the most daunting aspects of dealing with health information technology and informatics is the bewildering array of terminology used to describe and characterize this field of endeavor. In some respects, this represents a microcosm of the English language. English is unique among modern languages in the sheer number of entities it contains. Some estimates place the number of words in English at well over a million. This is more than five times the number of words in any other language. A century ago, the language of diplomacy was French, the language of medicine was Latin, the language of chemistry and engineering was German. Today, English has become dominant in all these fields. In reading texts that present the same information in two languages, in adjacent columns, I'm struck that that the English version is notably shorter than the foreign language text. English has such a large number of unique words that gradations of meaning can be conveyed with a single word, while (for example) the speaker of French must use two to three words to say the same thing.

When I began medical school, we were advised (correctly) that the first two years would be largely an intense vocabulary lesson. I still learn new words every day, and where I need a word to describe a concept, I sometimes invent one. But the words of both information technology and medicine out-do me.

Words permit us to precisely characterize a concept and communicate with others in a field of endeavor without resorting to multisyllabic circumlocutions. Information technology in general has created a vast number of new concepts, and clinical information technology and clinical informatics have been particularly prolific. Not surprisingly, the nexus of medicine (with a huge vocabulary) and information systems (with a rapidly growing and volatile terminology) makes for an explosion of expressions.

Given this plethora of words and terms, how does the ordinary health professional have any hope of coping? We believe that the compendium you now hold in your hands can be of assistance. This book focuses on terms emerging from the nexus of information technology and healthcare. For general information technology terms, we refer you to other sources, such as *Newton's Telecom Dictionary* (print only); *Online Dictionary for Library and Information Science* (print and online), and *Jones Media and Information Technology Encyclopedia* (online only). Given a concept that you want to express in a word, we refer you to the various online reverse-dictionaries, including www.onelook.com/reverse-dictionary.shtml or www.wordtree.com.

A particularly common source of obscure and unclear terms are the acronyms so prolific in the language of both medicine and information technology. The same acronym may refer to several different concepts. These have become so problematic in hospital charts that hospitals now publish lists of 'approved' abbreviations. In one Los Angeles hospital, we saw an apparent outbreak of Crimean hemorrhagic fever; upon investigation, these indeed were patients with 'CHF,' but congestive heart failure was the intended meaning.

When we operate at the intersection of two complex disciplines, the numbers of acronyms proliferate. For example, one's professional affiliations (organizational memberships, etc.) are often indicated by a string of acronyms following the name. In the first edition of this book, a daunting string followed my name: MD, FHIMSS, FACMI, HFAPI, FCAP. In a mere 32 characters, I provided (to the cognoscenti) knowledge of my professional degree, medical specialty, and distinctive recognition within three professional societies of clinical informatics. However, to the less initiated, I obfuscated my message in a meaningless alphabet soup. We must always be vigilant to use acronyms selectively, and only where absolutely necessary.

We are delighted to see that the third edition of the *HIMSS Dictionary of Healthcare Information Technology Terms, Acronyms and Organizations* is continuing a tradition established with the second edition—to enliven what might otherwise be a rather dry subject by incorporating a few humorous or frankly tongue-in-cheek terms. These describe challenging and sometimes frustrating aspects of our experience as healthcare informaticists; for example, 'TLAlgia.' This term is composed of 'TLA' (meaning 'three-letter acronym') and '-algia' (meaning 'pain'); thus, 'pain induced by excessive use of obscure three-letter acronyms.' Beware!

More than 50 volunteers reviewed the entries from the second edition and contributed new words to this dictionary.

In this third edition, we provide 283 new terms, 30 new organizations and 76 new references.

One of the troublesome aspects of this endeavor, and of any complex domain where 'newbie' practitioners attempt to use a complex lexicography to describe an even more complex realm, is that words are misused, or come—through usage—to assume two or three mutually exclusive meanings. In some cases, we have listed multiple meanings of a term; be aware, when you use that term, the listener may be thinking of a different definition than you.

With all of these caveats in mind, dive in, speak and write this new language we have invented at the intersection of medicine, management, and information technology.

Dr. Aller practices clinical informatics and laboratory medicine in Southern California, and is Clinical Professor and Director of Informatics for USC Pathology. He can be reached at raller@usc.edu.

Introduction

Welcome to the third edition of the *HIMSS Dictionary of Healthcare Information Technology Terms, Acronyms and Organizations*, which follows the anniversary of the dictionary's first publication in June 2006, and the second edition in 2009.

The third edition, while cumulative with the earlier publications, has added mature definitions to those same terms, as well as disaster recovery and organizational resilience terms. The terms and acronyms were gathered, refined, combined, and edited, using business rules that were ever watchful of consistency and terms eligible for the dictionary. The one unequivocal rule was no one was permitted to define terms themselves—editors included. Terms had to include an authoritative source.

Hundreds of new entries have been submitted. The third edition contains 2,900+ entries. Since the last edition, we have expanded and developed the dictionary with international as well as professional acronyms. And, in determining the dictionary structure, a new appendix has been added to the linear-alphabetical structure to make looking up numerous cross-references easy for the reader.

We would like to thank HIMSS for undertaking the 2013 revision publication of the dictionary. Our thanks also goes to people too numerous to mention for corresponding and giving us new ideas and suggestions, and helping us make a better dictionary.

Our dictionary audience is computer professionals, students and anyone who comes in contact with health information management and technology activities. We hope our readers will find the dictionary to be a useful reference in their everyday work.

Luann Whittenburg, PhD, RN, CPHIMS
Chair, 3rd Ed. Editorial Review Board

Acknowledgments

HIMSS sincerely thanks the Editorial Review Board: Dr. Luann Whittenburg, PhD, RN, CPHIMS, Editorial Review Chair, and the Work Group Team Leads, Dr. Raymond Aller; Dr. Asif Syed; and Mr. Erik Pupo. Without their leadership, expertise and consideration, this dictionary would not have become a reality.

Chair, Editorial Review Chair

Luann Whittenburg, PhD, RN, CPHIMS
Chair, 3rd Edition Editorial Review Board
Chief Nursing Informatics Officer
Medicomp Systems, VA

Work Group Team Leads

Raymond D. Aller, MD, FHIMSS
Clinical Professor and Director of Informatics
University of Southern California Pathology
e-mail: raller@usc.edu
Mailing: PO Box 2168, Vista, CA 92085

Asif A. Syed, MD, MPH
Director, Medical Informatics and Healthcare Strategy
American Medical Association

Erik Pupo
Specialist Leader | Federal Healthcare Consulting
Deloitte Consulting LLP

Definition of Terms

A

AA Attribute authority. Authority which assigns privileges by issuing attribute certificates.[121]

Abbreviated term Term resulting from the omission of any part of a term while designating the same concept.[3]

ABC Activity-based costing. An accounting technique that allows an organization to determine the actual cost associated with each product and service produced by the organization, without regard to organizational structure.[1]

ABC codes Terminology to describe alternative medicine, nursing, and other integrative healthcare interventions that include relative value units and legal scope of practice information.[52]

Abend Abnormal termination of software.[7]

Abort 1. Terminate. 2. In data transmission, an *abort* is a function invoked by a sending station to cause the recipient to discard or ignore all bit sequences transmitted by the sender since the preceding flag sequence.[7]

Abstract class 1. Virtual common parent to two or more classes which cannot itself be instantiated. 2. Closely related to interfaces. These are classes that cannot be instantiated and are either partially implemented or not at all implemented.[116,12]

Abstract message Associated with a particular trigger event. Includes data fields that will be sent within a message, the valid response messages, and the treatment of application level errors or the failure of the underlying communications system.[16]

Abstract syntax A formal description method that allows data types relevant to an application to be specified in terms of other data types, including basic data types, such as integer and octet string.[3]

Abstract syntax notation *See* **ASN.**

Abstracting An application that facilitates the collection and maintenance of coded patient information with selected patient demographic, clinical, and admissions data from the medical record, usually post-discharge. This information can be used for internal control, analysis, regulatory reports, etc.[2]

Abstraction The process of extracting essential properties while omitting inessential details.[22]

ACA Affordable Care Act. On March 23, 2010, President Obama signed the Patient Protection and Affordable Care Act, which extends healthcare coverage to an estimated 32 million uninsured individuals and makes coverage more affordable for many others. Section 1561 requests the Department of Health & Human Services (HHS), in consultation with the Health Information Technology (HIT) Policy Committee, and the HIT Standards Committee (the Committees), to develop interoperable and secure standards and protocols that facilitate electronic enrollment of individuals in federal and state health and human services programs.[178]

Acceptable downtime Predetermined maximum elapsed time between the disruption and restoration of service.[42]

Acceptable risk Level of risk at which, given costs and benefits associated with risk reduction measures, no action is deemed to be warranted at a given point in time.[118]

Acceptable use policy *See* **AUP.**

Acceptance testing A user-run testing event that demonstrates an application's ability to meet business objectives and system requirements.[6]

Access Providing a person the opportunity to approach, inspect, review, or make use of data, information, or an information system.[1]

Access control 1. A security policy to authenticate who can have access to what data or information, or policies and procedures preventing access by those who are not authorized to have it; a process that determines which data elements can be read, written, or erased by certain users of a system. **2.** The prevention of use of a resource by unauthorized entities.[1]

Access control decision function *See* **ACDF**.

Access control enforcement function *See* **AEF**.

Access control information *See* **ACI**.

Access control list *See* **ACL**.

Access control policy A set of rules, part of a security policy, by which human customers or representatives are authenticated, and by which access by the customers to applications and other services and security objects is granted or denied.[4]

Access control service *See* **ACS**.

Access decision function The combining of security functions with decision algorithms creating an access control matrix.[1]

Access level A level associated with an individual who may be accessing information, or with the information that may be accessed (e.g., a classification level).[1]

Access mode A distinct operation recognized by protection mechanisms as a possible operation on data or information. 'Read' and 'write' are possible modes of access to a computer file, 'execute' is an additional mode of access to a program, and 'create' and 'delete' are access modes for directory objects.[1]

Access point A wireless networking radio transceiver that allows an appropriately equipped computer or other device to connect to a data network.[2]

Access provider *See* **ISP**.

Access to radiology information *See* **ARI**.

Accessibility Ability of a patient or population to utilize needed healthcare services unrestricted by geographic, economic, social, cultural, organizational, or linguistic barriers.[123]

Accountability 1. Property that allows auditing of IT system activities to be traced to persons or processes that may then be held responsible for their actions. Accountability includes authenticity and non-repudiation. **2.** Refers to identifying the healthcare party (i.e., individuals, organizations, business units) or agent (e.g., software device, instrument, monitor) that is responsible for data origination, amendment, verification, translation, stewardship, access and use, disclosure, and transmission and receipt.[97,151]

Accountable Care Organization *See* **ACO**.

Accounting of disclosures Refers to the right of individuals, with limitations, to a listing of the uses and disclosures of their identifiable health information for a period of time not to exceed six years prior to the date of the request.[48]

Accreditation Formal declaration by a designated approving authority that an information system is approved to operate in a particular security mode using a prescribed set of safeguards at an acceptable level of risk.[97]

ACDF **Access control decision function.** Specialized function that makes access control decisions by applying access control policy rules to an access request, access control decision information (of initiators, targets, access requests, or that retained from prior decisions), and the context in which the access request is made.[125]

ACG **Ambulatory care group.** Preventative, diagnostic, therapeutic, surgical, and/or rehabilitative outpatient care, where the duration of treatment is less than 24 hours.[2] Also known as an *adjusted clinical group*.

ACI **Access control information.** Information used for access control purposes, including contextual information.[125]

ACID **Atomicity, consistency, isolation, and durability.** The basic properties of a database transaction: atomicity, consistency, isolation, and durability. Either all the steps in a transaction succeed, or the entire transaction is rolled back; partial completion should never be observed.[7]

ACK General acknowledgment message.[16]

ACL **Access control list.** A table that tells a computer operating system which access rights each user has to a particular system object, such as a file directory or individual file. Each object has a security attribute that identifies its access control list. The list has an entry for each system user with access privileges. The most common privileges include the ability to read a file (or all the files in a directory), to write to the file or files, and to execute the file (if it is an executable file, or program).[42]

ACO   Accountable   Care   Organization. Groups of doctors, hospitals, and other healthcare providers, who come together voluntarily to give coordinated high-quality care to the Medicare patients they serve. Coordinated care helps ensure that patients, especially the chronically ill, get the right care at the right time, with the goal of avoiding unnecessary duplication of services and preventing medical errors. When an ACO succeeds in both delivering high-quality care and spending healthcare dollars more wisely, it will share in the savings it achieves for the Medicare program.[102]

ACS   Access   control   service. Includes embedded security management capabilities (provided as precursor information to this construct), and all other user-side access control and decision-making capabilities (policy enforcement point, policy decision point, obligation service, etc.) needed to enforce user-side system-object security and privacy policy. The ACS is responsible for creating trustworthy credentials forwarded in cross-domain assertions regarding security information and attributes. Access control services may be hierarchical and nested, distributed, or local.[48]

Active directory   *See* **AD**.

Active server pages   *See* **ASP**.

Activities of daily living   *See* **ADL**.

Activity   An action for the creation, the acquisition, or the furnishing of a 'product' (e.g., register a patient).[4]

Activity-based costing   *See* **ABC**.

Actor   A system or application responsible for certain information or tasks (e.g., the order placer actor). Each actor supports a specific set of Integrating the Healthcare Enterprise (IHE) transactions to communicate with other actors. A vendor product may include one or more actors.[56]

Acute care   Providing or concerned with short-term medical care.[32]

Acute physiology and chronic health evaluation   *See* **APACHE**.

AD   Active directory. A Microsoft central directory service that manages user data, security, and other system-related resources. It is part of Windows Server operating system to centrally provide network administration and security across a domain.[12]

AD   Addendum. A portion added on to a document.[32]

Addendum   *See* **AD**.

Address   The unique location of: **1.** An Internet server. **2.** Identifies (as a computer peripheral or memory location) by an address or a name for information transfer.[32]

Address class   Five TCP/IP address classes [A, B, C, D, and E] were initially designed to accommodate networks of varying sizes. The class of address defines which bits are used for the network ID and which bits are used for the host ID. Also defines the possible number of networks and the number of hosts per network. Class A addresses are assigned to networks with a large number of hosts. The high-order bit in a class A address is always set to zero. The next seven bits (completing the first octet) complete the network ID. The remaining 24 bits (the last three octets) represent the host ID. This allows for 126 networks and 16,777, 214 hosts per network. (Class E is an experimental address that is reserved for future use. The high-order bits in a class E address are set to 1111.)[187]

Address resolution   Conversion of an Internet protocol address to the corresponding low-level physical address.[1]

Address resolution protocol   *See* **ARP**.

ADE   Adverse drug event. An injury resulting from the use of a drug. Under this definition, the term ADE includes harm caused by the drug (adverse drug reactions and overdose) and harm from the use of the drug (including dose reductions and discontinuations of drug therapy). Adverse drug events may result from medication errors, but most do not.[96]

Ad-hoc query   **1.** A query that is not determined prior to the moment it is run against a data source. **2.** A non-standard inquiry created to obtain information as the need arises and contrasts with a query that is predefined and routinely processed.[1,163]

ADL Activities of daily living. Activities that are considered a normal part of everyday life. Some of these are bathing, dressing, eating, toileting, and transferring (e.g., moving from and into a chair). These activities are used to measure the degree of impairment and can effect the eligibility for certain types for insurance benefits.[102]

Administrative code sets Code sets that characterize a general business situation, rather than a medical condition or service. Under HIPAA, these are sometimes referred to as non-clinical, or non-medical, code sets. Compare to code sets and medical code sets.[10]

Administrative record A record concerned with administrative matters, such as length of stay, details of accommodation, and billing.[4]

Administrative safeguards Administrative actions and policies and procedures to manage the selection, development, implementation, and maintenance of security measures to protect electronic protected health information; and to manage the conduct of the covered entity's workforce in relation to the protection of that information.[118]

Administrative services only See **ASO**.

Administrative simplification Title II, Subtitle F, of HIPAA, which authorizes HHS to: 1. Adopt standards for transactions and code sets that are used to exchange health data; 2. Adopt standard identifiers for health plans, healthcare providers, employers, and individuals for use on standard transactions; and 3. Adopt standards to protect the security and privacy of personally identifiable health information.[102]

Administrative users access level 1. The special rights given to the team of users who maintain and support a network. **2.** Level associated with an individual who may be accessing information (e.g., a clearance level) and information which may be accessed (e.g., a classification level).[1,3]

Admission date The date the patient was admitted for inpatient care, outpatient service, or start of care.[102]

Admitted term Term accepted as a synonym for a preferred term by an authoritative body.[3]

ADPAC Automated data processing application coordinator. The person assigned by a service to coordinate computer activities for that service.

ADR Adverse drug reaction. 1. Response to a drug which is noxious and unintended, and which occurs at doses normally used in humans for prophylaxis, diagnosis, or therapy of disease; or for the modification of physiological function. There is a causal link between a drug and an adverse drug reaction. In summary, an adverse drug reaction is harm directly caused by the drug at normal doses, during normal use. **2.** A complication caused by use of a drug in the usual (i.e., correct) manner and dosage.[96,18]

ADR ADT response message. Admission, discharge, and transfer response message.[16]

ADSL Asymmetric digital subscriber line. A high-speed line that allows voice and data to travel concurrently over a local copper loop (or pair), with speeds ranging from 2-8 Mbps downstream, and 640-960 Kpbs upstream.[1]

ADT Admission, discharge, and transfer message for patients in a healthcare facility.[102]

ADT response message See **ADR**.

Adult learning theory Based on the premise that for adults to learn, there must be a perceived need, practical application, and relevance to their situations.[6]

Advance directives Documentation allowing a person to give directions regarding his or her own healthcare in the event that the person loses decision-making capacity. This may include a Living Will and a Durable Power of Attorney for Healthcare.[102]

Advanced Technology Attachment See **ATA**.

Adverse drug event See **ADE**.

Adverse drug reaction See **ADR**.

Adverse event See **AE**.

AE   Adverse event. 1. Untoward incidents, therapeutic misadventures, iatrogenic injuries, or other adverse occurrences directly associated with care or services provided within the jurisdiction of a medical center, outpatient clinic, or other medical facility. **2.** An injury caused by medical management rather than by the underlying condition of the patient.[97]

AE title   Application entity title. An identifier utilized by picture archiving and communication systems (PACS) to uniquely name devices that can send and/or receive information to the imaging/PACS system.[192]

AEF   Access control enforcement function. Specialized function that is part of the access path between an initiator and a target on each access control request, and enforces the decision made by the access control decision function.[125]

Affinity domain policy Clearly defines the appropriate uses of the Integrating the Healthcare Enterprise (IHE) Cross-Enterprise Document Sharing (XDS) affinity domain. Within this policy is a defined set of acceptable use privacy consent policies that are published and understood.[56]

Affordable Care Act *See* **ACA.**

Agency specific data All data pertinent to the agency where care is provided and which are used for patient care, such as procedures, hours of operations, visiting hours, standards of care, pharmacy formulary, etc.[6]

Aggregate The collection or gathering of elements into a mass or whole.[6]

Aggregate data Data elements assembled into a logical format to facilitate comparisons or to elicit evidence of patterns.[151]

Aggregation logics Logic for aggregating detailed data into categories.[28]

AHT   Average handling time. The average duration of a call handled by a customer service associate.[15]

AIDC   Automatic identification and data capture. The ability to use unique numbers and other sets of standardized data shown in bar codes or other data carriers to identify different items automatically, without human intervention. Technologies typically considered part of AIDC include bar codes, radio frequency identification (RFID), biometrics, magnetic stripes, optical character recognition (OCR), smartcards, and voice recognition.

AIMS   Anesthesia Information Management System. An information system that allows integrated communication with other hospital and provider systems throughout the perioperative period (such as clinical information systems used by nurses, data clinical repositories used by hospitals, and professional billing systems).[2]

AIS privileges Automated information system. Permissions to perform specified functions within a computer system.[1]

Alert Written or acoustic signals to announce the arrival of messages and results and to avoid possible undesirable situations, such as contradictions, conflicts, erroneous entry, tasks that are not performed in time, or an exceptional result. A passive alert will appear on the screen in the form of a message. An active alert calls for immediate attention, and the appropriate person is immediately notified (e.g., by electronic pager).[4] *See* **Decision support**.

Alerting system Computer-based system that automatically generates alerts and advice as a consequence of monitoring, or other information-processing activities.[4]

Algorithm   1. A precise statement of a method of calculation. Sometimes expressed in programming language. **2.** A predetermined set of instructions for solving a problem in a finite number of steps.[4,6]

Alias   1. A link to another file in a file system. **2.** An indirect, usually unexpected effect on other data, when a variable or reference is changed.[7]

Alias domain name The practice of establishing an e-mail protocol within another e-mail protocol, to allow for the local identification of users within a larger enterprise.[1]

ALOS   Average length of stay. The American Hospital Association computes the average length of hospital stay by dividing the number of inpatient days by the number of admissions.

Alpha/beta testing A pre-production development stage comprised of an initial trial (alpha test) by a select set of users. This initial test is to ensure that the system is stable enough for a rigorous trial (beta test) by additional users, or in a variety of settings.[6] *See* **Beta testing**.

Alphanumeric Describes use of numbers, the letters of the alphabet, and punctuation markers. Normally used to describe the typewriter-style keyboard used by computers.[4]

ALU **Arithmetic logic unit.** Portion of the CPU that performs the following arithmetic operations: add, subtract, multiply, divide, and negate.[1]

Ambulatory care Medical care, including diagnosis, observation, treatment, and rehabilitation that is provided on an outpatient basis. Ambulatory care is given to persons who are able to ambulate or walk about.[102]

Ambulatory care group *See* **ACG**.

Ambulatory care information system Information systems used to improve the quality of care and promote business systems integration in the ambulatory care setting.[45]

Ambulatory EMR The EMR that supports the ambulatory/clinic/physician office environments. Provides all of the functions of an EMR; clinical documentation, order entry, clinical data repository, practitioner order entry, physician clinical documentation, etc.[2]

Ambulatory medical record *See* **AMR**.

Amendments and corrections In the final Privacy Rule, an amendment to a record would indicate that the data are in dispute while retaining the original information, while a correction to a record would alter or replace the original record.[10]

American Recovery and Reinvestment Act of 2009 *See* **ARRA**.

American standard code for information interchange *See* **ASCII**.

Amplifier A device used to increase the strength of broadband signals to travel greater distances.[1]

AMR **Ambulatory medical record.** An electronic or paper-based medical record used in the outpatient or ambulatory care setting.[45]

Analog Representing data by measurement of a continuous physical variable, as voltage or pressure, as opposed to digital, which represents data as discrete units.[7]

Analog signal A continuous transmission signal that carries information in the form of varying waveforms/frequencies.[1] *See* **Digital signal**.

Analog-to-digital conversion Analog-to-digital conversion is an electronic process in which a continuous variable analog is changed, without altering its essential content, into a multi-level digital signal.[1]

Ancillary service **1.** Providing necessary support to the primary activities or operation of an organization, institution, industry, or system. **2.** Ancillary services are healthcare services provided exclusive from room and board. Supplies and laboratory tests provided under home care, audiology, durable medical equipment (DME), ambulatory surgical centers (ASC), home infusion, hospice care, skilled nursing facility (SNF), cardiac testing, mobile lithotripsy, fitness center, radiology, pulmonary testing, sleep centers, and kidney dialysis are examples of ancillary services.[195,188]

Ancillary service information system Information systems designed to store, manipulate, and retrieve information for planning, organizing, directing, and controlling administrative activities associated with the provision and utilization of radiology, laboratory, pharmacy, and other services.[189]

Anesthesia information management system *See* **AIMS**.

Anonymization A process that removes or replaces identity information from a communication or record. Communications and records may be made pseudonymous, in which case the same subject will always have the same replacement identity, but cannot be identified as an individual.[193]

Anonymized data **1.** Originally identifiable data which have been permanently stripped of identifiers. **2.** Data from which the patient cannot be identified by the recipient of the information.[8,3]

Anonymous file transfer protocol
See **Anonymous FTP**.

Anonymous FTP Anonymous file transfer protocol. An FTP session that allows users to access designated public system resources or files.[1]

Anti-tearing The process or processes that prevent data loss when a smartcard is withdrawn during a data operation.[1]

Anti-virus software *See* **Virus scanner**.

APACHE Acute physiology and chronic health evaluation. **1.** A severity-of-disease classification scoring system widely used in the United States. APACHE II is the most widely studied version of this instrument (a more recent version, APACHE IV, is proprietary, whereas APACHE II is publicly available); it derives a severity score from such factors as underlying disease and chronic health status.[1,2] Other points are added for 12 physiologic variables (e.g., hematocrit, creatinine, Glasgow Coma Score, mean arterial pressure) measured within 24 hours of admission to the ICU. The APACHE II score has been validated in several studies involving tens of thousands of ICU patients. **2.** A widely-used web server platform written by the Apache Software Foundation (ASF). The Apache Web server browser had a key role in the initial growth of the World Wide Web.[186]

APC Ambulatory payment class. A payment type for outpatient PPS claims.[5]

API Application program interface. **1.** A set of standard software interrupts, calls, functions, and data formats that can be used by an application program to access network services, devices, applications, or operating systems. **2.** A set of pre-made functions used to build programs. APIs ask the operating system or another application to perform specific tasks. There is an API for almost everything, including messaging APIs for e-mail, telephony APIs for calling systems, Java APIs, and graphics APIs, such as DirectX.[1,12] *See* **Socket, SSL**.

APN Appendix.[32]

Application A program or set of programs that perform a task. The use of information resources (information and information

technology) to satisfy a specific set of user requirements.[1]

Application architecture Defines how applications are designed and how they cooperate; promotes common presentation standards to facilitate rapid training and implementation of new applications and functions. Good application architecture enables a high level of system integration, reuse of components, and rapid deployment of applications in response to changing business requirements.[8]

Application entity title *See* **AE title**.

Application integrator Software that is used between different managed-care applications to provide data conversion and transmission, without the need for special programming to interface two or more applications, thereby reducing the cost of systems interface.[1]

Application layer The seventh and highest layer of the OSI model. Provides resources for the interaction that takes place between a user and application.[1] *See* **OSI**.

Application metadata Data about a data dictionary concerning the structure and contents of application menus, forms, and reports.[1]

Application program interface *See* **API**.

Application protocol services These are services supporting application level protocols. Simple object access protocol (SOAP) will be supported. Other remoting protocols, such as remote method invocation, DICOM, etc., can be plugged into the application protocol service.[8]

Application role A characteristic of an application that defines a portion of its interfaces. It is defined in terms of the interactions (messages) that the role sends or receives in response to trigger events. Thus, it is a role played by a healthcare information system component when sending or receiving health information technology messages; a set of responsibilities with respect to an interaction.[8]

Application server **1.** Program on a distributed network that provides business logic and server-side execution environment for application programs. **2.** A computer that handles all operations between a company's back-end applications or databases and the users' computers' graphical user interface or web browsers.

3. The device that connects end users to software applications and databases that are managed by the server.[8,2]

Application service provider *See* **ASP.**

Appointment system System for the planning of appointments between resources, such as clinicians, facilities, and patients. **Note:** Used to minimize waiting time, prioritize appointments, and optimize the utilization of resources.[4]

Archetype **1.** A named content type specification with attribute declarations. **2.** Model (or pattern) for the capture of clinical information—a machine readable specification of how to store patient data.[33,190]

Archetype instance Metadata class instance of an archetype model, specifying the clinical concept and the value constraints that apply to one class of record component instances in an electronic health record extract.[116]

Archetype model Information model of the metadata to represent the domain-specific characteristics of electronic health record entries, by specifying values or value constraints for classes and attributes in the electronic health record reference model.[116]

Archetype repository Persistent repository of archetype definitions accessed by a client authoring tool, or by a run-time component within an electronic health record service.[116]

Architecture **1.** *Architecture* is a term applied to both the process and the outcome of specifying the overall structure, logical components, and the logical interrelationships of a computer, its operating system, a network, or other conception. **2.** A framework from which applications, databases, and workstations can be developed in a coherent manner, and in which every part fits together without containing a mass of design details. Normally used to describe how a piece of hardware or software is constructed and which protocols and interfaces are required for communications. Network architecture specifies the function and data transmission needed to convey information across a network.[8,4]

Archive Long-term, physically separate storage.[114]

Archiving Moving rarely- or never-accessed computer files to an off-line storage device, such as magnetic tape or optical disk system. Archiving is a good practice to provide backup of important files, as well as to save critical space on the system hard disk.[1]

Arden syntax A language created to encode actions within a clinical protocol into a set of situation-action rules for computer interpretation, and to facilitate exchange between different institutions.[13]

Argument **1.** The values that a formula uses; they may be entered by the user, or be functions provided by the software. **2.** The part of a command that specifies what the command is to do.[11,4]

ARI **Access to radiology information.** Specifies a number of query transactions providing access to radiology information, including images and related reports, in a DICOM format, as they were acquired or created. Such access is useful, both to the radiology department and to other departments, such as pathology, surgery, and oncology.[56] *See* **Profile.**

Arithmetic logic unit *See* **ALU.**

ARP **Address resolution protocol.** Used in TCP/IP networks to provide the physical address (MAC address) or a device from the assigned Internet provider (IP) address.[1]

ARPANET **Advanced research projects agency network. 1.** Developed by the Defense Advanced Research Projects Agency (DARPA), this distributed network grew into the Internet. **2.** The first operational packet-switching network.[18,7]

ARRA **American Recovery and Reinvestment Act of 2009.** An economic stimulus bill enacted by the 111th Congress that provides $30 billion for various health information technology investments. Some of this funding was allocated by CMS to encourage physicians and hospital providers to adopt certified EHRs.[2]

Array A set of sequentially indexed elements having the same intrinsic data type. Each element of an array has a unique identifying index number.[12]

Artificial intelligence A computer application that has been designed to mimic the actions of an intelligent human in a given situation, and to be capable of substituting for a human.[11]

ASA **Average speed of answer.** The average amount of time (measured in seconds) from when a caller calls customer service (enters the customer service queue) to when the caller begins speaking to a customer service associate.[140]

ASCII **American standard code for information interchange.** Extensively used bit standard information processing code that represents 128 possible standard characters used by PCs. In an ASCII file, each alphabetic, numeric, or special character is represented with a 7-bit number (a string of seven 0s or 1s), which yields the 128 possible characters.[1]

ASMOP **A simple matter of programming.** An expression used to convey the sense 'yes, it's possible, but it would require an unknown, and most likely large, expenditure of resources.'[7]

ASN **Abstract syntax notation.** A metadata standard to define standards, mainly used in the area of telecommunications.[119]

ASO **Administrative services only.** An arrangement whereby a self-insured entity contracts with a third-party administrator (TPA) to administer a health plan.[10]

ASP **Active server pages.** A protocol for creating and displaying web pages.[99]

ASP **Application service provider. 1.** An entity that provides some type of specialty automation service or access, under a service agreement for a customer, with the business model of being able to provide expertise and reliability at a desired lower cost than the customer could provide for itself within a local data center. **2.** Network administration includes the deployment, maintenance, and monitoring of active network gear: switches, routers, firewalls, etc. network administration commonly includes activities such as network address assignment, assignment of routing protocols, and routing table configuration, as well as configuration of authentication- and authorization-directory services. This function may be outsourced by the healthcare organization.[1,2]

Assembler A tool that reads source code written in assembly language and produces executable machine code; possibly together with

information needed by linkers, debuggers, and other tools.[7] *See* **Compiler**.

Assembly services A business request may include calls to various components providing multiple result sets. These result sets will be assembled together in the appropriate output format by the assembly service. This service will use assembly templates to carry out its function.[8]

Association Linking a document with the program that created it so that both can be opened with a single command (e.g., double-clicking a 'doc' file opens Word for Windows and loads the selected document).[105]

Assurance Measure of confidence that the security features, practices, procedures, and architecture of an IT system accurately mediate and enforce the security policy.[97]

Asymmetric **cryptographic** **algorithm** Algorithm for performing encipherment or the corresponding decipherment, in which the keys used for encipherment and decipherment differ.[121]

Asymmetric digital subscriber line *See* **ADSL**.

Asymmetric keys Independent review and examination of records and activities to assess the adequacy of system controls; to ensure compliance with established policies and operational procedures; and to recommend necessary changes in controls, policies, or procedures.[114]

Asymmetric multiprocessing Multiprocessing technique in which certain tasks are dedicated to specific processors. One processor executes the operating system, while another processor handles applications.[1]

Asynchronous communication Communication in which the reply is not made immediately after the message is sent, but when the recipient is available. E-mail is an example of asynchronous communication.[11]

Asynchronous transfer mode *See* **ATM**.

ATA **Advanced technology attachment.** Specifies the power and data signal interfaces between the motherboard and the integrated disk controller and drive. A disk drive interface standard based on the IBM PC ISA 16-bit bus and also used on other personal computers.[7]

Also known as *AT Attachment* or *Integrated Drive Electronics (IDE)*.

ATCB **Authorized testing and certification body.** An entity that tests and certifies that certain types of electronic health record (EHR) technology (base EHRs and EHR modules) are compliant with the standards, implementation specifications, and certification criteria adopted by the US Department of Health & Human Services Secretary and meet the definition of certified EHR technology.[178]

ATM **Asynchronous transfer mode.** A high-performance, cell-oriented, switching, and multiplexing technology that utilizes fixed-length packets to carry different types of traffic.[34] *See* **Frame relay, SONET**.

ATNA **Audit trail and node authentication.** Establishes the characteristics of a Basic Secure Note: **1.** Describes the security environment (user identification, authentication, authorization, access control, etc.). **2.** Defines basic security requirements for the communications of the node. **3.** Defines basic auditing requirements for the node. The profile also establishes the characteristics of the communication of audit messages between the Basic Secure Nodes and Audit Repository Nodes that collect audit information.[56] *See* **Profile. NOTE: ATNA is an Integrating the Healthcare Enterprise (IHE) Profile.**

Atomic concept **1.** Primitive concept. **2.** Concept in a formal system whose definition is not a compositional definition.[98,126]

Atomic data Data elements that represent the lowest level of possible detail in a data warehouse.[1]

Atomic level data The elemental, precise data captured at the source in the course of clinical care, which can be manipulated in a variety of ways. These data are collected once, but used many times.[6]

Atomicity The entire sequence of actions must be either completed or aborted. The transaction cannot be partially successful.[7]

Attachment unit interface *See* **AUI**.

Attack The act of aggressively trying to bypass security controls in a computer system.[1]

Attempted security violation An unsuccessful action to gain unauthorized access to computer resources.[1]

Attenuation The measurement of how much a signal weakens over distance on a transmission medium. The longer the medium, the more attenuation becomes a problem without the regeneration of the signal. Signal regeneration is usually accomplished through the use of hubs (baseband) and amplifiers (broadband).[1]

Attester Party (person) who certifies and records legal responsibility for a particular unit of information.[116]

Attribute **1.** An attribute expresses characteristics of a basic elemental concept. Attributes are also known as *roles* or *relationship types*. Semantic concepts form relationships to each other through attributes. **2.** Abstractions of the data captured about classes. Attributes capture separate aspects of the class and take their values independent of one another. **3.** Piece of information describing a particular entity.[16,19]

Attribute authority *See* **AA**.

Attribute certificate **1.** Data structure, digitally signed by an attribute authority, that binds some attribute values with identification about its holder. **2.** A digital document containing attributes associated to the holder by the issuer.[121,7]

Attribute relationship An attribute relationship consists of two semantic concepts related to each other through an attribute. When an attribute-value pair has been assigned to a concept, that relationship becomes part of the concept's logical definition. For this reason, attribute relationships are called 'defining characteristics' of semantic concepts.[19]

Attribute type The last part of an attribute name (suffix). Attribute type suffixes are rough classifiers for the meaning of the attribute.[16] *See* **Data type** for contrast in definition.

Attribute-value pair The combination of an attribute with a value that is appropriate for that attribute. Assigning attribute-value pairs to semantic concepts is known as 'authoring' or 'modeling' and is part of the process of semantic content development. Attributes and values are always used together as attribute-value pairs. Sometimes the entire relationship is referred to as an object-attribute-value triple, or 'OAV' triple.[19]

Audit Independent review and examination of records and activities to assess the adequacy of system controls; to ensure compliance with established policies and operational procedures; and to recommend necessary changes in controls, policies, or procedures.[114]

Audit data Chronological record of system activities to enable the reconstruction and examination of the sequence of events and changes in an event.[114]

Audit trail 1. Chronological record of system activity which enables the reconstruction of information regarding the creation, distribution, modification, and deletion of data. 2. Documentary evidence of monitoring each operation of individuals on health information. May be comprehensive or specific to the individual and information. Audit trails are commonly used to search for unauthorized access by authorized users.[8,1]

Audit trail and node authentication *See* **ATNA**.

Auditing Specific activities that make up an audit. This can be manual, automated, or a combination.[48] *See* **Audit**.

AUI Attachment unit interface. Connector port on network devices.[1]

AUP Acceptable use policy. Set of rules and guidelines that specify, in more or less detail, the expectations in regard to appropriate use of systems or networks.[48]

Authenticate To verify the identity of a user, user device, other entity, or the integrity of data stored, transmitted, or exposed to unauthorized modification in an information system.[1]

Authentication Security measure, such as the use of digital signatures, to establish the validity of a transmission, message, or originator, or a means of verifying an individual's authorization to receive specific categories of information. The process of proving that a user or system is really who or what it claims to be. It protects against the fraudulent use of a system, or the fraudulent transmission of information.[1]

Authenticity Ability to verify; confidence in the validity of a transmission, a message, or message originator.[48]

Authority certificate Certificate issued to a certification authority or to an attribute authority.[121]

Authorization 1. Process of determining what activities are permitted, usually in the context of authentication. 2. The permission to perform certain operations, or use certain methods or services.[8]

Authorization decision Evaluating applicable policy, returned by the PDP to the PEP. A function that evaluates to 'Permit,' 'Deny,' 'Indeterminate,' or 'Not Applicable,' and (optionally) a set of obligations Organization for the Advancement of Structured Information Standards (OASIS).[48]

Authorized access Mechanisms by which access to data is granted by challenges to the requesting entity, to assure proper authority based on the identity of the individual, level of access to the data, and rights to manipulate that data.[48]

Authorized testing and certification body *See* **ATCB**.

Automated data processing application coordinator *See* **ADPAC**.

Availability Assurance that the systems responsible for delivering, storing, and processing information are accessible when needed, by those who need them, and that the information it provides will be of acceptable integrity.[118]

Average handling time *See* **AHT**.

Average length of stay *See* **ALOS**.

Average speed of answer *See* **ASA**.

AVR Analysis, visualization, and reporting. Ability to analyze, display, report, and map accumulated data, and share data and technologies for analysis and visualization with other public health partners.[46]

B

b/w Between.[32]

B/W **Black and white.** Indicates a print image is being formulated to be readable in pure black and white, without the use of color (and perhaps without the use of grayscale).[7]

B2B **Business-to-business.** Healthcare commerce applications that support online business enhancements to standardize previous processes that involved paper, fragmented interfaces, or delay. The electronic commerce is conducted between the business of the hospital (or other healthcare entity) and the business of the supplier.[1]

B2C **Business-to-consumer. 1.** The electronic commerce (eCommerce) conducted between the business of the hospital (or other healthcare entity) and the consumer or patient. **2.** eCommerce transactions conducted over the Internet. **3.** Healthcare eCommerce applications that support online business enhancements to standardize previous processes that involved paper, fragmented interfaces, or delay.[1]

Back door Unauthorized, undocumented code in a program that gives special privileges.[1] *See* **Trap doors**.

Backbone The high-speed, high-performance main transmission path in a network; a set of paths that local or regional networks connect to as a node for interconnection.[1]

Background Application that is executing without user input on a multi-tasking machine.[1]

Background process A secondary process that runs concurrently behind the active process appearing on the computer terminal.[4]

Backup Creation or duplication of files from a hard disk drive to a tape medium for storage, security, or safekeeping.[1]

Backup domain controller *See* **BDC**.

BAN **Body area network.** A communication standard optimized for low-power devices and operation on, in, or around the human body (but not limited to humans) to serve a variety of applications, including medical, consumer electronics/personal entertainment, and others.[155]

Bandwidth The total range of frequency capacity that can pass over a network. The capacity of a channel to carry information as measured by the difference between the highest and lowest frequencies that can be transmitted by that channel.[1]

Bar chart A graphic display of data in the form of a bar showing the number of units (e.g., frequency, in each category).[123]

Bar code **1.** One-dimensional pattern of thick and thin parallel lines printed on objects and containing coded information, which can be read by a light pen or similar device and translated into an electronic form. **2.** Two-dimensional: Array of coded bars and/or dots in a two-dimensional (2-D) array, read by a laser, camera, or other imaging device, and translated into electronic form. A small 2-D bar code can store 200+ characters of information.[4,99]

Bar coding A code consisting of a group of printed and variously patterned bars and spaces, and sometimes numerals, that are designed to be scanned and read into computer memory as identification for the object it labels. Bar coding is used by materials management, nursing, and pharmacy in inpatient and outpatient settings.[2]

Bar code medication administration *See* **BCMA**.

Baseband The use of an entire bandwidth for digital bi-directional data transmission. Only one transmission at a time is possible in baseband networks. An Ethernet network is a baseband network.[1]

Baseline Compiled performance statistics for use in the planning and analysis of systems and networks.[1]

BASIC **Beginner's all-purpose symbolic instruction code.** Programming language. Originally devised as an easy-to-use programming language, it became widespread on home microcomputers in the 1980s, and remains popular to this day in a handful of heavily evolved dialects.[33]

Basic input output system *See* **BIOS**.

BAT Filename extension for a batch file.[1]

Batch Amount of material that is uniform in character and quantity, as shown by compliance with production and quality assurance test requirements, and produced during a defined validated process of manufacture.[117]

Batch mode A non-interactive mode of using a computer, in which customers submit jobs for processing and receive results on completion.[4]

Batch processing Batch processing is the sequential execution of a series of programs (jobs) on a computer. In many companies, batch jobs are scheduled on a timetable (e.g., end of day and end of quarter) and can be initiated automatically by, for example, the IBM mainframe job control language, or manually by an operator.[7]

Baud A measure of signal changes per second in a modem or other communications device.[1]

BBS Bulletin board service. A non-commercial dial-up service usually run by a user group or software company. One can exchange messages with other users and upload or download software.[1]

BCMA Bar code medication administration. Electronic system designed to prevent medication errors in healthcare settings and improve the quality and safety of medication administration. The overall goals of BCMA are to improve accuracy, prevent errors, and generate online records of medication administration.[7]

BDC Backup domain controller. 1. Secondary Windows NT server that contains a copy of the security database. Authenticates users of the primary domain controller (PDC) when the PDC is unavailable. **2.** When changes are made to the master accounts database on the PDC, the PDC pushes the updates down to the BDCs (read-only copy).[1,7]

Beaconing Token ring network signaling process that informs computers on the network that a serious error has occurred. A problem area ablation process.[1]

Beaming Transfer of data or software programs between devices, such as personal device assistants (PDAs), personal computers, and printers, using either infrared or radio-wave transmission.[107]

Bedside workstation Workstation in a patient room or examining room.[4]

Beginner's all-purpose symbolic instruction code See **BASIC**.

Behavioral risk factor surveillance system See **BRFSS**.

Benchmarking A process of searching out and studying the best practices that produce superior performance. Benchmarks may be established within the same organization (internal benchmarking), outside of the organization, and with another organization that produces the same service or product (external benchmarking), or with reference to a similar function or process in another industry (functional benchmarking).[123]

Best of breed An application buying philosophy that emphasizes buying the very best software application for the task regardless of compatibility, integration, or interoperability with other healthcare organization applications.[2]

Best of suite An application buying philosophy between 'best of breed' and 'single vendor' that emphasizes integration of segments, or suites, of applications, each segment normally purchased from a different vendor. Each suite is then interfaced. Examples of suites include financial applications, clinical applications, and revenue cycle applications.[2]

Best practice A way or method of accomplishing a business function, or process, that is considered to be superior to all other known methods.[123]

Best practices Best practices are the most up-to-date patient care interventions, which result in the best patient outcomes and minimize patient risk of death or complications.[138]

Beta testing The final stage in the testing of new software before its commercial release, conducted by testers other than its developers.[35]

BGI Binary gateway interface. Provides a method of running a program from a web server. Uses a binary Dynamic Link Library (DLL), which is loaded into memory when the server starts.[1]

BGP Border gateway protocol. Used to advertise the networks that can be reached within an autonomous system. Newer than the exterior gateway protocol (EGP).[1]

Binary A base two-numbering system consisting of two numbers (0 and 1), called *bits*.[1]

Binary gateway interface *See* **BGI**.

Binding 1. The linking of a protocol driver to a network adapter. 2. An affirmation by a certificate authority/attribute authority (or its acting registration authority) of the relationship between a named identity and its public key or biometric template.[1,114]

BinHex A file conversion format that converts binary files to ASCII test files.[1]

Bioinformatics An academic field involving the application of informatics to the biological sciences.[58]

Biomedical informatics The interdisciplinary field that studies and pursues the effective uses of biomedical data, information, and knowledge for scientific inquiry, problem solving, and decision making, motivated by efforts to improve human health.[183]

Biometric Pertaining to the use of specific attributes that reflect unique personal characteristics, such as a fingerprint, an eye blood-vessel print, or a voice print, to validate the identity of a person.[3]

Biometric authentication Use of technology to identify a person through recognition of specific or unique physical characteristics, such as retina, fingerprints, or voice patterns.[114]

Biometric identification Use of physiological characteristics, such as fingerprints or voice-print for identification.[11]

Biometric identifier An identifier based on some physical characteristic, such as a fingerprint.[5]

Biometric information The stored electronic information pertaining to a biometric. This information can be in terms of raw or compressed pixels, or in terms of some characteristic.[114]

Biometric system An automated system capable of the following: capturing a biometric sample from the end user, extracting biometric data from that sample, comparing the extracted biometric data with data contained in one or more references, deciding how well the samples match, indicating whether or not an identification or verification of identity has been achieved.[114]

BIOS **Basic input output system. 1.** The first operating system code that executes the open computer boot-up. This is contained in Flash memory or ROM firmware on the motherboard. **2.** Instructs the computer how to perform a number of basic functions, such as booting and keyboard control.[1,157]

Biosense A syndromic surveillance and situational awareness program being developed by the Centers for Disease Control and Prevention (CDC). Focuses on collecting data from many hospitals in the community, as well as other data sources, to develop an understanding of the current state of community health.[99]

Biosurveillance Surveillance programs in areas such as human health, hospital preparedness, state and local preparedness, vaccine research and procurement, animal health, food and agriculture safety, and environmental monitoring, that integrate those efforts into one comprehensive system.[48] *See* **Surveillance**.

Biosurveillance use case This HITSP Interoperability Specification (Interoperability Standard 02) is designed to meet the specific requirements of the Biosurveillance Use Case, defined as implementation of near real-time, nationwide public health event monitoring to support early detection, situational awareness, and rapid response management across care delivery, public health, and other authorized government agencies.[48]

Bioterrorism Terrorism using germ warfare; an intentional human release of a naturally occurring, or human-modified, toxin or biological agent.[7]

Bit **Binary digit.** First termed by John Tukey in 1949. Smallest unit of information associated with computers and information processing.[1]

Bit depth The number of bits used to represent each pixel in an image, determining its color or tonal range.[1]

Bitmap An image stored as a pattern of pixels corresponding bit-by-bit with the associated image. Used by computers because of its simplicity.[1] Also known as *bit-mapped data*.

Bitpipe Online resource for technical white papers, product literature, web casts, and case studies.[36]

Bits per second *See* **BPS**.

Block algorithms Formulas that encrypt data one block at a time.[1]

Blog A web site, usually maintained by an individual with regular entries of commentary, descriptions of events, or other material such as graphics or video.[182]

Bluetooth A protocol designed for short-range wireless communication, or networking, among a variety of devices.[107]

Body area network *See* **BAN**.

Boolean logic Form of logic seen in computer applications in which all values are expressed either as true or false. Symbols used to designate this are often called Boolean operators. They consist of equal to (=), more than (>), less than (<), and any combination of these, plus the use of 'AND,' 'OR,' and 'NOT.'[11]

Boot partition Partition that contains the operating system files.[1]

Border gateway protocol *See* **BGP**.

Bounce Act of gracefully shutting down a system and subsequent restarting or rebooting it. Ensures system changes are active and program areas are cleared due to the reboot process.[1]

Bound applications Programs compiled to run under DOS or operating system OS/2.[1]

Bourne shell Original and most widely used interactive command interpreter and programming language. UNIX shell.[1]

BPS **Bits per second.** The basic unit of speed associated with data transmission.[1]

Breach of security Any action by an authorized or unauthorized user that violates access rules and regulations, and results in a negative impact upon the data in the system or the system itself; or that causes data or services within a system to suffer unauthorized disclosure, modification, destruction, or denial of service.[1]

Breakthrough use case A use case selected for implementation which crosses boundaries and levels, intended to stimulate investment,

and delivers both immediate and long-term benefits.[48]

BRFSS **Behavioral risk factor surveillance system.** A state-based system of health surveys that collects information on health risk behaviors, preventive health practices, and healthcare access primarily related to chronic disease and injury.

Bridge Computer or device that connects or relates two or more similar networks or local area networks (LAN) that use the same protocols.[1]

Bridging router *See* **Brouter**.

Broadband **1.** The use of all bands of overall bandwidth for unidirectional data transmission. Multiple transmissions can occur at the same time in broadband networks. **2.** A signaling method which includes or handles a relatively wide range of frequencies that may be divided into channels or frequency bins.[1,2]

Broadcast A packet delivery technique that sends and delivers a single message for all nodes on a network.[1]

Broadcast storm Result of the number of broadcast messages on the network reaching or surpassing the bandwidth capability of the network.[1]

Broker Application system that acts as an intermediary between two collaborating systems or services.[8]

Brouter **Bridging router.** A device that provides both bridging and routing functions. Acts as a bridge for some protocols and a router for the rest.[1]

Browser A program that enables users to access information on the Internet. A software tool that supports graphics and hyperlinks, and is needed to navigate the Internet.[1]

Buffer Temporary storage holding areas for input or output data, mainly used to compensate for differences in data flows.[1]

Bug Unwanted or unintended programming mistake, or hardware error condition, that causes system failure, error, malfunction, or unpredictable system actions.[1]

Bulletin board service *See* **BBS**.

Bus **1.** A structure that is used for connecting processors and peripherals, either within a system or in a local area network (LAN). **2.** The internal wiring between and within the CPU and other motherboard subsystems.[4,1]

Business associate An individual or corporate 'person' who performs on behalf of the department any function or activity involving the use or disclosure of protected health information (PHI) and who is not a member of the department's workforce. The definition of function or activity includes claims processing or administration, data analysis, utilization review, quality assurance, billing, legal, actuarial, accounting, consulting, data processing, management, administrative, accreditation, financial services, and similar services. Business associates do not include licensees or providers, unless the licensee or provider also performs some 'function or activity' on behalf of the Department of Homeland Security.[118]

Business associate agreement Agreement between a covered entity and its business associate, in which the business associate agrees to restrict its use and disclosure of the covered entities' protected health information.[48]

Business intelligence system Business intelligence (BI) is a broad category of business processes, application software, and other technologies for gathering, storing, analyzing, and providing access to data to help users make better business decisions. It can be described as the process of enhancing data into information, and then into knowledge. Business intelligence is carried out to gain sustainable competitive advantage, and is a valuable core competence in some instances.[7] *See* **Decision support system**.

Business-to-business *See* **B2B**.

Business-to-consumer *See* **B2C**.

Byte Series of either 0 or 1 bits used to represent a character, and recognized by the computer as a single entity.[1]

C

C language A standardized imperative computer programming language, developed in the early 1970s by Dennis Ritchie, for use on the UNIX operating system. It has since spread to many other operating systems, and is one of the most widely used programming languages. C is prized for its efficiency, and is the most popular programming language for writing system software, though it is also used for writing applications. It is also commonly used in computer science education, despite not being designed for novices.[7]

C+/C++ An established programming language found in many operating systems, including UNIX. C++ is a daughter program based on objects, and is quickly becoming a favored programming language as object-oriented technology gains popularity.[107] *See* **JAVA**.

CA **Certification authority.** The official responsible for performing the comprehensive evaluation of the technical and non-technical security features of an IT system and other safeguards, made in support of the accreditation process, to establish the extent that a particular design and implementation meet a set of specified security requirements.[97]

caBIG™ **Cancer Biomedical Informatics Grid.**[37] An open source, open access information network initiative for the cancer community developed by the National Cancer Institute and maintained by the Center for Biomedical Informatics and Information Technology (CBIIT).[7]

Cache **1.** An area of temporary computer memory storage space that is reserved for data recently read from a disk, which allows the processor to quickly retrieve it, if it is needed again. A part of random access memory (RAM). **2.** A small, fast memory holding recently accessed data, designed to speed up access.[1,8]

Caching services Service used to manage the cache and provide functions related to cache responses based on configured settings. The settings may include time to live, persistence, cache cycling, parameter/role/facility-based caching, etc.[8]

CAD **Computer-aided design.** The use of a wide range of computer-based tools that assist engineers and architects in their design activities. It involves both software and special-purpose hardware.[7]

CAD **Computer-aided detection.** Combining elements of artificial intelligence and digital image processing with radiological image processing to assist in the interpretation of medical images.[7] Also called *computer-aided diagnosis (CADx)*.

CAH **Critical-access hospital.** Rural community hospitals that receive cost-based reimbursement. To be designated a CAH, a rural hospital must meet defined criteria that were outlined in the Conditions of Participation 42 CFR 485 and subsequent legislative refinements to the program through the Balanced Budget Refinement Act of 1999 (BBRA), Benefits Improvement and Protection Act (BIPA, 2000), the Medicare Modernization Act, the Medicare Improvements for Patients and Providers Act (MIPPA, 2008), and the Patient Protection and Affordable Care Act (ACA, 2010).[171]

CAL **Computer-assisted learning.** Refers to a system of educational instruction performed almost entirely by computer. Such systems typically incorporate functions, such as assessing student capabilities with a pre-test; presenting educational materials in a navigable form; providing repetitive drills to improve the student's command of knowledge; possibly, providing game-based drills to increase learning enjoyment; assessing student progress with a post-test; routing students through a series of courseware instructional programs; and recording student scores and progress for later inspection by a courseware instructor.[7] See **CBL**.

Call back A procedure in which a data processing system identifies a calling terminal, disconnects the call, and dials the calling terminal to authenticate the calling terminal.[3]

Canadian Health Outcomes for Better Information and Care *See* **C-HOBIC**.

Canonical Of, or relating to, a set of core, standard, irreducible, or foundational concepts, works, or documents.[38]

CAP **Capitation.** Pre-established payment of a set dollar amount to a provider on a per member basis for certain contracted services, for a given period of time. Amount of money paid to provider depends on number of individuals registered to their patient list, not on volume or type of service provided.[15]

CAP **Common alerting protocol.** A general format for exchanging all-hazard emergency alerts and public warnings over all kinds of networks.[91]

Capability Non-functional, observable system qualities that do not represent specific functions, and cannot be satisfied by any one component. These are emerging properties that are observed in a collection of components working together.[8]

Capacity The ability to run a number of jobs per unit of time.[8]

Capture **1.** The method of taking a biometric sample from an end user. **2.** Process or means of obtaining and storing external data for use at a later time.[42,114]

Card reader Equipment capable of reading the information on a smartcard, such as that in the magnetic stripe or chip.[1]

Care **1.** Watchful attention. **a.** Charge, supervision (under medical care). **b.** A person who is an object of attention. **2.** A therapeutic action.[27,32]

Care coordination The deliberate organization of patient care activities between two or more participants (including the patient) involved in a patient's care to facilitate the appropriate delivery of healthcare services. Organizing care involves the marshaling of personnel and other resources needed to carry out all required patient care activities, and is often managed by the exchange of information among participants responsible for different aspects of care.

Care management A set of activities that assures that every person served by the treatment system has a single approved care (service) plan that is coordinated, not duplicative, and designed to assure cost effective and good outcomes. Care managers will oversee a patient's journey through treatment.[133]

Care plan. *See* **Patient plan of care**.

Care transitions Movement of patients between different formal or informal healthcare providers over the course of an illness, encompassing the set of actions or processes designed to ensure the patient has continuity of care. Every change from provider or setting is another care transition.[128]

Cardiac catheterization workflow
See **CATH**.

Cardinality **1.** The number of rows in a table, or the number of indexed entries in a defined index. **2.** The number of elements in a set.[16] *See* **Multiplicity**.

Carrier sense multiple access with collision detection *See* **CSMA/CD**.

CAS **Computer-assisted surgery.** Represents a surgical concept and set of methods, that use computer technology for pre-surgical planning, and for guiding or performing surgical interventions.[7] Also known as *computer-aided surgery.*

CASE **Computer-assisted software engineering.** A computer-assisted method to organize and control the development of software. CASE allows developers to share a common view, allow checkpoint process, and serves as a repository.[42]

Case management A collaborative process involving the member and his or her family, the healthcare provider, and the health plan's case management nurse.[15]

Case mix management An application that provides integrated information from admission, discharge, transfer, utilization review, patient billing, and abstracting to monitor and understand the mix of types of patient services delivered.[2]

Casemix The mix of cases treated by a provider, based on the average weight (based on a relative scale) of case types treated. Originally used with DRGs, with weights calculated by the Centers for Medicare & Medicaid Services based on historical cost data, casemix was a rough measure of the complexity and severity of the cohort of patients treated by a particular provider.[4]

Casemix index A composite score derived from the average weight assigned by Medicare to individual DRGs. Initially based on costs by case type, the casemix index was used to establish base rates for payment that were then adjusted as the index changed for a given provider.[1]

Casemix systems An early form of analytic decision support system, which, for the first time, combined clinical and financial data for analysis. Sparked by the introduction of prospective payment (DRGs), the first system was developed at Rush-Presbyterian-St. Luke's, and was popularized by a system developed by New England Medical Center.[1]

Case-sensitive Programming languages that distinguish between uppercase and lowercase letters.[1]

CAT **Computerized axial tomography.** An x-ray procedure that combines many x-ray images with the aid of a computer to generate cross-sectional views and, if needed, three-dimensional images of the internal organs and structures of the body.[197] Also known as *CT*.

CAT-1-5 **Categories 1-5.** Categories of unshielded twisted pair cable (UTP). Allows voice grade only transmission rates below 100 Mbps up to 100 meters, or 328 feet, in length per segment.[1]

Categories 1-5 *See* **CAT-1-5**.

Categorization Process by which individual information products can be associated with other products, using vocabularies designed to help citizens locate and access information. There can be multiple attributes assigned to a product (e.g., multiple categorizations). Categorization is used to provide context to a specific product, and to define relationships across a group of information products.[17]

CATH **Cardiac catheterization workflow.** Establishes the continuity and integrity of basic patient data in the context of the cardiac catheterization procedure. This profile deals specifically with consistent handling of patient identifiers and demographic data, including that of emergency patient presentation where the actual patient identity may not be established until after the beginning of the procedure, or even a significant time after the completion of the procedure. It also specifies the scheduling and coordination of procedure data across a variety of imaging, measurement, and analysis systems, and its reliable storage in an archive form where it is available to support subsequent workflow steps, such as reporting. It also provides central coordination of the completion status of steps of a potentially multi-phase (diagnostic and interventional) procedure.[56]

Cause and effect diagram A display of the factors that are thought to affect a particular problem or system outcome. The tool is often used in a quality improvement program to group people's ideas about the causes of a particular problem in an orderly way. Also known as the *fishbone diagram* because of the shape that it takes when illustrating the primary and secondary causes.[123]

CBL Computer-based learning. Refers to the use of computers as a key component of the educational environment. While this can refer to the use of computers in a classroom, the term more broadly refers to a structured environment in which computers are used for teaching purposes. The concept is generally seen as being distinct from the use of computers in ways where learning is at least a peripheral element of the experience (e.g., computer games and web browsing).[7]

CBSA Core-based statistical area. Defined by the Census Bureau as a geographic area with an urbanized population of at least 50,000, or an urban cluster with a population of at least 10,000, plus the adjacent counties that have a high degree of social and economic integration with the core as measured through commuting ties.[2]

CCC Clinical care classification. A concept-oriented nursing terminology framework and coding structure for the electronic documentation and classification of the nursing practice and process. The nomenclature is discrete atomic level data elements about the nursing process, encompassing nursing assessment, diagnosis, intervention, actions, and actual and expected outcomes to measure patient outcomes over time, across population groups, and geographic locations. Recognized by American Nurses Association. *(Formerly known as the Home Health Care Classification, HHCC).*[27]

CCD Continuity of care document. A specification that is an XML-based markup standard (developed between HL7 and ASTM) intended to specify the encoding, structure, and semantics of a patient summary clinical document for exchange.[16]

CCO Chief compliance officer. Responsible for legal processes and procedures, maintaining industry standards, and ensuring compliance with healthcare regulations.[2]

CCoM Clinical context management. Coordinates different healthcare applications on a desktop, creating a user-driven, patient-centered information workspace.[7]

CCOW Clinical context object workgroup. Using a technique called context management, CCOW provides the clinician with a unified view on the information held in separate and disparate healthcare applications referring to the same patient, encounter, or user. This means that when a clinician signs onto one application within the group of disparate applications tied together by the CCOW environment, that same sign-on is simultaneously executed on all other applications within the group. Similarly, when the clinician selects a patient, the same patient is selected in all the applications. CCOW then builds a combined view of the patient on one screen. CCOW works for both client-server and web-based applications. The acronym CCOW is a reference to the standards committee within the HL7 group that developed the standard.[16]

CCR Continuity of care record. 1. A standard specification developed jointly by ASTM International, the Massachusetts Medical Society (MMS), the Healthcare Information and Management Systems Society (HIMSS), the American Academy of Family Physicians (AAFP), and the American Academy of Pediatrics (AAP). It is intended to foster and improve continuity of patient care, reduce medical errors, and assure at least a minimum standard of health information transportability when a patient is referred or transferred to, or is otherwise seen by another provider. **2.** A new XML document standard for a summary of personal health information that clinicians can send when a patient is referred, and that patients can carry with them to promote continuity, quality, and safety of care.[39]

CD Committee draft. The second internal technical committee balloting stage for international standards from ISO.[3]

CD Compact disc. Optical disk used to store digital data, originally developed for storing digital audio files.[7]

CDA Clinical document architecture. 1. An XML-based document markup standard that specifies the structure and semantics of clinical documents for the purpose of exchange. **2.** Known previously as the patient record architecture, CDA provides an exchange model for clinical documents, such as discharge summaries and progress notes, and brings the healthcare industry closer to the realization of an electronic medical record. By leveraging the use of XML, the HL7 Reference Information Model (RIM), and coded vocabularies, the CDA makes documents both machine-readable (so documents are easily parsed and processed electronically) and human-readable so documents can be easily retrieved and used by the people who need them.[2,16]

CDFS CD-ROM file system. A 32-bit file system used in conjunction with CD-ROMs on Windows 95 and Windows NT machines.[1]

CDMA Code division multiple access. A wireless technology that includes digital voice service with 9.6 Kpbs to 14.4 Kpbs data services, and includes enhanced calling features, such as caller ID, but lacks an 'always-on' data connection feature.[1]

CDPD Cellular digital packet data. A TCP/IP-based industry standard for data, which is compatible with nearly all TCP/IP applications. Data packets can follow the user from cell to cell of calling regions, keeping an 'always-on' data connection alive while the user is in motion.[1]

CDR Clinical data repository. 1. A structured, systematically collected storehouse of patient-specific clinical data. **2.** A centralized database that allows organizations to collect, store, access, and report on clinical, administrative, and financial information, collected from various applications within or across the healthcare organization that provides an open environment for accessing/viewing, managing, and reporting enterprise information.[12]

CD-ROM Compact disk read-only memory. Read-only optical disk storage used for imaging, reference, and database application with massive amounts of data and for multimedia.[1]

CD-ROM file system See **CDFS**.

CDS Clinical decision support. The use of automated rules based on clinical evidence to provide alerts, reminders, clinical guidelines, and other knowledge to assist in healthcare delivery.[151]

CDT Current Dental Terminology. Official coding system for dentists to report professional services and procedures to third parties for payment. CDT is produced by the American Dental Association.[151]

CDW Clinical data warehouse. Grouping of data accessible by a single data management system, possibly of diverse sources, pertaining to a health system or sub-system; and enabling secondary data analysis for questions relevant to understanding the functioning of that health system, and hence can support proper maintenance and improvement of that health system.[94]

CE Coded element. A data type that transmits codes and the text associated with the code.[16]

Cellular digital packet data See **CDPD**.

CEN European Committee for Standardization. Major provider of European standards and technical specifications. CEN is the only recognized European organization for the planning, drafting, and adoption of European standards in all areas of economic activity with the exception of electrotechnology (CENELEC) and telecommunication (ETSI).[86]

Centers for Medicare & Medicaid Electronic Health Record Incentive Program Program that provides incentive payments to eligible professionals, eligible hospitals and critical-access hospitals (CAHs) as they adopt, implement, upgrade, or demonstrate meaningful use of certified EHR technology.[102]

Central processing unit See **CPU**.

Central processing unit See **Microprocessor**.

CERT Computer emergency response team. A team of system specialists and other professionals, such as lawyers, who investigate computer break-ins and attacks.[1]

CERT Community emergency response team. Federal Emergency Management Agency (FEMA) disaster preparedness program that educates communities about hazards that may impact them, and trains communities in basic disaster response skills, such as fire safety, light search and rescue, team organization, and disaster medical operations.[225]

Certificate   Public key certificate.[121]

Certificate authority   An independent licensing agency that vouches for a patient/person's identity in encrypted electronic communication. Acting as a type of electronic notary public, a certified authority verifies and stores a sender's public and private encryption keys and issues a digital certificate, or seal of authenticity, to the recipient.[8]

Certificate distribution   Act of publishing certificates and transferring certificates to security subjects.[121]

Certificate extension   Extension fields (known as extensions) in X.509 certificates that provide methods for associating additional attributes with users or public keys, and for managing the certification hierarchy. **Note:** Certificate extensions may be either critical (i.e., a certificate-using system has to reject the certificate if it encounters a critical extension it does not recognize) or non-critical (i.e., it may be ignored if the extension is not recognized).[121]

Certificate generation   Act of creating certificates.[121]

Certificate issuer   Authority trusted by one or more relying parties to create and assign certificates and which may, optionally, create the relying parties' keys.[121] **Note 1:** Adapted from ISO 9594-8:2001. **Note 2:** 'Authority' in the Certificate Authority (CA) term does not imply any government authorization; it only denotes that the certificate authority is trusted. **Note 3:** *Certificate issuer* may be a better term, although *CA* is very widely used.

Certificate management   Procedures relating to certificates (i.e., certificate generation, certificate distribution, certificate archiving, and revocation).[121]

Certificate policy   *See* **CP**.

Certification   **1.** Comprehensive evaluation of the technical and non-technical security features of an IT system and other safeguards, made in support of the accreditation process, to establish the extent that a particular design and implementation meets a set of specified security requirements. **2.** Procedure by which a third party gives assurance that all, or part of, a data processing system conforms to security requirements. **3.** A defined process to ensure that EHR technologies meet the adopted standards, certification criteria, and other technical requirements to achieve meaningful use of those records in systems. [97,121,178]

Certification authority   *See* **CA**.

Certification practices statement   *See* **CPS**.

Certification profile   Specification of the structure and permissible content of a certificate type.[121]

Certification revocation   Act of removing any reliable link between a certificate and its related owner (or security subject owner) because the certificate is not trusted any more, even though it is unexpired.[121]

Certified EHR technology   A qualified electronic health record that is certified pursuant to Section 3001(c) (5) of the Public Health Service Act (PHSA) as meeting standards adopted under Section 3004 that are applicable to the type of record involved (as determined by the Secretary of HHS, such as an ambulatory electronic health record for office-based physicians or an inpatient hospital electronic health record for hospitals).[130,196]

CF   Conditional formatting/coded formatted element. 1. A tool that allows a user to apply formats to a cell or range of cells; and have that formatting change, depending on the value of the cell or the value of a formula.[41] **2.** Coded element with formatted values data type. This data type transmits codes and the formatted text associated with the code.[16,41]

CGI   Common gateway interface. A standard or protocol for external gateway programs to interface with information servers, such as HTTP servers. Part of the overall HTTP protocol.[1]

Challenge handshake authentication protocol   *See* **CHAP**.

Changing or moving   Presenting new directions and developing new behaviors and attitudes based on new information. A learning process and social support is critical to this phase.[6]

Channel   A path for the transmission of signals between a transmitting and receiving device.[1]

Channel sharing unit/data service unit *See* **CSU/DSU.**

CHAP   **Challenge handshake authentication protocol.** An authentication protocol used to log in a user to an Internet access provider.[1]

Character   A member of a set of elements that is used for representation. Organization or control of data.[3]

Character-based terminal   A type of computer terminal and system that supports only alphabetical or numeric characters, with the visual displays and 'mouse'-driven, bitmap software that most systems now utilize; the opposite of graphical user interface (GUI).[1]

Characteristic   Abstraction of a property of an object or a set of objects.[98]

Charge posting   *See* **CHG.**

Check digit   The resultant representation of a checksum operation.[1]

CHG   **Charge posting.** Specifies the exchange of information from the department system scheduler/order filler actor to the charge processor actor regarding charges associated with particular procedures, as well as communication between the ADT/patient registration and charge processor actors about patient demographics, accounts, insurance, and guarantors. The charge posted transaction contains all of the required procedure data to generate a claim. Currently, these interfaces contain fixed field formatted, or HL7-style, data. The goal of including this transaction in the IHE Technical Framework is to standardize the charge posted transaction to a charge processor, thus reducing system interface installation time between clinical systems and charge processors. Additionally, the charge posted transaction reduces the need of the billing system to have knowledge of the radiology internals. The result is that the charge processor will receive more complete, timely, and accurate data.[56] *See* **Profile. NOTE: CHG is an Integrating the Healthcare Enterprise (IHE) Profile.**

Chief compliance officer (CCO)   *See* **CCO.**

Chief information/informatics officer (CIO)   *See* **CIO.**

Chief medical information/informatics officer *See* **CMIO.**

Chief nursing informatics/information officer *See* **CNIO.**

Chief security officer (CSO)   *See* **CSO.**

Chief technology officer (CTO)   *See* **CTO.**

Child   Document subordinate to another, such as a parent document.[16]

CHIN   **Community health information network.** The service model for delivery of medical information across a local community, shared between providers, that was promulgated in the early 1990s. The movement failed to take hold due to concerns about aligning costs with benefits, with confidentiality of patient and propriety information, and other factors.[99] *See* **RHIO.**

Chip   A small piece of thin semiconductor material, such as silicon, that has been chemically processed to have a specific set of electrical characteristics, such as circuits, storage, and/or logic elements.[1]

C-HOBIC   **Canadian Health Outcomes for Better Information and Care.** Joint project between the Canadian Nurses Association (CNA) and Canada Health Infoway to begin the process of collecting standardized clinical outcomes that are reflective of nursing practice for inclusion in electronic health records.[200]

Chronic care model   Model developed by Edward Wagner and colleagues that provides a solid foundation from which healthcare teams can operate. The model has six dimensions: community resources and policies; health system organization of healthcare; patient self-management supports; delivery system redesign; decision support; and clinical information system. The ultimate goal is to have activated patients interact in a productive way with well-prepared healthcare teams. Three components that are particularly critical to this goal are adequate decision support, which includes systems that encourage providers to use evidence-based protocols; delivery system redesign, such as using group visits and same-day appointments; and use of clinical information systems, such as disease registries, which allow providers to exchange information and follow patients over time.[138]

Chronic disease   A sickness that is long-lasting or recurrent. Examples include diabetes, asthma, heart disease, kidney disease, and chronic lung disease.[138]

Chronic disease management   *See* **Disease management**.

CHV   Consumer health vocabulary initiative. Open-access, collaborative initiative that links everyday words and phrases about health to technical terms or jargon used by healthcare professionals.[199]

CIA   Confidentiality / integrity / availability. The *CIA triad* is one of the core principles of information security.[7]

CIO   Chief information officer. Responsible for the overall planning and management of the information technology department, including establishing strategic long-term goals and determining long-term systems needs and hardware acquisitions to accomplish business objectives.[2]

CIO   Chief informatics officer. Healthcare executive generally responsible for the health informatics platform required to work with clinical IT staff to support the efficient design, implementation, and use of health technology within a healthcare organization.[7]

Cipher text   Data produced through the use of encipherment, the semantic content of which is not available.[121]

Circuit switched   A type of network connection that establishes a continuous electrical connection between calling and called users for their exclusive use until the connection is released (e.g., telephone system); ideal for communications that require data to be transmitted in real-time.[1] *See* **Packet switching**.

CIS   Clinical information system. A system dedicated to collecting, storing, manipulating, and making available clinical information important to the delivery of healthcare. Clinical information systems may be limited in scope to a single area (e.g., lab system, ECG management system) or they may be comprehensive and cover virtually all facets of clinical information (e.g., electronic patient; the original discharge summary residing in the chart, with

a copy of the report sent to the admitting physician, another copy existing on the transcriptionist's machine).[8]

CISC   Complex instruction set computer processor. CISC computers use microprocessors with a large number of execution steps and many clock cycles to operate. Intel computers are CISC computers.[1]

Claim attachment   Any variety of hardcopy forms or electronic records needed to process a claim, in addition to the claim itself.[10]

Claim status category codes   A national administrative code set that indicates the general category of the status of healthcare claims. This code set is used in the Accredited Standards Committee (ASC) X12 248 claim status notification transaction, and is maintained by the healthcare code maintenance committee.[10]

Claim status codes   A national administrative code set that identifies the status of healthcare claims. This code set is used in the Accredited Standards Committee (ASC) X12 277 claim status notification transaction, and is maintained by the healthcare code maintenance committee.[10]

Class   A term used in programs written in the object-oriented paradigm. A class description will contain the code which describes the features (i.e., the data [properties] and behaviors [methods] of an object).[4]

Classification   The systematic placement of things or concepts into categories that share some common attribute, quality, or property. A classification structure is a listing of terms that depicts hierarchical structures.[4]

Clear text   Unencoded text that can easily be read.[1] *See* **Plain text**.

Clearance level   The security level of an individual who may access information.[1]

Clickable image   Any image that has instructions embedded on it so that clicking on it initiates some kind of action or result. On a web page, a clickable image is any image that has a URL embedded in it.[1]

Client   An individual who requests or receives services in healthcare. May be used in place of the word 'patient.'[118]

Client A single term used interchangeably to refer to the user, the workstations, and the portion of the program that runs on the workstation. If the client is on a local area network (LAN), the client can share resources with another computer (server).[8]

Client application A system entity, usually a computer process acting on behalf of a human user, that makes use of a service provided by a server.[114]

Client information Personal information relating to healthcare.[118]

Client records All personal information that has been collected, compiled, or created about clients, which may be maintained in one or more locations and in various forms, reports, or documents; including information that is stored or transmitted by electronic media.[118]

Client registry A client registry is the area where a patient/person's information (i.e., name, date of birth, Social Security number, health access number) is securely stored and maintained.[8]

Client/server model 1. A client application is one that resides on a user's computer, but sends requests to a remote system to execute a designated procedure using arguments supplied by the user. The computer that initiates the request is the client, and the computer responding to the request is the server. 2. A model for computing that splits the processing between clients and servers on a network, assigning functions to the machine most able to perform the function.[1]

Clinical algorithm Flow charts to which a diagnostician or therapist can refer for a decision on how to manage a patient with a specific clinical program.[14]

Clinical care classification CCC. Standardized, coded nursing terminology system that identifies the discrete elements of nursing practice. CCC provides a unique framework and coding structure for capturing the essence of patient care in all healthcare settings.[27]

Clinical context management See **CCoM**.

Clinical context object workgroup See **CCOW**.

Clinical data All relevant clinical and socio-economic data disclosed by the patient and others, as well as observations, findings, therapeutic interventions, and prognostic statements, generated by the members of the healthcare team.[1]

Clinical data information systems Automated systems that serve as a tool to inform clinicians about tests, procedures, and treatment in an effort to improve quality of care through real-time assistance in decision making, and to increase efficiency and decrease unnecessary utilization.[1]

Clinical data repository See **CDR**.

Clinical data warehouse See **CDW**.

Clinical decision support See **CDS**.

Clinical decision support system An application that uses pre-established rules and guidelines that can be created and edited by the healthcare organization, and integrates clinical data from several sources to generate alerts and treatment suggestions. Also known as *CDSS*.

Clinical document architecture See **CDA**.

Clinical documentation system An application that allows clinicians to chart treatment/therapy/health assessment results for a patient. This application provides the flow sheets and care plan documentation for a patient's course of therapy.[2]

Clinical informaticist A person who evaluates clinical data relative to improving patient safety, clinical outcomes, and protocols and guidelines for clinical services. The functions are usually performed by people with clinical degrees.[2]

Clinical informatics 1. Promotes the understanding, integration, and application of information technology in healthcare settings. 2. The application of informatics and information technology to deliver healthcare services.[45,183]

Clinical information or data Information/data related to the health and healthcare of an individual, collected from or about an individual receiving healthcare services.[1]

Clinical laboratory information system Information system that manages clinical laboratory data to support laboratory management, laboratory data collection and processing, patient care, and medical decision making. **Note:** May be part of a hospital information system, or may be independent.[4] *Also known as* **LIS**.

Clinical observation Clinical information, excluding information about treatment and intervention.[4] **Note:** Clinical information that does not record an intervention is, by nature, a clinical observation.

Clinical observation access service *See* **COAS**.

Clinical pathway A patient care management tool that organizes, sequences, and times the major interventions of nursing staff, physicians, and other departments for a particular case type, subset, or condition.[123]

Clinical performance measure This is a method or instrument to estimate or monitor the extent to which the actions of a healthcare practitioner or provider conform to practice guidelines, medical review criteria, or standards of quality.[102]

Clinical practice guidelines A set of systematically developed statements, usually based on scientific evidence, to assist practitioners and patient decision making about appropriate healthcare for specific clinical circumstances.[123]

Clinical protocol A set of rules defining a standardized treatment program or behavior in certain circumstances.[4]

Clinical quality measures *See* **CQM**.

Clinical record *See* **EHR**.

Clinical status Description of the individual by means of results for a specified set of measurable quantities.[4]

Clinical terminology Terminology required directly or indirectly to describe health conditions and healthcare activities.[59]

Clinical terminology system Consists of a collection of words or phrases organized together to represent the entities and relationships that characterize the knowledge within a given biomedical domain.[108]

Clinical trials Research studies that involve patients. Biotechnology companies typically use clinical trials to assess the efficacy and safety of new therapies and to answer scientific questions. Typically, there are three phases during a clinical trial. Phase I is designed to evaluate the safety of the product in humans; phase II analyzes the effects of dose escalation; and phase III definitively evaluates the clinical efficacy of the product.[104]

Clinical/medical code sets Code sets used to identify medical conditions and the procedures, services, equipment, and supplies used to deal with them. Non-clinical or non-medical or administrative code sets identify, or characterize, entities and events in a manner that facilitates an administrative process.[10]

Clipboard An area used to temporarily store cut or copied information; can store text, graphics, objects, and other data. Clipboard contents are erased when new information is placed on the clipboard, or when the computer is shut down.[1]

Clock speed Measure of how quickly a computer completes basic computations and operations. This is measured as a frequency in hertz (Hz) and most commonly refers to the speed of the computer's central processing unit.[170]

Closed card system A smartcard system in which the cards can only be used in a specified environment, such as a college campus.[1]

Closed loop medication administration An environment in which the medication process is electronic from initial entry by physicians using CPOE, to pharmacies for order validation and bar coding the medications, to the automatic dispensing machines, to the actual administration of the medication at the point of care by the nurse, the point at which the nurse scans patient bar code and the medication bar code, which initiates clinical decision support for the five rights of medication administration: right patient, right time, right drug, right dose, and right route.[2]

Cloud Cloud computing. A model for enabling ubiquitous, convenient, on-demand network access to a shared pool of configurable computing resources (e.g., networks, servers, storage, applications, and services) that can be rapidly provisioned and released with minimal management effort or service provider interaction.[57]

Cluster Disk storage unit of 1,024 bytes.[1]

CM Composite message/composite data type. A field that is a combination of other meaningful data fields. Each portion is called a component.[16]

CMD Command. File type: External Command Menu. Dot (.) CMD is similar to a DOS .bat (batch file) or an .exe (executable file). A way of giving command line (like DOS) prompts to the computer (e.g., to map the drive).[7]

CMET Common message element type. Reusable data types, which can be included in any number of messages without repeating the common internal structure.[16]

CMIO Chief medical information officer. Provides overall leadership in the ongoing development, implementation, advancement, and optimization of electronic information systems that impact patient care. Works in partnership with the organization's IT leadership to translate clinician requirements into specifications for new clinical and research systems.[2]

CMIO Chief medical informatics officer. Healthcare executive generally responsible for the health informatics platform required to work with clinical information technology staff to support the efficient design, implementation, and use of health technology within a healthcare organization.[7]

CMYK Cyan, magenta, yellow, and black. 1. Printing processes, such as offset lithography, use CMYK inks; digital art must be converted to CMYK color for print. **2.** The 'K' in CMYK stands for Key, since in four-color printing cyan, magenta, and yellow printing plates are carefully keyed or aligned with the key of the black key plate.[7,57]

CNCL Cancelled.

CNIO Chief nursing information officer. Leads the strategy, development, and implementation of information technology to support, nursing, nursing practice and clinical applications, collaborating with the chief nursing officer on the clinical and administration decision-making process.[2]

COA Compliance-oriented architecture. The virtues of service-oriented architectures (SOAs) applied to the specific business challenge of compliance, the result is a flexible architecture that can meet compliance challenges now and in the future. Compliance requirements can be expressed as a set of core services.[88]

COAS Clinical observations access service. Standardizes access to clinical observations in multiple formats, including numerical data stored by instruments, or entered from observations.[88]

Coaxial cable Network/communications cable medium, consisting of an inner conductor encased in a clear/white insulation and a braided outer conductor, surrounded by black PVC insulation.[1]

COB Close of business.[99]

COB Coordination of benefits. 1. The process by which a payer handles claims that may involve other insurance companies (i.e., situations in which an insured individual is covered by more than one insurance plan). **2.** Process of determining which health plan or insurance policy will pay first and/or determining the payment obligations of each health plan, medical insurance policy, or third-party resource when two or more health plans, insurance policies, or third-party resources cover the same benefits.[184]

Code 1. Concept identifier that is unique within a coding system. **2.** A representation assigned to a term so that the term may more readily be electronically processed.[126,151]

Code 128 A one-dimensional bar code symbology, using four different bar widths, used in blood banking and other health and non-healthcare applications.[99] *See* **ISBT 128.**

Code division multiple access *See* CDMA.

Code meaning Element within a coded set.[117]

Code set 1. A set of elements which is mapped onto another set according to a coding scheme. **2.** Clinical or medical code sets identify medical conditions, and the procedures, services, equipment, and supplies used to deal with them. Non-clinical or non-medical or administrative code sets identify, or characterize, entities and events in a manner that facilitates an administrative process.[3,9]

Code set maintaining organization Under the Health Insurance Portability and Accountability Act (HIPAA), this is an organization that creates and maintains the code sets adopted by the HHS Secretary for use in the transactions for which standards are adopted.[10]

Code value Result of applying a coding scheme to a code meaning.[117]

Codec Compression/decompression. An algorithm, or specialized computer program, that reduces the number of bytes consumed by large files and programs.[57]

Coded element *See* **CE.**

Coded formatted elements *See* **CF.**

Coded with exceptions *See* **CWE.**

Coding The activity of using a coding scheme to map from one set of elements to another set of elements. The products of classification and coding are often used for similar purposes and sometimes considered as the same; however, coding and classification are distinct concepts.[4]

Coding scheme The collection of rules that maps the elements of one set onto the elements of a second set.[3]

Coding system Combination of a set of concepts (coded concepts), a set of code values, and at least one coding scheme mapping code values to coded concepts.[126]

Collect and communicate audit trails Means to define and identify security relevant events and the data to be collected and communicated, as determined by policy, regulation, or risk analysis.[48]

Collect/collection The assembling of personal information through interviews, forms, reports, or other information sources.[48]

Collision detection The ability of a transmitting node to detect traffic on an Ethernet (baseband) shared network. If a transmitting station detects silence, it will transmit data. If a collision takes place, the transmitting station will wait a random amount of time before attempting to re-transmit the entire message.[1] *See* **CSMA/CD.**

Comm closet Room or location where network electronic equipment resides and where drops terminate.[1] Also known as a *wiring closet.*

Command A sequence of words and/or symbols that instructs the computer to perform a specific task.[4]

Command interpreter Program that accesses and executes user input.[1]

Committee draft *See* **CD.**

Common alerting protocol *See* **CAP.**

Common gateway interface *See* **CGI.**

Common message element type *See* **CMET.**

Common object request broker architecture *See* **CORBA.**

Common services A type of software service that can be shared across multiple applications. These include services such as messaging, security, logging, auditing, mapping, etc. Common services are part of the health information access layer.[8]

Common vulnerabilities and exposures *See* **CVE.**

Common weakness enumeration *See* **CWE.**

Communication bus Part of the health information access layer that allows applications to communicate according to standard messages and protocols.[8]

Communication network Configuration of hardware, software, and transmission facilities for transmission and routing of data carrying signals between electronic devices.[4]

Communications security *See* **COMSEC.**

Communities of interest Inclusive term to describe collaborative groups of users who must exchange information in pursuit of shared goals, interests, missions, or business process; and must have a shared vocabulary for the information exchanged. Communities provide an organization and maintenance construct for data.[18]

Community health information network *See* **CHIN.**

Compact disc *See* **CD.**

Compact disk read only memory *See* **CD-ROM.**

Comparability The ability of different parties to share precisely the same meaning for data.[151]

Comparison The process of comparing a biometric with a previously stored reference.[114]

Compatibility Suitability of products, processes, or services for use together under specific conditions to fulfill relevant requirements without causing unacceptable interactions.[4]

Competence Demonstrated performance and application of knowledge to perform a required skill or activity to a specific, predetermined standard.[123]

Compiler **1.** Programs written in high-level languages are translated into assembly language or machine language by a compiler. Assembly language programs are translated into machine language by a program called an assembler. Every CPU has its own unique machine language. Programs must be rewritten or recompiled, therefore, to run on different types of computers. **2.** A program that translates a program written in a high-level programming language to a machine-language program, which can then be executed.[4,7] *See* **Assembler**.

Complex instruction set computer processor *See* **CISC**.

Compliance Adherence to those policies, procedures, guidelines, laws, regulations, and contractual arrangements to which the business process is subject.[118]

Compliance date Under the Health Insurance Portability and Accountability Act (HIPAA), this is the date by which a covered entity must comply with a standard, an implementation specification, or a modification. This is usually 24 months after the effective date of the associated final rule for most entities; 36 months for small health plans. For future changes in the standards, the compliance date would be at least 180 days after the effective date, but can be longer for small health plans or for complex changes.[10]

Component An object-oriented term used to describe the building block of GUI applications. A software object that contains data and code. A component may or may not be visible.[4]

Component object model Used by developers to create reusable software components, link components together to build applications, and take advantage of Windows services.[12]

Composite message *See* **CM**.

Compression/decompression *See* **Codec**.

Compromise Disclosure of information to unauthorized persons, or a violation of the security policy of a system in which unauthorized intentional or unintentional disclosure, modification, destruction, or loss of an object may have occurred.[114]

Computed tomography *See* **CT**.

Computer-assisted coding Software solutions using natural language processing (NLP), which is an exclusive patented algorithmic software to electronically analyze entire medical charts to pre-code with both CPT procedure and ICD diagnostic nomenclatures.[2]

Computer emergency response team *See* **CERT**.

Computer network A collection of computers that are physically and logically connected together to exchange information.[1]

Computer readable card A card capable of storing information in a form that can be read by a computer. Information may be written to the card on manufacture, or may be added during the use of the card. If the card contains a processor, the card is known as a *smartcard*.[4]

Computer security The protection of data and resources from accidental or malicious acts, usually by taking appropriate actions.[3]

Computer system An integrated arrangement of computer hardware and software operated by customers to perform prescribed tasks.[4]

Computer telephony integration *See* **CTI**.

Computer-aided detection *See* **CAD**.

Computer-aided instruction, computer-based training The development and use of computer technology to facilitate training or education on a topic. One of the most important advantages of using computer-based training is that the learner is provided with a self-paced training module.[6] *See* **CAL, CBL**.

Computer-assisted learning *See* **CAL** and **CBL**.

Computer-assisted medicine Use of computers directly in diagnostic or therapeutic interventions (e.g., computer-assisted surgery).

Computer-assisted software engineering *See* **CASE**.

Computer-based learning *See* **CBL**.

Computer-based patient record Term coined by the Institute of Medicine in its work *The Computer-based Patient Record: An Essential Technology for Health Care* (Washington, DC: National Academy Press, 1991, p.11, rev. 1997). It may be used synonymously with *electronic medical record* or *electronic health record*. It is electronic patient medical record information that resides in a system specifically designed to support users by providing accessibility to complete and accurate data, alerts, reminders, clinical decision support systems, links to medical knowledge, and other aids.[151] *See* **EHR**.

Computerized axial tomography *See* **CAT**.

Computerized practitioner order entry *See* **CPOE**.

Computer-on-wheels *See* **COW**.

Computing environment The total environment in which an automated information system, network, or a component operates. The environment includes physical, administrative, and personnel procedures, as well as communication and networking relationships, with other information systems.[97]

COMSEC **Communications security.** Measures and controls taken to deny unauthorized persons information derived from telecommunications and ensure the authenticity of such telecommunications. Communications security includes cryptosecurity, transmission security, emission security, and physical security of COMSEC material.[97]

Concentrator Network device where networked nodes are connected. Used to divide a data channel into two or more channels of lower bandwidth.[1] *See* **Hub**.

Concept 1. A concept is an abstraction or a general notation that may serve as a unit of thought or a theory. In terminology work, the distinction is made between a concept and the terms that reference the concept. Where the concept is identified as abstract from the language and the term is a symbol that is part of the language. 2. A clinical idea to which a unique concept has been assigned. Each concept is represented by a row in the concepts table. Concept equivalence occurs when a post-coordinated expression has the same meaning as a pre-coordinated concept or another post-coordinated expression.[4,19] **Note 1:** Informally, the term 'concept' is often used when what is meant is 'concept representation'. However, this leads to confusion when precise meanings are required. Concepts arise out of human individual and social conceptualizations of the world around them. Concept representations are artifacts constructed of symbols.[96] **Note 2:** Concept representations are not necessarily bound to particular languages. However, they are influenced by the social or cultural context of use often leading to different categorizations.[96]

Concept harmonization Activity for reducing or eliminating minor differences between two or more concepts that are closely related to each other.[4] **Note:** Concept harmonization is an integral part of standardization.

Concept identifier Concept name, code, or symbol, which uniquely identifies a concept.[96]

Concept status A field in the concepts table that specifies whether a concept is in current use. Values include 'current,' 'duplicate,' 'erroneous,' 'ambiguous,' and 'limited.'[19]

Concept unique identifier *See* **CUI**.

Concepts table A data table consisting of rows, each of which represents a concept.[19]

Concurrent versioning system *See* **CVS**.

Conditional formatting *See* **CF**.

Confidentiality 1. Obligation of an entity that receives identifiable information about an individual as part of providing a service to that individual to protect that data or information; including not disclosing the identifiable information to unauthorized persons, or through unauthorized processes. 2. A property by which information relating to an entity or party is not made available or disclosed to unauthorized individuals, entities, or processes.[48,3]

Confidentiality/integrity/availability
See **CIA**.

Configuration The components that make up a computer system, including the identity of the manufacturer, model, and various peripherals; the physical arrangement of those components (what is placed and where). The software settings that enable two computer components to communicate with each other.[1]

Configuration control Process of controlling modifications to an IT system's hardware, firmware, software, and documentation to ensure the system is protected against improper modifications prior to, during, and after system implementation.[97]

Configuration management Management of security features and assurances through control of changes made to hardware, software, firmware, documentation, test, test fixtures, and test documentation, throughout the lifecycle of the IT.[97]

Configuration manager The individual or organization responsible for configuration control or configuration management.[97]

Configuration services This service is used to configure the EHRs. This includes configuration of the EHR data repository, the system, the metadata, the service components, EHR indexes, schema support, security, session, and caching mechanism, etc.[8]

Conformance The precise set of conditions for the use of options which must be implemented in a standard. There are two types of conformance: dynamic and static. Dynamic conformance requirements of a standard are all those requirements (including options) which determine the possible behavior permitted by the standard. Static conformance is a statement of what conforming implementation should be capable of doing (i.e., what is implemented).[3]

Conformance assessment process The complete process of accomplishing all conformance testing activities necessary to enable the conformance of an implementation or system to one or more standards to be assessed.[4]

Conformance testing Testing to determine whether a system meets some specified standard. To aid in this, many test procedures and test setups have been developed, either by the standard's maintainers or external organizations, specifically for testing conformance to standards. Conformance testing is often performed by external organizations, sometimes the standards body itself, to give greater guarantees of compliance. Products tested in such a manner are then advertised as being certified by that external organization as complying with the standard.[7]

Connectathon A testing event to which developers have registered their implementations for supervised interoperability testing with other implementations. Each participating system is tested for each registered combination of IHE actor and IHE integration or content profile.[93]

Connectivity The potential to establish links to, or interact with, another computer system or database.[1]

Consensus General agreement, characterized by the absence of sustained opposition to substantial issues by any important part of the concerned interests, and by a process that involves seeking to take into account the views of all parties concerned, and to reconcile any conflicting arguments.[4]

Consensus standards These are standards developed or adopted by consensus standards bodies, both domestic and international. Such work and the resultant standards are usually voluntary.[3]

Consent Under the Privacy Rule, consent is made by an individual for the covered entity to use or disclose identifiable health information for treatment, payment, and healthcare operations purposes only. This is different from consent for treatment, which many providers use and which should not be confused with the consent for use or disclosure of identifiable health information. Consent for use and/or disclosure of identifiable health information is optional under the Privacy Rule, although it may be required by state law, and may be combined with consent for treatment unless prohibited by other law.[48]

Consent directive The record of a healthcare consumer's privacy policy that grants or withholds consent for: one or more principals (identified entity or role); performing one or more operations (e.g., collect, access, use, disclose, amend, or delete); purposes, such as treatment, payment, operations, research, public health, quality measures, health status evaluation by third parties, or marketing; certain conditions (e.g., when unconscious); specified time period (e.g., effective and expiry dates); and certain context (e.g., in an emergency).[48]

Consent informed *See* **Informed consent**.

Consenter An author of a consent directive; and may be the healthcare consumer or patient, a delegate of the healthcare consumer (e.g., a representative with healthcare power of attorney), or a provider with legal authority to either override a healthcare consumer's consent directive, or create a directive that prevents a patient's access to protected health information (PHI) until the provider has had an opportunity to review the PHI with the patient.[48]

Consistency The transaction takes the resources from one consistent state to another.[7] *See* **ACID**.

Consistent presentation of images *See* **CPI**.

Consistent time *See* **CT**.

Consumer empowerment use case This HITSP Interoperability Specification (Interoperability Specification 03) is designed to meet the specific requirements of the consumer empowerment use case, defined as the active involvement of consumers (i.e., individuals) in managing their healthcare and gaining the benefits of having their health information in a format easily accessible to them. This includes having a personal health record (PHR) to track patient information, insurance, family history, medications, and other special conditions.[48]

Consumer health vocabulary initiative *See* **CHV.**

Contact An electrical connecting surface between an integrated circuit chip and its interfacing device that permits a flow of current.[1]

Content coverage The ability of a coding system to capture the meaning of a document.[1]

Content profile An IHE content profile specifies a coordinated set of standards-based information content, exchanged between the functional components of communicating healthcare IT systems and devices. An IHE content profile specifies a specific element of content (e.g., a document) that may be conveyed through the transactions of one or more associated integration profile(s).[93]

Continuity A performance dimension addressing the degree to which the care for a patient is coordinated among practitioners and organizations, and over time, without interruption, cessation, or unnecessary repetition of diagnosis or treatment.[123]

Continuity Strategic and tactical capability, preapproved by management, of an organization to plan for and respond to conditions, situations, and events in order to continue operations at an acceptable predefined level.[175]

Continuity of care document *See* **CCD.**

Continuity of care record *See* **CCR.**

Continuity strategy Approach by an organization intended to ensure continuity and ability to recover in the face of a disruptive event, emergency, crisis, or other major outage.[175]

Continuous improvement **1.** A management strategy to embed awareness of quality in all organizational processes. It has been widely used in healthcare (beginning in the 1990s), manufacturing, education, government, service industries, as well as NASA space and science programs. It employs teamwork, statistical techniques, and motivational factors. **2.** When applied to healthcare in the 1990s, the first generation of clinical decision support tools emerged, including casemix systems and rudimentary medical alerting systems.[7]

Control Means of managing risk, including policies, procedures, guidelines, practices, or organizational structures, which can be of administrative, technical, management, or legal nature.[124]

Control chart A graphic display of the results of a process over time and against established control limits. The dispersion of data points on the chart is used to determine whether the process is performing within prescribed limits, and whether variations taking place are random or systematic.[123]

Control rights The right of an individual to know where his/her data are stored, to authorize who can access his/her own data, to correct his/

her own record, to make certain segments inaccessible via standard process, and to know that the data keeper observes the laws and professional ethical tenets.[1]

Control unit *See* **CU.**

Controlled access Authorized user access limited to specific data and resources, according to that user's authorization.[1]

Controlled resource A resource to which an access control mechanism has been specifically applied.[1]

Controlled vocabulary An established list of standardized terminology for use in indexing and retrieval of information.[145]

Conventional memory The range of RAM used by MS-DOS to run real-mode (access to all system hardware) applications.[1]

Convergence The end point of any algorithm that uses iteration or recursion to guide a series of data processing steps. An algorithm is usually said to have reached convergence when the difference between the computed and observed steps falls below a predefined threshold.[104]

Cookies An amount of data generated by a web site and saved to the web browser. The purpose is to remember information about the web session, similar to a preference file created by a software application.[147]

Coordination of benefits *See* **COB.**

Coprocessor A chip designed specifically to handle a particular task, such as math calculations or displaying graphics on-screen; faster at its specialized function than the main processor; relieves the processor of some work.[1]

CORBA Common object request broker architecture. A language-independent object model and specification for a distributed applications development environment.[1]

Core-based statistical area. *See* **CBSA.**

Core values An organization's essential and enduring tenets—a small set of general guiding principles.[185]

Corporate executives or C-level *See* **CxO.**

Cost containment The process of planning in order to keep costs within certain constraints.[4]

Cost effectiveness A system contributing to cost savings in healthcare by efficiently collecting, storing, and aggregating data; and by providing decision support and augmented practices with appropriate and timely information.[6]

Cost-benefit analysis A comparison of the costs of a proposed course of action with its benefits, considering tangible and intangible economic impacts, and the time value of money.[6]

Countermeasure response administration *See* **CRA.**

Covered entity Health plans, healthcare clearinghouses, and healthcare providers who transmit any health information in electronic form, in connection with a transaction that is subject to federal Health Insurance Portability and Accountability Act (HIPAA) requirements, as those terms are defined and used in the HIPAA regulations, 45 CFR Parts 160 and 164.[118]

Covered function Functions that make an entity a health plan, a healthcare provider, or a healthcare clearing house.[10]

COW Computer-on-wheels.[16]

CP Certificate policy. Named set of rules that indicates the applicability of a certificate to a particular community and/or class of application with common security requirements.[121]

CPI Consistent presentation of images. Specifies a number of transactions that maintain the consistency of presentation for grayscale images and their presentation state information (including user annotations, shutters, flip/rotate, display area, and zoom). It also defines a standard contrast curve, the Grayscale Standard Display function, against which different types of display and hardcopy output devices can be calibrated. It thus supports hardcopy, softcopy, and mixed environments. *See* **Profile. NOTE: CPI is an Integrating the Healthcare Enterprise (IHE) Profile.**

CPM Control program for microcomputers. Introduced in the late 1970s, this was the first standard microcomputer operating system, and generally used by the first generation of microcomputers. It relied on an 8-bit architecture, and was configured to run on a variety of microprocessors. Usage decreased after the advent of MS-DOS and the Apple operating system.[99]

CPOE Computerized practitioner order entry. 1. An order entry application specifically designed to assist practitioners in creating and managing medical orders for patient services and medications. This application has special electronic signature, workflow, and rules engine functions that reduce or eliminate medical errors associated with practitioner ordering processes. **2.** A computer application that accepts the provider's orders for diagnostic and treatment services electronically, instead of the clinician recording them on an orders sheet or prescription pad.[2] Also known as *computerized physician order entry, computerized patient order entry,* and *computerized provider order entry.*

CPR Computer-based patient record. *See* **EHR**.

CPRS Computer-based patient record system. *See* **EHR**.[1]

CPS Certification practices statement. Statement of the practices that a certification authority employs in issuing certificates.[121]

CPT Current Procedural Terminology. 1. The official coding system for physicians to report professional services and procedures to third parties for payment. It is produced by the American Medical Association.[15] **2.** A medical code set, maintained and copyrighted by the AMA, that has been selected for use under HIPAA for non-institutional and non-dental professional transactions.[9,151]

CPU Central processing unit. 1. The component in a digital computer that interprets and executes the instructions and data contained in software. Microprocessors are CPUs that are manufactured on integrated circuits, often as a single-chip package. **2.** Brain of the computer. Main system board (motherboard) integrated chip that directs computer operations. Performs the arithmetic, logic, and controls operations in the computer.[1]

CQM Clinical quality measures. Tools that measure and track the quality of healthcare services provided by eligible professionals (EPs), eligible hospitals, and critical-access hospitals (CAHs) within the US healthcare system.

CRA Countermeasure response administration. Systems that manage and track measures taken to contain an outbreak or event, and to provide protection against a possible outbreak or event. This public health information network (PHIN) functional area also includes multiple dose delivery of countermeasures: anthrax vaccine and antibiotics; adverse events monitoring; follow-up of patients; isolation and quarantine; and links to distribution vehicles (such as the Strategic National Stockpile).[46]

Crash A data system error condition leading to a total termination of all computing activities, and requiring a restart procedure for recovering normal operational status.[1]

Crawler A program that automatically fetches web pages. Crawlers are used to feed pages to search engines.[1] *See* **Webcrawler**.

Credential Evidence attesting to one's right to credit or authority; in this standard, the data elements associated with an individual that authoritatively binds an identity (and, optionally, additional attributes) to that individual.[114]

Crisis An unstable condition involving an impending abrupt or significant change that requires urgent attention and action to protect life, assets, property, or the environment.[175]

Crisis management Holistic management process that identifies potential impacts that threaten an organization and provides a framework for building resilience. Includes the capability for an effective response that safeguards the interests of its key stakeholders, reputation, brand, and value-creating activities—as well as effectively restoring operational capabilities.[175]

Crisis management team Group of individuals functionally responsible for directing the development and execution of the response and operational continuity plan, declaring an operational disruption or emergency/crisis situation, and providing direction during the recovery process, both pre- and post-disruptive incident. The crisis management team may include individuals from the organization, as well as immediate and first responders, stakeholders, and other interested parties.[175]

Critical-access hospital *See* **CAH**.

Critical activity Any function or process that is essential for the organization to deliver its products and/or services.[174]

Critical path A tool that supports collaborative, coordinated practices. It provides for multidisciplinary communication, treatment and care planning, and documentation of caregiver's evaluations and assessments.[6]

Criticality The quality, state, or degree of being of the highest importance.[220]

Criticality assessment A process designed to systematically identify and evaluate an organization's assets based on the importance of its mission or function, the group of people at risk, or the significance of a disruption on the continuity of the organization.[175]

CRM Customer relationship management. The approach of establishing relationships with customers on an individual basis, then using collected information about customers and their buying habits to treat different customers differently.[1]

Cross-enterprise document sharing *See* **XDS**.

Cross map A reference from one concept in one terminology to another in a different terminology. A concept may have a single cross map or a set of alternative cross maps.[19]

Cross-platform Refers to software or network functionality that will work on more than one platform or type of computer.[1]

Crosstalk Signal overflow from one wire to an adjacent wire, with the possibility of causing information distortion. UTP cable is the most susceptible transmission medium to crosstalk.[1]

Crosswalk *See* **Data mapping**.

CRUD Create, read, update, and delete.[18]

Cryptographic algorithm cipher Method for the transformation of data in order to hide its information content, prevent its undetected modification, and/or prevent its unauthorized use.[121]

Cryptography The art of keeping data secret, primarily through the use of mathematical or logical functions that transform intelligible data into seemingly unintelligible data and back again.[1]

CSMA/CD Carrier sense multiple access with collision detection. A network control protocol in which a carrier-sensing scheme is used; and a transmitting data station that detects another signal while transmitting a frame, stops transmitting that frame, transmits a jam signal, and then waits for a random time interval (known as 'backoff delay' and determined using the truncated binary exponential backoff algorithm) before trying to send that frame again. Ethernet is the classic CSMA/CD protocol.[7]

CSO Chief security officer. The person with the responsibility for the security of the paper-based and electronic health information, as well as the physical and electronic means of managing and storing that information.

CSU/DSU Channel sharing unit/data service unit. A unit that shapes digital signals for transmission. The CSU is a device that performs protective and diagnostic functions for a telecommunications line.[1]

CT Computed tomography. Specialized x-ray imaging technique.[7] Also known as *computerized tomography.*

CT Consistent time. Mechanisms to synchronize the time base between multiple actors and computers. Various infrastructure, security, and acquisition profiles require use of a consistent time base on multiple computers. The consistent time profile provides a median synchronization error of less than one second.[56] *See* **Profile**. **NOTE: CT is an Integrating the Healthcare Enterprise (IHE) Profile.**

CTI Computer telephony integration. Systems that enable a computer to act as a call center, accepting incoming calls and routing them to the appropriate device or person.[1]

CTO Chief technology officer. 1. Has overall responsibility for managing technical vendor relationships and performance, as well as the physical and personnel technology infrastructure, including technology deployment, network and systems management, integration testing, and developing technical operations personnel. **2.** Develops technical standards and ensures compatibility for the enterprise-wide computer environment.[1,2]

CTS   Common terminology services. Specification developed as an alternative to a common data structure.[16]

CU   Control unit. Portion of the CPU that coordinates all computer operations through the machine cycle: fetch, decode, execute, and store.[1]

CUI   Concept unique identifier. The class of names that uniquely identify an instance of entity. Some examples of unique identifiers are the keys of tables in database applications and the International Standard Book Number (ISBN).[1]

Culture   The mindset of an organization (e.g., a culture may be collaborative vs. regimented, favor open vs. proprietary solutions, or be internally vs. externally focused).[1]

Cure letter   A letter sent by one party to another, proposing or agreeing to actions that a party will take to correct legal errors or defects that have occurred under a contract between the parties or other legal requirement.[118]

Current procedural terminology   *See* **CPT**.

Curriculum development centers program One component of the Office of the National Coordinator (ONC) Workforce Program is to provide funding to institutions of higher education (or consortia thereof) to support health information technology curriculum development.[178]

Cursor   The representation of the mouse location on the screen; may take many shapes.[1]

Custom, customized   Software that is designed or modified for a specific user or organization; may refer to all or part of a system. *See* **Vanilla**.[1]

Customer relationship management *See* **CRM**.[1]

Customer-centric   Placing the customer at the center or focus of design or service.[7]

Customer-driven   Systems design focused on user acceptance; focused on customer requirements.[7]

CVE   Common vulnerabilities and exposures. A list of standardized names for vulnerabilities and other information security exposures. CVE aims to standardize the names for all publicly known vulnerabilities and secure exposures.[125]

CVS   Concurrent versioning system. Keeps track of all work and changes in a set of files.[7]

CWE   Coded with exceptions. A data type coded with exceptions.[16]

CWE   Common weakness enumeration. A community-developed formal list of software weaknesses, idiosyncrasies, faults, and flaws.[125]

CxO   Corporate executives or **C-level.** A short way to refer, collectively, to corporate executives at what is sometimes called the C-level, whose job titles typically start with 'Chief' and end with 'Officer.'[42]

Cyberspace   The realm of communications and computation. A term used to refer to the electronic universe of information available through the Internet.[1]

Cyberspace shadow   The model in cyberspace of a person or of an organization (e.g., a person's medical files).[1]

D

Dashboard   User interface based on predetermined data fields that facilitate domain-specific data queries and are suited to regular use with minimal training.[94]

DAT   Digital audio tape. A magnetic tape that stores audio data converted to digital form.[47]

Data   1. Items representing facts, text, numbers, graphics, images, sound or video. Data are the raw material used to create information. **2.** Discrete entities that are described objectively without interpretation. **3.** Data are information that has been translated into a form that is more convenient to move or process.[177,204,42]

Data aggregation   1. A process by which information is collected, manipulated, and expressed in summary form. **2.** Combining protected health information by a business associate, on behalf of more covered entities than one, to permit data analysis related to the healthcare operations of the participating covered entities.[160,48]

Data architecture The component of the data resource framework that contains all activities, and the products of those activities, related to the identification, naming, definition, structuring, quality, and documentation of the data resource for an organization.[177]

Data center 1. A centralized repository, either physical or virtual, for the storage, management, and dissemination of data and information organized around a particular body of knowledge or pertaining to a particular business. 2. Computer facility designed for continuous use by several users, and well-equipped with hardware, software, peripherals, power conditioning, and backup, communication equipment, security systems, etc.[42,205]

Data circuit-terminating equipment *See* **DCE**.

Data classification The decision to assign a level of sensitivity to data as they are being created, amended, enhanced, stored, or transmitted. The classification of the data then determines the extent to which the data need to be controlled/secured and is indicative of its value in terms of information assets.[118]

Data cleaning/cleansing Manipulating data extracted from operational systems to make data usable by the data warehouse.[177]

Data collection The process of gathering and measuring information on variables of interest, in an established systematic fashion that enables one to answer stated research questions, test hypotheses, and evaluate outcomes. While methods vary by discipline, the emphasis is on ensuring the accurate collection of data.[179]

Data compression 1. The process of eliminating gaps, empty fields, redundancies, and unnecessary data to shorten the length of records or blocks so they take up less space when stored or transmitted. 2. The process of reducing the amount of data needed for the storage or transmission of a given piece of information, typically by the use of encoding techniques.[1,206] Also known as *compaction*.

Data condition A description of the circumstances in which certain data are required.[102]

Data content All the data elements and code sets inherent to a transaction, and not related to the format of the transaction.[10]

Data corruption A deliberate or accidental violation of data integrity.[1]

Data definition language *See* **DDL**.

Data dictionary An alphabetical listing of data elements, listings of recommended coded values and a cross-reference from data elements to segments.[16]

Data diddling Unauthorized data alteration; a common form of computer crime.[1]

Data element 1. The smallest named unit of information in a transaction or database. 2. A unit of data for which the definition, identification, representation, and permissible values are specified by means of a set of attributes.[3,10]

Data elements for emergency department systems *See* **DEEDS**.

Data encryption standard *See* **DES** and **DEA**.

Data entry Changing information from the original source into machine readable format.[1]

Data exchange Securing transmissions over communication channels.[1]

Data field 1. The physical unit of storage in a record. 2. A physical structure in a form, file, or database that holds data. A field is one or more bytes in size. The field is the common denominator for database searches.

Data flow diagram 1. A special form of flow chart intended to help illustrate a process by showing events, or by tracing the paths of data through a process or operation. 2. A graphical representation of the 'flow' of data through an information system (how the output data from a process serve as the input data for other processes).[6,7]

Data governance The overall management of the availability, usability, integrity, and security of the data employed in an enterprise. A sound data governance program includes a governing body or council, a defined set of procedures, and a plan to execute those procedures.[42]

Data granularity   *See* **Granularity**.

Data integration   Combining data residing in different sources and providing a unified data view.[7]

Data integrity   **1.** Assurance of the accuracy, correctness, or validity of data, using a set of validation criteria against which data is compared or screened. **2.** The property that data have not been altered or destroyed in an unauthorized manner or by authorized users; it is a security principle that protects information from being modified or otherwise corrupted either maliciously or accidentally.[6,151]

Data interchange   The process of transferring data from an originating system to a receiving system.[4]

Data leakage   The practically undetectable loss of control over, or possession of, information.[1]

Data link layer   Second layer in the OSI model. Consists of upper logical link control (LLC) and lower media access control (MAC) portions. Handles data flow control, the packaging of raw data in its frames, or frames into raw data bits, and retransmits frames as needed.[1]

Data manipulation language   *See* **DML**.

Data mapping   **1.** The process of matching one set of data elements of individual code values to their closest equivalents in another set of them. **2.** Describes the process of creating data element mappings between two distinct data models.[10,7]

Data mark   A derivation of a data warehouse that is focused on publishing data from a single subject area or departmental point of view.[1]

Data mart   **1.** A well-organized, user-centered, searchable database system. A data mart picks up where a data warehouse stops, by organizing the information according to the user's needs (usually by specific subjects), with ease of use in mind. **2.** A repository of data that serves a particular community of knowledge workers. The data may come from an enterprise-wide database or a data warehouse. **3.** Collection of data focusing on a specific topic or organization unit or department created to facilitate strategic business decisions.[1,8,203]

Data messaging   *See* **Messaging**.

Data migration   Steps taken to enable legacy data to be accessible as part of a system that uses a specific type of semantic content. Options for data migration include actual conversion of the data or provision of methods for accessing the data in its original form.[19]

Data mining   A decision support approach of analyzing data, and then extracting actionable information in the form of new relationships, patterns, clusters, predictive models, and trends.[1]

Data model   **1.** A conceptual model of the information needed to support a business function or process. **2.** Describes the organization of data in an automated system. The data model includes the subjects of interest in the system (or entities) and the attributes (data elements) of those entities. It defines how the entities are related to each other (cardinality) and establishes the identifiers needed to relate entities to each other. A data model can be expressed as a conceptual, logical, or physical model.[10,8]

Data modeling   A method used to define and analyze data requirements needed to support the business functions of an enterprise. Data modeling defines the data elements, their relationships, and their physical structure in preparation for creating a database.[1]

Data object   A collection of data that has a natural grouping and may be identified as a complete entity.[117]

Data origin authentication   Corroboration that the source of data are received as is claimed.[1]

Data originator   The person who generates data, such as the patient for symptoms, the physician for examination and decisions, the nurse for patient care, etc.[1]

Dataport   Telephone socket that provides an outside line for sending data or a fax via modem. Any socket used for data communications, which can include infrared, serial, and parallel ports.[220]

Data processing   The systematic performance of operations upon data, such as handling, merging, sorting, and computing. The semantic content of the original data should not be changed, but the semantic content of the processed data may be changed.[104]

Data quality **1.** A comprehensive view of the usefulness of data to support decision making. The measurements of data quality include completeness, correctness, comprehensibility, and consistency in support of intended use. **2.** The features and characteristics that ensure data are accurate, complete, and convey the intended meaning.[1,151]

Data registry An information resource by a registration authority that describes the meaning and representational form (metadata) of data units, including data element identifiers, definitions, units, allowed value domains, etc. HIPAA's proposed standards for electronic transactions call for a master data dictionary to be developed and maintained to ensure common data definitions across standards selected for implementation.[151]

Data repository *See* **Repository** and **Data warehouse**.

Data service unit *See* **DSU**.[1]

Data services Group of services that will hold metadata for operations that are carried out on repositories, and abstract data access services for specific database management systems.[8]

Data set ready *See* **DSR**.

Data set **1.** A known grouping of data elements. **2.** Usually describes a minimum group of data elements to be collected in a standardized manner for a specific purpose. Examples: Uniform Hospital Discharge Data Set (UHDDS), developed by the National Committee on Vital and Health Statistics (NCVHS); Uniform Ambulatory Care Data Set, also developed by NCVHS; Minimum Data Set (MDS) for Long-term Care and Resident Assessment Protocols, created by Health Care Financing Administration (HCFA)—now the Centers for Medicare & Medicaid Services—the Outcomes and Assessment Information Set (OASIS), created by HCFA for home health data; the Health Plan Employer and Information Set (HEDIS), established for managed care accreditation by the National Committee for Quality Assurance (NCQA).[57,151] *See* **PNDS, NMDS, NMMDS**.

Data standards Consensual specifications for the representation of data from different sources and settings; necessary for the sharing, portability, and reusability of data.[110]

Data structure A hierarchical description of a set of data elements. A data set can be described according to its data structure.

Data subject The person whose information is stored in the computer.[1]

Data synchronization The process of sending data between two or more computers so that each repository contains the identical information.[7]

Data tagging A formatted word that represents a wrapper for a stored value. The data tag is a small piece of scripting code, typically JavaScript, which transmits page-specific information via query string parameters. The process begins when a page containing a data tag is requested from the server. The tag is a piece of scripting code executed when the page is loaded into the browser. The data tag constructs the query string by scanning the document source for HTML, beginning with a specific identifier.[18]

Data terminal ready *See* **DTR**.

Data transformation Methods by which stored data or information is processed according to the needs of the end user.[6]

Data type **1.** A category of data. The broadest data types are alphanumeric and numeric. Programming languages allow for the creation of several data types, such as integer (whole numbers), floating point, date, string (text), logical (true/false), and binary. Data type usually specifies the range of values, how the values are processed by the computer and how the data type is stored. **2.** The categories of data that will be persisted in the EHR. They include voice, waveforms, clinical notes, and summaries, diagnostic imaging, lab, and pharmacy information.[8,163]

Data use agreement Confidentiality agreement between a covered entity and the recipient of health information in a limited data set.[48]

Data user The person or organization that has justified need for certain data to perform his or her legitimate tasks.[1]

Data validation A process used to determine if data are accurate, complete, or meet specified criteria. Data validation may include format checks, check key tests, reasonableness checks, and limit checks.[3]

Data visualization A decision support methodology for turning data into information by using the high capacity of the human brain to visually recognize patterns and trends using a wide variety of data plotting, graphing, and exploration techniques.[1]

Data warehouse **1.** A repository where all types of data (clinical, administrative, and financial) are stored together for later retrieval. Data mining and decision support systems are uses of a data warehouse. When the perspective of the strategy or user shifts from the enterprise view of aggregate data to the individual user or knowledge worker (who may need access to a specialized or local database), then the system is referred to, instead, as a data mart. **2.** A collection of clinical and/or financial data in a database designed to support management decision making.[1,8]

Database **1.** A file created by a database manager that contains a collection of information. The basic database contains fields, records, and files; a field is a single piece of information, a record is one complete set of fields, and a file is a collection of records. **2.** A collection of stored data, typically organized into fields, records, files, and associated descriptions (schema).[1,4]

Database administrator The person responsible for a database system, particularly for defining the rules by which data are accessed, modified, and stored.[1]

Database design The process of producing a detailed data model of a database. This logical data model contains all the needed logical and physical design choices and physical storage parameters needed to generate a design in a Data Definition Language, which can then be used to create a database. A fully attributed data model contains detailed attributes for each entity.[7]

Database management system *See* **DBMS.**

Datum Any single observation or fact. A medical datum generally can be regarded as the value of a specific parameter (e.g., a patient, at a specific time).[4]

Daughterboard A board that attaches to another board, such as the motherboard or an expansion card. A daughter card may contain additional memory to an accelerator card.[1]

DBMS **Database management system. 1.** A program that lets one or more computer users create and access data in a database. On personal computers, Microsoft Access is a popular example of a single or small group user DBMS. Microsoft's SQL server is an example of a DBMS that serves database requests from multiple users. **2.** A set of programs used to define, administer, store, modify, process, and extract information from a database.[2,1]

DCE **Data circuit-terminating equipment.** Typically a modem or other type of communication device.[90]

DDL **Data definition language.** A syntax similar to a computer programming language for defining data structures, especially database schemas.[7] Also known as *data description language.*

DEA **Data encryption algorithm.** A method for encrypting information.[7] *See* **DES.**

Debugging The process of discovering and eliminating errors and defects, or bugs, in program code.[1]

Decentralized hospital computer system *See* **DHCP.**

Decipherment decryption Process of obtaining, from a cipher text, the original corresponding data.[121]

Decision support (analytic) The collection of analysis tools, systems, models, and processes applied to organized information, in support of management decision making.[1]

Decision support (clinical) Software that taps into database resources and messages, presents data to assist users in making business decisions. A clinical decision support system gives physicians structured (rules-based) information to help make decisions on diagnoses, treatment plans, orders, and results.[8] *See* **Clinical decision support, CDS,** and **Alerts.**

Decision support system *See* **DSS.**

Decision tree A data mining predictive model-building algorithm that segregates data into factors with high association to the predicted variable. The resulting set of decision rules branch off each other and resemble a tree.[1]

Decompression The expansion of compressed image files.[1] *See* **Lossless compression, Lossy**.

Decryption The process of decoding a message so that its meaning becomes obvious. The reverse process of encryption in which cipher text is transformed back into the original plain text using a second complex function and a decryption key.[1]

Dedicated line A telephone or data line that is always available. This line is not used by other computers or individuals, is available 24 hours a day, and is never disconnected.[1]

DEEDS Data elements for emergency department systems. The recommended data set for use in emergency departments; it is published by the Centers for Disease Control and Prevention (CDC).[46]

Default gateway TCP/IP configuration option that specifies a device or computer to send packets out of a local subnet.[1] *See* **Gateway**.

Default route A routing table entry used to direct packets addressed to networks not explicitly listed in the routing table.[1]

Definition Statement that describes a concept and permits differentiation from other concepts within a system.[3]

Degaussing Exposure to high magnetic fields. One method of destroying data on a disk.[1]

De-identified health information Removal of individual identifiers so that they cannot be used to identify an individual. De-identified health information is not protected by HIPAA.[48]

Deliberate threat Threat of a person or persons to damage a computer system consciously and willingly.[1]

Deliverable Any tangible outcome that is produced by the project. These can be documents, plans, computer systems, buildings, aircraft, etc. Internal deliverables are produced as a consequence of executing the project, and are usually only needed by the project team. External deliverables are those that are created for clients and stakeholders.[12]

DELOS WP5 Network on Excellence on Digital Libraries (EURO), Knowledge Extraction & Semantic Interoperability.[142]

Demodulation Reverse of modulation. The analog-to-digital signal conversion process occurring in a modem at a receiving site. Analog signals are used to transfer data over phone lines. Digital signals are in a format that can be used by a computer.[1]

Demographic information Information concerning population statistics, such as birth date, birth place, sex, residence, etc. Collected and used for healthcare evaluation and planning purposes.[4]

Denial-of-service attack An attack in which a user (or a program) takes up so much of a shared resource that none of the resource is left for other users or uses.[1]

Derivative Any re-use of information at the application level. Captures the notion of 'collect once, use many times.' For example: detailed data information from an accounting system can be used for financial planning. Loosely adapted from mathematics, investing.[32]

DES Data encryption standard. An algorithm implemented in electronic hardware devices and used to protect computer data through cryptography.[1]

Description logics Description logics are a family of knowledge representation languages that can be used to represent the terminological knowledge of an application domain in a structured and formally well-understood way. The name *description logic* refers, on the one hand, to concept descriptions used to describe a domain; and, on the other hand, to the logic-based semantics which can be given by a translation into first-order predicate logic.[7]

Descriptor The text defining a code in a code set.[10]

Desiderata A list of things considered necessary or highly desirable (plural); a definitive list.[28]

Design 1. Phase of software development following analysis and concerned with how the problem is to be solved. **2.** The process and result of describing how a system or process is to be automated. Design must thoroughly describe the function of a component and its interaction with other components. Design usually also identifies areas of commonality in systems and optimizes reusability.[8]

Designated approving authority   Official with the authority to formally assume the responsibility for operating a system or network at an acceptable level of risk.[97]

Designated code set   Specified within the body of a rule.[10]

Designated record set   Healthcare provider's medical records and billing records about individuals, a health plan's enrollment, payment, claims adjudication, and case or medical management records, and any other records used by a covered entity to make decisions about individuals.[48]

Development process device   Any piece of equipment used in computer input/output operations.[1]

DHCP   Dynamic host configuration protocol.   Standard protocol that allows a network device to obtain all network IP configuration information automatically from host-based, pooled IP addresses. Alleviates manual static IP address assignment.[1]

DI   Diagnostic imaging.   The use of digital images and textual reports prepared as a result of performing diagnostic studies, such as x-rays, CT scans, MRIs, etc.[8]

Diagnosis related group   Group of patients defined using a case-mix approach. Note: Originally the approach involved coding with ICD-9-CM (Clinical Modification) or ICD-AM (Australia Modification) and grouping by homogeneous cost and used major diagnosis, length of stay, secondary diagnosis, surgical procedure, age, and type of services required.[4]

Diagnosis related group   *See* **DRG.**

Diagnostic and statistical manual   *See* **DSM.**

Diagnostic procedure   A procedure aimed to finding a diagnosis (the identification of diseases and other clinical conditions from the examination of signs and symptoms). A diagnostic procedure can involve an interview with a patient, physical examination, or the use of laboratory tests.[4]

Dial-up line   A communication connection from a computer to a host computer over standard phone lines. Unlike a dedicated line, user must dial the host computer to establish a connection.[1]

DICOM   Digital imaging and communications in medicine. 1. DICOM is a standard for the electronic communication of medical images and associated information. DICOM relies on explicit and detailed models of how patients, images, and reports involved in radiology operations are described and how the above are related. The DICOM standards contain information object definitions, data structure, data dictionary, media storage, file format, communications formats, and print formats. **2.** An ANSI-accredited standards development organization that has created a standard protocol for exchanging medical images among computer systems.[151]

Dictionary   Structured collection of lexical units with linguistic information about each unit.[4]

Digital   A digital system is one that uses numbers for input, processing, transmission, storage, or display, rather than a continuous spectrum of values (an analog system) or non-numeric symbols, such as letters or icons. The word 'digital' is commonly used in computing, especially where real-world information is converted to numeric form, as in digital audio and digital photography.[7]

Digital audio tape   *See* **DAT.**

Digital certificate   A digital document issued by a certification authority that contains the holder's name, serial number, public key, and the document's expiration date. Digital certificates are used in public key infrastructure to send and receive secure, encrypted messages.[8]

Digital envelope   Data appended to a message that allow the intended recipient to verify the integrity of the content of the message.[3]

Digital imaging and communications in medicine   *See* **DICOM.**

Digital radiography A form of x-ray imaging in which digital x-ray sensors are used instead of traditional photographic film. Advantages include time efficiency through bypassing chemical processing and the ability to digitally transfer and enhance images. Also less radiation can be used to produce an image of similar contrast to conventional radiography.[7]

Digital signal Transmission signal that carries information in the discrete value form of 0 and 1.[1] *See* **DS-2-3**.

Digital signature A means to guarantee the authenticity of a set of input data the same way a written signature verifies the authenticity of a paper document. A cryptographic transformation of data that allows a recipient of the data to prove the source and integrity of the data and protect against forgery. Specifically, an asymmetric cryptographic technique in which each user is associated with a public key distributed to potential verifiers of the user's digital signature used to encrypt messages destined for other uses; and a private key, which is known only to the user, and is used to decrypt incoming messages.[1] *See* **Private key, Public key**.

Digital signature standard Digital signatures provide a signature manifestation whereby signer identity, as well as document and signature attributes, are bound by a public key-based cryptographic process. Public key, or asymmetric, cryptography involves two mathematically related keys. A 'signature' key is used to encrypt a one-way hash or 'digest' of the electronic data to obtain a digital signature of that data; the unique mathematical inverse of the signature key. The security of a digital signature depends upon the ability of the signer to maintain exclusive control over the use of the signature key. Also known as the *verification key*; can be used to decrypt the digital signature. Verification of the digital signature follows from comparison of the decrypted hash with the verifier's application of the hashing function to the purportedly signed record. In digital signature applications, the signature key is uniquely associated with a particular signer by means of data structure, known as a verification certificate. The security of a digital signature depends upon the ability of the signer to maintain exclusive control over the use of the signature key.[3]

Digital subscriber line *See* **DSL**.

Digital subscriber line access multiplexer *See* **DSLAM**.

Digitize To convert an analog signal to a digital signal.[1]

Digitized signature An electronic image of an actual written signature. A digitized signature looks much the same as the original, but it does not provide the same protection as a digital signature, as it can be forged and copied.[1]

Dimension table A building block of a star schema data model; it contains the descriptive data regarding the data in a fact table that are used for column headings, query constraints, and OLAP dimensions.[1]

DIP switch **Dual in-line package switch.** A grouping of small on (1)/off (0) switches used in computers and associated devices to configure hardware options. DIP switches commonly allow a user to change the configuration of a circuit board to suit a particular computer.[1]

Direct connection A permanent communication connection between a computer system (either a single CPU or a LAN) and the Internet. This is also called a leased-line connection because the telephone connection is leased from the phone company. A direct connection is in contrast to a dial-up connection.[1]

Direct memory access *See* **DMA**.

DIRECT project Specifies a simple, secure, scalable, standards-based transportation mechanism that enables participants to send encrypted health information directly to known, trusted recipients over the Internet.[178]

Direct sequence spread spectrum *See* **DSSS**.

Directory A system that the computer uses to organize files on the basis of specific information.[1]

Directory services markup language *See* **DSML**.

DIS **Draft international standard.** The fourth balloting stage for a draft international standard document. This most important phase of balloting lasts five months.[3]

Disaster recovery system The processes, policies and procedures related to preparing for recovery or continuation of technical infrastructure critical to an organization after a natural or human-induced disaster.[2]

Disclosure history   Under the Health Insurance Portability and Accountability Act (HIPAA), this is a list of any entities that have received personally identifiable healthcare information for uses unrelated to treatment and payment.[10]

Disclosure/disclose   The release, transfer, relay, provision of access to, or conveying client information to any individual or entity outside a specific healthcare system.[118]

Discovery   Locating a resource on the enterprise, using a process (such as a search engine) to obtain knowledge of information content or services that exploit metadata descriptions of enterprise IT resources stored directories, registries, and catalogs.[4]

Discrete data   Data that can only take certain values.[143]

Disease episode   An episode of care focused on the treatment of a specific disease.[141]

Disease management   A system of coordinated healthcare interventions and communications for populations with conditions in which patient self-care efforts are significant.[101]

Disease registry   A large collection or registry belonging to a healthcare system that contains information on different chronic health problems affecting patients within the system. A disease registry helps to manage and log data on chronic illnesses and diseases. All data contained within the disease registry are logged by healthcare providers and are available to providers to perform benchmarking measures on healthcare systems.[138]

Disease staging   A type of severity system which maps progression through degrees of morbidity.[32] *See* **Severity system**.

Disk   Rotating magnetic device used for file storage. Can be magnetic floppy disk (diskette), hard disk, or optical CD.[1]

Disk duplexing   Fault-tolerant storage technique that mirrors the information from a primary drive to a secondary drive, while maintaining additional redundancy through the use of separate disk controllers. Mirrors data from a

primary drive to a secondary drive to make files accessible in the event of a drive failure.[1]

Disk mirroring   Fault-tolerant storage technique that mirrors data from a primary drive to a secondary drive to make files accessible in the event of a drive failure.[1]

Disk operating system   *See* **DOS**.

Disk striping with parity   Fault-tolerant storage technique that distributes data and parity across three or more physical disks. Storage technique that stripes data and parity in 64K blocks across all disks in the array. Striping provides fast data transfer and protection from a single disk failure by regenerating data for a failed disk through the stored parity. Minimum of three physical disks are required for disk striping with parity.[1] Also known as *RAID 5*.

Disk striping without parity   Storage technique that distributes data across two or more physical disks in 64K blocks across all disks in the array. Striping provides fast data transfer. Minimum of two physical disks are required for disk striping without parity.[1] Also known as *RAID 0*.

Diskette   Small, flexible, removable, magnetic storage media used for file storage.[1]

Display codes   **1.** A parameter users can set that allows for the display of classification codes on the selection list during searches. **2.** The 6-bit character set used by many computer systems manufactured by Control Data Corporation, notably the CDC 6600 in 1964. The CDC 6000 series, and follow-ons, had 60-bit words. As such, typical usage packed 10 characters per word.[7]

Disruption   An event that interrupts normal business, functions, operations, or processes, whether anticipated (e.g., hurricane, political unrest) or unanticipated (e.g., a blackout, terror attack, technology failure, earthquake). A disruption can be caused by either positive or negative factors that will disrupt normal functions, operations, or processes.[175]

Distance learning   Using communication technology to bring seminars and classes from distant locations into schools, offices, and homes. Distance learning technologies can range from one-way video to two-way video and audio transmission, with two or more PCs for the purpose of instruction. Distance learning provides virtual classroom, seminar, or meeting attendance, without the expense and difficulty of travel.[1]

Distinguished name A set of data that identifies a real-world entity, such as a person in a computer-based context.[114]

Distributed computing environment A client-server environment in which data are located in many servers that might be geographically dispersed but connected by a wide area network (WAN).[1]

Distributed database A database that is stored in more than one physical location. Parts or copies of the database are physically stored in one location, and other parts are stored and maintained in other locations.[1]

Distributed processing The distribution of computer processing work among multiple computers, linked by a communications network.[1]

Dithering Within the context of the 216-color, browser-safe palette for web engineering, the use of colors outside the selection of the 216 'safe' colors may bring distortion or dithering. This is caused by interpretation by another operating system, yielding a color not intended by the designer.[1]

DLC Dynamic link control. Protocol used for networked-enabled HP printers, and for connectivity to IBM mainframe machines from Windows NT.[1]

DLL Dynamic link library. A file of code containing functions that can be called from other executable code (either an application or another DLL). Programmers use DLLs to provide code that they can reuse and to parcel out distinct jobs. Unlike an executable file, a DLL cannot be directly run. DLLs must be called from other code that is already executing.[1]

DMA Direct memory access. Rapid data movement between computer subsystems. Accomplished through the use of the DMA controller without the use of the CPU.[1]

DMA controller Direct memory access controller. Integrated computer chip that handles direct memory operations without CPU intervention. Allows the CPU to concentrate on other computer operations.[1]

Database management system *See* **DBMS**.

DML Data manipulation language. A family of computer languages, including commands permitting users to manipulate data in a database. This manipulation involves inserting data into database tables, retrieving existing data, deleting data from existing tables, and modifying existing data. DML is most often incorporated into structured query language (SQL) databases.[156]

DNS Domain name server. An online database that resolves human readable names to IP addresses. The DNS is a distributed database used by TCP/IP applications to map between host names and IP addresses, and to provide electronic mail routing information. The DNS provides the protocol to allow clients and servers to communicate with each other.[1]

DNSSEC Domain name system security extension. 1. Secure Domain Name System (DNS) for authentication and integrity. **2.** A suite of Internet Engineering Task Force (IETF) specifications for securing certain kinds of information provided by the DNS as used on Internet protocol networks. DNSSEC is a set of extensions to DNS which provide to DNS clients (resolvers) origin authentication of DNS data, authenticated denial of existence, and data integrity; not availabilty or confidentiality.[1,7]

Document integrity To ensure the integrity of a document that is exchanged or shared.[48]

Document management Software systems allowing organizations to control the production, storage, management, and distribution of electronic documents, yielding greater efficiencies in the ability to reuse information and to control the flow of the documents, from creation to archiving.[2]

Document type definition *See* **DTD**.

Documentation and procedures test A testing event that evaluates the accuracy of user and operations documentation and determines whether the manual procedure will work correctly as an integral part of the system.[6]

Domain 1. The problem or subject to be addressed by a set of information technology messages or by a system ('application domain'). A particular area of interest in healthcare. **2.** Refers to a field of action, thought, or influence. In healthcare, domain is often used to describe a one of many different clinical areas.[8,151] Also known as *spheres of interest or concern.*

Domain information model The model describing common concepts and relationships for a problem domain.[4]

Domain name server *See* **DNS**.

Domain specific data Information and knowledge specific to a given discipline (nursing, medicine, physical therapy, nutrition, etc.). Examples include data banks, online consultants, side effects of patients' medications, knowledge retrieval systems, etc.[6]

Domain synchronization Process in which a primary domain controller (PDC) updates all backup domain controllers (BDCs) with an updated copy of the accounts database through the replication service. Default PDF-to-BDC synchronization occurs every five minutes. BDCs can also be manually synchronized with the PDC through server manager.[1]

DOS Disk operating system. The first widely installed operating system for personal computers.[42]

Dot bust Years of the 'Internet bust' (early 2000 to October 2003), in which many '.com' companies went bankrupt and many investors lost money.[32]

Dot com 1. An Internet-based business, or '.com.' **2.** Short for 'commercial,' the generic top-level domain used on the Internet's Domain Name System.[7]

Dot pitch A measurement (in millimeters) of the distance between dots on a monitor. The lower the number, the higher the clarity of the display.[11]

Dots per square inch *See* **DPI**.

Download To retrieve a file from another computer.[1]

DPI Dots per square inch. A measure of the resolution of a printer, scanner, or monitor. It refers to the number of dots per inch. The more dots per inch, the higher the resolution.[1]

Draft international standard *See* **DIS**.

Draft standard for trial use *See* **DSTU**.

Draft supplement for public comment A specification candidate for addition to an IHE Domain Technical Framework (e.g., a new profile) that is issued for comment by any interested party.[93]

Draft technical report *See* **DTR**.

DRAM Dynamic random access memory. RAM that must be continuously refreshed to maintain the current RAM value. Most RAM in microcomputers is dynamic RAM, although there is a trend toward synchronous dynamic random access memory (SDRAM).[1]

DRG *See* **DRG**.

DRG Diagnosis related group. Group of International Classification of Diseases (ICD) coded diagnoses, procedures, and other information used to group patients for reimbursement by Medicare.[102]

Drilldown Exploration of multidimensional data allows moving down from one level of detail to the next, depending on the granularity of data in the level.[94]

Driver A piece of software that tells the computer how to operate an external device, such as a printer, hard disk, CD-ROM drive, or scanner.[1]

Drop Wiring run made from a modular wall plate to a comm/wiring closet. Unshielded twisted pair (UTP) is the most common medium used in drops. Also identified as the connection between a computer and thicknet cabling.[1]

Drop-down list (or menu) A menu of commands or options that appears when you select an item with a mouse. The item you select is generally at the top of the display screen, and the menu appears just below it, as if you had it dropped down or you had pulled it down.[32]

Drug information system A computer-based system that maintains drug-related information, such as information concerning appropriate dosages and side effects, and may access a drug interaction database. A drug information system may provide, by way of a directed consultation, specific advice on the usage of various drugs.[4]

Drug interaction database Database containing information on drug interactions.[4]

Drug reference terminology A collection of drug concepts and information such as definitions, hierarchies, and other kinds of knowledge and relationships related to the drug concepts.[151]

Drug therapy The use of drugs to cure a medical problem, to improve a patient's condition, or to otherwise produce a therapeutic effect.[4]

DS-2-3 Digital signal. Digital Signal 2.6.312-3.45 Mbps synchronous digital 1 transmission.[1]

DSA Digital signature algorithm. *See* **Digital signature**.

DSG Document digital signature. *See* **Digital signature**.

DSL Digital subscriber line. 1. DSL technologies use sophisticated modulation schemes to pack data onto copper wires. **2.** A family of technologies that provides digital data transmission over the wires of a local telephone network.[1,2] Also known as *digital subscriber loop*.

DSLAM Digital subscriber line access multiplexer. A mechanism at a phone company's central location that links many customer DSL connections to a single high-speed ATM line. When the phone company receives a DSL signal, an asymmetric digital subscriber line (ADSL) modem with a plain old telephone system (POTS) splitter detects voice calls and data.[1]

DSM Diagnostic and Statistical Manual of Mental Disorders. Manual produced by the American Psychiatric Association to facilitate communication among mental health clinicians, researchers, and administrators to improve patient care by facilitating reliable and valid diagnoses and differential diagnoses; to facilitate education and training in psychopathology, and to facilitate collection of statistical data about mental disorders.[151]

DSML Directory services markup language. Combines the directory services technology Lightweight Directory Access Protocol (LDAP) with XML syntax to provide an easy way to share and use personalized data across company and technology boundaries.[7]

DSMO Designated standard maintenance organization. Designed to maintain ongoing updates to International Organization for Standardization (ISO) standards. Responsible to ISO Central Secretariat and the Technical Committee Secretariat.[3]

DSR Daily response message. Request and response messages may be exchanged between a client and server.[12]

DSR Data set ready. Modem control that indicates that the modem is attached to a communications line.[1]

DSS Decision support system. Computer tools or applications to assist in clinical decisions by providing evidence-based knowledge in the context of patient-specific data. Examples include drug interaction alerts at the time medication is prescribed and reminders for specific guideline-based interventions during the care of patients with chronic disease. Information should be presented in a patient-centric view of individual care and also in a population or aggregate view to support population management and quality improvement.[178]

DSTU Draft standard for trial use. An archaic term for any standard that has been approved.[10]

DSU Data service unit. Provides digital-to-digital communication.[1]

DSU/CSU Data service unit/channel service unit. Digital-interface device used to connect a Data Terminal Equipment device (DTE), such as a router to a digital circuit or a T1 line. The DSU/CSU implements two different functions. The CSU is responsible for the connection to the telecom network while the DSU is responsible for handling the interface with the DTE. A CSU/DSU is the equivalent of the modem for an entire local area network (LAN).[7]

DT Date data type (YYYYMMDD). 1. International method of writing the date. **2.** International format defined by ISO (ISO 8601) to define a numerical date system as follows: YYYY-MM-DD where YYYY is the year [all the digits, i.e. 2012], MM is the month [01 (January) to 12 (December)], DD is the day [01 to 31].[33]

DTD Document type definition. Defines the legal building blocks of an XML document. It defines the document structure with a list of legal elements.[1]

DTE Data terminal equipment. An end instrument that converts information into signals or reconverts received signals.[7]

DTR Data terminal ready. Modem control that indicates that a terminal is ready for transmission.[1]

DTR Draft technical report. A standards document containing only informative information ready for ballot.[3]

Dual-use technology Technology that has both civilian and military applications (e.g., cryptography).[1]

Dumb terminal Terminal with no localized processing, storage, or GUI capacity. VT-320s, VT-420s, and VT-510s are dumb terminals associated with Center for Healthcare Strategies. Mainly associated with mainframes and centralized computing.[1]

Durability A database property that ensures transactions are saved permanently and do not accidentally disappear or get erased, even during a database crash. This is usually achieved by saving all transactions to a non-volatile storage medium.[156] *See* **ACID**.

Duration A field within a certificate that is composed of two subfields: 'date of issue' and 'date of next issue.'[114]

DVD Digital video disk or digital versatile disk. Backwardly compatible with CD-ROMs (i.e., DVDs can read CD-ROMs). The DVD specification can support a disk with capacities from 4.7 gigabytes to 17 gigabytes.[11]

DXPlain A decision support system from Massachusetts General Hospital, which uses a set of clinical findings (signs, symptoms, laboratory data) to produce a ranked list of diagnoses which might explain, or be associated with, clinical manifestations.[141]

Dynamic host configuration protocol *See* **DHCP**.

Dynamic link control *See* **DLC**.

Dynamic link library *See* **DLL**.

Dynamic RAM *See* **DRAM**.

E

e-[text] or e-text Electronic. Short for 'electronic,' 'e' or 'e-' is used as a prefix to indicate that something is Internet-based, not just electronic. The trend began with e-mail in the 1990s, and now includes eCommerce, eHealth, e-GOV, etc.[32]

E-1-3 European digital signal. 2.048-3.139.254 Mbps digital transmission that is similar to Integrated Service Digital Network (ISDN).[1]

EAI Enterprise application integration. 1. The use of software and architectural principles to bring together (integrate) a set of enterprise computer applications. It is an area of computer systems architecture that gained wide recognition from about 2004 onwards. EAI is related to middleware technologies, such as message-oriented middleware (MOM), and data representation technologies, such as eXtensible markup language (HTML,XML). Newer EAI technologies involve using web services as part of service-oriented architecture as a means of integration. **2.** A presentation-level integration technology that provides a single point of access to conduct business transactions that utilize data from multiple disparate applications.[1,7] *See* **System integration**.

EAP Extensible authentication protocol. A general protocol for authentication that also supports multiple authentication methods, such as token cards, one-time passwords, certificate, public key authentication, and smartcards.[2]

Early event detection *See* **EED**.

EBB Eligibility-based billing. Process in which a payer bills a customer based on the eligibility. Clients are responsible for their own eligibility and data accuracy.

EBCDIC Extended binary coded decimal interchange code. A character set coding scheme that represents 256 standard characters. IBM mainframes use EBCDIC coding, while personal computers use American Standard Coding for Information Interchange (ASCII) coding. Networks that link personal computers to IBM mainframes must include a translating device to mediate between the two systems.[157]

EC Electronic commerce. Consists of the buying and selling of products or services over electronic systems such as the Internet and other computer networks.[158] Also known as *eCommerce*.

ECG Retrieve ECG for display. Specifies a mechanism for broad access throughout the enterprise to electrocardiogram (ECG) documents for review purposes. The ECG documents may include 'diagnostic quality' waveforms, measurements, and interpretations. This integration profile allows the display of this information without requiring specialized cardiology software or workstations, but with general purpose computer applications, such as a web browser. This integration profile is intended primarily for retrieving resting 12-lead ECGs, but may also retrieve ECG waveforms gathered during stress, Holter, and other diagnostic tests. This integration profile only addresses ECGs that are already stored in an information system. It does not address the process of ordering, acquiring, storing, or interpreting the ECGs.[56] *See* **Profile. NOTE: ECG is an Integrating the Healthcare Enterprise (IHE) Profile.**

ECHO Describes the workflow associated with digital echocardiography (diagnostic test that uses ultrasound waves to create an image), specifically transthoracic echo, transesophageal echo, and stress echo. As with the Cath Workflow integration profile, this profile deals with patient identifiers, orders, scheduling, status reporting, multi-stage exams (especially stress echo), and data storage. It also specifically addresses the issues of acquisition modality devices that are only intermittently connected to the network, such as portable echo machines, and addresses echo-specific data requirements.[56] *See* **Profile. NOTE: ECHO is an Integrating the Healthcare Enterprise (IHE) Profile.**

ECN Explicit congestion notifier. A 2-bit IP packet header field that allows reduction of the number of Transmission Control Protocol (TCP) retransmissions in the Internet.[1]

eCommerce Commonly known as *e-commerce* or *electronic commerce*, consists of the buying, selling, marketing and servicing of products or services over electronic systems, such as the Internet and other computer networks.[158] *See* **EC.**

ED Encapsulated data. The coupling or encapsulation of the data with a select group of functions that defines everything that can be done with the data.[7]

ED Evidence documents. Defines interoperable ways for observations, measurements, results, and other procedure details recorded in the course of carrying out a procedure step to be output by devices, such as acquisition systems and other workstations; to be stored and managed by archival systems; and to be retrieved and presented by display and reporting systems. This allows detailed non-image information, such as measurements, computer-aided detection (CAD) results, procedure logs, etc., to be made available as input to the process of generating a diagnostic report. The evidence documents may be used either as additional evidence for the reporting physician, or in some cases, for selected items in the evidence document to be included in the diagnostic report.[56] *See* **Profile. NOTE: ED is an Integrating the Healthcare Enterprise (IHE) Profile.**

EDC Electronic data capture system. A computerized system designed for the collection of clinical data in electronic format for use mainly in human clinical trials.[7]

EDDS Electronic document digital storage. Document management systems available online.[32] *See* **Decision support, clinical and analytic** and **Decision support system.**

EDI Electronic data interchange. 1. Even before HIPAA, the American National Standards Institute (ANSI) approved the process for developing a set of EDI standards known as the X12. EDI is a collection of standard message formats that allows businesses to exchange data via any electronic messaging service. **2.** The electronic transfer of data between companies using networks to include the Internet. Secure communications are needed in healthcare to exchange eligibility information, referrals, authorization, claims, encounter, and other payment data needed to manage contracts and remittance.[43]

EDI Electronic data interchange gateway. An electronic process to send data (claims, membership, and benefits) back and forth between providers and insurance companies.[15]

EDIT In the Centers for Medicare & Medicaid Services, the logic within the Standard Claims Processing System (or PSC Supplemental Edit Software) that selects certain claims, evaluates or compares information on the selected claims or other accessible source, and, depending on the evaluation, takes action on the claims, such as pay in full, pay in part, or suspend for manual review.[118]

EED **Early event detection.** This component of PHIN preparedness uses case and suspect case reporting, along with statistical surveillance of health-related data, to support the earliest possible detection of events that may signal a public health emergency.[46]

EDXL **Emergency Data Exchange Language.** A standard message distribution framework for data sharing among emergency information systems.[91]

EDXL–HAVE **Emergency Data Exchange Language - Hospital Availability Exchange.** The Hospital AVailability Exchange (HAVE) describes a standard message for data sharing among emergency information systems using the XML-based Emergency Data Exchange Language (EDXL).[91]

EEPROM **Electronically erasable programmable read only memory.** A reprogrammable memory chip that can be electronically erased and reprogrammed via a reader/writer device.[1]

Effective date This is the date that a federal agency final rule is effective, which is usually 60 days after it is published in the *Federal Register*.[10]

EGA **Enhanced graphics adapter.** Color display system providing 16 to 64 colors at a resolution of 640x480.[1]

E-GOV The E-Government Act of 2002 was signed into law by President George W. Bush in July 2002: 'This legislation builds upon the Administration's expanding E-Government initiative by ensuring strong leadership of the information technology activities of Federal agencies, a comprehensive framework for information security standards and programs, and uniform safeguards to protect the confidentiality of information provided by the public for statistical purposes. The Act also assists in expanding the use of the Internet and computer resources in order to deliver Government services, con-sistent with the reform principles I outlined on July 10, 2002, for a citizen-centered, results-oriented, and market-based Government.'[44]

EGP **Exterior gateway protocol.** An old protocol that advertises the networks that can be reached within an autonomous system by advertising its IP addresses to a router in another autonomous system.[1]

eHealth eHealth (also written *e-health*) is a term for healthcare practice which is supported by electronic processes and communication; some people would argue the term is interchangeable with *health informatics*. However, the term eHealth encompasses a whole range of services that is at the edge of medicine/healthcare and information technology, including electronic medical records, telemedicine, and evidence-based medicine.[7]

EHR **Electronic health record. 1.** A longitudinal electronic record of patient health information generated by one or more encounters in any care delivery setting. Included in this information are patient demographics, progress notes, problems, medications, vital signs, past medical history, immunizations, laboratory data, and radiology reports and images. The EHR automates and streamlines the clinician's workflow. The EHR has the ability to generate a complete record of a clinical patient encounter, as well as supporting other care-related activities directly or indirectly via interface; including evidence-based decision support, quality management, and outcomes reporting. **2.** Health-related information on an individual that conforms to nationally recognized interoperability standards and that can be created, managed, and consulted by authorized clinicians and staff across more than one healthcare organization. *See also* **CPR, EMR**, and the **EHR Appendix.**[45,84]

EHRS **Electronic health record system.**

EIDE **Enhanced or extended integrated drive electronics.** A standard interface for high-speed disk drives that operates at speeds faster than the standard Integrated Drive Electronics (IDE) interface. It allows the connection of four IDE devices.[1]

EIN **Employer** **identification** **number. 1.** Employers, as sponsors of health insurance for their employees, often need to be identified in healthcare transactions, and a standard identifier for employers would be beneficial for electronically exchanged transactions. Healthcare providers may need to identify the employer of the participant on claims submitted electronically to health plans. **2.** The HIPAA standard is the EIN, the taxpayer-identifying number for employers that is assigned by the Internal Revenue Service. This identifier has nine digits with the first two digits separated by a hyphen, as follows: 00-000000.[1,10]

EIP Enterprise information portal. **1.** A framework for integrating information, people and processes across organization boundaries. Provides a secure unified access point. **2.** An Internet-based approach to consolidate and present an organization's business intelligence and information resources through a single access point via an intranet.[7,1] Also known as an *Internet portal enterprise portal.*

EIS Enterprise information system. A class of decision-support systems that provide predefined and easy-to-use data presentation and exploration functionality to top-level executives.[1]

EIS Executive information system. A class of decision-support systems that provide predefined data presentation and exploration functionality to top-level executives. The system is intended to facilitate and support the information and decision-making needs of senior executives by providing ready access to both internal and external information relevant to meeting the strategic goals of the organization. Commonly considered a specialized form of decision-support systems (DSS). The emphasis of EIS is on graphical displays with reporting and drill-down capabilities. In general, an EIS is an enterprise-wide DSS that allows executives to analyze, compare, and highlight trends and important variables, as well as monitor performance and identify opportunities and problems.[2]

EISA Extended industry standard architecture. Thirty-two-bit internal bus. Introduced in 1988 to compete with the PS/2 (Micro Channel) line of computers.[1]

Electromagnetic interference *See* **EMI.**

Electronic *See* e-[text] or e-text.

Electronic attestation Verifies the identity of an individual by linking signature verification data to that person. The purpose of attestation is to show authorship and assign responsibility for an act, event, condition, opinion, or diagnosis. Every entry in the health record must be identified with the author and should not be made or signed by someone other than the author. Attestation functionality must meet applicable legal, regulatory, and other applicable standards or requirements.[2]

Electronic certificate *See* **Digital certificate.**

Electronic claim **1.** Electronic transactions sent to payers to receive payments for healthcare services covered by the payers. These are the HIPAA 837 transactions, responsible for remittance advice for claims payment made by payers. **2.** Any claim submitted for payment to the health plan by a central processing unit, tape diskette, direct data entry, direct wire, dial-in telephone, digital fax, or personal computer download or upload.[2,1] *See* **EDI.**

Electronic commerce *See* **EC** and **eCommerce.**

Electronic data Recorded or transmitted electronically, while non-electronic data would be everything else. Special cases would be data transmitted by fax and audio systems, which is, in principle, transmitted electronically, but which lacks the underlying structure usually needed to support automated interpretation of its contents.[10]

Electronic data capture system *See* **EDC.**

Electronic data interchange *See* **EDI.**

Electronic data interchange gateway *See* **EDI.**

Electronic forms management A software system that automatically generates forms and can be populated by importing data from another system and/or can export data that has been entered into another system.[2]

Electronic health record *See* **EHR** and **EHR Appendix.**

Electronic health record provider Entity in legitimate possession of electronic health record data, and in a position to communicate it to another appropriate entity.[116]

Electronic Health Records (EHR) Laboratory Results Reporting Use Case This Healthcare Information Technology Standards Panel (HITSP) Interoperability Specification (Interoperability Specification 01) is designed to meet the specific requirements of the electronic health record (EHR) use case, defined as sending laboratory test results and laboratory interpretations in an electronic format to clinicians for patient care. Laboratory test results and interpretations are then available for integration into an EHR, local or remote, or other clinical systems.[48]

Electronic media 1. Electronic storage media, including memory devices in computers (hard drives) and any removable/transportable digital memory media, such as magnetic tapes or disks, optical disks, or digital memory cards. 2. Transmission media used to exchange information already in electronic storage media; including, for example, the Internet (wide open), extranet (using Internet technology to link a business with information accessible only to collaborating parties), leased lines, dial-up lines, private networks, and the physical movement of removable/transportable electronic storage media. Certain transmissions, including paper via facsimile and voice via telephone, are not considered to be transmissions via electronic media because the information being exchanged did not exist in electronic form before the transmission.[118]

Electronic media claims *See* **EMC**.

Electronic medical record *See* **EMR**.

Electronic Medical Record Adoption Model *See* **EMRAM**.

Electronic medication administration record *See* **eMAR**

Electronic patient record *See* **EHR**.

Electronic personal health record *See* **ePHR** and **PHR**.

Electronic prescribing *See* **E-prescribing**.

Electronic protected health information. *See* **ePHI**.

Electronic purse A mechanism that allows end users to pay electronically for goods and services. The function of the electronic purse is to maintain a pool of value that is decremented as transactions are performed.[114]

Electronic remittance advice *See* **ERA**.

Electronic signature 1. An electronic signature creates the logical manifestation of a signature, including the possibility for multiple parties to sign a document and have the order of application recognized and proven and supply additional information, such as time stamp and signature purpose, specific to that user. 2. Verifying a signature on a document verifies the integrity of the document and associated attributes and verifies the identity of the signer. Several technologies are available for use authentication, including passwords, cryptography, and biometrics.[1]

Electronically erasable programmable read-only memory *See* **EEPROM**.

Eligible professional *See* **EP**.

Eligibility-based billing *See* **EBB**.

E-mail Electronic mail. Electronic messages sent via networks between users on other computer systems. A service that permits a message or response to be created on one computer and sent over a network to another machine, another person, a group, or a computer program.[1]

eMAR Electronic medication administration record. An electronic record keeping system that documents when medications are given to a patient during a hospital stay. This application supports the five rights of medication administration (right patient, right medication, right dose, right time, and right route of administration) and can be used with bar coding functionality, although bar coding is not required. eMAR functionality is normally found within a nursing documentation application.[2]

EMC Electronic media claims. This term usually refers to a flat file format used to transmit or transport claims.[10]

Emergency Sudden demand for action; a condition that poses an immediate threat to the health of the patient. This definition is further clarified to mean 'any potential denial of critical health services, or information, that could reasonably result in personal injury or death to an individual or the public.[11,39,48]

Emergency access Granting of user rights and authorizations to permit access to protected health information and applications in emergency conditions outside of normal workflows. (Emergency room access is considered to be a normal workflow.)[48]

Emergency care system An application that assists emergency department clinicians and staff in the critical task of managing patients quickly and efficiently; directs each step of the patient management/patient flow and patient documentation process, including triage, tracking, nursing and physician charting, disposition, charge capture, and management reporting.[2]

Emergency data exchange language *See* **EDXL**.

Emergency permission Permission granted to certain caregivers in advance that allows self-declaration of an emergency and assumption of an emergency role. Emergency permissions defined in standard ways, compliant with appropriate ANSI standards and Health Level Seven (HL7) healthcare permission definitions, are suitable for federated circumstances, where the person declaring the emergency is not a member of the organization possessing the requested information.[48]

Emergency repair disk *See* **ERD**.

Emergency respond data architecture *See* **ERDA**.

EMI Electromagnetic interference. Any disruption caused by electromagnetic waves.[1]

Emissions security *See* **EMSEC**.

Emoticons A combination word for 'emotional icon,' it is a small picture created with the normal keys on a keyboard meant to denote the writer's mood in an e-mail message.[11]

EMPI Enterprise master person index. A system that maintains on-line listings of patients and medical records across multiple facilities and/or hospitals. It includes admission, registration and discharge dates, as well as all data pertinent for re-registration. It provides for quick access to previous records and the ability to send new patient information to them.[2]

Employee Retirement Income and Security Act *See* **ERISA**.

Employee welfare benefit plan A plan, fund, or a program maintained by an employer, or an employee organization, that provides medical, surgical, or hospital care.[48]

Employer identification number *See* **EIN**.

EMR Electronic medical record. 1. An application environment that is composed of the clinical data repository, clinical decision support, controlled medical vocabulary, order entry, computerized practitioner order entry, and clinical documentation applications. This environment supports the patient's electronic medical record across inpatient and outpatient environments, and is used by healthcare practitioners to document, monitor, and manage healthcare delivery. 2. Health-related information on an individual that can be created, gathered, managed, and consulted by authorized clinicians and staff within one healthcare organization.[2,84]

EMRAM[SM] Electronic Medical Record Adoption Model. A tool developed by HIMSS Analytics guiding hospitals to improved clinical outcomes.[2]

EMSEC Emanations security. Measures taken to deny unauthorized persons information derived from intercept and analysis of compromising emanations from crypto-equipment of an IT system.[97]

Emulation A software program that allows a computer to imitate another computer with a differing operating system.[1]

EN European standard. Developed by the European Committee for Standardization (CEN). CEN is a major provider of European standards and technical specifications.[7]

EN 46000 Medical device quality management systems standard. EN 46000 is technically equivalent to ISO 13485:1996, an international medical device standard. The two are similar enough that if an organization is prepared to comply with one, it could easily comply with the other.[222]

Encapsulated data type *See* **ED**.

Encipherment encryption Cryptographic transformation of data to produce ciphertext.[121]

Encoded data Data represented by some identification of classification scheme, such as a provider identifier or a procedure code.[5]

Encoder This application enables health information management personnel to find and use complete and accurate codes and code modifiers for procedures and diagnosis to optimize billing and reimbursement. For example, 1234 is bronchitis, whereas 1235 is bronchitis with asthma, and 1236 is bronchitis with stomach flu.[2]

Encoding-decoding services This service will encode and/or decode message from and to different coding formats, such as Unicode, UTF-8, Base64, etc.[8]

Encounter Clinical encounter is: **1.** An instance of direct provider/practitioner to patient interaction, regardless of the setting, between a patient and practitioner vested with primary responsibility for diagnosing, evaluating, or treating the patient's condition, or both, or providing social worker services. **2.** A contact between a patient and practitioner who has primary responsibility for assessing and treating the patient at a given contact, exercising independent judgment. Encounter serves as a focal point linking clinical, administrative and financial information. Encounters occur in many different settings—ambulatory care, inpatient care, emergency care, home healthcare, field and virtual (telemedicine).[39]

Encounter data Detailed data about individual services provided by a capitated managed care entity. The level of detail about each service reported is similar to that of a standard claim form. Encounter data are also sometimes referred to as 'shadow claims.'[102]

Encryption 1. An application/technology that provides the translation of data into a secret code. Encryption is the most effective way to achieve data security. To read an encrypted file, you must have access to a secret key or password that enables you to decrypt it. Unencrypted data is called plain text; encrypted data is referred to as cipher text. **2.** Means of securing data by transforming/generating them into apparently meaningless random characters between source and destination. A process by which a message is encoded so that its meaning is not obvious. It is transformed into a second

message using a complex function and a special encryption key.[2,1]

Encryption-decryption services This encrypts and decrypts messages. It could use X.509 certificates and other cryptography mechanisms.[8]

Enhanced or extended integrated drive electronics *See* **EIDE**.

Enhanced small device interface *See* **ESDI**.

ENP® European nursing care pathways. Provides nursing knowledge for nursing professionals in terms of a nursing language implemented in a classification system for the illustration of the nursing process. The nursing classification ENP® consists of the vertical level of the classes nursing diagnoses, characteristics, resources, nursing objectives and nursing interventions, and intervention guiding specifications. Within the individual classes, the organizing principle is either hierarchical or coordinate. In the ENP® system, every single ENP® nursing diagnosis, supported by nursing literature, relates horizontally and class-spanning to other objects (characteristics, etiologies, resources, nursing objectives, and nursing interventions). According to the ENP® developers, these nursing diagnosis-related pathways represent up-to-date nursing knowledge and can be understood as a knowledge management system for nursing due to semantic networks. ENP® is among the pre-combined nursing classifications and is conceived for front-end use.[113]

Enterprise A business organization.[32]

Enterprise application integration *See* **EAI**.

Enterprise architecture 1. A strategic resource that aligns business and technology, leverages shared assets, builds internal and external partnerships, and optimizes the value of information technology services. **2.** A business-focused framework developed in accordance with the Clinger-Cohen Act of 1996 that identifies the business processes, systems that support processes, and guidelines and standards by which systems must operate.[178,23]

Enterprise architecture integration Tools and techniques that promote, enable, and manage the exchange of information and distribution of business processes across multiple application systems, typically within a sizeable electronic landscape, such as large corporations, collaborating companies, and administrative regions.[8]

Enterprise information portal *See* **EIP**.

Enterprise information system *See* **EIS**.

Enterprise master patient index A system that coordinates client identification across multiple systems, namely by collecting and storing IDs and person-identifying demographic information from source system (track new persons, track changes to existing persons). These systems also take on several other tasks and responsibilities associated with client ID management.[8]

Enterprise master person index *See* **EMPI**.

Enterprise network A network consisting of multiple servers and domains over a small or large geographical area.[1]

Enterprise network services Examples are security, messaging, administration, host connectivity, and wide area network communication.[1]

Enterprise resource planning *See* **ERP**.

Enterprise scheduling The ability to schedule procedures, exams, and appointments across multiple systems and/or locations spanning an entire jurisdiction.[8]

Enterprise user authentication *See* **EUA**.

Entity Something that has a distinct, separate existence, though an entity need not be a material existence.[7]

Entity identity assertion Ensure that an entity is the person or application that claims the identity provided.[48]

Entity-relationship diagram The entity-relationship model or entity-relationship diagram (ERD) is a data model or diagram for high-level descriptions of conceptual data models, and it provides a graphical notation for representing such data models in the form of entity-relationship diagrams. Such data models are typically used in the first stage of information system design; they are used, for example, to describe information needs and/or the type of information that is to be stored in the database during the requirements analysis.[7]

Entries Health record data in general (clinical observations, statements, reasoning, intentions, plans, or actions) without particular specification of their formal representation, hierarchical organization, or of the particular record component class(es) that might be used to represent them.[116]

EOB **Explanation of benefits.** A document detailing how a claim was processed according to the insured's benefits.[15]

EOP **Explanation of payment.** Generated to the provider in reply to a claim submission.[15]

EP **Eligible professional.** According to the Centers for Medicare & Medicaid Services eligible professionals may receive incentive payment under either the Medicare or Medicaid Incentive Programs. Eligible professionals (EPs) under the Medicare EHR Incentive Program include doctors of medicine or osteopathy, doctors of dental surgery or dental medicine, doctors of podiatry, doctors of optometry and chiropractors. Medicaid Eligible professionals include physicians (primarily doctors of medicine and doctors of osteopathy), nurse practitioners, certified nurse-midwives, dentists, and physician assistants who furnish services in a Federally Qualified Health Center or Rural Health Clinic that is led by a physician assistant.[130]

ePHI **Electronic protected health information.** Any protected health information (PHI) that is created, stored, transmitted, or received electronically.[48]

ePHR **Electronic personal health record.** A universally accessible, layperson comprehensible, lifelong tool for managing relevant health information, promoting health maintenance, and assisting with chronic disease management via an interactive, common data set of electronic health information and eHealth tools. The ePHR is owned, managed, and shared by the individual or his or her legal proxy(s) and must be secure to protect the privacy and confidentiality of the health information it contains. It is not a legal record unless so defined, and is subject to various legal limitations.[45] *See* **PHR**.

Episode of care Services provided by a healthcare facility or provider for a specific medical problem or condition or specific illness during a set time period. Episode of care can be given either for a short period or on a continuous basis or it may consist of a series of intervals marked by one or more brief separations from care.[188]

E-prescribing Electronic prescribing. The use of computing devices to enter, modify, review, and output or communicate drug prescriptions.[1]

EPROM Erasable programmable memory. Reusable firmware that can be programmed. Previous contents are erased by applying ultraviolet light through the window in the chip.[1]

ERA Electronic remittance advice. Any of several electronic formats for explaining the payments of healthcare claims.[10]

Erasable programmable memory
See **EPROM**.

ERD Emergency repair disk. Disk that contains machine-specific repair process information on registry (system, software, security, security accounts manager) and system files for use when failures occur.[1]

ERD Entity relationship diagram 1. A diagram showing entities and their relationships. Relates to business data analysis and database design. **2.** An entity relationship (ER) model shows how the sets of information contained in architectures are related to each other.[18,7]

ERISA Employee Retirement Income and Security Act of 1975. Most group health plans covered by ERISA are also health plans under Health Insurance Portability and Accountability Act.[48]

ERP Enterprise resource planning. Management information systems that integrate and automate many of the business functions associated with the operations or production aspects of an enterprise, such as general ledger, budgeting, materials management, purchasing, payroll, and human resources.[7,1]

Error An act of commission (doing something wrong) or omission (failing to do the right thing) that leads to an undesirable outcome or significant potential for such an outcome. For instance, ordering a medication for a patient with a documented allergy to that medication would be an act of commission. Failing to prescribe a proven medication with major benefits for an eligible patient (e.g., low-dose unfractionated heparin as venous thromboembolism prophylaxis for a patient after hip replacement surgery) would represent an error of omission. Errors of omission are more difficult to recognize than errors of commission but likely represent a larger problem. In other words, there are likely many more instances in which the provision of additional diagnostic, therapeutic, or preventive modalities would have improved care than there are instances in which the care provided quite literally should not have been provided. In many ways, this point echoes the generally agreed upon view in the healthcare quality literature that underuse far exceeds overuse, even though the latter historically received greater attention.[14] *See* **Underuse, Overuse, Misuse**.

Error chain Generally refers to the series of events that led to a disastrous outcome, typically uncovered by a root cause analysis. Sometimes the chain metaphor carries the added sense of inexorability, as many of the causes are tightly coupled, such that one problem begets the next. A more specific meaning of error chain, especially when used in the phrase 'break the error chain,' relates to the common themes or categories of causes that emerge from root cause analyses. These categories go by different names in different settings, but they generally include (1) failure to follow standard operating procedures; (2) poor leadership; (3) breakdowns in communication or teamwork; (4) overlooking or ignoring individual fallibility; and (5) losing track of objectives. Used in this way, 'break the error chain' is shorthand for an approach in which team members continually address these links as a crisis or routine situation unfolds, The checklists that are included in teamwork training programs have categories corresponding to these common links in the in the error chain (e.g., establish team leader, assign roles and responsibility, monitor your teammates).[14]

Error proofing Used to ensure products and processes are completed correctly the first time. Often relies on mechanisms built into tools or systems that automatically signal when problems occur or prevent the process from continuing until the proper conditions are met.[222] Also known as *mistake proofing*.[171]

ESDI Enhanced small device interface. Short-lived hard disk drive interface standard introduced by Compaq. Step-in technology after modified frequency modulation (MFM), and before Integrated Device Electronics (IDE).[1]

ESL eXtensible style sheet Language. A family of languages that allows one to describe how files encoded in the XML standard are to be formatted or transformed. XSL Transformation (XSLT) is used to transform the XML document, and XSL Formatting Objects (XSL-FO) is used to render the transformed document.[8]

Ethernet 1. The most common type of connection computers use within a local area network (LAN). An Ethernet port looks much like a regular phone jack, but it is slightly wider. This port can be used to connect the computer to another computer, a local network, or an external DSL or cable modem. **2.** A family of computer networking technologies and protocols for local area networks (LANs) commercially introduced in 1980. **3.** A frame-based computer networking technology for LANs. The name comes from the physical concept of ether. It defines wiring and signaling for the physical layer and frame formats and protocols for the media access control (MAC)/data link layer of the Open Systems Interconnection (OSI) model. Ethernet is mostly standardized as IEEEs 802.3. It has become the most widespread LAN technology in use during the 1990s to the present.[2,2,7]

Ethics Standards that dictate what humans ought to do in terms of obligations, rights, fairness, and virtues. Ethical standards include compassion, loyalty, and honesty.[20]

ETL Extraction transformation loading. A data warehousing term. The collection of methods, processes, and technology that perform the acquisition, cleansing, transformation, integration, and loading of raw data sources into a data warehouse.[1]

EUA Enterprise user authentication. A means to establish one name per user that can then be used on all of the devices and software that participate in this integration profile, greatly facilitating centralized user authentication management and providing users with the convenience and speed of a single sign-on. This profile leverages Kerberos (RFC 1510) and the HL7 clinical context object work group (CCOW) standard (user subject).[56]

European Committee for Standardization. *See* **CEN**.

European digital signal *See* **E-1-3**.

European nursing care pathways® *See* **ENP®**.

European standard. *See* **EN**.

Event Action or activity that occurs within a system and/or network scope, inclusive of its boundaries.[48]

Event aggregation Consolidation of similar log entries into a single entry, containing a count of the number of occurrences of the event.[48]

Event correlation Relationships between two or more log entries.[48]

Event filtering Suppression of log entries from analysis, reporting, or long-term storage, because their characteristics indicate that they are unlikely to contain information of interest.[48]

Event reduction Removal of unneeded data fields from all log entries to create a new log that is smaller.[48]

Evidence documents *See* **ED**.

Evidence-based medicine 1. The process of systematically finding, appraising, and using contemporaneous research findings as the basis for clinical decisions. **2.** Evidence-based medicine asks questions, finds and appraises the relevant data, and harnesses that information for everyday clinical practice. Evidence-based medicine follows four steps: formulate a clear clinical question from a patient's problem; search the literature for relevant clinical articles; evaluate (critically appraise) the evidence for its validity and usefulness; and implement useful findings in clinical practice. The term 'evidence-based medicine' was coined at McMaster Medical School in Canada in the 1980s to label this clinical learning strategy, which people at the school had been developing for over a decade.[151,5] *See* **Best practices**.

Evidence-based practice *See* **Evidence-based medicine**.

Exception A transaction that does not receive authorization by the accepted rules and procedures.[1]

Exchange format The representation of the data elements and the structure of a message, while in transfer between systems.[4]

Exclusive branching Splits a process in several branches, only one of which can be selected, based on the fulfillment of a condition associated with a given branch.[111]

Exclusive choice The divergence of a branch into two or more branches, such that when the incoming branch is enabled, the thread of control is immediately passed to precisely one of the outgoing branches, based on a mechanism that can select one of the outgoing branches.[112] *See* **Simple merge**.

Executive information system *See* **EIS**.

Expert system A software system with two basic components: a knowledgebase and an inference engine.[7]

Explanation of benefits *See* **EOB**.

Explanation of payment *See* **EOP**.

Explicit congestion notification *See* **ECN**.

Expression The textual means to convey a concept to the user. It can be a major concept, a synonym, or a lexical variant.[32]

Extended ASCII Extended American standard code for information interchange. Extensively used 8-bit standard information processing code with 256 characters.[1]

Extended binary coded decimal interchange code *See* **EBCDIC**.

Extended industry standard architecture *See* **EISA**.

Extended memory Additional area of memory beyond 1 MB associated with DOS machines.[1]

Extensibility **1.** System design feature that allows for future expansion without the need for changes to the basic infrastructure. **2.** The ability to economically modify or add functionality.[203,8]

Extensible authentication protocol *See* **EAP**.

Extensible markup language *See* **XML**.

Extensible stylesheet language *See* **XSL**.

Exterior gateway protocol *See* **EGP**.

External customer A person or organization that receives a product, service, or information; not part of the organization supplying the product, service or information.[220]

Extraction transformation loading *See* **ETL**.

Extranet An internal network or intranet opened to selected business partners to allow access to internal information in support of essential information for a business relationship, such as supply-chain management information.[1]

F

Facility directory Listing or reference document maintained by a healthcare provider, such as (but not limited to) a hospital, nursing home, or treatment center, of persons receiving care or treatment from that provider, and containing information about each individual patient or resident receiving care or treatment.[48]

Fact table In data warehousing, a fact table consists of the measurements, metrics, or facts of a business process. It is often located at the center of a star schema or a snowflake schema, surrounded by dimension tables.[7]

Failback The process of restoring operations to a primary machine or facility after they have been shifted to a secondary machine or facility during failover.[42]

Failover A backup operational mode in which the functions of a system component (such as a processor, server, network, or database, for example) are assumed by secondary system components when the primary component becomes unavailable through either failure or scheduled down time. Used to make systems more fault-tolerant, failover is typically an integral part of mission-critical systems that must be constantly available.[42]

Failsafe Pertaining to avoidance of compromise in the event of a failure.[3]

Failure The inability of an item, product or service to perform required functions on demand due to one or more defects.[222]

False acceptance rate *See* **FAR**.

Family set Group of backup tapes consisting of a single run of backup information.[1]

FAQ Frequently asked questions. A collection of information on any subject for which questions are typically asked. FAQ postings provide quick answers without the need or expense of a staff person answering the question on the phone or in writing and are viewed as a time-saving feature of web sites, which provides a return on investment.[1]

FAR False acceptance rate. Refers to the rate at which an unauthorized individual is accepted by the system as a valid user.[114]

Fast healthcare interoperability resources *See* **FHIR**.

Fast SCSI Fast small computer system interface. Ten Mbps high-speed 8-bit bus interface for connecting devices to the computer bus.[1]

Fast small computer system interface *See* **Fast SCSI**.

FAT File allocation table. Sixteen-bit file cluster system technique used by MS-DOS and Windows operating systems to manage disk space. Can also be used with Windows NT.[1]

FAT Client In a client/server system, a client that performs most of the necessary data processing itself, rather than relying on the server. Also called *thick, heavy,* or *rich client.*[107]

FAT32 File allocation table 32-bit. Thirty-two-bit file system technique used by the Windows 95 operating systems to manage disk space. Cannot be used with Windows NT.[1]

FCOE Fiber channel over Ethernet. An encapsulation of fiber channel frames over Ethernet networks. This allows a fiber channel to use 10 gigabit Ethernet networks (or higher speeds) while preserving the fiber channel protocol.[2]

FDDI Fiber distributed data interface. Fiber optic dual token ring network within the 802.8 standard. Provides 1,000 MHz of bandwidth at a distance of 200 km.[1]

Federal Health Architecture *See* **FHA**.

Federal Privacy Act of 1974 HIPAA. U.S.C. Section 552a. The Federal Privacy Act established a framework within which the government collects and uses information about individuals. Medicare recipients are protected because Medicare contractors are prohibited from releasing personal information, such as a person's health insurance claim number, claim data, diagnoses, etc., without written or verbal permission from the beneficiary or their official representative. Privacy rights of individuals were further strengthened in various revisions and through HIPAA.[1]

Fee for service *See* **FFS**.

Feeder systems Operational systems that will feed patient/person data to the EHR in the form of real-time single messages, multiple messages, or batch file uploads.[8] *See* **Source systems**.

FFS Fee for service. Contract method to pay a contracted fee for services performed by providers.[32]

FHA Federal Health Architecture. An E-government Line of Business initative managed by the Office of the National Coordinator for Health IT. Formed to coordinate health IT activities among the more that 20 federal agencies that provide health and healthcare services to citizens, including the Department of Health & Human Services (HHS), Department of Defense (DoD), Department of Veterans Affairs (VA), Department of Homeland Security (DHS), Environmental Protection Agency (EPA), Department of Agriculture (USDA), and Department of Energy (DOE). FHA provides a framework for linking health business processes to technology solutions and standards and for demonstrating how these solutions achieve improved health performance outcomes.[178]

FHIR Fast healthcare interoperability resources. Defines a set of resources for health. These resources represent granular clinical concepts that can be exchanged to quickly and effectively solve problems in healthcare and related process. The resources cover the basic elements of healthcare—patients, admissions, diagnostic reports, medications, and problem lists, with their typical participants, and also support a range of richer and more complex clinical models. The simple direct definitions of the resources are based on thorough requirements gathering, formal analysis and extensive cross-mapping to other relevant standards.[16]

Fiber channel over Ethernet   *See* **FCOE.**

Fiber channel   A gigabit-speed network technology primarily used for storage networking.[2]

Fiber distributed data interface   *See* **FDDI.**

Fiber optic cable   A pure glass cable used for the transmission of digital signals. It generates no radiation of its own and is resistant to electromagnetic interference. It is used in areas where security is of prime importance because tapping into the cable is detectable. Can be used over longer distances than copper cable.[1]

Fiber optics   Extremely fast communications technology that uses glass or plastic medium to transmit light pulses produced by LEDs or ILDs to represent data. Fiber optics are immune to electronic magnetic interference, but susceptible to chromatic dispersion. Information is transmitted through the fiber as pulsating light. The light pulses represent bits of information. Fiber optics give users of telecommunications added capacity, better transmission quality, and increased clarity.[1]

Fiber transceiver   Device that converts fiber optic signals to digital signals and vice versa. Usually used to make a connection from a fiber run to an Ethernet segment.[1]

Field   When a unit of data can be subdivided, the individual subdivisions are known as fields, or data elements.[1]

Field components   A field entry may also have discernable parts or components. For example, the patient's name is recorded as last name, first name, and middle initial, each of which is a distinct entity separated by a component delimiter.[16]

Field level security   Data protection and/or authorization of specified fields or data elements within files, rather than of entire files.[1]

FIFO   First in, first out.   An abstraction related to ways of organizing and manipulating data relative to time and prioritization.[7]

File   Electronic data collected in related records. Files have unique names and entities that allow for them to be stored, moved, and edited. Often, a file's suffix describes its type, such as a Microsoft document file (.doc) or an executable file (.exe).[1]

File allocation table   *See* **FAT.**

File allocation table 32-bit   *See* **FAT32.**

File extension   A group of characters appended to the end of a disk file name. File extensions usually consist of a full stop (dot) and one to three characters. Examples: .doc, .docx, or .pdf format.[4]

File server   A networked computer that provides file handling and storage for users with network access. A computer that each computer on a network can use to access and retrieve files that can be shared among the attached computers. Access to a file is usually controlled by the file server software, rather than by the operating system of the computer that accesses the file.[1]

File transfer protocol   *See* **FTP.**

Filmless radiology   Use of devices that replace film by acquiring digital images and related patient information, and transmit, store, retrieve, and display them electronically.[106]

Filter   A program that accepts a certain type of data as input, transforms the data in some manner, and then outputs the transformed data. Also defined as a pattern through which data passed. Only data that matches the pattern is allowed to pass through the filter.[58]

FIPS   Federal Information Processing Standard.   A standard for adoption and use by federal departments and agencies that has been developed within the Information Technology Laboratory and published by the National Institute of Standards and Technology (NIST), a part of the US Department of Commerce. A FIPS covers some topics in information technology to achieve a common level of quality or some level of interoperability.[114]

Firewall   1.   Used to prevent unauthorized access by blocking and checking all incoming network traffic. A firewall permits only authorized users to access and transmit privileged information and denies access to unauthorized users. **2.** Objective is to control the incoming and outgoing network traffic by analyzing the data packets and determining whether the packets should be allowed through based on a prede-termined rule set.[1,7]

Firmware   Computer instructions written to a read-only memory (ROM), programmable memory (PROM), or erasable programmable memory (EPROM) chip.[1]

First in, first out   *See* **FIFO**.

Fishbone diagram   **1.** The fishbone dia-gram, or cause-and-effect diagram, is a tool for capturing, displaying, and classifying the various theories about the causes of a problem. **2.** Referred to as the *Ishikawa diagram* and the *fishbone diagram* because the complete dia-gram resembles a fish skeleton. The diagram identifies many possible causes for an effect or problem and sorts ideas into useful catego-ries. The cause and effect diagram is one of the 'seven tools of quality.' [120,222]

Five rights of medication administration The Five Rights—administering the right medi-cation, in the right dose, at the right time, by the right route, to the right patient—are the corner-stone of traditional nursing teaching about safe medication practice.[14]

Fixed wireless   Refers to wireless devices or systems that are situated in fixed locations, such as an office or home, as opposed to devices that are mobile, such as cell phones and PDAs. The point-to-point signal transmissions occur through the air over a terrestrial micro-wave platform rather than through copper or fiber cables; therefore, fixed wireless does not require satellite feeds or local phone service. The advantages of fixed wireless over tradi-tional cabling infrastructure include the ability to connect with users in remote areas without the need for laying new cables and the capacity for broad bandwidth that is not impeded by fiber or cable capacities.[1] *See* **PDA**.

Flash drive   Portable memory in a space the size of a key. Also called memory key, jump drive, thumb drive, stick, removable drive, and other names.[7]

Flash memory   Non-volatile memory that provides read-only operations for computer boot-up. Contents can be updated. Smartcard memory technology that emulates a hard disk, except that the data are stored electronically, and there are no moving parts.[1]

Flat files   **1.** Files in which each record has the same length, whether or not all the space is used. Empty parts of the record are padded with a blank, or zero, depending on the data type of each field. **2.** Refers to a file that consists of a series of fixed-length records that include some sort of record type code.[1,10]

Flat table   One data element per field, tables are in the simplest form.[6]

Flexibility   The ability to support architec-tural and hardware configuration changes.[8]

Flexible spending account   *See* **FSA**.

Flip-flop   Digital signal circuit that can store one bit of information or be in a cleared state. One-bit memory.[1]

Flow chart   A diagram that combines sym-bols and abbreviated narratives to describe a sequence of operations and/or a process.[6]

Flow sheet   A tabular summary of informa-tion that is arranged to display the values of variables as changed over time.[4]

Foreground   Application or task that is exe-cuting and accepting user input and subsequent output on a multitasking machine.[1]

Foreign key   A primary key of one data table that is placed into another data table to represent a relationship among those tables. Foreign keys resolve relationships and support navigation among data structures.[1] *See* **Primary key**.

Formal system   In a concept representation, a set of machine processable definitions in a subject field.[90]

Format   Specifications of how data or files are to be characterized.[5]

Fortezza card   A credit card-sized electronic module that stores digital information that can be recognized by a network or system. It is used to provide data encryption and authentication services.[1]

Frame   A packet that can be 64- to 1,518-bytes long and contain header/data/trailer informa-tion, in addition to a preamble to mark the start of a frame.[1]

Frame relay   A packet-oriented communica-tion switching method used for local area net-work (LAN) interconnections and wide area network (WAN) connections. Used in both private and public networks. Frame relay networks in the US support data transfer rates at T-1 (1.544 Mbps) and T-3 (45 Mbps) speeds.[1] *See* **ATM**, **SONET**.

Framework **1.** A structured description of a topic of interest, including a detailed statement of the problem(s) to be solved and the goals to be achieved. An annotated outline of all the issues that must be addressed while developing acceptable solutions to the problem(s). A description and analysis of the constraints that must be satisfied by an acceptable solution, and detailed specifications of acceptable approaches to solving the problem(s). **2.** Provides a unified view of the needs and functionality of a particular service or application, thus allowing a coherent approach to the specification of protocols and protocol elements, as needed to realize the implementation of the service or application.[114,4]

Free text Unstructured, uncoded representations of information in text format (e.g., sentences describing the results of a patient's physical condition).[4]

Frequently asked questions *See* **FAQ**.

FSA **Flexible spending account.** A method of setting aside pre-tax dollars for healthcare reimbursement.[15]

FTF **Face to face.**

FTP **File transfer protocol. 1.** A standard high-level protocol for transferring files of different types between computers over a TCP/IP network. FTP can be used with a command line interface or graphical user interface. **2.** The name of a utility program available on several operating systems, which makes use of this protocol to access and transfer files on remote computers.[1]

Full duplex Communication channel/circuit that allows simultaneous two-way data transmission.[1]

Fully specified name A phrase that describes a concept uniquely and in a manner that is intended to be unambiguous.[19]

Functional health status Refers to a patient's ability to perform typical daily physical and social/role functions, plus other measures of self-perceived health status, such as well-being, vitality, and mental health.[120]

Functional requirements A statement of the system behavior needed to enforce a given policy. Requirements are used to derive the technical specifications of a system. Describes the performance expectations for a system.[1]

Functional role Role an individual is acting under when executing a function.[122]

Functional specifications A precise description of a computer system's functional requirements containing an overall picture of the proposed system's conditions, prerequisites, and restraints.[6]

G

Gantt chart A type of bar chart used in process or project planning, and control to display planned work targets for completion of work in relation to time. Typically, a Gantt chart shows the week, month, or quarter in which each activity will be completed, and the person or persons responsible for carrying out each activity.[123]

Gap analysis The comparison of a current condition to the desired state. Gap analysis is a term also used within process analysis to describe the variance between current and future state processes.[222]

Garbage in, garbage out *See* **GIGO**.

Gateway **1.** A computer or a network that allows access to another computer or network. **2.** A phrase used by web masters and search engine optimizers to describe a web page designed to attract visitors and search engines to a particular web site. A typical gateway page is small, simple, and highly optimized. **3.** A technical term for the software interface between a web-based shopping cart (or order form) and a merchant account.[7] *See* **Electronic commerce**.

GB **Gigabyte.**[1]

GBps **Gigabytes per second.** Transmission of a billion bits per second.[1]

GELLO **Guideline Expression Language, Object Oriented.**[30] An object-oriented query and expression language for clinical decision support.[92]

General order message The function of this message is to initiate the transmission of information about an order. This includes placing new orders, cancellation of existing orders, discontinuation, holding, etc. Messages can originate with a placer, filler, or interested third party.[16] Also known as *ORM messages*.

GIF Graphics interchange format. Standard for encoding, transmitting, decoding, and providing photo quality images. Introduced by CompuServe in 1987 to allow network transmission of photo-quality graphics images.[1]

GIFanim An animated picture created by including two or more .gif images in one file.[1]

GIG Global information grid. A globally interconnected, end-to-end set of information capabilities, associated processes, and personnel for collecting, processing, storing, disseminating, and managing information on demand.[23]

Gigabit 1. A measure of computer storage that is approximately equal to one billion bits, most commonly used to describe telecommunications transfer speeds. For example, gigabit Ethernet allows LAN transfer of about one billion bits, or discrete signal pulses, per second. **2.** A gigabit Ethernet is a term describing various technologies for transmitting Ethernet frames at a rate of gigabit per second (1,000,000,000 bits per second), as defined by IEEE 802.3-2008 standard.[1,2]

Gigabyte Approximately one billion (1,024 megabytes) bytes. Unit of computer storage capacity.[1]

Gigahertz One billion cycles per second.[1]

GIGO Garbage in, garbage out. Synonymous with the entry of inaccurate or useless data and processed output of worthless/useless information.[1]

Global information grid *See* **GIG**.

Global system for mobile communications *See* **GSM**.

Global unique device identification database *See* **GUDID**.

Glossary A list of terms (usually alphabetically sorted) with explanations pertaining to a particular field (glossary is synonymous with vocabulary).[4]

Gnutella A file-sharing network.[42] *See* **P2P**.

Google™ Internet search engine.[32]

Gopher Text-based menu-driven document retrieval information service used on the Internet. Has virtually been made obsolete by the introduction of graphical-based web browsers. A tool for finding data on the Internet that enables the user to locate essentially all textual information stored on Internet servers through a series of easy-to-use, hierarchical menus.[1]

Graduated security A security system that provides several levels of protection based on threats, risks, available technology, support services, time, human concerns, and economics.[114]

Granular 1. An expression of the relative size of a unit. The smallest discrete information that can be directly retrieved. In security, it is the degree of protection. Protection at the file level is considered coarse granularity, whereas protection at the field level is finer granularity. **2.** Refers to a high degree of detail. In particular, a vocabulary that is highly granular provides names and definitions for the individual data elements within the context of a broader concept.[1,151]

Graphical user interface *See* **GUI**.

Graphics interchange format *See* **GIF**.

Greenscreen Monochrome computer monitors. **1.** Named for the green phosphor commonly used in monitors in the 1970s and 1980s. **2.** Refers to a computer application based on a character-cell terminal, which typically displayed is about 80 characters wide by 24-25 lines tall, vs. the graphical user interfaces (GUI) commonly used in 2000 and later.[7]

Grid computing Grid computing uses the resources of many separate computers connected by a network (usually the Internet) to solve large-scale computation problems.[7]

Group health plan Under the Health Insurance Portability and Accountability Act, this is an employee welfare benefit plan that provides for medical care that either has 50 or more participants, or is administered by another business entity.[10]

GroupWare Network software that defines applications used by a group of people. Allows users on different systems to collaborate and interact. Electronic mail is an example.[1]

GSM   Global system for mobile communications. 1. A worldwide digital standard used in nearly all countries in the world except Japan and the US. GSM is a pure digital service that can transmit IP packets to the Internet and uses an array of fixed antennas in geographical cells that connect various mobile devices to the network. **2.** GSM uses 1,900 MHz in the US, and 800 to 900 MHz in Europe and Asia. GSM providers also offer wireless application protocol (WAP) services, such as connection of a GSM phone to a laptop with a PC card or cable at a data rate of 9.6 Kbps.[1]

GSNW   Gateway services for NetWare. Provides the ability to connect to and make NetWare server resources available to a Windows NT server.[1]

GUDID   Global unique device identification database. A proposed Food and Drug Administration (FDA) publically accessible database that would hold information about each medical device marketed in the United States.

GUI   Graphical user interface. 1. User interface that employs graphical images for the execution of resources as opposed to command line entry. Employs windows, icons, and menus in lieu of text to run programs and give commands to the computer. It is usually a window system accessed through a pointing device, such as a mouse. **2.** Options on how the mouse interacts with the objects on the screen allows a point-and-click interface to identify or activate an icon, or a drag-and-drop interface to move an item to another location. **3.** A type of display format that enables user to choose commands, initiate programs, and other options by selecting pictorial representation (icons) via a mouse or a keyboard.[1]

Guideline   1. A recommended approach, parameter, etc. for conducting an activity or task, utilizing a product. **2.** A description that clarifies what should be done and how, to achieve the objectives set out in policies.[123] *See* **Clinical practice guideline**.

H

Hacker   A person who gains unauthorized access to a computer network for profit, criminal mischief, or personal pleasure.[1]

Half duplex   Communication channel/circuit that allows data transmission in one direction at a time, but not in both directions simultaneously.[1]

HAN   Health alert network. To ensure that each community has rapid and timely access to emergent health information; a cadre of highly-trained professional personnel; and evidence-based practices and procedures for effective public health preparedness, response, and service on a 24/7 basis.[46]

Hand-held   A portable computer that is small enough to hold in one's hand. Used to refer to a variety of devices ranging from personal data assistance, such as the BlackBerry, to more powerful devices that offer many of the capabilities of desktop or laptop computers. Handhelds are used in clinical practice for such tasks as ordering prescriptions, accessing patients' medical records, and documenting patient encounters.[107]

Hard copy   File printed to a paper document.[1]

Hard disk   A hard disk is part of a unit, often called a 'disk drive' or 'hard disk drive,' that stores and provides relatively quick access to large amounts of data on an electromagnetically charged surface or set of surfaces.[1]

Hardware   The physical equipment of a computer system, including the central processing unit, data-storage devices, terminals, and printers.[4]

Hardware address   Unique   low-level address burned into each piece of network hardware.[1]

Harm   Physical injury or damage to the health of people, or damage to property or the environment.[68]

Harmonization   1. Harmonization of national standards is the prevention or elimination of differences in the technical content of standards having the same scope, particularly differences that may cause hindrances to trade. Processes to achieve harmonization include convergence, modeling, mapping, translation, and other technical specifications. **2.** The coordination processes by standard development organizations to make standards work together. Processes to achieve harmonization include convergence, modeling, mapping, translation, and other techniques.[4,151]

Hashing Iterative process that computes a value (referred to as a hashword) from a particular data unit in such a manner that, when the hashword is protected, manipulation of the data is detectable.[1]

Hazard Potential source of harm.[68]

Hazardous situation Circumstance in which people, property, or the environment are exposed to one or more hazards.[68]

HCO **Healthcare organization.** Coordinates the delivery of healthcare. The organization should equip healthcare personnel with the knowledge, tools, and expertise that they need to deliver care and act as a link to community resources. One approach to addressing healthcare systems is to divide them into the micro level (patient interaction), meso level (healthcare organization and community), and the macro level (policy).[25]

HCPCS **Healthcare Common Procedure Coding System. 1.** A set of healthcare procedure codes based on the American Medical Association Current Procedural Terminology. **2.** Currently incorporates CPT-4, national reporting certain healthcare supplies, durable medical equipment, and other services not listed in CPT-4, and local codes for Medicaid reporting.[102,151]

hData A specification for exchanging electronic health data.[16]

HDSL **High bit-rate digital subscriber line.** One of the earliest forms of DSL, used for wideband digital transmission within a corporate site and between the telephone company and a customer. The main characteristic of HDSL is that it is symmetrical: an equal amount of bandwidth is available in both directions.[1]

Heads-up An electronically generated display of flight, navigational, attack, or other data superimposed upon a military pilot's forward field of view; more recently, being adapted to medicine. Heads up is also used as a metaphor for an alert or forewarning.[35]

Health Refers to the general condition of the body or mind. When referencing the health system in general, the reference is to all actions contributing to health, including public health, healthcare, preventive care, health maintenance, and consumer health.[151]

Health alert network *See* **HAN**.

Health indicator **1.** Measure that reflects the state of health of a group of patients that have common characteristics. **2.** A single summary measure, most often expressed in quantitative terms, that represents a key dimension of health status, the healthcare system, or related factors. **Note:** A health indicator must be informative, and also be sensitive to variations over time and across jurisdictions. [94,166]

Health information Information, whether oral or recorded in any form or medium, that **(1)** is created or received by a healthcare provider, health plan, public health authority, employer, life insurer, school or university, or healthcare clearinghouse; and **(2)** relates to the past, present, or future physical or mental health or condition of an individual; the provision of healthcare to an individual; or the past, present, or future payment for the provision of healthcare to an individual.[48]

Health information exchange *See* **HIE**.

Health information organization *See* **HIO**.

Health information privacy An individual's right to control the acquisition, uses, or disclosures of his or her identifiable health data.[48]

Health information security Refers to physical, technological, or administrative safeguards or tools used to protect identifiable health data from unwarranted access or disclosure.[48]

Health information system Computer systems that capture, store, process, communicate, and present any healthcare information, including patient medical record information (PMRI).[151]

Health Information Technology Expert Panel *See* **HITEP**.

Health Information Technology for Economic and Clinical Health Act *See* **HITECH Act**.

Health Information Technology Policy Committee *See* **HITPC**.

Health insurance Insurance to cover the cost of healthcare. Health insurance can be privately managed or can be part of a government-managed scheme.[4]

Health insurance exchange *See* **HIEx**.

Health Insurance Portability and Accountability Act of 1996 *See* **HIPAA**.

Health Information Technology Standards Committee *See* **HITSC**.

Health maintenance organization *See* **HMO**.

Health outcome *See* **Outcome**.

Health Plan Employer Data and Information Set *See* **HEDIS**.

Health Plan Identifier *See* **HPID**.

Health services research The integration of epidemiologic, sociological, economic, and other analytic sciences in the study of health services. Health services research is usually concerned with relationships between need, demand, supply, use, and outcome of health services. The aim of the research is evaluation; particularly in terms of structure, process, output, and outcome.[1]

Healthcare Generally refers to the treatment of an illness or injury to the body or mind in order to restore good health or mitigate the effects of chronic disease or disability.[151]

Healthcare clearing house Organization that processes health information received from another entity in a nonstandard format or containing nonstandard data content, into standard data elements or a standard transaction, or vice versa.[48]

Healthcare Common Procedure Coding System *See* **HCPCS**.

Healthcare data card A machine readable card conformant to ISO 7810, intended for use within the healthcare domain.[117]

Healthcare enterprise Healthcare business organization (e.g., Hospital Corporation of America).[32]

Healthcare evaluation Methods for determining the success of healthcare delivery.[4]

Healthcare information framework High-level logical model of healthcare system.[4]

Healthcare Information Technology Standards Panel *See* **HITSP**.

Healthcare operations Operations, including quality assessment and improvement, peer review, underwriting, medical review audits, and business planning, management, and development.[48]

Healthcare organization *See* **HCO**.

Healthcare practitioner Person entrusted with the provision of healthcare services.[4]

Healthcare provider Person or organization that furnishes, bills, or is paid for healthcare in the normal course of business.[48]

Healthcare terminology 'A collective term used to describe the continuum of code set, classification, and nomenclature [or vocabulary].' A code is a representation assigned to a term so that it may more readily be processed. A classification arranges or organizes like or related terms for easy retrieval. A nomenclature, or vocabulary, is a set of specialized terms that facilitates precise communication by eliminating ambiguity. The term *controlled vocabulary* suggests only the set of individual terms in the vocabulary. A *structured vocabulary*, or *reference terminology*, relates terms to one another (with a set of relationships) that qualifies them (with a set of attributes) to promote precise and accurate interpretation.[151]

HEDIS Health plan employer data and information set. Set of standards for employers to use as a guide to compare health plans.[1] Also known as *Healthcare effectiveness data* and *information set. See* **MPI**.

Hercules graphics card *See* **HGC**.

Hexadecimal Base 16 numbering system where 4 bits are used to represent each digit. Uses the 0-9 digits and A-F letters for the representations of the 10-15 digits.[1]

HGC Hercules graphics card. Monochrome graphics display at a resolution of 720x348. Display type used before color graphics adapter (CGA) and enhanced graphics adapter (EGA).[1]

HIE   Health information exchange. 1. The sharing action between any two or more organizations with an executed business/legal arrangement that have deployed commonly agreed-upon technology with applied standards for the purpose of electronically exchanging health-related data between the organizations. **2.** A catch-all phrase for all health information exchanges, including RHIOs, QIOs, AHRQ-funded communities, and private exchanges. **3.** A concept evolved from the community health information exchanges of the mid-1990s. HIE provides the capability to electronically move clinical information among disparate healthcare information systems, and maintain the meaning of the information being exchanged. The goal of HIE is to facilitate access to and retrieval of clinical data to provide safer, more timely, efficient, effective, equitable, patient-centered care. HIE is also used by public health authorities to assist in the analysis of the health of populations.[45,15,84]

HIEx   Health insurance exchange. A set of state-regulated and standardized healthcare plans in the United States from which individuals may purchase health insurance eligible for federal subsidies. All exchanges must be fully certified and operational by January 1, 2014, under federal law.[7]

Hijacking   The ability of a hacker to misuse a system by gaining entry through the computer of a user who failed to logoff from a previous use.[1]

HIO   Health information organization. An organization that oversees and governs the exchange of health-related information among organizations according to nationally recognized standards. The purpose of an HIO is to perform oversight and governance functions for health information exchanges (HIEs).[84]

HIPAA   Health Insurance Portability and Accountability Act of 1996. According to the Centers for Medicare & Medicaid Services (CMS) web site, Title I of HIPAA protects health insurance coverage for workers and their families when they change or lose their jobs. Title II of HIPAA, the Administrative Simplification (AS) provisions, requires the establishment of national standards for electronic healthcare transactions and national identifiers for providers, health insurance plans, and employers. The AS provisions also address the security and privacy of health data. The standards are meant to improve the efficiency and effectiveness of the nation's healthcare system by encouraging the widespread use of electronic data interchange in healthcare. Also known as the *Kennedy-Kassebaum Bill, K2, Public Law 104-91.*[7]

HIPAA administrative code sets   Code sets that characterize a general business situation, rather than a medical condition or service.[1] Also called *non-medical code sets.*

HIPAA   administrative   simplification HIPAA, Title II, Subtitle F, gives the Department of Health & Human Services the authority to mandate the use of standards for the electronic exchange of healthcare data; specify what medical and administrative code sets should be used within those standards; require the use of national identification systems for healthcare patients, providers, payers (or plans), and employers (or sponsors); and specify the types of measures required to protect the security and privacy of personally identifiable healthcare information.[1]

HIPAA chain of trust   A term used in the HIPAA Security Notice of Proposed Rulemaking (NPRM) for a pattern of agreements that extend protection of healthcare data by requiring that each covered entity sharing healthcare data provide comparable protections offered by the original covered entity.[1]

HIPAA clearinghouse (or healthcare clearinghouse)   Under HIPAA, this is a public or private entity that reformats health information, especially billing transactions, from a non-standard format into a standard and approved format.[1]

HIPAA data dictionary   A data dictionary that defines and cross-references the contents of all X12 transactions included in the HIPAA mandate. The dictionary is maintained by the X12N/TG3.[1]

HIPAA standard   Any data element or transaction that meets each of the standards and implementation specifications adopted or established by the Secretary of the Department of Health & Human Services.[1]

HIPAA standard setting organization   An organization accredited by the American

National Standards Institute (ANSI) to develop information transactions or data elements for health plans, clearinghouses, and/or providers.[1]

HIPAA unique identifier A standard unique health identifier for each individual, employer, health plan, and healthcare provider, for use in the healthcare system.[1]

HIS Health information system. The National Committee on Vital and Health Statistics (NCVHS) describes HIS as a comprehensive, knowledge-based system, capable of providing information to all who need it to make sound decisions about health.[103]

Histogram A graphic display used to plot the frequency with which different values of a given variable occur. Histograms are used to examine existing patterns, identify the range of variables, and suggest a central tendency in variables.[123]

HIT Health information technology. A 'marriage' between the clinical healthcare activities and computer science for the benefit of patients and those who provide healthcare services.[138]

HIT analysis An analysis that uses the collected detail transactions of an organization's web site to determine how, when, why, and what visitors did during their web site visits. Within the analysis, the number of clicks, or hits, is shown from various perspectives; includes which search engine may have referred them to the site, how long they stayed, and how many different pages were viewed.[1]

HITECH Act Health Information Technology for Economic and Clinical Health Act. Part of the American Recovery and Reinvestment Act of 2009 (ARRA) that addresses privacy and security concerns related to the transmission of electronic health information. The HITECH Act broadened the scope of privacy and security measures for personal health records (PHRs) under Health Insurance Portability and Accountability Act (HIPAA), and also increased certain legal liabilities for noncompliance.[130]

HITEP Health Information Technology Expert Panel. Expert panel charged with recommending a standardized Quality Data Model for data representation to enable quality mea-

surement through improved data flows within and across care settings.[208]

HITPC Health Information Technology Policy Committee. A federal advisory committee charged with making recommendations to the National Coordinator for Health IT for the development and adoption of a nationwide health information infrastructure, including standards for the exchange of patient medical information.[130]

HITSC Health Information Technology Standards Committee. A federal advisory committee charged with making recommendations to the National Coordinator for Health Information Technology on standards, implementation specifications, and certification criteria for the electronic exchange and use of health information.[130]

HITSP Healthcare Information Technology Standards Panel. A multi-stakeholder coordinating body, based on a contract by the Department of Health & Human Services (DHHS), Office of National Coordinator for Health Information Technology (ONC), and the American National Standards Institute (ANSI) designed to provide the process within which affected parties can identify, select, and harmonize standards for communicating healthcare information throughout a National Nationwide Healthcare Information Network (NHIN).[48]

HMO Health maintenance organization. An entity that provides, offers, or arranges for coverage of designated health services needed by plan members for a fixed, prepaid premium.[15]

Home page The first and main view of a web document, under which a series of pages may be placed. A top-level document of an organization, or a document that a user frequently visits.[1]

Hospital AVailability Exchange *See* EDXL-HAVE.

Host An end user computer that is connected to at least one network.[1]

Host file Text file that maps remote host names to IP addresses. Acts as a local DNS equivalent to provide a static type of DNS service.[1]

HPID (Unique) health plan identifier. Health & Human Services (HHS) proposed a 2012 rule to establish a unique health plan identifier under the HIPAA standards for electronic healthcare transactions. The adoption of HPID and other entity identifier (OEID) would increase standardization within HIPAA standard transactions and would eliminate problems that several hospitals and healthcare providers experience frequently, such as improper routing of transactions, rejected transactions due to insurance identification errors, difficulty in determining patient eligibility and other claims processing challenges.[209]

HTML Hypertext markup language. **1.** American Standard Code for Information Exchange (ASCII)-based language used for creating files to display documents or web pages to web browsers. **2.** Hypertext markup language is the standard provided by World Wide Web Consortium (W3G) used for web pages on the Internet.[1,4]

HTTP Hypertext transfer protocol. **1.** Communication link protocol used by web servers and browsers to transfer/exchange HTML documents or files (text, graphic images, sound, video, and other multimedia files) over the Internet. **2.** Protocol with lightness and speed necessary for a distributed collaborative hypermedia information system. It is a generic, stateless, object-oriented protocol, which may be used for many similar tasks, such as name servers; and distributed object-oriented systems, by extending the commands or 'methods' used.[1,16] *See* **S-HTTP**.

HTTP over SSL/HTTPS HTTPS is a secure way of using HTTP. It supplements HTTP's transport layer, the insecure transmission control protocol (TCP), with Secure Socket Layer (SSL), a secure transport layer. HTTPS is a web protocol developed by Netscape and built into its, and other browsers, that encrypts and decrypts user page requests, as well as the pages that are returned by the web server.[8]

Hub Electronic network device to which multiple networked computers are attached. Divides a data channel into two or more channels of lower bandwidth. Hubs function at the physical layer (first layer) of the open systems interconnection (OSI) model.[1] *See* **Concentrator**.

Hybrid network Type of LAN topology in which networked nodes are connected to a hub, where star and ring topologies are combined into one overall topology.[1]

Hybrid smartcard A card that combines both optical and smartcard technologies.[1]

Hype cycle Hype Cycle of Emerging Technology (Gartner Group), a five-stage progression concerning 'the visibility' of an emerging technology (e.g., in the popular press): 1. Technology trigger; 2. peak of inflated expectations; 3. trough of disillusionment; 4. slope of enlightenment; and 5. plateau of productivity. Relative values on a 0-10 scale: 0, 9, 2, 3, 4. Used to convey the sense that new technologies are always oversold at first. Though they eventually are useful, they seldom live up to initial expectations.[47]

Hypertext markup language *See* **HTML**.

Hypertext transfer protocol *See* **HTTP**.

Hz Hertz. One cycle per second. Processing speeds for CPUs are measured in MHz.[1]

I

I/O Input/output device. Allows computer to communicate with external devices, such as printers.[4]

IAM Identity access management. Set of services to include authentication, user provisioning (UP), password management, role matrix management, enterprise single sign-on, enterprise access management, federation, virtual and meta-directory services, and auditing.[48]

IAP Internet access provider. Company that provides basic Internet connection access. No additional services are provided, such as e-mail hosting.[1]

ICC Integrated circuit chip. Another name for a chip, an integrated circuit is a small electronic device made out of a semiconductor material. Integrated circuits are used for a variety of devices, including microprocessors, audio and video equipment, and automobiles. Integrated circuits are often classified by the number of transistors and other electronic components they contain.[1]

ICD   The International Classification of Diseases. ICD is the standard diagnostic tool for epidemiology, health management, and clinical purposes, including the analysis of the general health situation of population groups. Also used to monitor the incidence and prevalence of diseases and other health program and to classify diseases and other health problems records on the many types of health and vital records include death certificates and health records. And, used for reimbursement and resource allocation decision-making by countries. It is published by the World Health Organization.[25]

ICIDH   International   Classification   of Improvements, Disability, and Health. Classification system issued by the World Health Organization, for common language for clinical use, data collection, and research.[151]

Icon   A picture or symbol that graphically represents an object or a concept.[32]

ICON   The ICON is an informational tool to describe nursing practice and provides data representing nursing practice in comprehensive health information systems. A combinatorial terminology for nursing practice that includes nursing phenomena, nursing actions, and nursing outcomes, and facilitates cross-mapping of local terms and existing vocabularies and classifications.[49]

ICR   Intelligent call routing. Capability that automatically routes each call, based on caller profile, to the best available agent to handle the need, anywhere in the network.[1] *See* **PING.**

ICR   Intelligent character recognition. The computer translation of manually entered text characters into machine-readable characters.[1]

ICR   Internet relay chat. A program that allows 'live' conversations between people all over the world by typing messages back and forth across the Internet.[1]

ICU   Intensive care unit. A specialized section of a hospital containing the equipment, medical and nursing staff, and monitoring devices necessary to provide intensive care. Also known as *critical care unit*, or may have a specialty name such as *cardiac care unit*.[32]

IDE   Integrated device electronics. A standard ISA 16-bit bus interface for high-speed disk drives that operates at 5 Mbps with two attached devices (master and slave). Invented in 1986 and introduced in microcomputers in 1989-1990.[1]

Identification   The process of discovering the true identity of a person or item from the entire collection of similar persons or items.[114]

Identification authentication   1. The process of determining the identity of a user who is attempting to access a physical location or computer resource. Authentication can occur through a variety of mechanisms, including challenge/response, time-based code sequences, biometric comparison, or other techniques. **2.** Use of a password, or some other form of identification, to screen users and to check their authorization.[114,1]

Identifier   Unique data used to represent a person's identity and associated attributes. A name or a card number are examples of identifiers.[114]

Identity   The set of physical and behavioral characteristics by which an individual is uniquely recognizable.[114]

Identity access management   *See* **IAM.**

Identity digital management   *See* **IDM.**

Identity proofing   The process of providing sufficient information (e.g., identity history, credentials, documents) to a personal identity verification (PIV) registrar when attempting to establish an identity.[114]

Identity verification   The process of confirming or denying that a claimed identity is correct by comparing the credentials of a person requesting access with those previously proven and stored in the personal identity verification (PIV) card/system, and associated with the identity being claimed.[114]

IDM   Identity digital management. Composed of the set of business processes, and a supporting infrastructure, for the creation, maintenance, and use of digital identities within a legal and policy context.[48]

IDMS   Identity   management   system. 1. Composed of one or more systems or applications that manages identity verification, validation, and issuance process. **2.** Software that is used to automate administrative tasks such as resetting user passwords. It enables users to reset their own passwords. There is also identity management 'password synchronization' software that enables users to access resources across the system with a single password, or single sign-on. In an enterprise setting, identity management is used to increase security and productivity, while decreasing cost and redundant effort. [114,2]

IDN Integrated delivery network. Commonly used to refer to an integrated delivery system but may also be used when referring more to the network of providers vs. the system as a whole.[1]

IDR Intelligent document recognition. 1. Based on intelligent character recognition, the IT system automatically identifies structural features of a document to allow for a more rapid creation of the document text. **2.** Provides the ability to make sense of and help manage the unstructured, untagged information that is coming into the corporation or organization. It can provide the front-end understanding needed to feed business process management (BPM) and business intelligence (BI) applications, as well as traditional accounting and document or records management systems.[17,226]

IDS Integrated delivery system. A healthcare organization (HCO) that owns at least two hospitals.[2]

IGP Interior gateway protocol. Used to advertise routing information within an autonomous system.[1]

IHE Integrating the Healthcare Enterprise. An initiative by healthcare professionals and industry to improve the way computer systems in healthcare share information. IHE promotes the coordinated use of established standards such as DICOM and HL7 to address specific clinical need in support of optimal patient care. Systems developed in accordance with IHE communicate with one another better, are easier to implement, and enable care providers to use information more effectively.[56] *See* **Appendix B**.

IHE profile Provides a common language for purchasers and vendors to discuss the integration needs of healthcare sites and the integration capabilities of healthcare IT products. IHE profiles offer developers a clear implementation path for communication standards supported

by industry partners and carefully documented, reviewed, and tested. They give purchasers a tool that reduces the complexity, cost, and anxiety of implementing operating systems.[56]

IIF Information in identifiable form. Any representation of information that permits the identity of an individual to whom the information applies to be reasonably inferred by either direct or indirect means.[114]

IIS Internet information server. Server that provides HTTP and FTP services to web browsers.[1]

IKE Internet key exchange. A key management protocol standard that is used in conjunction with the IPSec standard. IPSec is an IP security feature that provides robust authentication and encryption of IP packets.[1]

ILD Injection laser diode. Laser diode that provides the light pulses used with single-mode fiber to convey data transmission information.[1]

Image compression Used to reduce the amount of memory required to store an image (e.g., an image that has a resolution of 640x480 and is in the RGB color space at 8 bits per color requires 900 Kbytes of storage). If this image can be compressed at a compression ratio of 20:1, the amount of storage required is only 45 Kbytes. There are several methods of image compression, including iVEX, JPEG, MPEG, H.261, H.263, and Wavelet.[1]

Imaging The process of capturing, storing, displaying, and printing graphical information, such as the capturing of paper documents for archival purposes. Can be used to store and call up documents from centralized image storage systems.[1]

IMP Internet control message protocol. An extension to the Internet protocol, or IP, that supports packets containing error, control, and information messages. The PING command uses IMP to test an Internet connection.[1]

Impact analysis Process of analyzing all operational functions and the effect that an operational interruption might have upon them.[175]

Implementation The carrying out, execution, or practice of a plan, a method, or any design for doing something. Implementation is the action that must follow any preliminary thinking in order for something to actually happen.[8]

Implementation guide 1. A document explaining the proper use of a standard for a specific purpose. **2.** Method for standardized installation and maintenance of computer software and hardware. The implementation guidelines include recommended administrative processes and span the devices' lifecycle.[10,7]

Implementation specification Specific instructions for implementing a standard.[10]

In-band Communications that occur together in a common communications method or channel. For example, a privacy label that applies to a clinical document will be sent in-band with the document.[48]

Incident Event that has the capacity to lead to human, intangible, or physical loss, or a disruption of an organization's operations, services, or functions—which, if not managed, can escalate into an emergency, crisis, or disaster.[175]

Indicator A measurable variable (or characteristic) that can be used to determine the degree of adherence to a standard or the level of quality achieved.[123]

Individual Person who is the subject of information collected, used, or disclosed by the entity holding the information.[48]

Individual practice association *See* **IPA**.

Individually identifiable data Data that can be readily associated with a specific individual. Examples would be a name, a personal identifier, or a full street address.[5]

Individually identifiable health information That which relates to an individual's physical or mental health; the provision of healthcare to an individual; or the payment for healthcare provided to an individual that identifies the individual or could be used to identify the individual.[48]

Individually identifying information Single item or compilation of information or data that indicates or reveals the identity of an individual, either specifically (such as the individual's name or Social Security number), or that does not specifically identify the individual but from which the individual's identity can reasonably be ascertained.[48]

Industry standard architecture *See* **ISA**.

Infiltration Entry into the system via the communication lines of an inactive user that is still connected to the computer. Canceling a user's sign-off signal and then continuing to operate his password and authorization.[1] *See* **Piggyback**.

Infobutton A simple alerting system that provides information on request. The information may be keyed to topic and/or user. May or may not be linked to decision support system.[146]

Informatics 1. The discipline concerned with the study of information and manipulation of information via computer-based tools. **2.** Information science or informatics is the science of information. It is often, though not exclusively, studied as a branch of computer science and information technology and is related to database, ontology, and software engineering.[4,7]

Information 1. Knowledge derived from study, experience, or instruction; a collection of facts or data; the act of informing or the condition of being informed. **2.** Data to which meaning is assigned, according to context and assumed conventions.[60,1]

Information access model Depicts access to key processes and organization information for reporting and/or security purposes.[127]

Information asset Refers to any information in any form (e.g., written, verbal, oral, or electronic) upon which the organization places a measurable value. This includes information created by the entity holding the information, gathered for the entity, or stored by the entity for external parties.[48]

Information compromise An intentional or accidental disclosure or surrender of clinical data to an unauthorized receiver.[1]

Information exchange initiative Attempts by two or more independent healthcare organizations (HCOs) in a geographic area to collaborate to share common patient information for the improvement in community health status, patient care, or viability of the HCOs. A common variety of information exchange initiatives is regional healthcare information networks (RHINs).[2]

Information flow model Visually depicts information flows in the business-to-business functions, business organizations, and applications.[127]

Information infrastructure 1. The combination of computers and an information system. 2. The standards, laws, regulations, business practices, and technologies needed to facilitate unauthorized sharing of comparable data in a safe and secure manner.[1,151]

Information in identifiable form See **IIF**.

Information interchange Information interchange (American Standard Code) is a code for information exchange between computers made by different companies; a string of seven binary digits represents each character; used in most microcomputers.[147]

Information model 1. A conceptual model of the information needed to support a business function or process. 2. A representation of concepts, relationships, constraints, rules and operations to specify data semantics for a chosen domain.[5,57]

Information modeling The building of abstract models for the purpose of developing an abstract system.[4]

Information privacy The contractual right of a person to know that his/her recorded personal medical information is accurate, pertinent, complete, up-to-date, and that effective steps have been taken to restrict access to mutually agreed-upon purposes by authorized data users.[1]

Information resource department See **IRD**.

Information resource management See **IRM**.

Information security The result of effective protection measures that safeguard data or information from undesired occurrences and exposure to accidental or intentional disclosure to unauthorized persons, accidental or malicious alteration, unauthorized copying, loss by theft and/or destruction by hardware failures, software deficiencies, operating mistakes, or physical damage by fire, water, smoke, excessive temperature, electrical failure, or sabotage.[1]

Information system A system that takes input data (data keyed in, transferred from other systems, etc.), processes it, and provides information as output (reports, screen displays, etc.).[6]

Information system architecture A framework from which applications, system software, and hardware can be developed in a coherent manner, and in which every part fits together without containing a mass of design details.[4]

Information systems A general description that may include any combination of hardware, software, and network components that comprise the ability to store, process, and retrieve information.[1]

Information technology The hardware, firmware, and software used as part of the information system to perform information functions. This definition includes computers, telecommunications, automated information systems, and automatic data processing equipment. Information technology (IT) includes any assembly of computer hardware, software, and/or firmware configured to collect, create, communicate, compute, disseminate, process, store, and/or control data or information.[97]

Information Technology Management Reform Act of 1996 See **ITMRA**.

Information technology security See **ITSEC**.

Information warfare Deliberate attacks on data confidentiality and possession, integrity and authenticity, and availability and utility.[1]

Informed consent Refers to the requirement that all researchers explain the purposes, risks, benefits, confidentiality protections, and other relevant aspects of a research study to potential human subjects, so that they may make an informed decision regarding their participation in the research. Institutional Review Boards (IRBs) review informed consent processes and forms documenting the consent to ensure compliance with research regulations and policies.[48]

Infrared Data Association See **IrDA**.

Infrastructure-centric A security management approach that considers information systems and their computing environment as a single entity.[97]

Initiator An (authenticated) entity (e.g., human user or computer-based entity) that attempts to access other entities.[125] Also known as *claimant* or *principal*.

Injection laser diode   *See* **ILD**.

Inpatient   Patient who is admitted to a health-care facility in order to receive healthcare.[4]

Inpatient record   Healthcare record of a hospitalized patient.[4]

Inputs   The resources needed to carry out a process or provide a service. Inputs required in healthcare are usually financial, physical structures, such as buildings, supplies and equipment, personnel, and clients.[123]

Institutional Review Board   *See* **IRB**.

Integrated call management   An important strategy to improve speed and efficiency in many healthcare applications through the use of multiple automated system components for telecommunications support or medical information systems design.[1]

Integrated circuit chip   *See* **ICC**.

Integrated client   Existing applications in hospitals and other medical facilities that will provide EHR functionality by integrating with the EHR using specified HL7 v3 messages.[8]

Integrated delivery network   *See* **IDN**.

Integrated delivery system   *See* **IDS**.

Integrated device electronics   *See* **IDE**.

Integrated networks   Proposal to provide seamless access to unified data across multiple care delivery sites to support patient care.[6]

Integrated service digital network *See* **ISDN**.

Integrating the Healthcare Enterprise *See* **IHE**.

Integration   **1.** The process of bringing together related parts into a single system. To make various components function as a connected system. **2.** Combining separately developed parts into a whole, so that they work together. The means of integration may vary, from simply mating the parts together at an interface to radically altering the parts or providing something to mediate between them.[8]

Integration layer   Software component that presents a single, consolidated point of access to several systems and/or services.[8]

Integration profile   A precise description of how standards are to be implemented to address a specific clinical integration need. Each integration profile includes definition of the clinical use case, the clinical information and workflow involved, and the set of actors and transactions that address that need. Integration profiles reference the fully detailed integration specifications defined in the IHE technical framework in a form that is convenient to use in requests for proposals and product descriptions.[56]

Integration services   This group of services is made up of services that manage the integration, message brokering, and service catalog functions.[8]

Integration testing   A testing event that seeks to uncover errors in the interactions and interfaces among application software components when they are combined to form larger parts of a system.[6]

Integrity   **1.** Quality of an IT system reflecting the logical correctness and reliability of the operating system; the logical completeness of the hardware and software implementing the protection mechanisms; and the consistency of the data structures and occurrence of the stored data. It is composed of data integrity and system integrity. **2.** Knowledge that a message has not been modified while in transit. May be done with digitally signed message digest codes. Data integrity, the accuracy and completeness of the data, program integrity, system integrity, and network integrity are all components of computer and system security.[97,1]

Intelligent agent   A program that can learn from its owner and complete a task according to the owner's personal preferences. These programs incorporate artificial intelligence technology, which allows them to be able to offer intuitive suggestions and make judgments.[1]

Intelligent call routing   *See* **ICR**.

Intelligent character recognition   *See* **ICR**.

Intelligent document recognition   *See* **IDR**.

Intended use/intended purpose   Use for which a product, process, or service is intended according to the specifications, instructions, and information provided by the manufacturer.[68]

Intensive care unit   *See* **ICU**.

Intentionally unsafe acts   Any events that result from a criminal act, a purposefully unsafe act, an act related to alcohol or substance abuse by an impaired provider and/or staff, or events involving alleged or suspected patient abuse of any kind.[96]

Interaction model   Logical diagram or narrative describing the exchange of data and sequence of method invocation between objects to perform a specific task within a use case.[8]

Interactive services   Services that allow customers to decide which information they will be presented with next, such as requesting a search, or conducting business-to-business or electronic commerce.[1]

Interactive video disk   *See* **IVD**.

Interactive voice response   *See* **IVR**.

Interface   Computer hardware or software that is designed to communicate information between devices, between programs, or between a computer and a user.[151]

Interface engine   Tool that translates functions from different systems and protocols into a common format to facilitate information sharing. It is a translator for data or files to pass between systems.[2]

Interface terminology   Support interactions between healthcare providers and computer-based applications. They aid practitioners in converting clinical 'free text' thoughts into the structured, formal data representations, used internally by application programs.[108]

Interior gateway protocol   *See* **IGP**.

Internal protocol   An Internet working protocol that executes in hosts and routers to interconnect a number of packet networks.[1]

International standard   Standard that is adopted by an international standardizing/standards organization and made available to the public.[4]

Internet   A global network interconnecting thousands of dissimilar computer networks and millions of computers worldwide.[1]

Internet access provider   *See* **IAP**.

Internet control message protocol   *See* **ICMP**.

Internet Explorer™   A graphical web browser developed and distributed by Microsoft to allow web pages to incorporate sound, graphics, movies, and Java applets along with text.[1]

Internet information server   *See* **IIS**.

Internet key exchange   *See* **IKE**.

Internet Network Information Center   *See* **InterNIC**.

Internet protocol   *See* **IP**.

Internet protocol address   *See* **IP address**.

Internet protocol datagram   *See* **IPsec**.

Internet protocol security   *See* **IPsec**.

Internet relay chat   *See* **IRC**.

Internet service provider   *See* **ISP**.

Internet work packet exchange/sequence   A network of computer networks.[1]

InterNIC   Internet Network Information Center. Agency that provides and coordinates Internet services, such as IP addresses. In addition, the center also handles registration of IP addresses and domain names.[1] Also known as *NIC*.

Interoperability   There are three levels of health information technology interoperability: foundational, structural, and semantic. **1.** 'Foundational' interoperability allows data exchange from one information technology system to be received by another and does not require the ability for the receiving information technology system to interpret the data. **2.** 'Structural' interoperability is an intermediate level that defines the structure or format of data exchange (i.e., the message format standards) where there is uniform movement of health data from one system to another such that the clinical or operational purpose and meaning of the data is preserved and unaltered. Structural interoperability defines the syntax of the data exchange. It ensures that data exchanges between information technology systems can be interpreted at the data field level. **3.** 'Semantic' interoperability provides interoperability at the highest level, which is the ability of two or more systems or elements to exchange information and to use the information that has been exchanged. Semantic interoperability takes advantage of both the structuring of the data exchange and the codification of the data including vocabulary so that the receiving information technology systems can interpret the data. This level of interoperability supports the electronic exchange of health-related financial data, patient-created wellness data, and patient summary information among caregivers and other authorized parties. This level of interoperability is possible via potentially disparate EHR systems, business-related information systems, medical devices, mobile technologies, and other systems to improve wellness, as well as the quality, safety, cost-effectiveness, and access to healthcare delivery.[229,230]

Interpreted language   Code that is not compiled. A line-by-line interpretation of code takes place each and every time an interpreted language program is run. Tends to run slowly.[1]

Interrupt   A request for service from an external device seeking attention. The external device requests service by asserting an interrupt request line connected to the processor.[1]

Interrupt request   *See* **IRQ**.

Intervention   Treatment, procedure, or activity designed to achieve an outcome.[27]

Intranet   Private computer network that uses Internet protocols and Internet-derived technologies, including web browsers, web servers, and web languages, to facilitate collaborative data sharing within an enterprise.[2]

Intrusion detection   The act of detecting actions that attempt to compromise the confidentiality, integrity, or availability of a resource.[2]

I/O bus   A signal route to which a number of input and output devices can be connected in parallel.[193]

iOS   (originally) **iPhone Operating System.** Mobile operating system developed and distrib-

uted by Apple. Apple does not license iOS for installation on non-Apple hardware.[7]

IP   Internet protocol. Basic Internet transmission protocol based on a connectionless best-effort packet delivery.[1]

IP address   Internet protocol address. The equivalent of an Internet mailing address, which identifies the network, the subnet, and the host, such as 168.100.209.246. A specific 32-bit (4 octet) unique address assigned to each networked device.[1]

IP datagram   Internet protocol datagram. Basic unit of information that passes across the Internet. Contains data and source and destination address information.[1]

IPA   Individual practice association. Health maintenance organization (HMO) model that contracts with an entity, which in turn contracts with physicians to provide healthcare services in return for a negotiated fee. Physicians continue in their existing individual or group practices and are compensated on a per capita, fee schedule, or fee-for-service basis.[15]

iPhone operating system   *See* **iOS**.

IPsec   Internet protocol security. 1. A developing low-level protocol for encrypting the Internet protocol packet layer of a transmission instead of the application layer to provide improved confidentiality, authentication, and integrity. IPsec can be handled without requiring changes to individual user computers. **2.** IPSec virtual private network (VPN) is a compilation of standards created by the Internet Engineering Task Force to help the user filter encrypted data packet.[1,2]

IRB   Institutional review board. A specially constituted review body established or designated by an entity, in accordance with 45 CFR Part 46, to protect the welfare of human subjects recruited to participate in biomedical or behavioral research.[118]

IRD   Information resource department. Department within a facility that provides data automation, hardware, software, and user support. Usually associated with US Army facilities.[1]

IrDA   Infrared Data Association. A group of device manufacturers that worked on the development of a standard for transmitting data via infrared light waves, the IrDA port.[143]

IRM Information resource management. Department within a facility that provides data automation, hardware, software, and user support. Usually associated with US Air Force and Marine Corps facilities.[1]

IRQ Interrupt request. Standard interrupt assignment for the system timer.[1]

ISA Industry standard architecture. Eight- and 16-bit internal bus, or used to identify an Internet server application.[1]

ISDN Integrated service digital network. A data transfer technology that can transfer data significantly faster than a dial-up modem. ISDN enables wide-bandwidth digital transmission over the public telephone network, which means more data can be sent at one time. A typical ISDN connection can support transfer rates of 64K or 128K of data per second.[2]

ISO/TC 215 International Organization for Standardization (ISO) Technical Committee for Health Informatics. Standardization in the field of information for health, and Health Information and Communications Technology (ICT). Promotes interoperability between independent systems, to enable compatibility and consistency for health information and data, as well as to reduce duplication of effort and redundancies.[3]

Isolation 1. A transaction's effect is not visible to other transactions until the transaction is committed. **2.** Transaction isolation levels specify what data are visible to statements within a transaction. These levels directly impact the level of concurrent access by defining what interaction is possible between transactions against the same target data source.[22,82] *See* **ACID**.

ISP Internet service provider. Company that provides Internet connectivity and Internet-related services, online computer access, web site hosting, and domain name registration, for an added fee beyond their costs with the InterNIC or other registration retailers.[1]

ITMRA Information Technology Management Reform Act of 1996. Former name of the Clinger-Cohen Act of 1996.[1]

ITSEC Information Technology Security. Protection of information technology against unauthorized access to or modification of information, whether in storage, processing, or transit, and against the denial of service to authorized users, including those measures necessary to detect, document, and counter such threats. Protection and maintenance of confidentiality, integrity, availability, and accountability.[97]

IVD Interactive video disk. A combination of computer and laser disk technology, which can be rapidly accessed through instructions on the computer disk to hold still and motion pictures; useful for providing simulation experiences.[6]

IVR Interactive voice response. Ability to access information over the phone (claim payments, claim status, and a patient's eligibility).[15]

J

JAD Joint Application Development. A development methodology that involves continuous interaction with users and designers of the system in development. JAD centers on workshop sessions that are structured and focused to improve the quality of the final product by focusing on the up-front portion of the development lifecycle, thus reducing the likelihood of errors that are expensive to correct later.[58]

Java A language for adding interactivity to web pages.[1]

JavaScript 1. JavaScript is used in web site development to do such things as automatically change a formatted date on a web page, cause a linked-to page to appear in a popup window, or cause text or graphic images to change during a mouse rollover. **2.** JavaScript is an interpreted programming or script language.[8]

J-codes A subset of the Healthcare Common Procedure Coding System (HCPCS) level II code set with a high-order value of 'J' that has been used to identify certain drugs and other items. The final HIPAA transactions and code sets rule states that these J-codes will be dropped from the HCPCS and that NDC codes will be used to identify the associated pharmaceuticals and supplies.[10]

Joins A data query operation performed on data tables in a relational database management system (DBMS), in which the data from two or more tables are combined using common data elements into a single table. Typically performed using Structured Query Language (SQL).[1]

Joint application development *See* **JAD.**

Joint photographic experts group *See* **JPEG.**

Journaling Recording of all computer system activities and uses of a computer system. Used to identify access violations and the individual accountable for them, determine security exposures, track the activities of selected users, and adjust access control measures to changing conditions.[1]

JPEG Joint photographic experts group. Standard for encoding, transmitting, and decoding full-color and grayscale still images. JPEG is a graphic file format that has a sophisticated technique for compressing full-color bitmapped graphics, such as photographs.[1]

JPEG compression A generic algorithm to compress still images.[1]

JTC Joint Technical Committee. A standards body straddling the International Organization for Standardization (ISO) and International Electrotechnical Commission (IEC).[220]

JWG Joint Working Group. A harmonization initiative of Health Informatics Standards organizations: CEN/TC251, ISO/TC215 and HL7 formed at an inaugural Joint Working Group meeting in Brisbane hosted by ISO/TC215 and Standards Australia.[16]

K

KB Kilobyte. Equal to 1,024 bytes of digital data.[1]

Kbps Kilobits per second. Transmission of a thousand bits per second.[1]

Kennedy-Kassebaum Bill Original name for the Health Insurance Portability and Accountability Act of 1996 (HIPAA).[1]

Kerberos Network security service for securing higher-level applications and providing confidentiality and authentication. Kerberos was developed in the Athena Project at the Mas-

sachusetts Institute of Technology. The name is taken from Greek mythology; Kerberos was a three-headed dog who guarded the gates of Hades.[1]

Kernel The core components of most operating systems. It is the part of the system that manages files, peripherals, memory, and system resources. It runs the processes and provides communication between the processes.[1]

Key **1.** A value that particularizes the use of a cryptographic system. **2.** An input that controls the transformation of data by an encryption algorithm.[114,1]

Key image notes *See* **KIN.**

Key management services As data are brought in from various sources, there will be cases where certain primary source identity keys are not unique across source systems. The key management service will generate and manage keys during insert and update operations in the EHR repository.[8]

Keystroke verification The determination of the accuracy of data entry by the re-entry of the same data through a keyboard.[3]

Keyword Specified words used in text search engines. Through the use of multiple keywords, an organization increases its chances that search engines will locate its web page and serve it up to the requesting user.[1]

KHz Kilohertz. One thousand cycles per second.[1]

Kickstand An accessory or an attachment that props up a mobile device up so it stands and the user does not have to hold it.[42]

Kill UNIX command to stop a process.[1]

KIN Key image notes. Specifies transactions that allow a user to mark one or more images in a study as significant by attaching to them a note managed together with the study. This note includes a title stating the purpose of marking the images and a user comment field. Physicians may attach key image notes to images for a variety of purposes: referring physician access, teaching files selection, consultation with other departments, and image quality issues, etc.[56] *See* **Profile**. **NOTE: KIN is an Integrating the Healthcare Enterprise (IHE) Profile.**

Klugey Clunky, inefficient, inelegant. 'It's kind of a klugey solution, but we don't have the cycles to clean it up.' Also used in noun form as *kluge* or *kludge*.[148]

Knowledge Knowledge can be considered as the distillation of information that has been collected, classified, organized, integrated, abstracted, and value-added. Knowledge is at the level of abstraction higher than the data and information on which it is based and can be used to deduce new information and new knowledge.[4]

Knowledge acquisition The process of eliciting, analyzing, transforming, classifying, organizing, and integrating knowledge; and representing that knowledge in a form that can be used in a computer system.[4]

Knowledge engineering Converting knowledge, rules, relationships, heuristics, and decision-making strategies into a form understandable to the artificial software upon which an expert system is built.[6]

Knowledge representation The process and results of formalization of knowledge in such a way that the knowledge can be used automatically for problem solving.[4]

Knowledgebase Data tables, databases, and other tools designed to assist the process of care.[151]

L

LIS Laboratory information system. An application to streamline the process management of the laboratory for basic clinical services, such as hematology and chemistry. This application may provide general functional support for microbiology reporting but does not generally support blood bank functions. Provides an automatic interface to laboratory analytical instruments to transfer verified results to nurse stations, chart carts, and remote physician offices. The module allows the user to receive orders from any designated location, process the order and report results, and maintain technical, statistical, and account information. It eliminates tedious paperwork, calculations, and written documentation, while allowing for easy retrieval of data and statistics.[2] Also known as

LIS, laboratory information management system (LIMS), and *laboratory management system (LMS).*

Laboratory information system *See* **LIS**.

Laboratory information management system *See* **LIS**.

Laboratory scheduled workflow *See* **LSWF**.

LAN Local area network. A single network of physically interconnected computers that is localized within a small geographical area. Operates in a span of short distances (office, building, or complex of buildings).[1,2] *See* **MAN, WAN, WLAN**.

LAN adapter Allows access to a network, usually wireless network.[100]

Laser printer Desktop printers that use the dry toner and Xerographic printing process.[1]

Laserdisc A 12-inch disk that is similar to an audio CD but holds visual images (such as high-quality movies), as well as music.[1] Also known as a *videodisc*.

Last in, first out *See* **LIFO**.

LAT Local-area transport. Non-routable and bridgeable protocol used by the Digital Equipment Corporation to support terminal servers.[1]

LCD Liquid crystal display. The display screen of an electronic device.[1]

LEAP Lightweight and efficient application protocol. One of several protocols used with the International Electrical and Electronics Engineers (IEEE) 802.1 standard for local area network (LAN) port access control. In the IEEE framework, a LAN station cannot pass traffic through an Ethernet hub or wide local area network (WLAN) access point until it successfully authenticates itself. The station must identify itself and prove that it is an authorized user before it is actually allowed to use the LAN.[2]

Leased line Permanent communications link owned by the telephone companies, leased for dedicated customer use.[1]

Legacy systems 1. Usually refers to computers that have been in use for a long period of time, that contain many years of data, and have been used over many years of software development. 2. Data that were collected and maintained using a 'previous' system, but are now preserved on a 'current' system.[1,116]

Level Seven   Level Seven refers to the highest level of International Standards Organization's (ISO) communications model for Open Systems Interconnection (OSI)—the application level. Issues within the application level include definition of the data to be exchanged, the timing of the interchange, and communication of certain errors to the application.[16]

Lexicon   A group of related terms used in a particular profession, subject area, or style.[32]

Lexicon query service   *See* **LQS**.

License   Authorization to use a software product.[1]

Licensure   A process by which a governmental authority grants permission to individual practitioners or healthcare organizations to operate or to engage in an occupation or profession.[123]

Lifecycle   All phases in the life of a medical device or system, from the initial conception to final decommissioning and disposal.[68]

LIFO   Last in, first out. A queue that executes last-in requests before previously queued requests.[1] Also known as a *stack*.

Lightweight and efficient application protocol   *See* **LEAP**.

Limited data set   Specifies health information from which identifiers have been removed. Information in a limited data set is protected but may be used for research, healthcare operations, and public health activities without the individual's authorization.[48]

LIMS   Laboratory information management system. *See* **LIS**.

Line-of-sight   Propagation along an unobstructed path.[1]

Link   A connection between two network devices.[1] Also known as *anchors*, *hotlinks*, and *hyperlinks*.

Liquid crystal display   *See* **LCD**.

LIS   *See* **Laboratory information system.**

LISTSERV   A distribution list management package whose primary function is to operate mailing lists. An e-mail program that allows multiple computer users to connect onto a single system, thus creating an online discussion.[1]

LLC   Logical link control. Upper part of the second layer of the open systems interconnection (OSI) model. Oversees and controls the exchange of data between two network nodes.[1]

LMHOSTS   LAN manager hosts. Text file that maps IP addresses to Windows computer names (NetBIOS names) to network computers outside the local subnet. Acts as a local WINS equivalent to provide a static type of WINS service.[1]

Local area network   *See* **LAN**.

Local area transport   *See* **LAT**.

Local codes   Generic term for code values that are defined for specific payers, providers, or political jurisdictions.[15]

Local talk   Networking cabling standard used by Macintosh computers. Transmits 230kb per second over STP at distances up to 300 feet. Supports only 32 computers per segment.[1]

Log   Record that is created by an event(s).[48]

Log analysis   Studying log entries to identify events of interest or suppress log entries for insignificant events.[48]

Log archival   Retaining logs for an extended period of time, typically on removable media, a storage area network (SAN), or a specialized log archival appliance or server.[48]

Log clearing   Removal of all entries from a log that precede a certain date and time.[48]

Log compression   Storing a log file in a way that reduces the amount of storage space needed for the file without altering the meaning of its contents.[48]

Log conversion   The process of parsing a log in one format and storing its entries in a second format.[48]

Log entry   Individual record within a log.[48]

Log management   Process for generating, transmitting, storing, analyzing, and disposing of log data.[48]

Logging   Activities involved in creating logs.[48]

Logic board   A logic board is a computer component made by the company Apple. The logic board houses the internal circuitry of the computer.[202]

Logic bomb   A program deliberately written or modified to produce unexpected results when certain conditions are met.[1]

Logical access control   An automated system that controls an individual's ability to access one or more computer system resources, such as a workstation, network, application, or database.[114]

Logical drive   Subdivision of a large physical drive into numerous smaller drives.[1]

Logical link control   See **LLC**.

Logical observation identifiers names and codes.   See **LOINC**.

Logical threat   A threat of the possibility of destruction or alteration of software or data. Would be realized by logical manipulation within the system, rather than by physical attack.[1]

Logical unit   See **LU**.

Login   To enter and identify yourself as a proper customer of the computer.[4]

Login controls   Specific conditions users must meet for gaining access to a computer system.[1]

Login/Logging into   Action performed by an end user, when authenticating into a computer system.[48]

Logoff   Process of closing an open server session.[1]

Logon   Process of opening a server session through authentication.[1]

Logon process   The interaction between a user and the clinical computer system that enables the user to utilize the computer system.[1]

Logout   To formally exit from the computer's environment.[4]

LOINC   Logical observation identifiers names and codes. Universal identifiers for laboratory and clinical observations, including such things as vital signs, hemodynamic measures, intake/output, EKG, obstetric ultrasound,

cardiac echo, urologic imaging, gastro endoscopic procedures, pulmonary ventilator management, selected survey instruments, and other clinical observations.[50]

Longitudinal lifetime patient record   The concept of access to health information across an individual's lifetime.[1] See **EHR**.

Long-term care   See **LTC**.

Loop   1. A repeating structure or process. 2. A collection of segments that can repeat.[5,59]

Loophole   An incompleteness or error in a computer program, or in the hardware that permits circumventing the access control mechanism.[1]

Loosely coupled   Loosely coupled application roles do not assume that common information about the subject classes participating in a message is available to system components outside of the specific message.[8]

Lossless compression   Method of data compression that permits reconstruction of the original data exactly, bit-for-bit. The graphics interchange file (GIF) is an image format used on the web that provides lossless compression.[57]

Lossy compression   Method of data compression that permits reconstruction of the original data approximately, rather than exactly. JPEG is an example of lossy compression.[57]

LQS   Lexicon query service. Standardizes a set of read-only interfaces able to access medical terminology system definitions, ranging from sets of codes, to complex hierarchical classification and categorization schemes.[124]

LSWF   Laboratory scheduled workflow. Establishes the continuity and integrity of clinical laboratory testing and observation data throughout the healthcare enterprise. It involves a set of transactions to maintain the consistency of ordering and patient information, to control the conformity of specimens, and to deliver the results at various steps of validation.[56] See **Profile**. NOTE: LSWF is an Integrating the Healthcare Enterprise (IHE) Profile.

LTC   Long-term care. The segment of the healthcare continuum that consists of maintenance, custodial, and health services for the chronically ill or disabled; may be provided on an inpatient (rehabilitation facility, nursing home, mental hospital) or outpatient basis, or at home.[1]

LU   Logical unit. Portion of the arithmetic logic unit (ALU) within the CPU that coordinates logical operations.[1]

Luminance   Brightness; the amount of light, in lumens, that is emitted by a pixel or an area of the computer screen.[57]

M

MAC   Mandatory access control. A system of access control that assigns security labels or classifications to system resources and allows access only to entities (people, processes, devices) with distinct levels of authorization or clearance.[1]

MAC   Media access control. Lower portion of the second layer of the open systems interconnection (OSI) model. Identifies the actual physical link between two nodes.[1]

MAC   Message authentication code. A digital code generated using a cryptographic algorithm, defined in an International Organization for Standardization (ISO) standard that establishes that the contents of a message have not been altered or generated by an unauthorized party.[3]

MAC address   Media   access   control address. 1. Synonym for unique hardware physical address of a network device identified at the media access control layer and stored in ROM. **2.** A hardware identification number that uniquely identifies each device on a network. The MAC address is manufactured into every network card, such as an Ethernet card or wi-fi card, and therefore cannot be changed.[1,156]

Machine code   The elemental language of computers, consisting of a stream of 0s and 1s. Ultimately, the output of any programming language analysis and processing is machine code.[1]

Machine language   The lowest-level programming language (except for computers that utilize programmable microcode), machine languages are the only languages understood by computers. While easily understood by computers, machine languages are almost impossible for humans to use because they consist entirely of numbers. Programmers, therefore, use either a high-level programming language or an assembly language. An assembly language contains the same instructions as a machine language, but the instructions and variables have names instead of being just numbers.[7]

Macro   Small program that automates a function for an application program. Although many of these are supplied with the purchase of a program, in many applications, users can create their own by either recording keystrokes or writing the commands using the language that the application program provides. (This process is usually very similar to the Basic language.)[11]

Magnetic resonance imaging   *See* **MRI**.

Magnetic stripe card   A   smartcard containing a magnetic stripe that can store about 800 bits (100 bytes) of information. Largely used as banking cards and for security access applications.[1]

Mail merge   The merging of database information, such as names and addresses, with a letter template in a word processor to create personalized letters.[1]

Mailing list   A list of e-mail users who are members of a group. A mailing list can be an informal group of people who share e-mail with one another, or it can be a more formal LISTSERV group that discusses a specific topic.[1]

Mailslots   Connection-oriented interprocess messaging interface between clients and servers in a Windows NT environment.[1]

Malicious software   Software, e.g., a virus, designed to damage or disrupt a system.[118]

MAN   Metropolitan-area network. 1. Provides high-speed data transfer regional connectivity through multiple physical networks. Operates over distances sufficient for a metropolitan area. An IEEE 802.6 standard. **2.** A backbone network that covers a metropolitan area and is regulated by state or local utility commissions. Suppliers that provide MAN services are telephone companies and cable services.[1,2] *See* **LAN, WAN, WLAN**.

Manage consent directives   Ensure   that protected health information is only accessed with a consumer's consent.[48]

Managed care Use of a planned and coordinated approach to providing healthcare with the goal of quality care at a lower cost. Usually emphasizes preventive care, and often associated with a health management organization.[6]

Management information department *See* **MID**.

Management information system (service) *See* **MIS**.

Management service organization *See* **MSO**.

Mandatory access control *See* **MAC**.

Manufacturer Natural or legal person with responsibility for the design, manufacture, packaging, or labeling of a medical device, assembling a system, or adapting a medical device before it is placed on the market or put into service, regardless of whether these operations are carried out by that person, or on that person's behalf by a third party.[68]

Manufacturing automation protocol *See* **MAP**.

Map A relationship between a concept in a terminology and a concept in the same or another terminology, according to a mapping scheme or rules.[98]

MAP **Manufacturing automation protocol.** A set of protocols developed by General Motors based on Token Bus (IEEE 802.4) and giving predictable real-time response. [220]

Mapping **1.** Assigning an element in one set to an element in another set through semantic correspondence. **2.** A rule of correspondence established between data sets that associates each element of a set with an element in the same or another set.[126,32] *See* **Data mapping, Crosswalk**.

Mapping services The mapping service helps create a map file that translates a source document format to the destination format. This service can be used to map from XML to flat file and other formats, and vice versa.[8]

Marketing Communications that encourage the purchase or use of a product or service. This does not include a covered entity's communications about its own products, services, or benefits, or communications for treatment, case management, care coordination, or referral for care.[48]

Masquerading Obtaining proper identification through improper means (such as wiretapping), and then accessing the system as a legitimate user.[1]

Massachusetts General Hospital Utility Multi-programming System *See* **MUMPS**.

Massively parallel processing *See* **MPP**.

Master browser Computer on a network that maintains a list of all computers and services available on the network.[1]

Master data **1.** Core data is data that is essential to operations in a specific business or business unit and varies by industry and company. **2.** Often refers to data units that are non-transactional that an organization may reuse across a variety of software programs and technologies.[42,156] Also known as *reference data*.

Master patient index *See* **MPI**.

Match/matching The process of comparing biometric information against a previously stored biometric data, and scoring the level of similarity.[114]

Math co-processor Accompanying integrated chip to the CPU that performs arithmetic functions, which allows the CPU to perform system functions.[1]

MAU **Media access unit.** A token-ring network hub.[1]

Maximum defined data set All of the required data elements for a particular standard based on a specific implementation specification. An entity creating a transaction is free to include whatever data any receiver might want or need. The recipient is free to ignore any portion of the data that is not needed to conduct his or her port of the associated business transaction, unless the inessential data is needed for coordination of benefits.[10]

Mb **Megabit.** 1,048,576 bits or 1,024kb.[1]

MBDS **Minimum basic data set.** A set of data that is the minimum required for a healthcare record to conform to a given standard.[4]

Mbps   Megabits per second. Transmission of a million bits per second.[1]

MDA   Model-driven architecture. A platform independent model providing for separate business and application functionality from the technology-specific code, while enabling interoperability within and across platform boundaries.[111]

MDI-X port   Hub port that can be configured to provide a crossover function that reverses the transmit and receive wire pairs. Used to connect hubs together with a standard drop cable. Alleviates creating a crossover cable to perform the same function.[1]

MDM   Medical   document   management message.

MDS   Minimum data set. A core of elements to use in performing comprehensive assessments in long-term care facilities.[102]

Mean time between failure   See **MTBF**.

Mean time to diagnose   See **MTTD**.

Mean time to repair   See **MTTR**.

Meaningful Use   See **MU Stage 1, MU Stage 2, MU Stage 3**.

Measure   A number assigned to an object or an event. Measures can be expressed as counts (45 visits), rates (10 visits/day), proportions (45 primary healthcare visits/380 total visits=.118), percentage (12 percent of the visits made), or ratios (45 visits four health workers= 11.25).[123]

MedDRA   Medical Dictionary for Regulatory Activities. 1. Used by regulatory agencies and drug manufacturers. **2.** A terminology developed under the auspices of the International Conference on Harmonization of Technical Requirements for Registration of Pharmaceuticals for Human Use. MedDRA is a standard international terminology for regulatory communication in the registration, documentation, and safety monitoring of medical products throughout all phases of their regulatory cycle. As a standard, MedDRA is expected to promote the harmonization of regulatory requirements and documentation for medical products in the US, Japan, and European Union.[14,151]

Media access control   See **MAC**.

Media access control address   See **MAC address**.

Media access unit   See **MAU**.

Medicaid information technology architecture   See **MITA**.

Medicaid management information system   See **MMIS**.

Medical code sets   Codes that characterize a medical condition to treatment. These code sets are usually maintained by professional societies and public health organizations.[10]

Medical device   Any instrument, apparatus, implement, machine, appliance, implant, in vitro reagent or calibrator, software, material, or other similar or related article, intended by the manufacturer to be used, alone or in combination, for human beings for one or more of the specific purposes(s) of diagnosis, prevention, monitoring, treatment, or alleviation of disease; diagnosis, monitoring, treatment, alleviation of, or compensation for an injury; investigation, replacement, modification, or support of the anatomy or of a physiological process; supporting or sustaining life; control of conception; disinfection of medical devices; providing information for medical purposes by means of in vitro examination of specimens derived from the human body; and which does not achieve its primary intended action in or on the human body by pharmacological, immunological, or metabolic means, but which may be assisted in its function by such means.[68]

Medical error   1. The failure of a planned action to be completed as intended, or the use of a wrong plan to achieve an aim in the healthcare delivery process. **2.** A mistake that harms a patient. Adverse drug events, hospital-acquired infections and wrong-site surgeries are examples of preventable medical errors.[107,138]

Medical home   1. A model of delivering primary care that is accessible, continuous, comprehensive, family centered, coordinated, compassionate, and culturally effective. **2.** In a medical home model, primary care clinicians and allied professionals provide conventional diagnostic and therapeutic services, as well as coordination of care for patients who require services not available in primary care settings. The goal is to provide a patient with a broad spectrum of care, both preventive and curative, over a period of time and to coordinate all of the care the patient receives.[134,135]

Medical informatics Scientific discipline concerned with the cognitive, information processing, and communication task of healthcare practice, education, and research, including the information science and technology to support healthcare tasks.[4]

Medical information BUS *See* **MIB**.

Medical logic model *See* **MLM**.

Medical record *See* **EHR, EMR**.

Medical subject heading *See* MeSH.

Medical terminology/controlled medical vocabulary A vocabulary server application that normalizes various medication vocabularies used by system applications in a healthcare delivery environment.[2]

Medication error Mishaps that occur during prescribing, transcribing, dispensing, administering, adherence, or monitoring a drug.[96]

MEDIX A terminology developed for use in monitoring medical products throughout all phases of their regulatory cycle.[111]

MEDS Minimum emergency data set. A standardized view of the critical components of a patient's past medical history.[1]

Megabyte One million bytes of data used as a measure of computer processor storage and real and virtual memory. A megabyte is actually 2 to the 20th power of 1,048,576 bytes.[1]

Memorandum of understanding *See* **MOU**.

Memory 1. The part of a system which holds program instructions and information being processed. Sometimes referred to as RAM (random access memory). 2. Area of a computer used to store data. Can be RAM or ROM. Another word for dynamic RAM, the chips where the computers store system software, programs, and data currently being used.[1] *See* **RAM, ROM**.

Menu A list of options listed on the screen from which to choose. Usually labeled, and customer is asked to press the key corresponding to a choice.[4]

Merchant status Term used to indicate a business is authorized to accept credit cards in payment for goods and services.[1]

MeSH Medical subject heading. A thesaurus of concepts and terms used for the indexing of biomedical literature.[4]

Message An organized set of data exchanged between people or computer processes.[4]

Message authentication Ensuring that a message is genuine, has arrived exactly as was sent, and comes from the stated source.[4]

Message authentication code *See* **MAC**.

Message format standards Protocols that make communication between disparate systems possible. These message format standards should be universal enough that they do not require negotiation of an interface agreement between the two systems in order to make the two systems communicate.[151]

Message syntax System of rules and definitions specifying the basic component types of messages, interrelationships, and arrangement.[4]

Message type An identified, named, and structured set of functionally related information that fulfills a specific business purpose.[4]

Message, instant A package of information communicated from one application to another.[8]

Messaging Creating, storing, exchanging, and managing data messages across a communications network. The two main messaging architectures are publish-subscribe and point-to-point.[57]

Messaging services A group of services that handle messages. Services in this group include parsing, serialization, encryption, and decryption, encoding and decoding, transformation, and routing.[8]

Meta tag A special HTML command that provides information about a web page. Unlike normal HTML tags, meta tags do not affect how the page is displayed.[1]

Metadata 1. Machine understandable information for the web. Metadata describes the content, quality, condition, and other characteristics of the data. Fundamentally, metadata describes who, what, when, where, why, and how about a data set. Without proper documentation, a data set is incomplete. Metadata is critical to preserving the usefulness of data over time. Metadata captures important information on how data was collected and/or processed so that future users of that data understand these details.[18]

Metadata customer Individuals who need to access metadata (e.g., information system designers and survey form developers who ensure products meet national reporting requirements, analysts who need information to interpret data, and information managers who advise clinicians on how to report data).[18]

Metadata developers Individuals responsible for developing and proposing new metadata content and revising existing metadata.[18]

Metadata registry A metadata registry is a system that contains information that describes the structure, format, and definitions of data.[18]

Metadata stewards Organizations that have the responsibility for the ongoing maintenance of a metadata item.[18]

Metathesaurus The National Library of Medicine's Unified Medical Language System (UMLS) Metathesaurus cross-references national and international medical vocabularies.[151] *See* **UMLS**.

Metropolitan-area network *See* **MAN**.

mHealth **Mobile health.** A term used for the practice of medicine and public health, supported by mobile devices (written as *m-health* or *mobile health*).[7]

MHz **Megahertz.** One million times, cycles, occurrences, alterations, or pulses per second. Used to describe a measurement of CPU or processor speed.[1]

MIB **Medical information BUS. 1.** A hardware and software standard (IEEE P1073) that enables standardized connections between medical monitoring devices and clinical information systems. **2.** Institute of Electrical and Electronics Engineers (IEEE) P1073 (standard designation) standard for data exchange in a medical environment.[227,51]

Micro channel Micro channel architecture. IBM 32-bit multi-processing system and interface hardware bus standard for PS/2 computers.[1]

Micro channel architecture *See* **Micro channel**.

Microcomputer Desktop or laptop/notebook computer employing a microprocessor.[1]

Microprocessor **Central processing unit.** A microprocessor is a computer processor on a microchip. It is the 'engine' that goes into motion when you turn your computer on. Designed to perform arithmetic and logic operations that make use of small number-holding areas called *registers*.[1] *See* **CPU**.

Microsecond One millionth of a second.[1]

Microsoft disk operating system *See* **MS-DOS**.

MID **Management information department.** Department within a facility that provides data automation, hardware, software, and user support.[1]

Middleware Software systems that facilitate the interaction of disparate components through a set of commonly defined protocols. The purpose is to limit the number of interfaces required for interoperability by allowing all components to interact with the middleware using a common interface.[8]

Migration tool for NetWare Utility included in Windows NT to migrate NetWare user accounts, group accounts, files, and directories from a NetWare server environment to a Windows NT server environment. Gateway services for NetWare (GSNW) and NWLink must be installed before a migration can take place.[1]

Millions of instructions per second *See* **MIPS**.

Millisecond One thousandth of a second.[1]

MIME **Multipurpose Internet mail extensions.** A format originally developed for attaching sounds, images, and other media files to electronic mail, but now also used with web applications.[1]

Minicomputer Small-to-medium-scale computer that often uses dumb terminals.[1]

Minimum basic data set *See* **MBDS**.

Minimum emergency data set *See* **MEDS**.

Minimum necessary Minimum amount of protected health information necessary to accomplish permitted use or disclosure for payment or healthcare operations.[48]

Minimum scope of disclosure The principle that, to the extent practical, individually identifiable health information should only be disclosed to the extent needed to support the purpose of the disclosure.[10]

MIPS **Millions of instructions per second.** Rate that a processor executes instructions. Used as a measurement of processing power and computer speed.[1]

Mirror set **Redundant array of independent disks (RAID) Level 1.** Two-disk array where one disk shadows the contents of the original disk to maintain instant redundancy.[1]

Mirror site A file transfer protocol (FTP) site that is created after the contents of an original FTP archive server are copied to it. Usually, mirror sites use larger and faster systems than the original, so it is easier to obtain material from the mirror.[1]

MIS **Management information system (or service).** A class of software that provides manager with tools for organizing and evaluating their department, or the staff that supports information systems.[1]

Mission critical Activities, processing, etc., which are deemed vital to the organization's business success, and possibly, its very existence.[48]

Misuse Occurs when an appropriate process of care has been selected, but a preventable complication occurs and the patient does not receive the full potential benefit of the service. Avoidable complications of surgery or medication use are misuse problems. A patient who suffers a rash after receiving penicillin for strep throat, despite having a known allergy to that antibiotic, is an example of misuse. A patient who develops a pneumothorax after an inexperienced operator attempts to insert a subclavian line would represent another example of misuse.[138]

MITA **Medicaid information technology architecture.** A national framework to support improved systems development and healthcare management for the Medicaid enterprise.[102]

Mitigation Limitation of any negative consequence of a particular incident.[174]

MLM **Medical logic model.** Arden Syntax for Medical Logic Systems Version 1.0 was adopted by ASTM in 1992.[39]

MMIS **Medicaid management information system.** An integrated group of procedures and computer processing operations (subsystems) developed at the general design level to meet the principal objectives of the Medicaid program.[102]

Mobile devices A portable device that uses wireless technologies to transmit and exchange data.[2]

Mobile health *See* **mHealth**.

Model A very detailed description or scaled representation of one component of a larger system that can be created, operated, and analyzed to predict actual operational characteristics of the final produced component.[114]

Model driven architecture *See* **MDA**.

Modeling The process of defining concepts to reflect their unique definition and meaning.[19] *See* **Data modeling**.

Modem **Modulator/demodulator.** Device that converts digital data to analog signals for transmission over a telephone line, and performs analog-to-digital signals conversion for the receiving node.[1]

Modified frequency modulation *See* **MFM**.

Modify/modification Under the Health Insurance Portability and Accountability Act (HIPAA), this is a change adopted by the Secretary, through regulation, to a standard or an implementation specification.[10]

Modularity The design goal of separating code into self-sufficient, highly cohesive, low coupling pieces.[1]

MOLAP **Multidimensional online analytical processing (OLAP).** A technical OLAP approach in which data are pre-summarized using specialized multi-dimensional DBMS technology in a very structured manner within pre-determined dimensions, allowing for very high performance.[1]

Moore's Law The empirical observation that at our rate of technological development, the complexity of an integrated circuit, with respect to minimum component cost, will double in about 18 months. It is attributed to Gordon E. Moore, a co-founder of Intel, and published in 1965.[7]

Motherboard **1.** Main system board of the computer that consists of the central processing unit (CPU), I/O Bus, and built-in peripherals. **2.** A printed circuit board (PCB) found in many modern computers that holds many of the crucial components of the system, such as the central processing unit (CPU) and memory, and provides connectors for other peripherals.[1,7] Also known as the *logic board*. *See* **Daughterboard**.

Motion Picture Expert Group *See* **MPEG**.

MOU **Memorandum of understanding. 1.** A document providing a general description of the responsibilities that are to be assumed by two or more parties in their pursuit of some goals. More specific information may be provided in an associated statement of work (SOW). **2.** A document describing an agreement between parties that expresses a convergence of will and indicates an intended common line of action. Often used when parties do not wish to imply a legal commitment or in situations where the parties cannot create a legally enforceable agreement.[7]

Mouse Desktop input device used with graphical user interface (GUI) systems providing cursor control and program execution features.[1]

Mousing-around The non-productive activity required by many graphic user interface software designs where the hands must leave the keyboard many times during entry of a page of information.[99]

MOV **QuickTime Video.** A file extension that denotes the file is a movie or video in Quick-Time format.[1]

MPEG **Motion Picture Expert Group.** Standard for digital encoding, transmitting, decoding, and presentation of video recorder quality motion video.[1]

MPI **Master patient index. 1.** The unique numerical index identity of a patient that may contain the patient's Social Security number or any other locally derived or system-generated unique number. **2.** The MPI is important because it serves as the centerpiece for all subsequent functionality and software applications, such as links to the patient clinical record, the patient schedule for appointments, reporting results of lab, x-ray, pharmacy, patient-related images, etc. **3.** As part of HIPAA's unique identifier codes, a mandated standard was controversial due to patient concern about these numbers being accidentally made available providing potential means for, and thereby identifying, the confidential records to other persons.[1]

MPP **Massively parallel processing.** A computing platform technology that clusters multiple independent servers, each managed by its own operating system.[1]

MRI **Magnetic resonance imaging.** Magnetic fields and radio waves to construct 2-D images or 3-D models of internal body structures.[2]

MS-DOS **Microsoft disk operating system.** Set of 16-bit software programs that direct system-level computer operation. Developed by Microsoft in the early 1980s for the 8086 CPU.[1]

MTBF **Mean time between failure.** The average device operating time, as measured between the last failure until the next failure occurs.[1]

MTTD **Mean time to diagnose.** The time taken to diagnose a problem.[1]

MTTR **Mean time to repair.** The time it takes to restore a device to service from a failure.[1]

MU **Meaningful Use.** The set of standard defined by the Centers for Medicare & Medicaid Services (CMS) Incentive Programs that governs the use of electronic health records and allows eligible providers and hospitals to earn incentive payments by meeting specific criteria.[178]

MU Stage 1 Data capture and sharing.[178]

MU Stage 2 Advance clinical processes.[178]

MU Stage 3 Improved outcomes.[178]

Multi-axial taxonomy Taxonomy that requires terms on more than one axis to create a term describing the phenomenon.[11]

Multicast Network transmission meant for multiple, but not all, network nodes. Technique that allows copies of a single packet to be passed to a select number of nodes within a subnet.[1]

Multidimensional online analytical processing *See* **MOLAP.**

Multi-homed host Computer that is physically connected to two networks. Has two IP addressees assigned to it, one for each network interface.[1]

Multimedia Communications that combine voice, video, and graphics that require large amounts of disk space for storage and large amounts of bandwidth for transmission.[1]

Multiple station access unit *See* **SMA.**

Multiplex The division of a single transmission medium into multiple logical channels, supporting many apparently simultaneous sessions.[1]

Multiplexer, multipleXer, or multipleXor *See* **MUX.**

Multiplicity In mathematics, the multiplicity of a member of a multiset is the number of times the member appears in the multiset, the number of times a given polynomial equation has a root at a given point. The notion of multiplicity is important to be able to count correctly, without specifying exceptions (e.g., *double roots* counted twice). Hence the expression 'counted with (sometimes implicit) multiplicity.'[16]

Multipurpose Internet mail extensions *See* **MIME.**

Multi-site testing A testing event that determines the ability of the application or its subsystems to function in multiple geographical settings.[6]

MUMPS Massachusetts General Hospital Utility Multi-programming System. A procedural, interpreted general-purpose programming language oriented toward database applications, with built-in multi-user/multi-tasking support.[1]

Murphy's Law 'If anything can go wrong, it will.'[32]

Mutual aid agreement Pre-arranged agreement developed between two or more entities to render assistance to the parties of the agreement.[174]

Mutual authentication Occurs when parties at both ends of a communication activity authenticate each other.[48]

MUX Multiplexer, multipleXer, or multipleXor. A network device in which multiple streams of information are combined from different sources onto a common medium for transmission.[1]

N

NAHDO National Association of Health Data Organizations. A group that promotes the development and improvement of state and national health information systems.[9]

Name Designation of an object by a linguistic expression.[4]

Name resolution The process of mapping a name into a corresponding address. The domain name system provides a mechanism for naming computers in which programs use remote name servers to resolve a machine name into an IP address.[1]

Named pipes One- or two-way pipe used for connectionless interprocess messaging interface between clients and servers.[1]

NANDA taxonomy II A taxonomy of nursing diagnostic concepts that identify and code a patient's responses to health problems or life processes.[52]

Narrowband A telecommunications medium that uses (relatively) low-frequency signals, exceeding 1.544 Mbps.[106]

NAS Network attached storage. A hard disk storage system that has its own network address rather than being attached to the department computer that is serving applications to a network's workstation users. By removing storage access and its management from the department server, both application programming and files can be served faster because they are not competing for the same processor resources.[2]

NAT Network address translation. Involves rewriting the source and/or destination addresses of IP packets as they pass through a router or firewall. Most systems using NAT do so in order to enable multiple hosts on a private network to access the Internet using a single public IP address. According to specifications, routers should not act in this way, but many network administrators find NAT a convenient technique and use it widely. Nonetheless, NAT can introduce complications in communication between hosts. Also known as *network masquerading* or *IP-masquerading*.[7]

National drug codes *See* **NDC**.

National Emergency Medical System (EMS) Information System *See* **NEMSIS**.

National employer ID A system for uniquely identifying all sponsors of healthcare benefits.[9]

National Health Information Infrastructure *See* **NHII**.

National Health-Related Item Code *See* **NHRIC**.

National member body *See* **NMB**.

National patient identification (ID) A system for uniquely identifying all recipients of healthcare services.[1] Sometimes referred to as the *National Individual Identifier*, or as the *healthcare ID. See* **MPI**.

National payer ID A system for uniquely identifying all organizations that pay for healthcare services.[10]

National provider file *See* **NPF**.

National provider identifier *See* **NPI**.

National provider registry The organization envisioned for assigning national provider IDs.[10]

National standard format *See* **NSF**.

National standardization Standardization that takes place at the level of a specific country.[4]

National standards body Standards body recognized at the national level that is eligible to be the national member of the corresponding international and regional standards organization.[4]

National standards system network *See* **NSSN**.

Nationwide Health Information Network *See* **NHIN** and **NwHIN**.

Native format The native format is generally readable only by that application, but other programs can sometimes translate it using filters.[1]

Natural language Spoken or written language in contrast to a formal language.[4]

Natural language processing *See* **NLP**.

NAV Notification of document availability. A mechanism allowing notifications to be sent point-to-point to systems and users within an affinity domain, eliminating the need for manual steps or polling mechanisms.[56] *See* **Profile**. NOTE: NAV is an Integrating the Healthcare Enterprise (IHE) Profile.

Navigation tools Allows users to find their way around a web site or multimedia presentation. They can be hypertext links, clickable buttons, icons, or image maps.[1]

NCPDP National Council for Prescription Drug Programs. Develops business solutions, including ANSI-accredited standards, and guidance for promoting information exchanges related to medications, supplies, and services within the healthcare system.[54]

NCPDP batch standard 1. A National Council for Prescription Drug Programs (NCPDP) standard designed for use by low-volume dispensers of pharmaceuticals, such as nursing homes. Use of Version 1 of this standard has been mandated under Health Insurance Portability and Accountability Act (HIPAA). 2. Created to use the functionality of the NCPDP Telecommunication Standard. Uses the same syntax, formatting, data set, and rules as the Telecommunication Standard. The Batch Standard wraps the Telecommunication Standard around a detail record; then adds a batch header and trailer. This allows implementers to code one. It was intended that once a NCPDP Data Record (containing the Telecommunication Standard transaction) was built, it could then be wrapped with the Detail Data Record. Then, the Transmission Header Record and The Transmission Trailer Record are created. The Batch consisting of Header, Detail Data Records, and Trailer are formed into a batch file.[10,54]

NCPDP Telecommunication Standard 1. A National Council for Prescription Drug Programs (NCPDP) standard designed for use by high-volume dispensers of pharmaceuticals, such as retail pharmacies. Use of Version 5.1 of this standard has been mandated under HIPAA. 2. Developed to provide a standard format for the electronic submission of third-party drug claims. The development of the standard was to accommodate the eligibility verification process at the point-of-sale and to provide a consistent format for electronic claims processing.[10,54]

NDC **National Drug Code.** The Drug Listing Act of 1972 requires registered drug establishments to provide the Food and Drug Administration (FDA) with a current list of all drugs manufactured, prepared, propagated, compounded, or processed by it for commercial distribution. (*See* Section 510 of the Federal Food, Drug, and Cosmetic Act [Act] [21 U.S.C. § 360]). Drug products are identified and reported using a unique, three-segment number, called the National Drug Code (NDC), which is a universal product identifier for human drugs.[1]

NDIS **Network driver interface specification.** For writing device drivers for network interface cards. Using the NDIS specification, multiple protocols can be bound to a single network adapter.[1]

Near miss An event or situation that could have resulted in an adverse drug event, or an adverse event, but did not, either by change or through timely intervention.[96]

NEDSS **National Electronic Disease Surveillance System.** An initiative that promotes the use of data and information system standards to advance the development of efficient, integrated, and interoperable surveillance systems at federal, state, and local levels. It is a major component of the Public Health Information Network (PHIN).[48]

Needs assessment The identification, definition, and description of the problems to be addressed for selected system.[6]

Need-to-know The explicit specification of the kind of data to be made available to a qualified, authorized user or an authorized computer system.[1]

NEMSIS **National EMS Information System.** Framework for collecting, storing, and sharing standardized emergency medical system (EMS) data from states nationwide.[211]

Nesting Placing documents within other documents. Nesting allows a user to access material in a non-linear fashion. This is the primary factor needed for developing hypertext.[1]

NetBEUI **NetBIOS extended user interface.** Fast, easy to install, non-configurable, non-routable network protocol for use with up to 200 network nodes. Resides at the open systems interconnection (OSI) transport layer.[1]

NetBIOS **Network basic input output system.** Standard interface to networks employing IBM and compatible PCs. Implemented at the application layer. NetBIOS names cannot exceed 15 characters.[1]

NetBIOS extended user interface *See* **NetBEUI**.

Net-centric The realization of a robust, globally interconnected, networked environment, in which data are shared timely and seamlessly among users, applications, and platforms.[18]

Network A collection of hardware, such as printers, modems, servers, and terminals/personal computers, that enables users to store and retrieve information, share devices, and exchange information.[2]

Network adapter card Computer hardware adapter card that provides an interface between the computer and the network.[1]

Network address translation *See* **NAT**.

Network administration The process of managing all components of network operations. This may include WANs as well as LANs. Network administration includes the deployment, maintenance and monitoring of active network gear: switches, routers, firewalls, etc. Network administration includes activities such as network address assignment, assignment of routing protocols and routing table configuration as well as configuration of authentication and authorization-directory services.[2]

Network architecture Specifies the function and data transmission needed to convey information across a network.[4]

Network attached storage *See* **NAS**.

Network basic input output system *See* **NetBIOS**.

Network computer A computer with minimal memory, disk storage, and processor power designed to connect to a network, especially the Internet. The idea behind network computers is that many users who are connected to a network do not need all the computer power they get from a typical personal computer. Instead, they can rely on the power of the network servers.[58]

Network drive A shared disk drive available to network users.[1]

Network driver interface specification *See* **NDIS.**

Network file system *See* **NFS.**

Network information center *See* **NIC.**

Network layer Third layer of the OSI model. Routes data from source to destination across networks, and handles addressing and switching.[1] Also known as the *Internet layer.*

Network operating system *See* **NOS.**

Network operation center *See* **NOC.**

Network printer Shared printer available to network users. Can be connected to a print server, directly connected to the network, or shared from a workstation.[1]

Network protocol services The network protocol service will provide communication capabilities over the physical network. The primary network protocol that will be supported is TCP/IP.[8]

Network redirector Operating system feature that intercepts requests from the computer and directs them to the local or remote machine for processing. Resides at the OSI presentation layer.[1]

Network server A network server supports the sharing of peripheral devices among the workstations in the network. Network servers provide printing, file sharing, and messaging services to end users' personal computers.[2]

Network service provider *See* **NSP.**

Network topology The pattern of links connecting pairs of nodes of a network. A given node has one or more links to others, and the links can appear in a variety of different shapes. The simplest connection is a one-way link between two devices. A second return link can be added for two-way communication. Modern communications cables usually include more than one wire in order to facilitate this, although very simple bus-based networks have two-way communication on a single wire. Network topology is determined only by the configuration of connections between nodes; it is, therefore, a part of graph theory. Distances between nodes, physical interconnections, transmission rates, and/or signal types are not a matter of network topology, although they may be affected by it in an actual physical network.[7]

Network traffic Data transmitted on a network for the purpose of sending information from one node to another, or from one network to another.[1]

Network weaving A penetration technique in which different communication networks are used to gain access to a data processing system to avoid detection and trace back.[3]

Neural network A data mining predictive model-building algorithm that is composed of connected logical nodes with inputs, outputs, and processing at each node. The neural network is particularly useful for pattern recognition.[1]

New work item proposal *See* **NWIP.**

NFS Network file system. A protocol developed by Sun Microsystems that allows a computer system to access files over a network as if they were on its local disks.[1]

NHII National health information infrastructure. A healthcare standardization initiative for the development of an interoperable health information technology system. First proposed under President George W. Bush, the goal of NHII was to build an interoperable system of clinical, public health and health information technology that encouraged public-private collaboration with the federal government in a leadership role. The NHII has evolved to become the Nationwide Health Information Network.[42]

NwHIN Nationwide health information network. 1. A secure, nationwide, interoperable health information infrastructure to connect providers, consumers, and others involved in supporting health and healthcare. 2. A web-services series of specifications designed to securely exchange healthcare-related data. The Nationwide Health Information Network, often abbreviated as NHIN or NwHIN. **3.** Provides for the exchange of health information across the nation, between and among various organization and constituents, and is facilitated by nationally established standards for this exchange. NwHIN components include authentication, delivery protocols, security, directories, and vocabulary/documents/message standards.[178,7,2]

Nationwide Health Information Network
See **NwHIN**.

NwHIN Direct The Direct Project was launched to specify a simple, secure, scalable, standards-based way for participants to send authenticated encrypted health information directly to known, trusted recipients over the Internet. The Direct Project expands existing Nationwide Health Information Network (NwHIN) standards and service descriptions to address the key Stage 1 requirements for Meaningful Use, and to provide an on-ramp to nationwide exchange for a wide set of providers and organizations.

National health-related item code
See **NHRIC**.

NHRIC National health-related items code. A system for identification and numbering of marketed device packages that is compatible with other numbering systems such as the National Drug Code (NDC) or Universal Product Code (UPC). In the early 1970s, the Drug Listing Branch of FDA set aside a block of numbers that could be assigned to medical device manufacturers and distributors. Those manufacturers who desire to use the NHRIC number for unique product identification may apply to FDA for a labeler code.[207]

Nibble First or last half of an 8-bit byte. A half byte.[1]

NIC Nursing intervention classification. A comprehensive, research-based, standardized classification of interventions that nurses perform. NIC is useful for clinical documentation, communication of care across settings, integration of data across systems and settings, effectiveness research, productivity measurement, competency evaluation, reimbursement, and curricular design.[26]

NIC Network information center. 1. An organization that provides information, assistance, and services to network users. 2. A computer circuit board or card that is installed in a computer so that it can be connected to a network.[1]

NIC Network interface card. A card that allows one to access a network. *See* **LAN adapter**.

NLP Natural language processing. A subfield of artificial intelligence and linguistics. It studies the problems inherent in the processing and manipulation of natural language, and natural language understanding devoted to making computers 'understand' statements written in human languages.[7]

NM Nuclear medicine image integration. Specifies how nuclear medicine images should be stored by acquisition modalities and workstations, and how image displays should retrieve and make use of them. It defines the basic display capabilities that image displays are expected to provide, and also how result screens, both static and dynamic, such as those created by NM cardiac processing packages, should be stored using DICOM objects that can be displayed on general purpose image display systems.[56] *See* **Profile**. **NOTE: NM is an Integrating the Healthcare Enterprise (IHE) Profile.**

NMB National member body. The standards institute in each country that is a member of International Organization for Standardization (ISO).[3]

NMDS Nursing minimum data set. 1. The foundation for nursing languages development that identified nursing diagnosis, nursing intervention, nursing outcomes, and intensity of nursing care as unique nursing components of the Uniform Hospital Discharge Data Set (UHDDS). 2. Essential set of information items that has uniform definitions and categories concerned with nursing. It is designed to be an abstraction tool or system for collecting uniform, standard, compatible, minimum nursing data.[52,6]

NMMDS Nursing management minimum data set. A data set used to describe environment at unit level of service related to nursing delivery (unit/service, patient/client population, care delivery method), as well as nursing care resources and financial resources.[52]

NOC Nursing outcome classification. A comprehensive, standardized classification of patient/client outcomes developed to evaluate the effects of nursing interventions. Standardized outcomes are necessary for documentation in electronic records, for use in clinical information systems, for the development of nursing knowledge, and the education of professional nurses.[26]

NOC Network operation center. A location from which the operation of a network or Internet is monitored. Additionally, this center usually serves as a clearinghouse for connectivity problems and efforts to resolve those problems.[1]

Node 1. Originating or terminating point of information or signal flow in a telecommunications network. **2.** Computer or device connected to a network. Also known as a *host*.[48,1]

NOI Notice of intent. A document that describes a subject area for which the federal government is considering developing regulations. It may describe the presumably relevant considerations and invite comments from interested parties. These comments can then be used in developing a notice of proposed rulemaking (NPRM) or a final regulation.[10]

Nomenclature A consistent method for assigning names to elements of a system.[6]

Nonconformity Deviation from a specification, a standard, or an expectation.[7]

Non-overwriting virus A computer virus that appends the virus code to the physical end of a program, or moves the original code to another location.[1]

Non-repudiation Cryptographic receipts created so that an author of a message cannot falsely deny sending a message. Proof to a third party that only the signer could have created a signature. A basis of legal recognition of electronic signatures.[1]

Non-uniform memory architecture *See* **NUMA.**

Nonvolatile memory Memory that retains its content when power is removed.[1]

Normalization 1. The process of creating a uniform and agreed-upon set of standards, policies, definitions, and technical procedures to allow for interoperability. **2.** The process of organizing the fields and tables of a relational database to minimize redundancy.[8,7]

Normalization services This service will take various concepts from different sources, normalize, and store them in the EHR's internal form. This service could be extended to include normal values based on incoming and outgoing profiles.[8]

Normative document Document that provides rules, guidelines, or characteristics for activities or results.[4]

NOS Network operating system. Operating system that includes special functions for connecting computers and devices into a LAN. The term *network operating system* is generally reserved for software that enhances a basic operating system by adding networking features. Novell Netware, Artisoft's LANtastic, Microsoft Windows Server, and Windows NT are examples of an NOS.[58]

Notice of Intent *See* **NOI.**

Notice of proposed rulemaking *See* **NPRM.**

Notification of document availability *See* **NAV.**

NPF National provider file. The database envisioned for use in maintaining a national provider registry.[10]

NPI National provider identifier. 1. A system for uniquely identifying all providers of healthcare services, supplies, and equipment. **2.** A Health Insurance Portability and Accountability Act (HIPAA) Administrative Simplification Standard. The NPI is a unique identification number for covered healthcare providers. Covered healthcare providers and all health plans and healthcare clearinghouses must use the NPIs in the administrative and financial transactions adopted under HIPAA. The NPI is a 10-position, intelligence-free numeric identifier (10-digit number). This means that the numbers do not carry other information about healthcare providers, such as the state in which they live or their medical specialty. The NPI must be used in lieu of legacy provider identifiers in the HIPAA standards transactions.[10,102]

NPRM   Notice of proposed rulemaking. A document that describes and explains regulations that the federal government proposes to adopt at some future date and invites interested parties to submit comments related to them. These comments can then be used in developing a final regulation.[10]

NSF   National standard format. Generically, this applies to any nationally standardized data format, but it is often used in a more limited way to designate the professional flat file record format used to submit professional claims.[10]

NSP   Network service provider. A company providing consolidated service for some combination of e-mail, voice mail, phone, and fax configurations on broadband or wireless handheld devices.[1] Also known as *unified messaging solutions*.

NSSN   National standards system network. A National Resource for Global Standards is a search engine that provides users with standards-related information from a wide range of developers, including organizations accredited by the American National Standards Institute (ANSI), other US private sector standards bodies, government agencies, and international organizations.[43]

Nuclear medicine image integration *See* NM.

Null modem cable Serial cable with transmit and receive pins crossed to simulate a modem for a direct connection between computers.[1]

NUMA   Non-uniform memory architecture. A computing platform technology that clusters multiple symmetrical multi-processing (SMP) nodes together, similar to massively parallel processing (MPP) technology.[1] *See* SMP, MPP.

Nursing informatics The specialty that integrates nursing science, computer science, and information science in identifying, collecting, processing, and managing data and information to support nursing practice, administration, education, and research, and to expand the knowledge of nursing.[52]

Nursing information system Part of the healthcare information system that deals with nursing aspects, particularly the maintenance of the nursing record.[4]

Nursing intervention classification *See* NIC.

Nursing management minimum data set *See* NMMDS.

Nursing minimum data set *See* NMDS.

Nursing outcome classification *See* NOC.

Nursing procedure Systematic activity directed at, or performed on, an individual patient, with the object of providing nursing care or treatment.[4]

NWIP   New work item proposal. First balloting phase for draft standards and draft technical specifications. During this phase, at least five experts from five participating ISO/TC 215 countries are chosen to work on the document.[3]

O

OASIS   Outcome and Assessment Information Set. A group of data elements that represent core items of a comprehensive assessment for an adult home care patient, and form the basis for measuring patient outcomes for purposes of outcome-based quality improvement. This assessment is performed on every patient receiving services of home health agencies that are approved to participate in the Medicare and/or Medicaid programs.[102]

Object A block of information that is self-contained and has additional information that describes the data, the application that created it, how to format it, and the location of related information stored in a separate disk file.[1]

Object identifier *See* OID.

Object linking and embedding *See* OLE.

Object model Conceptual representation, typically in the form of a diagram, which describes a set of objects and their relationship.[8]

Object request broker The common interface that permits object-to-object communication.[1]

Object reuse Securing resources for the use of multiple users.[1]

Objective evidence Data supporting the existence or verity of something.[92]

Object-oriented Applied to analysis, design, and programming. The basic concept in this approach is that of objects, which consist of data structures encapsulated with a set of routines, often called 'methods,' which operate on the data. Operations on the data must be performed via these methods, which are common to all instances of objects of a particular class. Thus, the interface to objects is well-defined and allows the code implementing the methods to be changed, so long as the interface remains the same.[18]

Object-oriented programming *See* **OOP**.

Obligation Operations specified in a policy, or policy set, that should be performed by the PEP in conjunction with the enforcement of an authorization decision.[48]

Observation **1.** Information derived from performance of a health-related activity. **2.** A clinical statement or series of statements about a subject, usually a patient.[165,16]

OC **Optical carrier.** Used to specify the speed of fiber optic networks conforming to the Synchronous Optical Networking (SONET) standard.[2]

OCR **Optical character recognition.** A technology that scans a printed page and converts it into an electronic document that can be edited on a computer.[1]

OCSP **Online certificate status protocol.** An Internet protocol used for obtaining the revocation status of an X.509 digital certificate.[7]

Octal Base eight numbering system where three bits are used to represent each digit. Uses the 0-7 digits for representations.[1]

Octet Eight-bit or 1 byte unit of data. Four octets are used in an IP address.[1]

ODA **Open document architecture.** A standard document file format created by the International Telecommunications Union-Telecommunication Standardization (ITU-T) to replace all proprietary document file formats. It

should not be confused with the OASIS Open Document Format for Office Applications.[7] Also known as *open document*.

Odd parity **1.** A technique of checking whether data have been lost or written over during transmission. **2.** In asynchronous communication systems, odd parity refers to parity checking modes, where each set of transmitted bits has an odd number of bits. If the total number of ones in the data plus the parity bit is an odd number of ones, it is called odd parity. If the data already has an odd number of ones, the value of the added parity bit is 0; otherwise it is 1.[1,156]

ODS **Operational data store.** A subject-oriented, integrated, real-time, volatile store of detailed data, in support of operational and tactical decision making.[1]

OEID **Other entity identifier.** Proposed data element for entities needing to be identified in standard transactions that are not health plans, healthcare providers, or individuals.[103]

OEM **Original equipment manufacturer.**[1]

Off-line Device not available to be connected to or controlled by a computer.[1]

OID **Object identifier.** An identifier used to name an object, usually strings of numbers. In computer programming, an object identifier generally takes the form of an implementation-specific integer or pointer that uniquely identifies an object.[7]

OLAP **Online analytical processing.** A high-level concept that describes a category of tools that aid in the analysis of multi-dimensional queries.[156]

OLE **Object linking and embedding.** **1.** A document standard developed by Microsoft that allows for the creation of objects within one application, and linking them into a second application. **2.** OLE is used for compound document management, as well as application data transfer via drag-and-drop and clipboard operations.[1,156]

OLTP **Online transaction processing.** A class of systems that supports or facilitates high transaction-oriented applications. OLTP's primary system features are immediate client feedback and high individual transaction volume.[156]

OM Outbreak management. The capture and management of information associated with the investigation and containment of a disease outbreak or public health emergency.[46]

Omaha nursing diagnosis/intervention *See* **Omaha system**.

Omaha system Omaha nursing diagnosis/ intervention. A research-based, comprehensive and standardized taxonomy designed to enhance practice, documentation, and information management. It consists of three relational, reliable, and valid components: the Problem Classification Scheme, the Intervention Scheme, and the Problem Rating Scale for Outcomes. The components provide a structure to document client needs and strengths, describe multidisciplinary practitioner interventions, and measure client outcomes in a simple, yet comprehensive, manner.[29]

On-chip applications Applications that reside on the integrated circuit chip.[1]

One-to-many Synonym for identification.[114]

Online Device available to be connected to, or controlled by, a computer. Actively connected to other computers or devices. A device is online when it is logged on to a network or service.[1]

Online analytical processing *See* **OLAP**.

Online certificate status protocol *See* **OCSP**.

Online service provider An entity that provides a service online. It can include Internet service providers and web sites, such as message board operators. In its original, more limited definition, it referred only to a commercial computer communication service in which paid members could dial via a computer modem the service's private computer network and access various services and information resources, such as bulletin boards, downloadable files and programs, news articles, chat rooms, and electronic mail services. The term 'online service' was also used in reference to these dial-up services.[7]

Online transaction processing *See* **OLTP**.

Onsite concurrent review A process to evaluate inpatient hospital services at delivery to determine that the member's clinical care is being provided in the appropriate hospital setting and facilitates timely discharge.[15]

Ontology 1. A specification of a conceptualization of a knowledge domain. An ontology is a controlled vocabulary that describes objects and the relations between them in a formal way, and has a grammar for using the vocabulary terms to express something meaningful within a specified domain of interest. The vocabulary is used to make queries and assertions. Ontological commitments are agreements to use the vocabulary in a consistent way for knowledge sharing. Ontologies can include glossaries, taxonomies, and thesauri, but normally have greater expressivity and stricter rules than these tools. A formal ontology is a controlled vocabulary expressed in an ontology representation language. **2.** An information model that provides the structure to enable all forms of available knowledge to be used in integrated applications with semantic understanding. A reference terminology is a form of ontology. **3.** Represents knowledge as a set of concepts within a domain and the relationships between those concepts.[1,151,7]

OOA Out of area. Not within the market geographic bounds.[15]

OON Out of network. In the geographic bounds, but not contracted.[7]

OOP Out of pocket. An amount patient pays at time of service.[8]

OOP Object-oriented programming. 1. An approach to software development that combines data and procedures into a single object. **2.** A computer program composed of a collection of individual units or objects, as opposed to a traditional view in which a program is a list of instructions to the computer. Each object is capable of receiving messages, processing data, and sending messages to other objects. **3.** Software programming model constructed around objects. This model compartmentalizes data into objects (data fields) and describes object contents and behavior through the declaration of classes (methods).[1,156] *See* **SOA**.[7]

OpArc Operational architecture. Describes the mission, functions, information requirements, and business rules (operational requirements) for healthcare delivery. Further defined in the Department of Defense Architecture Framework (DoDAF).[20] *See* **Architecture**.

Open access A type of network that allows a member to self-refer.[15]

Open card system The open system model envisions that consumers will obtain from an independent third party, a single certificate, which certifies that consumer's identity. Consumers will then use that certificate to facilitate transactions with potentially numerous merchants.[1]

Open source Software in which the source code is available free to users, who can read and modify the code.[107]

Open systems architecture In telecommunications, the term 'open systems architecture' means the layered hierarchical structure, configuration, or model of a communications or distributed data processing system that (1) enables system description, design, development, installation, operation, improvement, and maintenance to be performed at a given layer or layers in the hierarchical structure; (2) allows each layer to provide a set of accessible functions that can be controlled and used by the functions in the layer above it; (3) enables each layer to be implemented without affecting the implementation of other layers; and (4) allows the alteration of system performance by the modification of one or more layers without altering the existing equipment, procedures, and protocols at the remaining layers.[7]

Open systems environment Software systems that can operate on different hardware platforms because they use components that follow the same standards for user interfaces, applications, and network protocols.[1]

Open systems interconnection *See* **OSI**.

Operating system *See* **OS**.

Operating system (O/S) interface layer The layer that allows for the interconnection and interrelationship among the various operating systems in the form of two or more devices, applications, and the user interfacing with an application or device.[1]

Operating system 2 *See* **OS/2**.

Operation system certification A guarantee based on an objective and closed process or assessment that no design and/or implementation flaw is present, and that the occurrence of a random hardware and/or software error is below a specified value.[1]

Operational architecture Describes the mission, functions, information requirements, and business rules (operational requirements) for healthcare delivery.[20] *See* **Architecture, Enterprise architecture**.

Operational data store Repository of clinical data used by client applications to create, update, and process encounter specific information at the points of service.[8]

Optical card An optical memory card with laser-recorded and laser-read information that can be edited or updated.[1]

Optical Carrier *See* **OC**.

Optical character recognition *See* **OCR**.

Optical disc **1.** An electronic data storage medium that is read or recorded using a low-powered laser beam. There has been a constant succession of optical disc formats, first in CD formats, followed by a number of DVD formats. Optical disc offers a number of advantages over magnetic storage media. An optical disc holds much more data. **2.** A disk read or written by light, generally laser light; such a disk may store video, audio or digital data.[2,47]

Optical resolution The built-in resolution of a scanning device. Contrast with 'interpolated resolution' or 'digital resolution' which enhances an image by software. Both resolutions are given as dots per inch (dpi), thus a 2,400 dpi scanner can be the true resolution of the machine or a computed resolution.[163]

Optical video disk Compact discs that use lights to read information.[1]

Opt-in Mechanism that states data collection and/or use methods, and provides user choice to accept such collection and/or use.[36]

Opt-out Mechanism that states data collection and/or use methods, and provides user choice to decline such collection and/or use.[36]

OR Logical gating operation that provides a high output if any input is high.[1]

Order Request for a certain procedure to be performed.[4]

Order entry system System for recording and processing orders.[4] *See* **CPOE.**

Organizational resilience management Systematic and coordinated activities and practices through which an organization manages its operational risks and the associated potential threats and impacts.[175]

Organizational resilience management program Ongoing management and governance process supported by top management; resourced to ensure that the necessary steps are taken to identify the impact of potential losses; maintain viable recovery strategies and plans; and ensure continuity of functions/products/services through exercising, rehearsal, testing, training, maintenance, and assurance.[175]

Organized healthcare arrangement Organized system of healthcare in which more than one covered entity participates, and in which the participating covered entities hold themselves out to the public as participating in a joint arrangement; and participate in joint utilization review, quality assurance, or financial risk for healthcare services.[48]

OS Operating system. Software that manages basic computer operations, and supervises and controls tasks, such as Windows 95, 98, NT, Windows 2000, Me, CE, Linus, Palm OS, MAC OS X, OS/2, and UNIX.[1]

OS/2 Operating system/2. IBM's 32-bit GUI multi-tasking operating system with the ability to run DOS, Win16, Win 32, OS/2 16, and OS/2 32 applications, for 80286 and 80386 computers.[1]

OSI Open systems interconnection. A reference model to the protocols in the seven-layer data communications networking standards model and services performed at each level. The OSI standard is defined by the International Organization for Standardization (ISO). The seven layers from the bottom are physical, data link, network, transport, session, presentation, and application.[1]

Out of area *See* **OOA.**

Out of network *See* **OON.**

Out of pocket *See* **OOP.**

Outbreak management *See* **OM**.

Outcome The valued results of care as experienced primarily by the patient, but also by physicians, and all other participants in the processes contributing to the outcomes.[120]

Outcome and assessment information set *See* **OASIS.**

Outcome assessment Research aimed at assessing the quality and effectiveness of healthcare, as measured by the attainment of a specified end result or outcome. Measures include parameters, such as improved health, lowered morbidity or mortality, and improvement of abnormal states (such as elevated blood pressure).[5]

Outcome data Data that measure the health status of patients resulting from specific medical and health interventions.[102]

Outcome indicator An indicator that assesses what happens or does not happen to a patient following a process; agreed-upon desired patient characteristics to be achieved; undesired patient conditions to be avoided.[102]

Outcome measure A parameter for evaluating the success of a system; the parameter reflects the top-level of goals of the system.[4]

Outcomes-based practice Multidisciplinary clinical practice, based on evidence that specific treatments will improve patient outcomes.[120]

Out-of-band Communications that occur outside of a communications method or channel (e.g., the communication of security policies that will be applied to data in the future are communicated out-of-band; they communicated prior to, not at the same time as, the data).[48]

Outpatient Patient who does not reside in a healthcare facility.[4]

Outpatient record Healthcare record of an outpatient.[4]

Output The direct result of the interaction of inputs and processes in the system; the types and qualities of goods and services produced by an activity, project, or program.[123]

Overuse Providing a process of care in circumstances where the potential for harm exceeds the potential for benefit. Prescribing an antibiotic for a viral infection like a cold, for which antibiotics are ineffective, constitutes overuse. The potential for harm includes adverse reactions to the antibiotics and increases in antibiotic resistance among bacteria in the community. Overuse can also apply to diagnostic tests and surgical procedures.[14]

Overwriting virus A virus that reproduces by overwriting the first parts of the program with itself. Because important parts of the program are effectively destroyed, it will not ever run, but the virus code will. These viruses are dangerous and can cause damage to computers.[35]

OWL Web ontology language. Designed for use by applications that need to process the content of information instead of just presenting information to humans. OWL facilitates greater machine interpretability of web content that that support by extensible markup language (XML), resource description framework (RDF) and RDF Schema (RDF-S) by providing additional vocabulary along with a formal semantics.[33]

P

P2P Peer-to-peer. **1.** A network structure in which the computers share processing and storage tasks as equivalent members of the network. Different from a client/server network, in which computers are assigned specific roles. **2.** A general term for popular file-sharing systems like Gnutella, in which there is no central repository of files. Instead, files can be stored on, and retrieved from, any user's computer.[107]

P4P Pay for performance. Refers to the general strategy of promoting quality improvement by rewarding providers (meaning individual clinicians or, more commonly, clinics or hospitals) who meet certain performance expectations with respect to healthcare quality or efficiency. Performance can be defined in terms of patient outcomes but is more commonly defined in terms of processes of care (e.g., the percentage of eligible diabetic patients who have been referred for annual retinal examinations, the percentage of children who have received immunizations appropriate for their age, patients admitted to the hospital with pneumonia who receive antibiotics within six hours).[14]

Packet 1. The unit of data that is routed between an origin and a destination on the Internet or any other packet-switched network. Packets have no set size. **2.** A typical packet contains 1,000 or 1,500 bytes.[1,215]

Packet format Contains three sections: the header, data, and trailer.[1]

Packet header First three octets of an X.25 packet that specifies packet destination, source, and contains an alert.[1]

Packet Internet groper *See* **PING**.

Packet sniffing A technique in which attackers surreptitiously insert a software program at remote network switches or host computers. The program monitors information packets as they are sent through networks, and sends a copy of the information retrieved to the hacker.[1]

Packet switched Transmission technique in which data are broken up into packets and sent along multiple destination paths using store and forward techniques. Once all the packets forming a message arrive at the destination, they are recompiled into the original message.[1] *See* **Circuit switched**.

Packet-switched telephone network *See* **PSTN**.

Packet switching Data are coded into small units and sent over an electronic communication network. Most traffic over the Internet uses packet switching, and the Internet is basically a connectionless network.[1]

Packet-filtering firewall A computer that decides packet-by-packet whether a packet should be copied from one network to another.[1]

PACS Picture archiving and communication systems. A system that begins by converting the standard storage of x-ray films into digitized electronic media that can later be retrieved by radiologists, clinicians, and other staff to view exam data and medical images. Computers or networks are dedicated to the storage, retrieval, distribution, and presentation of images. Full PACS handle images from various modalities, such as ultrasonography, magnetic resonance imaging, positron emission tomography, computed tomography, and radiography (plain x-rays).[1] Small-scale systems that handle images from a single modality (usually connected to a single acquisition device) are also known as *mini-PACS*.

PAN Personal-area network. Personal wireless devices, such as mobile phones, headsets, and notebook PCs, connected together wirelessly via protocol such as Bluetooth.[47]

PAP Password authentication protocol. Allows the use of clear text passwords at its lowest level.[1]

Parallel branching Specifies that two or more tasks are executed independently of each other.[111] *See* **Exclusive branching**.

Parallel cable A cable used to connect peripheral devices through a computer's parallel port.[1]

Parallel port A type of port that transmits data in parallel, with several bits side by side.[1]

Parallel split The divergence of a branch into two or more parallel branches, each of which execute concurrently.[112]

Parameter A word, number, or symbol that is typed after a command to further specify how the command should function.[1]

Parameter RAM *See* **PRAM**.

Pareto chart 1. A graphic representation of the frequency with which certain events occur. It is a rank-order bar chart that displays the relative importance of variables in data sets and may be used to set priorities regarding opportunities for improvement. **2.** Chart named after Vilfredo Pareto contains both bars and a line graph, where individual values are represented in descending order by bars, and the cumulative total is represented by the line.[123,7]

Pareto principle 1. States that for many phenomena, 80 percent of consequences stem from 20 percent of the causes. **2.** Describes a phenomenon in which 80 percent of the variation can be explained by 20 percent of the causes of that variation.[7,123] Also known as the *80-20 percent rule, the law of the vital few,* and the *principle of factory sparsity.*

Parity 1. Parity is used to check a unit of data for errors during transmission through phone lines or modem cables. **2.** Refers to a technique of checking whether data has been lost or written over when it is moved from one place in

storage to another or when transmitted between computers.[1,42]

Parser 1. A function that recognizes valid sentences of a language by analyzing the syntax structure of a set of tokens passed to it from a lexical analyzer. **2.** A software tool that parses programs or other text, often as the first step of assembly, compilation, interpretation, or analysis.[8]

Parser services This service will parse the messages that come in through the protocol layer. The parser will provide support for input formats such as XML, flat files positional, flat file fixed field length, etc.[8]

Partitioning code Applications can be broken into three logical parts: presentation, logic, and data. These are areas in which the program can be separated to facilitate execution of each logical piece on a different machine. Each segment is known as a partition. For example, the thin-client web model requires that interface presentation be handled by the browser, application logic by the web server and other application servers, and data by a database server. Developers are responsible for determining where the separation occurs.[47]

PAS Publicly available specification. Standards from the International Organization for Standardization (ISO) freely available for standardization purposes. PAS is protected by ISO copyright.[3]

Passive threat A potential breach of security, the occurrence of which would not change the state of the system. Such threat could arise from unauthorized reading of files or use of the computer system for an unauthorized application.[1]

Password A special code word, or a string of characters, that a user must present before gaining access to a data system's resources. A sequence that an individual presents to a system for purposes of authentication.[1]

Password authentication protocol *See* **PAP**.

Password cracking A technique in which attackers try to guess or steal passwords to obtain access to computer systems.[1]

Patch Vendors, in response to the discovery of security vulnerabilities, provide sets of files that have to be installed on computer systems. These files 'fix' or 'patch' the computer system or programs and remove the security vulnerability.[118]

Pathway *See* **Clinical pathway.**

Patient Person who is the focus of healthcare activity.[4]

Patient administration system Information system or subsystem used for patient administration, billing, and reimbursement purposes.[4]

Patient care data set *See* **PCDS.**

Patient care management *See* **PCM.**

Patient-centered medical home *See* **PCMH.**

Patient-centric A design goal or characteristic that establishes that all information in an application system shall be grouped and/or indexed according to the patient/person.[8]

Patient classification A classification of patients based on specific criteria or data elements.[4]

Patient demographic query *See* **PDQ.**

Patient identifier domain A single system or a set of interconnected systems that all share a common identification scheme for patients. Such a scheme includes (1) a single identifier-issuing authority; (2) an assignment process of an identifier to a patient; (3) a permanent record of issued patient identifiers with associated traits; and (4) a maintenance process over time. The goal of patient identification is to reduce errors.[56]

Patient experience Comprised of research reports and administrative information that reflect quality from the perspective of patients by capturing observations and opinions about what happened during the process of healthcare delivery. Patient experience encompasses various indicators of patient-centered care, including access (whether patients are obtaining appropriate care in a timely manner), communication skills, customer service, helpfulness of office staff and information resources.[138]

Patient flow The movement of patients who seek care through the admission process. This is the process through which patients are granted entry for care at the hospital.[138]

Patient information reconciliation *See* **PIR.**

Patient portal A web application that provides access to various interactive service functions such as medical content for patients/consumers in a healthcare delivery organization. The portal may provide functions such as pre-registration, pre-scheduling of procedures or outpatient services, bill payment services, access to diagnostic results, or access to a personal health record.[2]

Patient plan of care 1. A roadmap to guide all services that are involved with a patient's care. The plan of care contains goals or outcomes related to treatment options. 2. Based on the six steps/standards of the nursing process: (1) Assessment, (2) Nursing diagnoses/problems, (3) Outcomes Identification, (4) Planning, (5) Implementation, (6) Evaluation.[26,52]

Patient privacy consent The act of a patient consenting to a specific privacy consent policy.[56]

Patient Protection and Affordable Care Act *See* **PPACA** and **ACA.**

Patient record Systematic record of the history of the health of a patient kept by a physician or other healthcare practitioner.[4]

Patient record system The set of components that form the mechanism by which patient records are created, used, stored, and retrieved; a patient record system is usually located within a healthcare provider setting. Includes people, dates, rules and procedures, processing and storage devices, and communication and support facilities.[30]

Patient registry 1. A patient database maintained by a hospital, provider's office, or health plan that allows the identification of patients according to a condition, demographic characteristics, and other factors. Patient registries can help providers better coordinate care for their patients, monitor treatment and progress, and improve overall quality of care. 2. Patient registries are also maintained by local and state governments (e.g., immunization registry), specialty societies (cardiovascular disease registry of American College of Cardiology), and some patient support organizations.[138,216]

Patient safety Freedom from accidental or preventable injuries produced by medical care.[14]

Patient synchronized applications *See* **PSA**.

Patient-centered care Considers patients' cultural traditions, personal preferences and values, family situations, and lifestyles. Responsibility for important aspects of self-care and monitoring is put in patients' hands—along with the tools and support they need. Patient-centered care also ensures that transitions between different healthcare providers and care settings are coordinated and efficient. When care is patient-centered, unneeded and unwanted services can be reduced.[138]

Patient-specific data All data captured and stored in the system pertaining to a patient, such as clinical assessments, medications, insurance information, etc.[6]

Pay for performance *See* **P4P**.

Payer Indicates a third-party entity that pays for or underwrites coverage for healthcare expenses. A payer may be an insurance company, a health maintenance organization (HMO), a preferred provider organization (PPO), a government agency, or an agency such as a third-party administrator (TPA).[16] *See* **NPI**.

PBM Pharmacy benefit manager. A company that administers drug benefit programs for employers and health insurance carriers.[47]

PC Personal computer. A computer designed for use by one person at a time. PC is also commonly used to describe an IBM-compatible personal computer in contrast to an Apple Macintosh computer.[1]

PC card slot The port in a computer in which a smartcard is inserted via a 68-pin socket connector. They are available in type I, II, and III form factors. Type II form factor is the most prevalent.[1] *See* **PCMCIA**.

PCB Printed circuit board. Used to mechanically support and electrically connect electronic components using conductive pathways, tracks, or signal traces etched from copper sheets laminated onto a non-conductive substrate. Printed circuit boards are used in virtually all but the simplest commercially produced electronic devices.[7] Also known as a *printed wiring board* (*PWB*) or *electronic wiring board*.

PCDS Patient care data set. A compilation of pre-coordinated terms used in patient records

to record patients' problems, therapeutic goals, and care actions.[151]

PCI Peripheral component interconnect. Standard CPU to I/O device interface with 32-, 64-, and 128-bit data paths. PCI motherboards automatically configure interrupts. Introduced in 1993.[1]

PCM Patient care management. A system that enrolls or assigns patients to interventions across the continuum of health and illness. It includes wellness exams and routine screenings, utilization reviews, event focus, short-term case management, and the management of long-term chronic conditions.[47]

PCMCIA Personal computer memory card international. Association that has worked to standardize and promote PC card technology.[1]

PCMH Patient-centered medical home. 1. A healthcare setting that facilitates partnerships between individual patients, and their personal physicians, and when appropriate, the patient's family. Care is facilitated by registries, information technology, health information exchange, and other means to assure that patients get the indicated care when and where they need and want it in a culturally and linguistically appropriate manner. **2.** A model for transforming the organization and delivery of primary care.[191,14] Also known as the *Primary care medical home*.

PCO Physician contracting organization. A legal entity representing multiple physicians, practices, and clinics that contracts with other entities to provide healthcare services.[47]

PCP Primary care provider. 1. PCPs specialize in internal medicine, pediatrics, family practice, or obstetrics/gynecology. They provide primary care to members and make referrals to specialty care providers. **2.** A nurse practitioner or a licensed physician's assistant can also provide this basic level of healthcare.[15,102]

PDA Personal digital assistant. A hand-held computing device capable of containing streamlined versions of healthcare software that is compatible with other major systems, and capable of communicating through a direct serial connection, modem, or wireless interface.[2]

PDC Primary domain controller. First operational computer in a Windows NT domain, and only PDC in a domain. Authenticates all users, and maintains the master security accounts database.[1]

PDF Portable document format. A PDF file in an electronic facsimile of a printed document; the filename extension for a packed data file.[1]

PDF 417 A 2-dimensional bar code symbology, enabling error-free transmission of larger blocks of data than is feasible with a 1-dimensional bar code.[99]

PDI Portable data for imaging. Specifies actors and transactions that provide the distribution of diagnostic and therapeutic imaging information on interchange media. The goal of this profile is to provide reliable interchange of evidence objects and diagnostic reports for import, display, or print by a receiving actor.[56] *See* **Profile**. NOTE: PDI is an Integrating the Healthcare Enterprise (IHE) Profile.

PDP Policy decision point. The system entity that evaluates applicable policy and renders an authorization decision.[125] *See* **ACS**.

PDQ Patient demographic query. Provides ways for multiple distributed applications to query a central patient information server for a list of patients, based on user-defined search criteria. Patient demographics data can be entered directly into the application from which the user is querying by picking the appropriate record from a list of possible matches called a patient pick list.[56] *See* **Profile**. NOTE: PDQ is an Integrating the Healthcare Enterprise (IHE) Profile.

Peer review organization *See* **PRO**.

Peer-to-peer network LAN with no central computer where 10 or fewer user computers are connected together. This network setup allows every computer to both offer and access network resources, such as shared files.[1] Also known as a *work group*.

Penetration A successful and repeatable extraction and identification of recognizable privileged (i.e., clinical) data from a protected resource of a data system.[1]

PEP Policy enforcement point. The system entity that performs access control, by making decision requests and enforcing authorization decisions.[125] *See* **ACS**.

Performance assessment Involves the analysis and interpretation of performance measurement data to transform it into useful information for purposes of continuous performance improvement.[102]

Performance indicator Measure that allows observing the progress of a particular change and evaluating its impact.[94]

Performance measure Sets of established standards against which healthcare performance is measured. Performance measures are now widely accepted as a method for guiding informed decision making as a strong impetus for improvement.[138]

Perioperative nursing data set *See* **PNDS**.

Peripheral A piece of hardware that is outside the main computer. It usually refers to external hardware, such as disk drives, printers, and scanners.[1]

Perl Practical extraction and report language. An interpreted procedural programming language designed by Larry Wall. Perl has a unique set of features, some borrowed from imperative computer programming language (C), and from others.[1] *See* **CGI**.

Permanent virtual circuit *See* **PVC**.

Persistent data Data which are stored on a permanent basis.[116]

Person identification service *See* **PIDS**.

Personal computer *See* **PC**.

Personal computer memory card international *See* **PCMCIA**.

Personal digital assistant *See* **PDA**.

Personal health information *See* **PHI**.

Personal health management tool *See* **PHMT**.

Personal health record *See* **PHR** and **ePHR**.

Personal identification number *See* **PIN**.

Personal identification verification *See* **PIV**.

Personal representative Person(s) who has the authority, under applicable state law, to act on behalf of an individual who is an adult or an emancipated minor in making decisions related to the program, service, or activity that an entity provides to the individual. If, under applicable state law, a parent, guardian, or other person acting in loco parentis has authority to act on behalf of an individual who is an un-emancipated minor in making decisions related to the program, service, or activity, this person should be treated as the personal representative of the individual.[48]

Personal-area network. *See* **PAN**.

Personally identifiable health information Health information that contains an individual's identifiers (e.g., name, Social Security number, birth date) or contains a sufficient number of variables to allow identification of an individual.[1]

Personnel White Pages *See* **PWP**.

Pervasive computing Promoters of this idea hope that embedding computation into the environment would enable people to move around and interact with computers more naturally than they currently do. One of the goals of ubiquitous computing is to enable devices to sense changes in their environment, and to automatically adapt and act based on these changes, based on user needs and preferences. Some simple examples of this type of behavior include GPS-equipped automobiles that give interactive driving directions, and RFID store checkout systems.[7] *See* **Ubiquitous computing**.

PET scan **Positron emission tomography scan.** A digital imaging modality capable of detecting subtle differences in temperature.[36]

PGP **Presentation of grouped procedures.** Addresses what is sometimes referred to as the linked studies problem: viewing image subsets resulting from a single acquisition with each image subset related to a different requested procedure (e.g., CT chest, abdomen, and pelvis). It provides a mechanism for facilitating workflow when viewing images and reporting on individual requested procedures that an operator has grouped (often for the sake of acquisition efficiency and patient comfort). A single acquired image set is produced, but the combined use of the scheduled workflow transactions and the consistent presentation of images allow separate viewing and interpretation of the image subsets related to each of the requested procedures.[56] *See* **Profile**. **NOTE:**

PGP is an Integrating the Healthcare Enterprise (IHE) Profile.

PGP **Pretty good privacy.** A public key encryption program used to encrypt and decrypt e-mail over the Internet. Also, PGP may be used for digital signatures to let the receiver know the sender's identity and that the transmission was not changed en route.[1]

Pharmacy benefit manager *See* **PBM**.

Pharmacy informatics Pharmacy informatics is the scientific field that focuses on medication-related data and knowledge within the continuum of healthcare systems, including its acquisition, storage, analysis, use, and dissemination, in the delivery of optimal medication-related patient care and health outcomes.[45]

Pharmacy information systems Health information system that deals with the pharmacy. Such systems can be linked to prescribing system for electronic processing of requests for medications and can provide inventory control.[4]

Pharmacy management system **1.** An application used by a pharmacy to manage fulfillment of prescriptions, claims processing, and other administrative functions. **2.** An application that provides support to the pharmacy department from an operational, clinical, and management perspective, helping to optimize patient safety, streamline workflow, and reduce operational costs.[8,2]

PHI **Protected/personal health information.** Any individually identifiable health information, whether oral or recorded in any form or medium that is created or received by a healthcare provider, health plan, public health authority, employer, life insurer, school or university, or healthcare clearinghouse; and relates to the past, present, or future physical or mental health or condition of an individual; the provision of healthcare to an individual; or the past, present, or future payment for the provision of healthcare to an individual. Any data transmitted or maintained in any other form or medium by covered entities, including paper records, fax documents, and all oral communications, or any other form (i.e., screen prints of eligibility information, printed e-mails that have identified individual's health information, claim, or billing information, hard copy birth or death certificate). Protected health information excludes school records that are subject to the Family Educational Rights and Privacy Act, and employment records held in Department of Homeland Security's role as an employer.[118]

PHIN Public health information network. CDC's vision for advancing fully capable and interoperable information systems in the many organizations that participate in public health. PHIN is a national initiative to implement a multi-organizational business and technical architecture for public health information systems.[46] *See* **CDC.**

PHIN-MS Public health information network-messaging system. A protocol for secure transmission of data, based on the ebXML model. Developed and supported by Centers for Disease Control and Prevention (CDC), the protocol allows for rapid and secure messages to send sensitive health information over the Internet to other local, state, and federal organizations, as well as the CDC.[46]

PHMT Personal health management tool. A set of functions that assist a consumer in managing his or her health status or healthcare.[47]

PHO Physician hospital organization. A management service organization in which partners are physicians and hospitals.[220]

PHR Personal health record. 1. An electronic personal health record ('ePHR') is a universally accessible, layperson comprehensible, lifelong tool for managing relevant health information, promoting health maintenance, and assisting with chronic disease management via an interactive, common data set of electronic health information and e-health tools. The ePHR is owned, managed, and shared by the individual or his or her legal proxy(s) and must be secure to protect the privacy and confidentiality of the health information it contains. It is not a legal record unless so defined and is subject to various legal limitations. **2.** Usually used when referring to the version of the health/medical record owned by the consumer/patient. **3.** An electronic record of health-related information on an individual that conforms to nationally recognized interoperability standards and that can be drawn from multiple sources while being managed, shared, and controlled by the individual.[45,15,84] *See* **Appendix E.**

Physical access The ability and the means to approach and use any hardware component of a clinical data system.[1]

Physical access control Refers to an automated system that controls an individual's ability to access to a physical location, such as a building, parking lot, office, or other designated physical space. A physical access control system requires validation of an individual's identity through some mechanism, such as a personal identification number (PIN), card, biometric, or other token prior to providing access. It has the capability to assign different access privileges to different persons, depending on their roles and responsibilities in an organization.[114]

Physical layer First layer in the OSI model. Defines the physical characteristics of a link between communicating devices.[1]

Physical safeguards The physical measures, policies, and procedures to protect a covered entity's electronic information systems and related buildings and equipment from natural and environmental hazards and unauthorized intrusion.[118]

Physical security The measures taken against all physical threats to a clinical data system, including its remote facilities and operational area; including control of access and exit, protection against fire, explosion, natural disaster, sabotage, social protests, and power problems, and protection of all the stored clinical data from malicious destruction or theft.[1]

Physician contracting organization *See* **PCO.**

Physician hospital organization *See* **PHO.**

Picosecond One trillionth of a second.[1]

Picture archiving and communication system *See* **PACS** and **Radiology PACS.**

PIDS Person identification service. Defines a set of interfaces to an interchangeable set of services that provides a best match or ordered list of best matches to possibly incomplete or conflicting data about a person.[124]

Piggyback Interception of messages between a user and the computer system and then releasing them, modifying them, or returning error messages.[1]

PIM Platform independent model. A model of a software or business system that is independent of the specific technological platform used to implement it. For example, HTML defines a model for hypertext that includes concepts such as title, headings, paragraphs, etc. This model is not linked to a specific operating system or web browser and is, therefore, being successfully implemented on a variety of different computing systems. The term *platform-independent model* is most frequently used in the context of model-driven architectures.[144]

PIN Personal identification number. Used to authenticate or identify a user.[1]

PING Packet INternet Groper. Utility used to test destination reachability. Sends an Internet control message protocol (ICMP) echo request to the destination and waits for a reply.[1]

PIP Policy information point. Point that can provide external information to a policy decision point.[125] *See* **ACS**.

PIR Patient information reconciliation. Extends the scheduled workflow integration profile by offering the means to match images, diagnostic reports, and other evidence objects acquired for a misidentified or unidentified patient (e.g., during a trauma case) with the patient's record.[56] *See* **Profile. NOTE: PIR is an Integrating the Healthcare Enterprise (IHE) Profile.**

PIV Personal identification verification. A physical artifact (e.g., identity card, 'smart' card) issued to an individual that contains stored identity credentials (e.g., photograph, cryptographic keys, digitized fingerprint representation) so that the claimed identity of the cardholder can be verified against the stored credentials by another person (human readable and verifiable) or an automated process (computer readable and verifiable).[227]

PIX Patient identifier cross-referencing. Provides cross-referencing of patient identifiers from multiple patient identifier domains. These patient identifiers can then be used by identity consumer systems to correlate information about a single patient from sources that know the patient by different identifiers.[56] *See* **Profile. NOTE: PIX is an Integrating the Healthcare Enterprise (IHE) Profile.**

Pixel The smallest unit of data for defining an image in the computer. The computer reduces a picture to a grid of pixels.[1]

Pixel skipping A means of reducing image resolution by simply deleting pixels throughout the image.[1]

PKC Public key certificate. X.509 public key certificates (PKCs), which bind an identity and a public key; the identity may be used to support identity-based access control decisions after the client proves that it has access to the private key that corresponds to the public key contained in the PKC.[121]

PKI Public key infrastructure. 1. Technology, facilities, people, operational procedures, and policy to support public key-based security mechanisms. It is an enabler for these encryption and digital signatures. **2.** Infrastructure used in the relation between a key holder and a relying party that allows a relying party to use a certificate relating to the key holder for at least one application using a public key dependent security service, and that includes a certification authority, a certificate data structure, means for the relying party to obtain current information on the revocation status of the certificate, a certification policy, and methods to validate the certification practice.[1,121]

Plan of care The plan of care (also *interdisciplinary plan of care*) is a plan, based on data gathered during patient assessment, that identifies the participant's care needs, describes the strategy for providing services to meet those needs, documents treatment goals and objectives, outlines the criteria for terminating specified interventions, and documents the participant's progress in meeting goals and objectives. Patient-specific policies and procedures, protocols, clinical practice guidelines, clinical paths, care maps, or a combination thereof, may guide the format of the plan in some organizations. The care plan may include care, treatment, habilitation, and rehabilitation.[31] **NOTE: Patient Plan of Care (PPOC) is an Integrating the Healthcare Enterprise (IHE) Profile.**

Platform independent model *See* **PIM.**

Plenum cable Fire-resistant cable that is installed in false ceilings. Uses a coating that will not emit toxic fumes in the event of a fire.[1]

Plotter Output device that produces graphs and diagrams.[1]

Plug-and-play Software that can be plugged into the operating system, or other software, and used immediately, without any adaptation or reconfiguration on the part of the user.[1]

Plug-in A software tool that extends the capabilities of a web browser, allowing the browser to run multimedia files.[1]

PNDS Perioperative nursing data set. A standardized nursing vocabulary of nursing diagnoses, nursing interventions, and nurse-sensitive patient outcomes, that addresses the perioperative patient experience from pre-admission to discharge.[52]

PNG Portable network graphics. A bit-mapped image format that employs lossless data compression. PNG was created to improve upon and replace graphic interchange format (GIF) as an image-file format not requiring a patent license.

Point-of-care system Hospital information system that includes bedside workstations or other devices for capturing and entering data at the locations where patients receive care.[4]

Point-to-multipoint connection A communications architecture in which multiple devices are connected to a link that branches from a single point called an intelligent controller, which manages the flow of information.[1]

Point-to-point connection A communications link between two specific end devices, such as two computers or two modems.[1]

Point-to-point protocol *See* **PPP**.

Point-to-point tunneling protocol *See* **PPTP**.

Policy Overall intention and direction as formally expressed by management.[124]

Policy decision point *See* **PDP**.

Policy enforcement point *See* **PEP**.

Policy information point *See* **PIP**.

POP Post office protocol. A server using this protocol to hold users' incoming e-mail until they read or download it.[1]

Pop To remove data from the top of a stack.[1]

POP server Point-of-presence server. A description for a server supporting POP, serving as a dial-up modem for an Internet service provider (ISP) or e-mail service provider.[1] *See* **ISP**.

Pop-down list box In a graphical user interface (GUI) environment, the list box that appears when the user selects an icon that represents a box with various choices.[1]

PORT Patient outcomes research teams.

Portability The capability of a program to be executed on various types of data processing systems with little or no modification, and without converting the program to a different language.[8]

Portability The ability of a program to run on systems with different architectures.[4]

Portable data for imaging *See* **PDI**.

Portable document format *See* **PDF**.

Portable network graphics *See* **PNG**.

Portable open systems interface *See* **POSIX**.

Portal *See* **Web portal**.[7]

Porting Moving software and data files to other computer systems.[4]

POS Physician office system.[8]

POS Point of service. A type of health maintenance organization (HMO) plan that offers limited coverage for care received outside the HMO's network.[47]

Positron emission tomography *See* **PET** scan.

POSIX Portable open systems interface. IEEE standard for UNIX-like program implementation. Capable of case-sensitive file naming, last-access time stamping, and hard links. A standard, not an operating system. Windows NT supports POSIX.[1]

Post office protocol *See* **POP**.

Post processing workflow *See* **PWF**.

Post-coordination **1.** Describes representation of a concept using a combination of two or more codes. **2.** Using more than one concept from one or many formal systems, combined using mechanisms within or outside the formal systems.[19,59]

Post-production Part of the lifecycle of the product after the design has been completed and the medical device has been manufactured and released.[68]

POTS Plain old telephone system. *See* **PSTN.**[1]

Power PC RISC microprocessor developed by IBM with built-in features that allow the personal computer to emulate other microprocessors.[1]

PPACA **Patient Protection and Affordable Care Act (Public Law 111-148).** Focuses on provisions to expand healthcare coverage, control healthcare costs, and improve the healthcare delivery system.[228]

PPO **Preferred provider organization.** A list of preferred providers that members utilize at a discounted fee.[1]

PPP **Point-to-point protocol.** Protocol that links two networks for serial data transfer. Supports multiple network protocols (TCP/IP, IPX/SPX, and NetBEUI) compression and encryption.[1]

PPS **Prospective payment system.** A system for paying for services that is not based on costs or charges, but on clinical characteristics of a case. DRGs are an example.[15]

PPTP **Point-to-point tunneling protocol.** Protocol for data transfer over the Internet supporting secure communication through encryption.[1]

Practical extraction and report language *See* **Perl.**

Practice management system Generic term used to reference a management system.[8] *See* **Pharmacy management system, Physician management system.**

PRAM **Parameter RAM.** A small portion of the RAM set aside to hold basic information, such as the date and time, speaker volume, desktop pattern, and keyboard and mouse settings.[1]

Pre-coordination Describes representation of a potentially complex concept using a single code.[19]

Predicate migration Steps taken to enable pre-existing data retrieval predicates (including queries, standard reports, and decision support protocols) to be converted or utilized in a system using a mappable vocabulary.[19]

Predictive modeling A statistical technique to predict future behavior. Predictive modeling solutions are a form of data-mining technology that works by analyzing historical and current data and generating a model to help predict future outcomes.[47]

Preferred provider organization *See* **PPO.**

Preferred term The term that is deemed to be the most clinically appropriate way of expressing a concept in a clinical record. Preferred term is one of the three types of terms that can be indicated by the description type field.[19]

Preparedness Activities, programs, and systems developed and implemented prior to an incident that may be used to support and enhance mitigation of, response to, and recovery from disruptions, disasters, or emergencies.[175] Also known as *readiness*.

Prescriber Healthcare person authorized to issue prescriptions.[117]

Prescribing system An information system used in healthcare for processing the prescription of medication by a physician; such a system links the physician with pharmacies and others engaged in prescription of medication.[4]

Prescription Direction created by an authorized healthcare person to instruct a dispensing agent regarding the preparation and use of a medicinal product or medicinal appliance to be taken or used by a patient.[117]

Prescription set Collection of one or more prescription items prescribed and/or dispensed as a unit.[117]

Presentation layer Sixth layer of the open systems interconnection (OSI) model. Provides services to interface applications to the communications system in the form of encryption, compression, translation, and conversion. The network redirector resides here.[1]

Presentation of grouped procedures *See* **PGP.**

Presentation services **1.** Service that provides user interface capabilities and deals with formatting and presenting data to the user. May use user profiles/preferences, personalization, style sheets, etc. **2.** Client application systems that allow authorized users to access and view patient EHR data in an easily customizable manner.[8] Also known as *presentation systems* or *EHR portal*.

Pretty good privacy *See* **PGP**.

Prevalence The number of existing cases of a disease or condition, in a given population, at a specific time.[102]

Prevention Measures that enable an organization to avoid, preclude, or limit the impact of a disruption.[175]

Preventive action Action to eliminate the cause of a potential nonconformity.[175]

PRG Procedure-related group.[9]

Primary care-centered medical home *See* **PCMH**.

Primary care physician *See* **PCP**.

Primary domain controller *See* **PDC**.

Primary key A data element or combination of data elements in a table whose values uniquely identify a row or record. The primary key must have a unique value for each record or row in the table.[1]

Primary patient record Primary record of care. The primary legal record documenting the healthcare services provided to a person in any aspect of healthcare delivery. This term is synonymous with medical record, electronic health record, client record, and resident record.[1]

Primitive A concept is primitive if its defining characteristics are insufficient to define it relative to its immediate supertype(s). For example, if the concept 'red sports car' is defined as [is a=car] + [color=red], this is the primitive, but the same definition applied to the concept 'red car' is fully defined.[19]

Print server A computer that manages print requests from many different users by holding them in a queue until they can be printed. It sends print requests to the appropriate printer in a multi-printer environment.[1]

Printed circuit board *See* **PCB**.

Privacy **1.** The right to have all records and information pertaining to healthcare treated as confidential. **2.** Freedom from intrusion into the private life or affairs of an individual, when that intrusion results from undue or illegal gathering and use of data about that individual.[6,3]

Privacy consent policy One of the acceptable-use privacy consent policies that are agreed to and understood in the affinity domain.[56]

Privacy consent policy identifier An affinity domain assigned object identifier (OID) that uniquely identifies the affinity domain, privacy consent policy. There is one unique OID for each privacy consent policy within the affinity domain.[56]

Privacy impact assessment Tells the 'story' of a project or policy initiative from a privacy perspective, and helps to manage privacy impacts.[115]

Privacy officer Appointed by a covered entity to be responsible for developing and implementing policies and procedures for complying with the health information privacy requirements of the Health Insurance Portability and Accountability Act.[48]

Privacy rights Specific actions that an individual can take, or request to be taken, with regard to the uses and disclosures of their information.[48]

Private key A key in an asymmetric algorithm; the possession of this key is restricted, usually to one entity. Used for signing one's signature to a block of data, which is an HTML document, an e-mail message, or a photograph.[1] *See* **Digital signature**.

Private key cryptography Encryption methodology in which the encryptor and decryptor use the same key, which must be kept secret.[1]

Privilege An individual's right to hold private and confidential the information given to a healthcare provider in the context of a professional relationship. The individual may, by overt act of consent or by other means, waive the right to privilege.[1]

Privileged information A datum or data combination for which adequate technological and administrative safeguards for handling, disclosure, storage, and disposal are required by law or by administrative policy.[1]

PRO   Professional review organization, or peer review organization. A group that provides utilization review and quality oversight to provider organizations.[32]

Problem domain   The field of healthcare under consideration in a modeling process.[4]

Problem-oriented medical record   Healthcare record in which all data may be linked to a list of health problems of an individual patient.[4]

Procedure   Act or conduct of diagnosis, treatment, or operation. Method or technique.[32]

Procedure-related group   *See* **PRG**.

Process   Set of interrelated or interacting activities which transform inputs into outputs.[68]

Process model   A number of tasks that have to be carried out, and a set of conditions that determine the order of the tasks.[111]

Process standard   Standard that specifies requirements to be fulfilled by a process, to establish fitness for purpose.[4]

Processor   The logic circuitry that responds to and processes the basic instructions that drive a computer. The term *processor* has generally replaced the term *central processing unit*.[1]

Product standard   Standard that specifies requirements to be fulfilled by a product or groups of products to establish fitness for purpose.[4]

Professional review organization, or Peer review organization   *See* **PRO**.

Profile   A set of selected parameters that describes a particular reimplementation of a standard.[4]

Program   A set of instructions that can be recognized by a computer system and used to carry out a set of processes.[4]

Program manager   The person ultimately responsible for the overall procurement, development, integration, modification, or operation and maintenance of an IT system.[97]

Program security controls   Controls designed to prevent unauthorized changes

to programs in systems that are already in production.[1]

Programmable read-only memory
See **PROM**.

Programmers   Highly trained technical specialists who write computer software instructions.[1]

Project management   A set of principles, methods, tools, and techniques for effective planning of work, thereby establishing a sound basis for effective scheduling, controlling, and preplanning in the management of programs and products.[6]

Project Sentinel   A project of the National Biosurveillance Testbed. Project Sentinel takes de-identified HIPAA compliance data from participating emergency departments, aggregates it for a specific area, and allows for regional and national comparison for identification of emerging diseases and bioterrorism threats.[1]

PROM   Programmable read-only memory. Subclass of ROM, non-volatile memory chip used in control devices because it can be programmed once.[1]

Prompt   A message displayed on the monitor screen, which asks the customer to perform some action and shows that the computer is ready to accept a command or instruction.[4]

Properties   Information about an object or file, including settings or options for that object. For example, user looks at properties of a file for information, such as the date created, file size, file type, and file attributes.[1]

Proprietary   Privately owned and controlled, typically by a single party. In the computer industry, proprietary is the opposite of open. A proprietary design or technique is one that is owned by a company. It also implies that the company has not divulged specifications that would allow other companies to duplicate the product.[1]

Protected health information   *See* **PHI**.

Protocol   In information technology, a protocol is a special set of rules using end points in a telecommunication connection for communication. Protocols exist at several levels.[14]

Protocol stack Set of combined protocols that accomplish the communications process.[1]

Provider Any supplier of a healthcare service.[8]

Proximity Refers to a technology used to provide physical access control. This technology uses a contact-less interface with a card reader.[114]

PSA Patient synchronized applications. A means for viewing data for a single patient using independent and unlinked applications on a user's workstation, reducing the repetitive tasks of selecting the same patient in multiple applications. Data can be viewed from different identifier domains when used with the Patient Identifier Cross-referencing Integration Profile to resolve multiple identifications for the same patient. This profile leverages the HL7 CCOW standard specifically for patient subject context management.[56] *See* **Profile. NOTE: PSA is an Integrating the Healthcare Enterprise (IHE) Profile.**

PSTN Packet-switched telephone network. Regular dial-up telephone lines. Also known as *plain old telephone system* (POTS). The international telephone system, based on copper wires carrying analog voice data, in contrast to newer telephone networks, based on digital technologies.[1]

Psychotherapy notes Recorded in any medium by a healthcare provider who is a mental health professional, documenting or analyzing the contents of conversation during a private counseling session, or a group, joint, or family counseling session, when notes are separated from the rest of the individual's record.[48]

Public health agency An agency that performs or conducts one or more of the following essential functions that characterize public health programs, services, or activities: **(a)** monitor health status to identify community health problems; **(b)** diagnose and investigate health problems and health hazards in the community; **(c)** inform, educate and empower people about health issues; **(d)** mobilize community partnerships to identify and solve health problems; **(e)** develop policies and plans that support individual and community health efforts; **(f)** enforce laws and regulations that protect health and ensure safety; **(g)** link people to

needed personal health services and ensure the provision of healthcare when otherwise unavailable; **(h)** ensure a competent public health and personal healthcare workforce; **(i)** evaluate effectiveness, accessibility, and quality of personal and population-based health services; and **(j)** research for new insights and innovation solutions to health problems.[118]

Public health information network *See* **PHIN**.

Public information Data which, by their nature, require non-specific handling, limited disclosure, protected storage, and disposal.[1]

Public key A key in an asymmetric algorithm that is publicly available. Used for verifying a signature after it has been signed. *See also* **Digital signature**.[1]

Public key algorithms A method of cryptography in which one key is used to encrypt a message and another key is used to decrypt it.[1]

Public key certificate *See* **PKC**.

Public key cryptography Encryption system that uses a linked pair of keys; one key encrypts, the other key decrypts.[1]

Public key infrastructure *See* **PKI**.

Publicly Available Specification *See* **PAS**.

Push Putting data on a stack.[1]

PVC Permanent virtual circuit. A fixed circuit between two users in a packet-switched network. PVCs are more efficient for connections between hosts that communicate frequently.[1] *See* **SVC**.

PWF Post-processing workflow. Addresses the need to schedule, distribute, and track the status of typical post-processing workflow steps, such as computer-aided detection or image processing. Work lists for each of these tasks are generated and can be queried, work items can be selected, and the status returned from the system performing the work to the system managing the work.[56] *See* **Profile. NOTE: PWF is an Integrating the Healthcare Enterprise (IHE) Profile.**

PWP Personnel White Pages. Provides access to basic human workforce user directory information. This information has broad use among many clinical and non-clinical applications across the healthcare enterprise. The information can be used to enhance the clinical workflow (contact information), enhance the user interface (user friendly names and titles), and ensure identity (digital certificates). This Personnel White Pages directory will be related to the user identity provided by the Enterprise User Authentication (EUA) Integration Profile previously defined by IHE.[56] *See* **Profile**. **NOTE: PWP is an Integrating the Healthcare Enterprise (IHE) Profile.**

Q

QDM   Quality Data Model. An information model that defines concepts used in quality care and is intended to enable automation of EHR use.[208]

QMF   Query management facility. Ad hoc query tool to extract data from some mainframe systems.[15]

QMR   Quick medical reference. Search system for the National Library of Medicine.[141]

QoS   Quality of service. A negotiated contract between a user and a network provider that renders some degree of reliable capacity in the shared network.[47]

QR codes   Quick response codes. High-density, two-dimensional bar codes that are readable by mobile phones and computer cameras with the correct software.[47]

Qualified certificate   In public key infrastructure security information technology, a qualified certificate is used to describe a certificate with a certain qualified status within applicable governing law.[121]

Quality   The totality of features and other characteristics of a product or service that bear on its ability to satisfy stated or implied needs.[123]

Quality assessment   The act of detecting and measuring the differences between efficacy and effectiveness that can be attributed to care, including variations across regions and people.[4]

Quality assurance   The formal and systematic exercise of identifying problems in medical care delivery, designing activities to overcome the problems, and carrying out follow-up steps to ensure that no new problems have been introduced and that corrective actions have been effective.[4]

Quality control   A process to control the quality of care and services.[4]

Quality data model   *See* **QDM**.

Quality design   Systematic approach to service design that identifies the key features needed or desired by both external and internal clients, creates design options for the desired features, and then selects the combination of options that will maximize satisfaction within available resources.[123]

Quality improvement   An approach to the study and improvement of the processes of providing healthcare services to meet needs of clients.[123]

Quality indicator   An agreed-upon process to outcome measurement that is used to determine the level of quality achieved. A measurable variable, or characteristic, that can be used to determine the degree of adherence to a standard or achievement of quality goals.[123]

Quality management   An ongoing effort to provide services that meet or exceed customer expectations through a structured, systematic process for creating organizational participation in planning and implementing quality improvements.[123]

Quality measures   Mechanisms used to assign a quantity to quality of care by comparison to a criterion.[138]

Quality monitoring   The collection and analysis of data for selected indicators thatenable managers to determine whether key standards are being achieved as planned, and are having the expected effect on the target population.[123]

Quality of care   Degrees of excellence of care in relation to actual medical knowledge, identified by quality tracers based on outcomes of care, as well as on structure and process.[4]

Quality of Service   *See* **QoS**.

Quantity   Attribute of a phenomenon, body, or substance that may be distinguished qualitatively and determined quantitatively (e.g., length).[4]

Query   1. The process by which a web client requests specific information from a web server, based on a character string that is passed along. **2.** A request for information that results in the aggregation and retrieval of data.[1,6]

Query management facility *See* **QMF.**

Queue A storage concept in which data are ordered in such a manner that the next data item to be retrieved is the one stored first. This concept is characterized as 'first in, first out' (FIFO).[8]

Queuing services This service provides store and forward capabilities. It can use message queues, as well as other persistence mechanisms, to store information. This service can be used for asynchronous types of operations.[8]

Quick medical reference *See* **QMR.**

Quick response codes *See* **QR codes.**

QWERTY Keyboard layout named after the first six letters on the top left row of keys.[1]

R

R&C **Reasonable & customary.** An amount charged by a provider for services or supplies that is not in excess of the charge made by most providers in the same locality.[15]

RA **Registration authority. 1.** Body responsible for assigning healthcare coding scheme designators and for maintaining the Register of Health Care Coding Schemes as described in a standard. **2.** Entity that is responsible for identification and authentication of certificate subjects, but that does not sign or issue certificates (i.e., an RA is delegated certain tasks on behalf of a CA).[4,121]

RAD **Rapid application development.** An application development approach that includes small teams—typically two to six people using joint application development (JAD) and iterative-prototyping techniques to construct interactive systems of low to medium complexity within a timeframe of 60 to 120 days.[47]

Radio frequency identification *See* **RFID.**

Radio frequency interference Disruption caused by radio and television. A subset of electromagnetic interference.[1]

Radiology information system *See* **RIS.**

Radiology PACS **Radiology picture archiving communications system.** Rather than using film, computed radiography uses an imaging plate. This plate contains photostimulable storage phosphors, which retain the latent image. When the imaging plate is scanned with a laser beam in the digitizer, the latent image information is released as visible light. This light is captured and converted into a digital stream to compute the digital image.[2]

RAID **Redundant array of independent disks.** A method of storing data on multiple hard disks. When disks are arranged in a RAID configuration, the computer sees them all as one large disk. However, they operate much more efficiently than a single hard drive. Since the data are spread out over multiple disks, the reading and writing operations can take place on multiple disks at once, which can speed up hard-drive access time significantly.[2]

RAM **Random access memory. 1.** Primary storage of data or program instructions that can directly access any randomly chosen location in the same amount of time. **2.** The data in RAM stay there only as long as your computer is running. When you turn the computer off, RAM loses its data.[1]

Random access memory *See* **RAM.**

Rapid application development *See* **RAD.**

RARP **Reverse address resolution protocol.** Discovers the IP address of a device by broadcasting a request on a network. Hardware address to IP address resolution.[1]

RAS **Remote access server.** Dial-in capability of Windows NT providing remote access to the server or the entire network from a remote location. Allows the use of modems, ISDN, and X.25 adapters for connectivity.[1]

Raster A synonym for grid. Sometimes used to refer to the grid of addressable positions in an output device.[1]

Raster graphics Digital images created or captured as a set of samples of a given space. A raster is a grid of x and y coordinates on a display space. Examples of raster image file types are BMP, TIFF, GIF, and JPEG files.[1]

Rate A special form of proportion that includes specification of time.[123]

Ratio The relationship between two numbers.[123]

RBAC Role-based access control. An approach to restricting system access to authorized users.[7]

RDBMS Relational database management system. A type of database management system that stores data in the form of related tables. Relational databases are powerful because they require few assumptions about how data are related or how they will be extracted from the database. As a result, the same database can be viewed in many different ways.[1] *See* **DBMS**.

RDF Resource description framework. A family of World Wide Web Consortium (W3C) specifications originally designed as a metadata model. Used as a general method for conceptual description or modeling of information that is implemented in web resources, using a variety of syntax formats.[7]

RDISK Repair disk utility. Windows NT command to initiate the creation or updating of an emergency repair (rescue) disk (ERD).[1]

Read codes Clinical terminology system used in the United Kingdom, now National Health Service (NHS) Clinical Terms, Version 3.[73]

Reader/writer A smartcard reader/writer device provides a means for passing information from the smartcard to a larger computer, and for writing information from the larger computer onto the smartcard.[1]

Reader/writer driver layer The layer in various reader and writer devices that pulls information from, writes to, or erases segments and/or zones of a smartcard.[1]

Readiness *See* **Preparedness**.

Read-only memory *See* **ROM**.

Real-time location service *See* **RTLS**.

Realm A sphere of authority, expertise, or preference that influences the range of concepts and descriptions required, or the frequency with which they are used. A realm may be a nation, an organization, a professional discipline, a specialty, or an individual user.[19]

Real-time system Online computer that generates a nearly simultaneous output from the inputs received.[1]

Reasonable & customary *See* **R&C**.

REC Recommendation.

Record 1. Document stating results achieved or providing evidence of activities performed. 2. A collection of fields that are related to, or associated with, a focal point.[68,6]

Records management *See* **RM**.

Recovery time objective *See* **RTO**.

Red, green, blue color model *See* **RGB**.

Redaction tools Software used to edit content, i.e., selectively and reliably remove information from documents or web sites before sharing the remaining content with someone who is not authorized to see the entire original document.[47]

Reduced instruction set computer *See* **RISC**.

Redundant array of independent disks *See* **RAID**.

Reference architecture Generalized architecture of several end systems that share one or more common domains. The reference architecture defines the infrastructure common to the end systems and the interfaces of components that will be included in the end systems. The reference architecture is then instantiated to create a software architecture of a specific system.[8]

Reference information model *See* **RIM**.

Reference model A structure used to describe a logical process.[4]

Reference model for open distributed processing *See* **RM-ODP**.

Reference terminology 1. Standardized terminology that comprises a set of terms to which the terminology in the interface terminologies is mapped, enabling comparisons to be made even when different terminologies are used. 2. Relates terms to one another (with a set of relationships) and qualifies them (with a set of attributes) to promote precise and accurate interpretation.[11,151]

Reference terminology model *See* **RTM**.

Refreezing Integrating the changes with existing behavioral frameworks to recreate a natural, whole, and stable entity.[6]

Regional health information organization *See* **RHIO**.

Registration authority *See* **RA**.

Registry Directory-like system that focuses solely on managing data pertaining to one conceptual entity. In an EHR, registries store, maintain, and provide access to peripheral information not categorized as clinical in nature, but required to operationalize an EHR. The primary purpose of a registry is to respond to searches using one or more pre-defined parameters in order to find and retrieve a unique occurrence of an entity.[8]

Regression model A data mining statistical method that predicts a value based on the correlation between two or more independent predictor values.[1]

Regression testing **1.** A hypothesis testing event that attempts to determine whether a recent change in one part of the application affects another specific event. **2.** A type of software testing that seeks to uncover new software bugs, or regressions, in existing functional and non-functional areas of a system after changes, such as enhancements, patches, or configuration changes have been made to them. The intent of regression testing is to ensure that a change, such as a bugfix, did not introduce new faults.[6,7]

Relational data model A logical database model that treats data as if they were stored in two-dimensional tables. It can relate data stored in one table to data in another, as long as the two tables share a common data element.[1]

Relational database A flexible collection of data stored in various locations that are held together by common elements.[6]

Relational database management system *See* **RDBMS**.

Relational online analytical processing *See* **ROLAP**.

Relationship Link between two or more concepts.[4]

Relationships table A data table consisting of rows, each of which represents a relationship.[19]

Relative value unit *See* **RVU**.

Reliability A measure of consistency of data items based on their reproducibility and an estimation of their error of measurement.[1]

Relying party Recipient of a certificate who acts in reliance on that certificate and/or digital signature verified using that certificate.[121]

Remote access Access to a system or to information therein, typically by telephone or communication network, by a customer who is physically removed from the system.[4]

Remote access server *See* **RAS**.

Remote access software The software that enables remote or mobile users to dial into a network and access the network resources.[1]

Remote boot Windows NT network service that can boot MS-DOS and Windows 95 computers from across the network.[1]

Remote hosting A form of outsourcing where a client's personal computers are networked into a vendor's remote data processing center via high-speed phone lines. Rapid response times allow the client to access software at the vendor's site. Thus, a client avoids hardware costs, and shares processing and software costs with the vendor's other remote processing clients. If this is done with a web-based architecture, it is referred to as application service provisioning (ASP).[2]

Remote method invocation *See* **RMI**.

Remote network monitor *See* **RMON**.

Remote procedure call *See* **RPC**.

Remote service A support service (e.g., testing, diagnostics, software upgrades) that is not physically or directly connected to the device (e.g., remote access via modem, network, Internet).[45]

Removable media *See* **Electronic media**.

Rendering Process of formatting a print job by the print processor in Windows NT before delivery to a print device.[1]

Repeater Device that extends a LAN by increasing the signal of a LAN segment and joining it with another. The repeater forwards every packet appearing on one network to another.[1]

Repetition separator The repetition separator is used in some data fields to separate multiple occurrences of a field. It is used only where specifically authorized in the descriptions of the relevant data fields.[16]

Replication Periodic push duplication of specific data over the network from one server (export) to another (import).[1]

Reporting workflow *See* **RWF**.

Repository 1. A repository is a central place where data are stored and maintained. A repository can be a place where multiple databases or files are located for distribution over a network, or a repository can be a location that is directly accessible to the user without having to travel across a network. 2. An implementation of a collection of information along with data access and control mechanisms, such as search, indexing, storage, retrieval, and security.[7,8]

Repudiation Denial by one of the entities involved in a communication of having participated in all, or part of, the communication.[1]

Request for information *See* **RFI**.

Request for proposal *See* **RFP**.

Request to send *See* **RTS**.

Requirements A set of needs, functions, and demands which need to be satisfied by a particular software implementation or specification.[4]

Research Systematic investigation, including research development, testing, and evaluation, designed to develop or contribute to generalized knowledge.[48]

Resident virus A computer virus that installs itself as part of the operating system to infect all suitable hosts that are accessed.[1]

Residual risk Risk remaining after risk control measures have been taken.[68]

Resilience The adaptive capacity of an organization in a complex and changing environment. The ability to resist being affected by an event or the ability to return to an acceptable level of performance in an acceptable period of time after being affected by an event. The capability of a system to maintain its functions and structure in the face of internal and external change and to degrade gracefully when it must.[175]

Resolution Measure of graphical image dot density sharpness on a monitor. The higher the density, the sharper the display.[1]

Resource description framework *See* **RDF**.

Response plan The documented collection of procedures and information developed, compiled, and maintained in readiness for use in an emergency.[175]

Response team Group of individuals responsible for developing, executing, rehearsing, and maintaining the response plan, including the processes and procedures.[175]

Response time The time period between a terminal operator's completion of an inquiry and the receipt of a response. Response time includes the time taken to transmit the inquiry, process it by the computer, and transmit the response back to the terminal. Response time is frequently used as a measure of the performance of an interactive system.[47]

Retention The maintenance and preservation of information in some form (e.g., paper, microfilm, or electronic storage) for a given period of time. There are no federal laws outlining timeframes for the retention of health information.[1]

Retrieve information for display *See* **RID**.

Return on investment *See* **ROI**.

Reusability The ability to use code developed for one application in another application, traditionally achieved using program libraries.[8]

Reverse address resolution protocol *See* **RARP**.

Revocation The process of permanently ending the operational period of a certificate from a specified time forward. Generally, revocation is performed when a private key has been compromised.[114]

RFI **Request for information.** A standard business process, the purpose of which is to collect written information about the capabilities of various suppliers. Normally it follows a format that can be used for comparative purposes.[7]

RFID   Radio frequency identification. The RFID tag is attached to the patient, medications, or supplies. The tag consists of a microchip with an antenna, and an interrogator or reader with an antenna. The reader sends out electromagnetic waves. The tag antenna is tuned to receive these waves. A passive RFID tag draws power from the field created by the reader and uses it to power the microchip's circuits. The chip then modulates the waves that the tag sends back to the reader, and the reader converts the new waves into digital data.[2]

RFP   Request for proposal. An RFP typically asks for more than a price, including basic corporate information and history, financial information, and product information, such as stock availability and estimated completion period. The bidder returns a quote or proposal by a set date and time, known as a tender closing. The proposals are used to evaluate the suitability as a supplier, vendor, or institutional partner.[7]

RGB   Red, green, blue color model. A device-dependent color model. Different devices detect or reproduce a given RGB value differently since the color elements (such as phosphors or dyes) and response to the individual R, G, and B levels vary from manufacturer to manufacturer, or even in the same device over time. The name of the model comes from the initials of the three additive primary colors, red, green, and blue. The RGB color model is used in color image-producing technology for sensing, representation, and display of images in electronic systems, such as televisions and computers.[7]

RHIN   Regional health information network. *See* **RHIO**.[1]

RHIO   Regional health information organization. 1. A network of stakeholders within a defined region who are committed to improving the quality, safety, access, and efficiency of healthcare through use of health IT. No two RHIOs look alike, and each reflects the unique nature and interests of its region and resources. **2.** A group of organizations with a business stake in improving the quality, safety, and efficiency of healthcare. **3.** A health information organization that brings together healthcare stakeholders within a defined geographic area

and governance health information exchange among them for the purpose of improving health and care in that community.[45,84]

Rich text format *See* **RTF**.

Release of information *See* **ROI**.

RID   Retrieve information for display. A simple and rapid read-only access to patient information necessary for provision of better care. It supports access to existing persistent documents in well-known presentation formats, such as CDA, PDF, JPEG, etc. It also supports access to specific key patient-centric information, such as allergies, current medications, summary of reports, etc., for presentation to a clinician.[56] *See* **Profile**. **NOTE: RID is an Integrating the Healthcare Enterprise (IHE) Profile.**

RIM   Reference information model. A static model of health and healthcare information as viewed within the scope of HL7 standards development activities. It is the combined consensus view of information from the perspective of the HL7 working group and the HL7 international affiliates. The RIM is the ultimate source from which all HL7 Version 3.0 protocol specification standards draw their information-related content.[16]

Ring network Network topology in which all computers are linked by a closed loop in a manner that passes data in one direction, from one computer to another.[1]

RIP   Routing information protocol. Used to advertise and exchange information between routers within an autonomous system.[1]

RIS   Radiology information system. 1. The components of radiology software, hardware, and network infrastructure to support patient documentation, retrieval, and analysis. **2.** An automated RIS manages the operations and services of the radiology department. The functionality includes scheduling, patient and image tracking, and rapid retrieval of diagnostic reports.[1,2] *See also* **PACS**.

RISC   Reduced instruction set computer. Non-microcode computer that uses a simplified set of instructions in internal firmware to speed operation. Digital Equipment Corporation (DEC, now a part of Compaq), Alpha, IBM, Power PC, and MIPS are RISC computers.[1]

Risk Combination of the probability of an event and its consequences.[124]

Risk analysis A method for assessing risk. This may be used to subsequently compare the cost of achieving something (such as hospital system security) against the risk of losing something.[4]

Risk assessment 1. Process of analyzing threats to, and vulnerabilities of, an IT system, and the potential impact that the loss of information or capabilities of a system would have on national security. The resulting analysis is used as a basis for identifying appropriate and effective measures. 2. Overall process of risk analysis and risk evaluation.[97,124]

Risk control Process in which decisions are made and measures implemented by which risks are reduced to, or maintained within, specified levels.[68]

Risk estimation Process used to assign values to the probability of occurrence of harm and the severity of that harm.[68]

Risk evaluation Process of comparing the estimated risk against given risk criteria to determine the significance of the risk.[124]

Risk management 1. Systematic application of management policies, procedures, and practices to the tasks of analyzing, evaluating, controlling, and monitoring risk. 2. Coordinated activities to direct and control an organization with regard to risk.[68,124]

Risk tolerance Organization's readiness to bear the risk after risk treatments in order to achieve its objectives.[175]

Risk treatment Process of selection and implementation of measures to modify risk.[124]

RM Records management. Technologies that enable organizations to enforce policies and rules for the retention and disposition of required business transaction content. RM strategies and policies are an essential part of the organization-wide lifecycle management of records. RM principles and technologies apply to both physical and electronic content. The US National Archives and Records Administration (NARA) is the nation's RM agency for RM training to federal employees and contractors on RM topics from archive schedules to emergency preparedness. [47]

RMI Remote method invocation. An adaptation of the remote procedure call paradigm for object-oriented environments.[32]

RM-ODP Reference model for open distributed processing. The RM-ODP efforts began in 1987 as part of the International Organization for Standardization (ISO) Object Management Group (OMG), to enable the inter-working of applications and sharing of data across computer networks spanning organizational and national boundaries. As it relates to the healthcare domain, the uppermost two of five layers deal with the information viewpoint (such as HL7, X12, DICOM, CPT) and the enterprise viewpoint (such as patient registration, order communications, results retrieval).[1]

RMON Remote network monitor. Device that collects network traffic information for use by remote monitoring stations.[1]

Roadmap Technology road mapping is a technology management tool that attempts to plan and forecast the necessary steps toward achieving one or more technology goals. Technology roadmaps are different from project plans, in that roadmaps attempt to emphasize the uncertainty in the forecast rather than create a linked set of tasks. The value of a technology roadmap includes communicating vision, encouraging collaborative thinking, garnering necessary resources to solve technology challenges, creating contingency approaches, and consensus view for decision making. One of the most common extensions of the technology roadmap is to link it to product roadmaps and market roadmaps to provide the complete picture of 'what, why, and how' in relation to the achievement and delivery of a particular technology goal.[7] See **Transition plan**.

ROI Return on investment. A calculation used to determine whether a proposed investment is wise and how well it will repay the investor. It is calculated as the ratio of the amount gained (taken as positive) or lost (taken as negative), relative to the basis.[7]

ROI Release of information. Formal process to request to release health information to other healthcare providers and authorized users, ensuring that the information is timely, accurate, complete and confidential.[62]

ROLAP Relational online analytical processing (OLAP). A technical OLAP approach where data are presented dimensionally, but stored and accessed using traditional 2-dimensional relational DBMS technology allowing for very high flexibility.[1] *See* **OLAP**.

Role 1. Roles are attributes. These terms are synonymous. 2. Set of behaviors that are associated with a task.[19,121]

Role based access control *See* **RBAC**.

ROM Read-only memory. Non-volatile permanent memory written in firmware. Contents usually cannot be changed.[1]

Root cause analysis A process for identifying the basic or causal factors that underlie variation in performance, including the occurrence, or possible occurrence, of an adverse event.[31]

Root directory System base directory. All other directories and files are found under the root directory.[1]

Router 1. Device that attaches multiple networks, LANs, and WANs, and routes packets between the networks through the use of software. 2. Allows two devices connected to LANs or WLANs (wireless local area networks) of different types to access each other. Router's function is similar to a bridge, but it must be able to communicate between different LAN/WLAN protocols and choose the best path where multiple paths exist between nodes on the network.[1,2] *See* **Routing switch**.

Routing information protocol *See* **RIP**.

Routing services This service will route messages to the various internal integration channels, based on a publish/subscribe model.[8]

Routing switch Device that attaches multiple networks, LANs, and WANs, and routes packets between the networks through the use of hardware. Ten times faster than a conventional router.[1]

Routing table Lists maintained by routers that include the most recent information on routes advertised by other routers for different destinations.[1]

RSA A public key crypto-system, invented and patented by Ronald Rivest, Ade Shamir, and Leonard Adelman, based on large prime numbers. RSA is the best-known asymmetric algorithm.[1]

RTF Rich-text format. A minimum file format for text files that includes formatting instructions, the text itself, and very little additional information.[1] Also known as *interchange format.*

RTLS Real-time location service. Provides actionable information regarding the location, status and movement of equipment and people. Advanced RTLS search capabilities allow searching by specific location (floor, area, room) or unique asset identifiers (department owner, type, manufacturer, model number, asset control number or employee ID number). The detailed asset information and reporting capabilities of RTLS allow further analysis to support a variety of uses including equipment utilization data to identify inefficiencies that have required excess equipment inventory purchases.[2]

RTM Reference terminology model. Integration of a reference terminology model for nursing is an essential first step in creating comparable nursing data across settings and countries. Without such data, it is impossible to identify and implement 'best nursing practices' (i.e., those most likely to result in positive health outcomes for patients, families, and communities, or to determine how scarce nursing resources should be spent).[3]

RTO Recovery time objective. Time goal for the restoration and recovery of functions or resources based on the acceptable down time and acceptable level of performance in case of a disruption of operations.[175]

RTS Request to send. Modem control operation from data terminal equipment requesting clearance to transmit.[1]

Rule A formal way of specifying a recommendation, directive, or strategy, expressed as 'IF premise THEN conclusion' or 'IF condition THEN action.'[4]

Run chart A visual display of data that enables monitoring of a process to determine whether there is a systematic change in that process over time.[123]

RVU   Relative value unit. A comparable service measure used by hospitals to permit comparison of the amounts of resources required to perform various services within a single department or between departments. It is determined by assigning weight to such factors as personnel time, level of skill, and sophistication of equipment required to render patient services. RVUs are a common method of physician bonus plans based partially on productivity.[139]

RWF   Reporting workflow. Addresses the need to schedule, distribute, and track the status of the reporting workflow tasks, such as interpretation, transcription, and verification. Work lists for each of these tasks are generated and can be queried; work items can be selected, and the resulting status returned from the system performing the work to the system managing the work.[56] *See* **Profile. NOTE: RWF is an Integrating the Healthcare Enterprise (IHE) Profile.**

S

S/MIME   Secure MIME. Extends the Multipurpose Internet Mail Extensions (MIME) standard to allow for encrypted e-mail.[1]

SaaS   Software as a Service. 1. A software delivery model in which software and associated data are centrally hosted on the cloud. Typically accessed using a thin client via a web browser. **2.** Software that is owned, delivered and managed remotely by one or more providers. The provider delivers software based on one set of common code and data definitions, which are consumed in a one-to-many model by all contracted customers at any time on a pay-for-use basis or as a subscription based on metrics.[7,47] Also known as *on-demand software.*

Sabotage   Damage to another's system(s) on purpose.[1]

Safeguard   A protective measure to mitigate against the effect of system vulnerability.[1]

Safety   Freedom from unacceptable risk of harm.[4]

Salami   A technique by which criminals steal resources a little at a time. Programs may adjust payroll deductions by just a few cents in each transaction and then collect the funds. This type of transaction is very difficult to detect.[1]

SAML   Security assertion markup language. An XML standard for exchanging authentication and authorization data between security domains; that is, between an identity provider and a service provider.[91]

Sample   One or more parts taken, or to be taken from a system, and intended to provide information on that system or a subsystem, or to provide a basis for decision on either.[4]

SAN   Storage area network. A high-speed special purpose network (or sub-network) that interconnects different kinds of data storage devices with associated data servers on behalf of a larger network of users. Typically, a storage area network is part of the overall network of computing resources for an enterprise.[2]

Sanitization   Erasing all identifiers from certain files (i.e., clinical files).[1]

SATA   Serial Advanced Technology Attachment (ATA). De facto standard for internal PC storage, SATA is the evolutionary replacement for the Parallel ATA storage interface. A serial interface that can operate at speeds up to 6 Gb/s.[218]

SATAN   Security administrator tool for analyzing networks. A testing and reporting toolbox that collects a variety of information about networked hosts.[1,157]

SBAR   Situation-background-assessment-recommendation. Institute for Healthcare Improvement (IHI) technique that provides a framework for communication between members of the healthcare team about a patient's condition. [213]

Scalability   The ability to support the required quality of service as load increases.[8]

Scanner   1. A device used to digitize a picture of a document so that it can be stored in memory and on a disk. Fax machines use this process to transmit documents to other fax machines. **2.** An electronic device that generates a digital representation of an image for data input to a computer.[1,2]

Scatter diagram   A graphic display of data plotted along two dimensions.[123]

Scenario   Formal description of a class of business activities, including the semantics of business agreements, conventions, and information content.[4]

Scheduled workflow   *See* **SWF**.

Scheduler   Portion of the operating system that moves programs from input to ready.[1]

Schema   In general, a schema is an abstract representation of an object's characteristics and relationship to other objects. An XML schema represents the interrelationship between the attributes and elements of an XML object (e.g., a document or a portion of a document). To create a schema for a document, one would analyze its structure, defining each structural element as it is encountered (e.g., within a schema for a document describing a web site, one would define a web site element, a web page element, and other elements that describe possible content divisions within any page on that site). Just as in XML and HTML, elements are defined within a set of tags.[33,42]

Schmeist head   Person who executes a system command without knowing what the command will do.[1]

Science of clinical informatics   The transformation of clinical data into information, then knowledge, which supports clinical decision making. This transformation requires an understanding of how clinicians structure decision making and what data are required to support this process.[6]

SCOS   Smartcard operating system. Organizes data on the integrated circuit chip into files and protects them from unauthorized access.[1]

Screen saver   A moving picture or pattern that is displayed on the screen when no activity takes place for a specified period of time.[1] Also called a *time out*.

Script   A type of code or program that consists of a set of instructions for another application or utility to use.[1]

SCSI   Small computer system interface. Set of standards for physically connecting and transferring data between computers and peripheral devices.[7]

SCUI   Smartcard user interface. Provides a standard interface between applications and the data on the chip. Multiple applications can reside on the chip, and the SCUI allows an application to access its own data without affecting another application's data.[1]

SDLC   System design lifecycle. The process used by a systems analyst to develop an information system, including requirements, validation, training, and user ownership through investigation, analysis, design, implementation, and maintenance. An SDLC should result in a high-quality system that meets or exceeds customer expectations, within time and cost estimates, works effectively and efficiently in the current and planned information technology infrastructure, and is inexpensive to maintain and cost-effective to enhance.[7] Also known as *information systems development* or *application development*.

SDO   Standard development organization. Standardization in the field of information for health, and health information and communications technology, to achieve compatibility and interoperability between independent systems. Also, to ensure compatibility of data for comparative statistical purposes (e.g., classifications) and to reduce duplication of effort and redundancies.[3]

SDXC   Secure digital extended capacity. A flash memory card that resembles a Secure Digital (SD) card with greater storage capacity. SD and SDXC cards make storage portable among devices such as smartphones, eBooks, digital cameras, camcorders, music players, and computers.[42]

Search engine   A type of software that creates indexes of databases or Internet sites based on the titles or files, keywords, or the full text of files. The result of a search on the engine is a list of documents in which the keywords were found.[1]

Search/resolution services   This service is used to interface with resolution services present in registries, such as client, provider, and other registries. It is also used to resolve situations where clinical data about a client resides in different locations and systems across an interoperated network of EHRs.[8]

Searchable identifiers   Characteristics that uniquely identify an information object, support persistent access to that object, and support access to information about the object (i.e., metadata).[44]

Seat license The fee is paid per user or 'per seat,' or per concurrent user, through negotiations with a vendor to allow a fixed number of copies of copyrighted software.[1] *See* **Site license**.

SEC Security. Establishes basic security measures that can, as part of an institution's overall security policies and procedures in the enterprise, help protect the confidentiality of patient information. It also provides institutions with a mechanism to consolidate audit trail events on user activity across several systems interconnected in a secure manner.[56] *See* **Profile**. **NOTE: SEC is an Integrating the Healthcare Enterprise (IHE) Profile.**

Secondary data use Use of data for additional purposes than the primary reason for their collection, adding value to this data.[94]

Secondary record A record that is derived from the primary record and contains selected data elements.[1]

Secrecy The intentional concealment or withholding of information.[1]

Secret key A key in a symmetric algorithm; the possession of this key is restricted, usually to two entities.[1]

Secure communications channel Ensure the authenticity, the integrity, and the confidentiality of transactions, and the mutual trust between communicating parties.[48]

Secure digital extended capacity *See* **SDXC**.

Secure electronic transmission *See* **SET**.

Secure HTTP *See* **S-HTTP**.

Secure MIME *See* **S/MIME**.

Secure shell *See* **SSH**.

Secure socket layer *See* **SSL**.

Secure web server A program that implements certain cryptographic protocols to prevent eavesdropping on information transferred between a web server and a web browser. A server resistant to a determined attack over the Internet or from corporate insiders.[1]

Security Measures and controls that ensure confidentiality, integrity, availability, and accountability of the information processed and stored by a computer.[97]

Security administration control Includes all management control measures and appropriate policies necessary to provide an acceptable level of protection of data stored in the data system.[1]

Security administrator A member of the data system management team trained in data security matters, authorized to enforce the data security measures, and to create a confidentiality/privacy conscious working environment.[1]

Security and control testing A testing event that examines the presence and appropriate functioning of the application's security and controls to ensure integrity and confidentiality of data.[6]

Security architecture A plan and set of principles for an administrative domain and its security domains that describe the security services that a system is required to provide to meet the needs of its users, the system elements required to implement the services, and the performance levels required in the elements to deal with the threat environment.[8]

Security assertion markup language *See* **SAML**.

Security compromise A specific loss of a component of the security system, due to an unauthorized person obtaining classified information.[1]

Security incident The attempted or successful unauthorized access, use, disclosure, modification, or destruction of information or interference with system operations in an information system.[118]

Security level Categorization of a controlled resource or defined data user.[1]

Security manager The person assigned responsibility for management of the organization's security program.[1]

Security overhead The total cost, in dollars, of the added hardware features and software drafting/running to serve the safeguarding purposes.[1]

Security policy The framework within which an organization establishes needed levels of information security to achieve the desired confidentiality goals.[1]

Security process The series of activities that monitor, evaluate, test, certify, accredit, and maintain the system accreditation throughout the system lifecycle.[97]

Security requirements Types and levels of protection necessary for equipment, data, information, applications, and facilities to meet security policy.[97]

Security service A processing or communication service that is provided by a system to give a specific kind of protection to resources, where said resources may reside with said system or reside with other systems (e.g., an authentication service, or a public key infrastructure-based document attribution and authentication service).[8]

Security system of a data system The integrated combination of technological means, security administrator's activities, and the related statutory laws intended to prevent accidental or unauthorized disclosure of clinical data, modification, or destruction of stored clinical data, or damage to the clinical data system, or at least to reduce the risk to an acceptable level.[1]

Security tool A program run to evaluate or enhance the security of a site.[1]

Security design-in The provision of hardware and software features for security from the inception of the system.[1]

Segment A logical grouping of data fields. Segments of a message may be required or optional. They may occur only once in a message or they may be allowed to repeat. Each segment is identified by a unique character code known as the segment identifier.[16]

Semantic Pertains to the meaning or interpretation of a word, sign, or other representation.[151]

Semantic correspondence Measure of similarity between concepts.[126]

Semantic interoperability 1. Ability for data shared by systems to be understood at the level of fully defined domain concepts. **2.** The

ability to preserve the meaning of exchanged information.[124]

Semantic link Formal representation of a directed associative relation or partitive relation between two concepts.[126]

Semantic network A formalism (often expressed graphically) for representing relational information, the arcs of the network representing the relationships, and the nodes of objects in the network.[4]

Semantic web The Semantic web is a project that intends to create a universal medium for information exchange by giving meaning (semantics), in a manner understandable by machines, to the content of documents on the web. Currently under the direction of the web's creator, Tim Berners-Lee of the World Wide Web Consortium, the semantic web extends the ability of the web through the use of standards, markup languages, and related processing tools.[7]

Semantics Meaning of symbols and codes.[4]

Sensitivity label A security level associated with the content of the information. Society has historically considered as sensitive that information which has a heightened potential for causing harm to the patient or data subject, or to others, such as the subject's spouse, children, friends, or sexual partners.[1]

Sentinel event Unexpected occurrences involving death, serious physical or psychological injury, or risk thereof. Serious injury specifically includes loss of limb or function. The phrase 'risk thereof' includes any process variation for which a recurrence would carry a significant chance of serious adverse outcomes.[31]

Sequence A task in a process is enabled after the completion of a preceding task in the same process.[112]

Serial ATA *See* **SATA**.

Serial line Internet protocol *See* **SLIP**.

Serial transmission Sequential transmission of the signal elements of a group representing a character or other entity of data. The characters are transmitted in a sequence over a single line, rather than simultaneously over two or more lines, as in parallel transmission.[57]

Server   Centralized network computer that provides an array of resources and services to network users. Also, a program that responds to a request from a client.[1]

Service   Discrete units of application logic that expose loosely coupled message-based interfaces suitable for being accessed across a network.[8]

Service event   The act of providing a health-related service.[8]

Service-oriented architecture   *See* **SOA**.

Session   A period of interaction. **1.** In computer science, in particular, networking. A session is either a lasting connection using the session layer of a network protocol or a lasting connection between a user (or user agent) and a peer, typically a server. **2.** In healthcare, a period of treatment, a 'therapy session.' **3.** Government: legislative, judicial, or executive session.[8]

Session layer   Fifth layer of the open systems interconnection model. Provides file management needed to support intersystem communication through the use of synchronization and data stream checkpoints. Also responsible for the establishment, management, and termination of sessions.[1]

Session management service   This service manages user sessions. A user session will contain information such as ticket number, function and role information, authorization information, and other information that the system may choose to store to provide efficient access to information.[8]

SET   Secure electronic transmission.   A cryptographic protocol designed for sending encrypted credit card numbers over the Internet.[1]

Severity   Measure of the possible consequences of a hazard.[68]

Severity system   Expected likelihood of disease progression independent of treatment. Systems attempting to measure severity may use diagnostic codes, such as ICD, and/or additional clinical information.[53]

sFTP   Secure file transport protocol.   Standard for secure transfer of packets of information from one computer system to another.

Commonly used in the transport of files of information containing confidential information.[99]

SGML   Standardized general markup language.   A metalanguage in which one can define markup languages for documents. SGML is a descendant of IBM's Generalized Markup Language (GML), developed in the 1960s by Charles Goldfarb, Edward Mosher, and Raymond Lorie (whose surname initials also happen to be GML). SGML should not be confused with the Geography Markup Language (GML) developed by the Open Geographic Information System (Open GIS) Consortium, cf, or the Game Maker scripting language, GML. SGML provides a variety of markup syntaxes that can be used for many applications.[3]

SGMP   Simple gateway monitoring protocol.   Allows commands to be issued to application protocol entities to set or retrieve values (integer or octet string types), for use in monitoring the gateways on which the application protocol entities reside. SGMP was replaced by SNMP (simple network management protocol).[7]

Shared environment   A computing environment in which computers at a remote location provides the information systems processing for several clients.[2]

Shared service   An approach to computerization provided by a service organization that offers remote computer services with supporting software functions for the full range of hospital business and clinical applications.[2]

Shared space   A mechanism that provides storage of, and access to, data for users with bounded network space. Enterprise-shared space refers to a store of data that is accessible within or across security domains on the global information grid. A shared space provides virtual access to any number of data assets (catalogs, web sites, registries, document storage database). Any user, system, or application that posts data uses shared space.[18]

Shareware   Software that can be tried before purchase. It is distributed through online services and user groups.[1]

Shielded twisted pair   *See* **STP**.

Shockwave   A set of programs that allows Macromedia Director animation files to be played over the Internet with a web browser.[1]

Short Message Service   *See* **SMS**.

S-HTTP   Secure HTTP. A system for signing and encrypting information sent over the web's HTTP protocol.[1] *See* **HTTP**.

SIG   Special interest group. Subset of professional computer organizations that concentrates on a specific technical computing area.[1]

SIMM   Single in-line memory module. A type of RAM chip.[1]

Simple gateway monitoring protocol
See **SGMP**.

Simple image and numeric report
See **SINR**.

Simple mail transfer protocol   *See* **SMTP**.

Simple merge   The convergence of two or more branches into a single subsequent branch, such that each enablement of an incoming branch results in the thread of control being passed to the subsequent branch.[112] *See* **Exclusive choice**.

Simple network monitoring protocol
See **SNMP**.

Simple object access protocol   *See* **SOAP**.

Simplex   Communication channel/circuit that allows data transmission in one direction only.[1]

Simulation   Resembles a real-life situation that the learner might encounter; learners can engage in safe decision making.[6]

Simulation exercise   Test performed under conditions as close as practicable to real-world conditions.[174]

Simultaneous peripheral operation online
See **SPOOL**.

Single in-line memory module   *See* **SIMM**.

Single sign-on   A specialized form of software authentication that enables a user to authenticate once and gain access to the resources of multiple software systems.[2]

Single sign-on   *See* **SSO**.

SINR   Simple image and numeric report. Facilitates the growing use of digital dictation, voice recognition, and specialized reporting packages by separating the functions of reporting into discrete actors for creation,

management, storage, and viewing. Separating these functions while defining transactions to exchange the reports between them enables a vendor to include one or more of these functions in an actual system.[56] *See* **Profile**. NOTE: SINR is an Integrating the Healthcare Enterprise (IHE) Profile.

Site license   A renewable fee that has been paid through negotiations with a vendor to allow a fixed number of copies of copyrighted software at one site.[1] *See* **Seat license**.

Situation-background-assessment-recommendation   *See* **SBAR**.

Six Sigma   A business management strategy, originally developed by Motorola in 1986, that seeks to improve the quality of process outputs by identifying and removing the causes of defects (errors) and minimizing variability in manufacturing and business processes. Combines statistical process control, experimental design, and failure mode and effects analysis into a methodology.[7]

SLIP   Serial line Internet protocol. Minimal overhead protocol for TCP/IP-only data transfer over serial links, such as telephone circuits or RS-232 cables. Does not support multiple protocols, encryption, or compression. The precursor to point-to-point protocol.[1]

Slow-scan video   A device that transmits and receives still video pictures over a narrow telecommunications channel.[106]

Smartcard   An integrated circuit card that incorporates a processor unit. The processor may be used for security algorithms, data access, or for other functions according to the nature and purpose of the card.[4]

Smartcard operating system   *See* **SCOS**.

Smartcard user interface   *See* **SCUI**.

Smartphone   A device licensed to be a telephone using US Federal Communications Commission (FCC) authorized frequencies, which has Internet browser capabilities; web-enabled applications, the ability to view e-mail file attachments that include documents and images, file storage capability to support calendaring, e-mail and texting.[2]

SMAU   Multiple station access unit. A token-ring network hub.[1]

SME **Subject-matter expert.** An individual who has expertise on a particular topic.[7]

SMP **Symmetrical multi-processing.** A computing platform technology in which a single server uses multiple CPUs in a parallel fashion managed by a single operating system.[1]

SMS **Short message service. 1.** A mechanism of delivery of short messages over the mobile networks. **2.** Part of the Global System for Mobile Communications (GSM) standard developed by the European Telecommunications Standards Institute that enables a mobile device to send, receive and display messages of up to 160 characters in Roman text and variations for non-Roman character sets. Messages received are stored in the network if the subscriber device is inactive and are relayed when it becomes active. SMS has become available increasingly in Code Division Multiple Access (CDMA) technology networks.[7,47]

SMTP **Simple mail transfer protocol.** Protocol used to transfer mail between systems and from one computer to another. SMTP specifies how two mail systems interact, and the format of control messages they exchange to transfer mail.[1]

SNA **System network architecture.** Network architecture developed by IBM for mainframe networking. Does not interoperate with TCP/IP.[1]

Sniffer Network tool that collects network traffic packets to provide analysis on network and protocol usage, and generates statistics to assist in monitoring and optimizing networks.[1]

Sniffers Programs used to intercept clear text data in packets transmitted through local area networks. A method of eavesdropping on communications.[1]

SNMP **Simple network monitoring protocol.** Used to monitor hosts, routers, and networks. Enables a monitoring management station to configure, monitor, and receive alarms from network devices.[1]

SNMP **System network management protocol.** Forms part of the Internet protocol suite as defined by the Internet Engineering Task Force. The protocol can support monitoring of network-attached devices for any conditions that warrant administrative attention.[7]

SNOMED CT **Systematized Nomenclature of Medicine Clinical Terms.** A controlled healthcare terminology developed by the College of American Pathologists in collaboration with the United Kingdom's National Health Service. SNOMED CT includes comprehensive coverage of diseases, clinical findings, therapies, procedures, and outcomes.[19]

SOA **Service-oriented architecture. 1.** An infrastructure where many N-tier applications are deployed, sharing common software services that are accessible from any user interface. In this environment, any application can access any service, provided the application has the proper security permissions. **2.** A software architectural concept that defines the use of services to support the requirements of software users. In an SOA environment, nodes on a network make resources available to other participants in the network as independent services that the participants access in a standardized way.[7,8]

SOAP **Simple object access protocol.** A third-generation programmable web service built on top of standards-based Internet protocols that can be implemented on any platform, in any language.[1]

SOAP **Subjective, objective, assessment, and plan.** A method of documentation employed by healthcare providers to write notes in a patient's chart.[7]

Socket The logical address of a communications access point to a specific device or program on a host. A socket is defined as the endpoint in a connection. Also, the communication between a client program and a server program in a network.[1] *See* **API, SSL.**

Soft copy File maintained on disk in electronic storage format.[1]

Software A computer program encoded in such a fashion that the program (the instruction set) contents can be changed with minimal effort. Computer software can have various functions, such as controlling hardware, performing computations, communication with other software, human interaction, etc., all of which are prescribed in the program.[7]

Software access The ability and the means to communicate with the operating system or any file/database controlled by the operating system of a clinical data sytem.[1]

Software architecture   The software architecture of a program or computing system is the structure or structures of the system, which comprise software components, the externally visible properties of those components, and the relationships among them.[8]

Software as a service   *See* **SaaS**.

Software asset management   A management process for making software acquisition and disposal decisions. It includes strategies that identify and eliminate unused or infrequently used software, consolidating software licenses, or moving toward new licensing models.[1]

Software security system   A computer operating system certified as incorporating those hardware and software functions and features that are necessary to prohibit accidental or malicious access.[1]

SONET   Synchronous optical network. American National Standard Institute (ANSI) standard for connecting high-speed, high-quality, digital fiber-optic transmission systems. The international equivalent of SONET is synchronous digital hierarchy.[1] *See* **ATM, Frame relay**.

SOP   Standard operating procedure. Formalized way of uniformly carrying out a process.[15]

Source systems   Application systems where service encounter data are collected (e.g., laboratory information systems, pharmaceutical information systems, immunization systems). These clinical data are extracted from the source system and transformed prior to being used in the electronic health record.[8] *See* **Feeder systems**.

SOW   Statement of work. A document describing the specific tasks and methodologies that will be followed to satisfy the requirements of an associated contract or memorandum of understanding.[10]

SP   Subportal. A subportal provides highly targeted aggregate content and interactive capabilities that focus on a specific vertical healthcare market segment, as opposed to overall portals, such as Yahoo or Microsoft Network.[1]

Spam   Trash e-mail. The practice of blindly or intentionally posting commercial messages or advertisements to a large number of unrelated and uninterested newsgroups.[1]

SPD   Summary plan description. Document that explains the product and services a subscriber purchased.[15]

Special interest group   *See* **SIG**.

Specification   An explicit statement of the required characteristics for an input used in the healthcare system. The requirements are usually related to supplies, equipment, and physical structures used in the delivery of health services.[123]

Spider   *See* **Web crawler**.[7]

SPIN   Standard prescriber identification number. National Council for Prescription Drug Programs (NCPDP) sponsored the Standard Prescriber Identification Number from the early to mid 1990s in an effort to address the need for a unique prescriber identifier for the retail pharmacy industry. However, the Health Insurance Portability and Accountability Act of 1996 (HIPAA) contained a provision for a National Provider Identifier (NPI). Years passed with no NPI. Unfortunately, the need that NCPDP and others had identified in the early to mid 1990s did not diminish, but steadily grew over these years. By early 2001, NCPDP launched the HCIdea™ project. On January 23, 2004, HHS published the Final Rule for the HIPAA NPI in the *Federal Register*.[54]

SPOOL   Simultaneous peripheral operation online. It refers to putting jobs in a buffer, a special area in memory, or on a disk where a device can access them when it is ready. This is similar to a sewing machine spool, which a person puts thread onto, and a machine pulls at its convenience. Spooling is useful because devices access data at different rates. The buffer provides a waiting station where data can reside while the slower device catches up. Material is only added and deleted at the ends of the area; there is no random access or editing. This also allows the CPU to work on other tasks, while waiting for the slower device to do its task.[7]

Spooler   Service that buffers data for low-speed output devices.[1]

Spreadsheet   A spreadsheet is a rectangular table (or grid) of information, often financial information. (It is, therefore, a kind of matrix.) Spreadsheet programs can be used to tabulate many kinds of information, not just financial records; so the term 'spreadsheet' has developed a more general meaning as information (= data = facts) presented in a rectangular table, usually generated by a computer.[7]

Sprite   An element that can be manipulated in an animation. Each different object in an animation is called a sprite.[57]

SQL   **Structured query language.** A syntax used by many database programs to retrieve and modify information (pronounced either *see-kwell* or as separate letters). SQL is a standardized query language for requesting information from a database.[1]

SRAM   **Static random access memory.** A type of memory that is faster and more reliable than the more common dynamic RAM or DRAM. The term *static* is derived from the fact that it does not need to be refreshed like dynamic RAM.[1]

SSH   **Secure shell.** Encrypted remote terminal that provides confidentiality and authentication.[1]

SSL   **Secure socket layer.** Secure method and protocol for managing the secure transfer of data between a web browser and a web server.[1] *See* **Socket, API**.

SSO   **Single sign-on.** A specialized form of software authentication that enables a user to authenticate once and gain access to the resources of multiple software systems.[2]

Stack   Last in, first out (LIFO) data holding structure.[1]

Standard   **1.** A prescribed set of rules, conditions, or requirements established by consensus and approved by a recognized body that provides, for common and repeated use, rules, guidelines, or characteristics for activities or their results, aimed at the achievement of the optimum degree of order in a given context. **2.** A definition or format that has been approved by a recognized standards organization, or is accepted as a de facto standard by the industry. Standards exist for programming languages, operating systems, data formats, communications protocols, and electrical interfaces.[151,7]

Standard development organization   *See* **SDO**.

Standard of care   **1.** The standard of care is the expected level and type of care provided by the average caregiver under a certain given set of circumstances. These circumstances are supported through findings from expert consensus and based on specific research and/or documentation in scientific literature. **2.** In the law of negligence, the degree of care which a reasonable, prudent, or careful person should exercise under the same or similar circumstances. If the standard falls below that established by law for the protection of others against unreasonable risk of harm, the person may be liable for damages resulting from such conduct.[138]

Standard operating procedure   *See* **SOP**.

Standard prescriber identification number   *See* **SPIN**.

Standardization   Activity of establishing, with regard to actual or potential problems, provisions for common and repeated use, aimed at the achievement of the optimum degree of order in a given content.[4]

Standardization of terminology   Official recognition of a terminology by an authoritative body.[4]

Standardized general markup language   *See* **SGML**.

Standardized taxonomy   Use of common standardized definitions, criteria, terminology, and data elements for treatment processes, outcomes, data collection, and electronic transmission, with the goal of saving much time, effort, and misunderstanding in communicating these elements.[1]

Standards body   Body that is recognized at national, regional, or international level that has as a principle function, by virtue of statutes, for the preparation, approval, or adoption of standards that are made generally available.[4]

Standing orders   Physicians' orders pre-established and approved for use by nurses and other professionals under specific conditions, in the absence of a physician.[123]

Star network   Type of LAN topology in which networked nodes are connected to a hub at a central point.[1]

Star schema   A data-modeling technique and relational database management system extension that is optimized for ad hoc, unpredictable, and denormalized data queries. It facilitates simple and speedy access to information by decision support users.[1] *See* **OLTP**.

Start of care   *See* **Admission date**.

Statement of work   *See* **SOW**.

Static audit tool   System scanner that looks for and reports weaknesses.[1]

Static memory   Memory that does not need to be refreshed while power is maintained. Faster than dynamic memory.[1]

Static random access memory   *See* **SRAM**.

Statistical   healthcare   classification Exhaustive set of mutually exclusive categories to support aggregation of data at a pre-prescribed level of specialization for specific healthcare purposes.[126]

Stealth virus   A type of resident virus that attempts to evade detection by concealing its presence in infected files. To achieve this, the virus intercepts system calls, which examine the contents and attributes of infected files.[1]

Steganography   Hiding   information   in innocuous files and documents (e.g., insertion of instructions that modify portions of a program's output to carry information).[1]

Stemming   A process that determines the morphological root of a given inflected (or, sometimes, derived) word form. A stemmer for English, for example, should identify the string 'cats' (and possibly 'catlike,' 'catty,' etc.) as based on the root 'cat,' and 'stemmer,' 'stemming,' and 'stemmed,' as based on 'stem.' Used by search engines and for natural language processing.[7]

Storage   The function of storing records for future retrieval and use.[95]

Storage area network   *See* **SAN**.

Store-and-forward   Transmission of static images or audio-video clips to a remote data storage device, from which they can be retrieved by a medical practitioner for review and consultation at any time, obviating the need for the simultaneous availability of the consult-

ing parties and reducing transmission costs due to low bandwidth requirements.[106]

Storyboard   Originally developed by Disney Studios in the 1930s, storyboards allow action elements to be identified and organized into various sequences to form a story. Storyboards are used to brainstorm and capture all the ideas before taking action. The process of visual thinking and planning allows a group of people to brainstorm together, placing their ideas on storyboards, and then arranging the storyboards on the wall. This fosters more ideas and generates consensus inside the group.[7]

STP   Shielded twisted pair. Type of cabling 1.5 inches in diameter, in which the wire pairs are twisted together in a shielded protective jacket to reduce the effects of electromagnetic interference. Used to implement 10BaseT - 100BaseT networks.[1]

Stream algorithms   Algorithms that encrypt data byte by byte.[1]

Streaming   A technique for delivering data used with audio and video in which the recipient is able to hear or see part of the file before the entire file is delivered. Involves a method for the recipient computer to be able to do a smooth delivery, despite the uneven arrival of data.[11]

Stress testing   A type of performance testing focused on determining an application's robustness, availability, and reliability under extreme conditions. The goal of stress testing is to identify application issues that arise or become apparent only under extreme conditions. These conditions can include heavy loads, high concurrency, or limited computational resources.[12]

Structural role   Role of an individual within an organization.[122]

Structured data   Coded, semantically interoperable data that are based on a reference information model. The consent directive may be captured as a scanned image, which is not semantically interoperable and would preclude the ability of the consent repository to analyze the data for conflicts with previously persisted consent directives.[48]

Structured query language   *See* **SQL**.

Structured vocabulary Relates terms to one another (with a set of relationships) and qualifies them (with a set of attributes) to promote precise and accurate interpretation.[151] *See* **Healthcare terminology**.

Subject field Domain field of special knowledge.[98]

Subject-matter expert *See* **SME**.

Subject of care Person or defined groups of persons receiving, or registered as eligible to receive, healthcare services, or having received healthcare services.[117]

Subject of care identifier A unique number or code issued for the purpose of identifying a subject of (health)care.[95]

Subnet mask 32-bit portion of an IP address that identifies a specific network or host within a subnetwork.[1]

Subportal *See* **SP**.

Subscription services Services that provide capabilities to subscribe to events and manage the alerts and notifications functions when enabled.[8]

Subset Subsets represent groups of components that share specified characteristics that affect the way they are displayed or otherwise accessible within a particular realm, specialty, application, or context.[19]

Substitution A method of cryptography based on the principle of replacing each letter in the message with another one.[1]

Substitution cipher A cipher that replaces the characters of the original plain text. The characters retain their original position, but are altered.[1]

Subtype A specialization of a concept, sharing all the definitional attributes of the parent concept, with additional granularity. For example, bacterial infectious disease is a subtype of infectious disease. Bacterial septicemia, bacteremia, bacterial peritonitis, etc., are subtypes of bacterial infectious disease (and infectious disease as well).[19]

Summary plan description *See* **SPD**.

Sundial A common type of electronic mail used over the Internet.[1]

Super user Individuals identified within the end user groups as advocates for the new system; individuals better able to interact with, teach, and provide peer support for the new system.[6]

Super video graphics array *See* **SVGA**.

Superzapping The unauthorized use of utility computer programs to modify, copy, disclose, destroy, insert, use, or deny use of data stored in a computer or computer media. Type of computer crime.[1]

Surge suppressor A device to protect systems against power spikes.[1]

Surveillance The word 'surveillance' is commonly used to describe observation from a distance by means of electronic equipment or other technological means.[7] *See* **Biosurveillance**.

Surveillance data source Application system or services that provide clinical and demographic data to be used by health surveillance systems.[8]

SVC Switched virtual circuit. A temporary virtual circuit that is set up and used only as long as data are being transmitted. Once the communication between the two hosts is complete, the SVC disappears. In contrast, a permanent virtual circuit (PVC) remains available at all times.[1]

SVGA Super video graphics array. Color display system providing high-resolution graphics of multiple colors at various resolutions.[1]

SWF Scheduled workflow. Establishes the continuity and integrity of basic departmental imaging data acquired in an environment where examinations are generally being ordered. It specifies a number of transactions that maintain the consistency of patient and ordering information, as well as defining the scheduling and imaging acquisition procedure steps. This profile also makes it possible to determine whether images and other evidence objects associated with a particular performed procedure step have been stored (archived), and are available to enable subsequent workflow steps, such as reporting. It may also provide central coordination of the completion of processing and reporting steps.[56] *See* **Profile**. **NOTE: SWF is an Integrating the Healthcare Enterprise (IHE) Profile.**

Switch Within the Open Systems Intercon-nection (OSI) standard, as defined by the Inter-national Organization for Standardization, a switch is a high throughput network communi-cations device that functions within the second layer, or data-link layer, to direct packets of information to specific destinations or network nodes.[1]

Switched virtual circuit *See* **SVC**.

Symbol Designation of a concept by letters, numerals, pictograms, or any combination thereof.[4]

Symmetric digital subscriber line
See **Symmetric DSL/SDSL**.

Symmetric DSL/SDSL **Symmetric digital subscriber line.** A new technology that allows more data to be sent over existing copper tele-phone lines.[1] *See* **DSL**.

Symmetric key algorithms Encryption algorithm in which the same key is used to encrypt and decrypt the message.[1]

Symmetric multiprocessing Multiprocess-ing technique that utilizes all available pro-cessors in a computer to execute the operating system and applications.[1]

Symmetrical multi-processing *See* **SMP**.

Synchronization The convergence of two or more branches into a single subsequent branch, such that the thread of control is passed to the subsequent branch when all input branches have been enabled.[112]

Synchronous optical network *See* **SONET**.

Synchronous transmission High-speed simultaneous transmission of large blocks of data.[1]

Synonym A term which is an acceptable alternative to the preferred term as a way of expressing a concept.[19]

Synonymy Relation between designations representing only one concept in one language.[3]

Syntax **1.** The rules of grammar; an orga-nized set of rules for use. The rules and con-ventions that one needs to know or follow in order to validly record information, or interpret previously recorded information, for a spe-cific purpose. Thus, syntax is grammar. Such

rules and conventions may be either explicit or implicit. In the American National Standards Institute Accredited Standards Committee X12 (ASC X12), the X12 transactions, the data-ele-ment separators, the sub-element separators, the segment terminators, the segment identifiers, the loops, the loop identifiers (when present), the repetition factors, etc., are all aspects of the X12 syntax. When explicit, such syntactical elements tend to be the structural, or format-re-lated; data elements that are not required when a direct data entry architecture is used. **2.** Pertains to the patterns, rules for forming sentences, phrases, or fields from words, abbreviations, codes, and other elements. Syntax is the basic structure of a message format standard.[10,151]

System The combination of hardware and software which processes information for the customer.[4]

System administrator A person who is responsible for managing a multi-user com-puting environment, such a local area network. The responsibilities typically include installing and configuring system hardware and soft-ware, establishing and managing user accounts, upgrading software and backup and recovery tasks.[42] Also known as *sysadmin* or *systems administrator*.

System architecture Describes the sys-tems, capabilities, and information exchanges to support the business requirements and processes.[20]

System analysis The process of determin-ing how a set of interconnected components whose individual characteristics are known will behave in response to a given input of set of inputs. Closely related to requirements analysis and operations research.[35]

System audit A systematic investigation of the effectiveness of an information resource in meeting its original goals.[6]

System design A specification of human factors, and hardware and software require-ments, for an information system.[6]

System design lifecycle *See* **SDLC**.

System developmental lifecycle A struc-tured and systematic process for the devel-opment and installation of an information system composed of the following phases: analysis, design, development, implementation, and evaluation.[6]

System integration **1.** The composition of a capability by assembling elements in a way that allows them to work together to achieve an intended purpose. **2.** The process of creating a complex information system that may include designing or building a customized architecture or application, integrating it with new or existing hardware, packaged and custom software, and communications.[169,47] *See* **EAI.**

System integrator A firm that delivers the various services of systems integration.[1]

System network architecture *See* **SNA.**

System network management protocol *See* **SNMP.**

System security The result of all safeguards, including hardware, software, personnel policies, information practice policies, disaster preparedness, and oversight of these components.[1]

System security administrator The person who controls access to computer systems by entering commands to perform such functions, such as assigning user access codes and privileges, revoking user access privileges, and setting file protection parameters.[1]

System testing A multi-faceted testing event that evaluates the functionality, performance, and fit of the whole application. System testing encompasses usability, final requirements, volume and stress, security and controls, recovery, documentation and procedures, and multi-site testing.[6]

Systematized Nomenclature of Medicine Clinical Terms *See* **SNOMED CT.**

T

Table Database object with a unique name, and structured in columns and rows.[1]

Tablet A computing device that typically weighs less than four pounds and is operated by direct screen contact via a pen or touch interface.[47]

TAG Technical advisory group. A group of topic experts working in a particular area and building consensus among the group for specific positions. Used mainly in consensus standards work.[3,48]

Tag image file format *See* **TIFF.**

Tags Information within a web page contained between angle brackets (<>) which indicate document elements, structure, formatting, and hyperlinks. HTML tags are generally used to surround the text that they affect.[1]

Tampering Unauthorized modification that alters the proper functioning of a smartcard.[1]

Task A logical unit of work that is carried out as a whole. Tasks can be executed based on sequential, parallel, or conditional routing.[111]

Task manager Provides information on CPU usage, memory usage, and physical memory statistics.[1]

Taxonomy A method of classifying a vocabulary of terms for a specific topic according to specific laws and principles.[6]

TC Technical committee. A term, often used by consensus standards organizations, including Health Level Seven (HL7), European Committee for Standardization (CEN), and International Organization for Standardization (ISO) to describe a formal group of subject matter experts who work together in a committee structure to solve problems.[3,48]

T-Carrier High-speed, point-to-point, full duplex communications line identified in different levels: T-1, T-2, T-3, and T-4.[1]

TCO Total cost of ownership. A document that describes the cost of a project or initiative that usually includes hardware, software, development, and ongoing expenses.[15]

TCP Transmission control protocol. Connection-oriented data transmission mode portion of TCP/IP.[1]

TCP/IP Transmission control protocol/Internet protocol. 1. Routable protocol required for Internet accesses. TCP portion is associated with data. IP is associated with source to destination packet delivery. **2.** A set of communication protocols encompassing media access, packet transport, session communications, file transfer, electronic mail, and terminal emulation. It is supported by a large number of hardware and software vendors and is the basis for Internet transactions.[1,2]

TDR Time-domain reflectometer. Testing device that sends sound waves along cabling to detect shorts or breaks in the cable.[1]

Technical advisory group *See* **TAG**.

Technical architecture Describes the minimal set of rules governing the arrangement, interaction, and interdependence of system parts or elements.[20]

Technical committee *See* **TC**.

Technical framework The document that defines integration profiles, the problems and use cases they address, and the actors and transactions involved. It provides detailed implementation instructions for each transaction.[56]

Technical report A collection of informative data on a particular topic. Examples are survey data, implementation guide, a literature review of a specific topic, an overview of a technical product or service.[3]

Technical safeguards Policies and procedures to protect electronic health information and control access.[48]

Technical specification A second level International Organization for Standards (ISO) deliverable. Contains both normative and informative knowledge.[3]

Technical specification A technical description of the desired behavior of a system, as derived from its requirements. A specification is used to develop and test an implementation of a system.[1]

Telecommunications The use of wire, radio, optical, or other electromagnetic channels to transmit or receive signals for voice, data, and video communications.[106]

TELecommunications NETwork
See **TELNET**.

Teleconsultation Geographic separation between two or more providers during a consultation.[106]

Telediagnosis The detection of a disease by evaluating data transmitted to a receiving station from instruments monitoring a distant patient.[106]

Telehealth Using communication networks to provide health services, including, but not limited to, direct care, health prevention, consulting, and home visits to patients in a geographical location different than the provider of these services. Any delivery of health services to a client in a geographical location different than that of the provider.[11]

Telematics The use of computer-based information processing in telecommunications, and the use of telecommunications to allow computers to transfer programs and data to one another.[106]

Telemedicine 1. Part of telehealth that is defined as a health professional in one location, using electronic technologies for the diagnosis and/or treatment of a patient in another location. **2.** The transfer of information via telecommunication technologies and specifically designed devices for the purpose of consulting or for remote medical procedures or examinations.[11,2]

Telementoring The use of audio, video, and other telecommunications and electronic information processing technologies to provide individual guidance or instruction (e.g., involving a consultant guiding a distant clinician in a new medical procedure).[106]

Telemonitoring The use of audio, video, and other telecommunications and electronic information processing technologies to monitor patient status at a distance.[106]

Telenursing Practice of nursing over distance using telecommunications technology.[11]

Telepresence The use of robotic and other devices that allow a person (e.g., a surgeon) to perform a task at a remote site by manipulating instruments (e.g., lasers or dental hand pieces) and receiving sensory information or feedback (e.g., pressure akin to that created by touching a patient) that creates a sense of being present at the remote site, and allows a satisfactory degree of technical performance (e.g., dexterity).[106]

TELNET TELecommunications NETwork. Protocol for remote terminal service connectivity. Connectivity from one site to interact with a remote system. A method of logging one computer onto another. A program that allows users to remotely use computers across networks.[1]

Temporal key integrity protocol *See* **TKIP**.

Terabyte Approximately one trillion bytes; unit of computer storage capacity.[1]

Term **1.** Verbal designation of a concept in a specific subject field. **2.** The word or phrase in a particular language used to represent a concept (e.g., the concept *doctor* is represented in English by the term 'doctor' or 'physician,' and in Italian by the term '*il medico*').[98,4]

Terminal Any computer display or workstation that connects with limited capabilities to a network.[42] *See* **Workstation**.

Terminal printing suppression Suppressing the printing of passwords or other access control information.[1]

Terminal server Network communications device that allows one or more serial devices to connect to an Ethernet LAN. Used extensively throughout CHCS with the LAT protocol.[1]

Terminology A system of words used to name things in a particular discipline.[32]

Terminology identifier Unique permanent identifier of a healthcare terminology for use in information interchange.[98]

Test log A thorough record of testing, results, and follow-up.[6]

Test objectives Descriptions of what a specific testing event seeks to validate. The objectives state each feature of function to be tested and described, at a high level, the expected results.[6]

TFTP **Trivial file transfer protocol.** Minimal overhead file transfer used to upload or download bootstrap files to diskless workstations through the use of UDP.[1]

Thesaurus The vocabulary of a controlled indexing language, formally organized so that the *a priori* relationships between concepts (e.g., broader and narrower) are made explicit.[3]

Thin client/dumb terminal A computer or computer program that depends heavily on some other computer (such as an application or network server) to fulfill its traditional computational roles. A thin client is used to access data; does not process data.[2]

Third party Party, other than data originator or data recipient, required to perform a security function as part of a communication protocol.[121]

Third-party administrator *See* **TPA**.

Third-party vendor *See* **TPV**.

Thread A collection of any number of online posts defined by a title. A thread is a component of an Internet forum.[7]

Threat **1.** Any circumstance or event with the potential to cause harm to an IT system in the form of destruction, disclosure, adverse modification of data, and/or denial of service. **2.** Exploitation or compromise of a security of systems or networks.[97,48]

Threshold A level of achievement that determines the difference between what is deemed to be acceptable quality or not.[123]

Thunking Translation that takes place from 32- to 16-bit code.[1]

TIFF **Tag image file format.** A common format for exchanging raster graphics (bitmap) images between application programs, including those used for scanner images.[57]

Tightly coupled Tightly coupled application roles assume that common information about the subject classes participating in a message is available to system components outside of the specific message.[8]

Time bomb A subclass of logic bombs that explode at a certain event, such as a certain date. Can be used to damage disk directories on a certain date.[1]

Time to live *See* **TTL**.

Time-domain reflectometer *See* **TDR**.

TKIP **Temporal key integrity protocol.** Security protocol used in the IEEE 802.11 wireless networking standard.[2]

TLAlgia Term composed of 'TLA' for three-letter acronym and '-algia' meaning 'pain'; thus, pain induced by excessive use of three-letter acronyms.[99]

tn3270 The tn3270 program is a TELNET program used to connect to an IBM mainframe and emulate a 3270 terminal, which is dumb terminal.[1] *See* **TELNET**.

Token 1. A physical authentication device that the user carries (e.g., smartcard, SecureID™). Often combined with a PIN to provide a two-factor authentication method that is generally thought of as superior to simple password authentication. **2.** Packet used for LAN access in a token-based network. The node that possesses the token controls the transmission medium, and is allowed to transmit on the network.[45,1]

Token-bus network Type of LAN topology in which networked nodes are connected to the main cable of the network and uses a token for transmission access.[1]

Token-ring network Type of proprietary LAN topology in which network nodes are connected at points to form a ring in which data packets travel. Uses a token for transmission access.[2]

Top-level concept A concept that is directly related to the root concept by a single relationship of the relationship type 'ISA.' All other concepts are descended from one top-level concept via at least one series of relationships of the relationship type 'ISA' (i.e., all other concepts are subtypes of one top-level concept).[19]

Topology Physical layout or architecture of a network. Bus, star, ring, and hybrid are network topologies.[1]

Total cost of ownership *See* **TCO**.

Total quality management *See* **TQM**.

Touch screen Input technology that permits the entering or selecting of commands and data by touching the surface of a sensitized video display monitor with a finger or pointer.[1]

TPA Third-party administrator. A company that provides claim processing and administrative services for hospital or physicians groups.[15]

TPV Third-party vendor. A company designated to support specific services for healthcare.[15]

TQM Total quality management. An approach to quality assurance that emphasizes to all members of a production unit of the needs and desires of the ultimate service recipients in

the chain of service, and acknowledges how to use specific data-related techniques to assess and improve the quality of their own and the team's outputs.[123]

Traceroute A command causing the utility to initiate the sending of a packet, including in the packet a time limit that is designed to be exceeded by the first router that receives it, which will return a 'time exceeded' message.[1]

Trading partner agreement Related to the exchange of information in electronic transactions, specifically the communications protocols and transaction standards to be used.[48]

Train the trainer A core group of individuals are trained and then used to train other individuals who will be using the system. This is a common strategy when there are hundreds of users to be trained in a matter of weeks.[6]

Transaction 1. The exchange of information between two parties to carry out clinical, financial, and administrative activities related to healthcare. **2.** An exchange of information between actors. For each transaction, the technical framework describes how to use an established standard, such as HL7, DICOM, or W3C.[10,56]

Transaction standard A standard specifying the format of messages being sent from or received by a system, rather than for how the information is stored in the system.[10]

Transactional data The movement or exchange of data that completes a single interaction.[159]

Transition plan A strategy/map to guide the adoption of systems or technologies. A written plan for a transition from the current organization structure to a design that will minimize disruption, adverse impacts, capitalization, and startup requirements.[150]

Transitions of care *See* **Care transitions**.

Transmission The exchange of data between person and program, or program and program, when the sender and receiver are remote from each other.[1]

Transmission confidentiality Process to ensure that information in transit is not disclosed to unauthorized individuals, entities, or processes.[48]

Transmission control protocol *See* **TCP**.

Transmission control protocol/Internet protocol *See* **TCP/IP**.

Transmission integrity Process to guard against improper information modification or destruction while in transit.[48]

Transparent background Transparent GIF images can have one color designed to be transparent. Since all graphic images are stored as either square or rectangular shapes, even the background color will show up on a web page.[1] *See* **GIF**.

Transport layer Fourth layer of the OSI model. Handles the interface between hardware levels and software levels. Provides for end-to-end flow control and ensures that messages are delivered error-free.[1]

Transposition A method of cryptography based on the principle of scrambling the characters that are in the message.[1]

Transposition cipher A cipher in cryptography that rearranges the characters of the original plain message. Thus, the characters are unchanged but their position is altered, making the text unintelligible.[1]

Trap doors Hardware features, software limitations, or specially planted entry points that can provide an unauthorized source with access to the system.[1] *See* **Back door**.

Treatment The total bundle of services rendered to a patient to cope with a specific problem.[4]

Treatment protocols Precise and detailed plans for the study of a medical or biomedical problem and/or plans for a regimen of therapy.[5]

Trial implementation supplement A specification candidate for addition to an IHE Domain Technical Framework (e.g., a new profile) that is issued for early implementation by any interested party. The authoring technical committee expects developers' feedback.[93]

Trigger event An event, such as the reception of a message or completion of a process, which causes another action to occur.[56]

Trivial file transfer protocol *See* **TFTP**.

Trojan horse A program that appears to have one ubiquitous function, but actually has a hidden malicious function. A program that performs a desired task, but also includes unexpected and usually undesirable functions. Does not replicate.[1]

Trunk Single circuit between two switching center points. Handles many channels simultaneously.[1]

Trust Windows NT domain association with another Windows NT domain, where the domains trust each other with resources.[1]

Trust-based security Security management and access provision based on trusted domains or facilities.[8]

Trusted system A system delivered to enforce a given set of attributes to a stated degree of assurance or confidence.[1]

Trusted third party *See* **TTP**.

Trusted user access level A system user who needs access to sensitive information.[1]

TTL **Time to live.** Length of active Internet time technique used to avoid endless loop packets. Every packet is assigned a decrementing TTL. Packets with expired TTLs are discarded by routers.[1]

TTP **Trusted third party.** Third party that is considered trusted for purposes of a security protocol. (ENV 13608-1). **Note:** This term is used in many ISO/IEC International Standards and other documents describing mainly the services of a certification authority (CA). The concept is, however, broader and includes services such as time-stamping and possibly escrowing.[121]

Tunneling *See* **Virtual private network**.[8]

Turnkey portal Refers to a web application that provides access to various applications or content within a healthcare organization, or to its consumers, that has been developed by a vendor to facilitate easier implementation and support of the environment. The turnkey portal can have applications to support physicians and clinicians, patients/consumers, employers, etc. It can be used by internal employees (clinicians, executives, business and marketing professionals), or external customers (patients/consumers, employers, payers, etc.).[7]

Tutorial A type of computer assisted learning (CAL) providing information that the learner interacts with by answering questions. Responses provided by the learner may generate additional tutoring, or allow the learner to advance in the program.[6]

Twisted-pair cable Cable consisting of copper core wires surrounded by an insulator. A pair, consisting of two wires twisted together, forms a circuit that can transmit data. The twisting helps to prevent interference.[1]

U

UART Universal asynchronous receiver transmitter. The microchip with programming that controls a computer's interface to its attached serial devices.[42]

Ubiquitous computing Ubiquitous computing (ubicomp, or sometimes ubiqcomp) integrates computation into the environment, rather than having computers, which are distinct objects. Another term for ubiquitous computing is 'pervasive computing.' Promoters of this idea hope that embedding computation into the environment will enable people to move around and interact with computers more naturally than they currently do. One of the goals of ubiquitous computing is to enable devices to sense changes in their environment and to automatically adapt and act based on these changes, based on user needs and preferences. Some simple examples of this type of behavior include GPS-equipped automobiles that give interactive driving directions and RFID store checkout systems.[7]

UCC Uniform Code Council. In 2005, the organization changed its name to GS1. An administrative and educational organization whose mission is to promote multi-industry standards for product identification and related electronic communications. The Universal Product Code (UPC) is a bar code symbol used by companies in North America to uniquely identify themselves and their products worldwide.[7]

UDDI Universal description, discover, and integration. An XML-based registry for businesses worldwide to list themselves on the Internet. Its ultimate goal is to streamline online transactions by enabling companies to find one another on the web and make their systems interoperable for eCommerce. UDDI is often compared to a telephone book's White, Yellow, and Green pages. The project allows businesses to list themselves by name, product, location, or the web services they offer.[8]

UDI Unique device identifier. A method of knowing a specific object apart from other objects like itself.[109]

UDK User-defined keys. Used to store frequently used commands through the F6 to F20 keys on a video terminal keyboard.[1]

UDP User datagram protocol. A connectionless protocol that resides at the same level on the OSI model as TCP. Since it is connectionless, there is no handshaking or authentication.[1]

UI User interface. 1. The part of the application that allows the user to access the application and manipulate its functionality. It can include menus, forms, command buttons, etc. **2.** The part of the information system through which the end user interacts with the system; type of hardware and the series of on-screen commands and responses required for a user to work with the system.[107,1]

UM Utilization management. The evaluation of the necessity, appropriateness, and efficiency of the use of healthcare services, procedures, and facilities.[15]

UMDNS Universal medical device nomenclature system. The purpose of UMDNS is to facilitate identifying, processing, filing, storing, retrieving, transferring, and communicating data about medical devices. The nomenclature is used in applications ranging from hospital inventory and work order controls to national agency medical device regulatory systems, and from eCommerce and procurement to medical device databases.[55]

UML Unified Modeling Language. A language for specifying, visualizing, constructing and documenting the artifacts of software systems. UML is a standard notation for the modeling of real-world objects.[47]

UMLS The Unified Medical Language System. A large project sponsored by the United States National Library of Medicine (NLM) to produce a unified thesaurus and cross reference linking various medical nomenclatures, including the MeSH headings, ICD-9-CM, SNOMED, and the Terminology of DXPlain and QMR.[4]

UMS Unified messaging system. The handling of voice, fax, and regular text messages as objects in a single mailbox that a user can access either with a regular e-mail client, or by telephone.[1]

UNC Universal naming convention. Text-based method to identify the path to a remote device, server, directory, or file. Implemented as: \\computername\sharename\directoryname\filename.[1]

Underuse Refers to the failure to provide a healthcare service when it would have produced a favorable outcome for a patient. Standard examples include failures to provide appropriate preventive services to eligible patients (e.g., Pap smears, flu shots for elderly patients, screening for hypertension) and proven medications for chronic illnesses (e.g., steroid inhalers for asthmatics, aspirin, beta-blockers, and lipid-lowering agents for patients who have suffered a recent myocardial infarction).[14]

Undirected information Information that is broadcast without regard to who reads it. Usenet and mailing lists are undirected.[1]

Unfreezing Requires information which discontinues the current behaviors or attitudes. It also requires some sense that change can be safely made.[6]

Unicode A standard character set that represents most of the characters used in the world using a 16-bit encoding. Unicode can be encoded in using UTF-8 (USC Transformation Format) to more efficiently store the most common ASCII characters.[19]

Unified messaging system See **UMS**.

Unified modeling language See **UML**.

Uniform Code Council See **UCC**.

Uniform data standards Methods, protocols, or terminologies agreed to by an industry to allow disparate information systems to operate successfully with one another.[151]

Uniform resource locator See **URL**.

Uninterruptible power supply See **UPS**.

Unique device identifier See **UDI**.

Unique health plan identifier See **HPID**.

Unique identifier See **NPI**.

Unit testing A document that guides a tester through a testing event and ensures consistency among separate executions of the testing event.[6]

Universal asynchronous receiver transmitter See **UART**.

Universal identifier A means to provide positive recognition of a particular individual for all people in a population. A universal healthcare or patient identifier provides the identifier for use in healthcare transactions.[1]

Universal medical device nomenclature system See **UMDNS**.

Universal naming convention See **UNC**.

Universal product code See **UPC**.

Universal product number See **UPN**.

Universal resource locator See **URL**.

Universal serial bus See **USB**.

UNIX Operating system for microcomputers, minicomputers, and mainframes that is machine-independent and supports multi-user processing, multi-tasking, and networking. UNIX was developed at AT&T's Bell Laboratories in 1969.[1]

UPC Universal product code. A unique 12-digit number assigned to retail merchandise that identifies both the product and the vendor that sells the product. The UPC on a product typically appears adjacent to its bar code, the machine-readable representation of the UPC. The first six digits of the UPC are the vendor's unique identification number. All of the products that one vendor sells will have the same first six digits in their UPCs. The next five digits are the product's unique reference number that identifies the product within any one vendor's line of products. The last number is called the check digit that is used to verify that the UPC for that specific product is correct.[58]

UPI **Unique patient identifier. 1.** The identity of an individual consists of a set of personal characters by which that individual can be recognized. Identification is the proof of one's identity. Identifier verifies the sameness of one's identity. Patient identifier is the value assigned to an individual to facilitate positive identification of that individual for healthcare purposes. Unique patient identifier is the value permanently assigned to an individual for identification purposes and is unique across the entire national healthcare system. Unique patient identifier is not shared with any other individual. **2.** A form of identification and access control that identifies humans by their characteristics or traits. Biometric identifiers (or biometric authentication) are the distinctive, measurable characteristics used to label and describe individuals. Two categories of biometric identifiers include physiological and behavioral characteristics.[1,7]

Upload To send a file to another machine.[1]

UPN **Universal product number.** *See* **UPC.**

UPS **Uninterruptible power supply.** Device that keeps a computer running by protecting against power outages and power sags by maintaining constant power via battery. Provides the opportunity for a graceful shutdown in a commercial power-out condition.[1]

UR **Utilization review.** An organized procedure carried out through committees to review admissions, duration of stay, professional services furnished, and to evaluate the medical necessity of those services and promote their most efficient use.[5]

URI **Uniform resource identifiers.** Provides a simple and extensible means for identifying a resource. A URI can be further classified as a locator, a name, or both.[8]

URL **Uniform resource locator.** Provides the unique location information by using a naming convention of protocol type, followed by a specific service.[1]

URL **Universal resource locator.** A standardized address name layout for resources, such as documents or images, on the Internet or elsewhere.[7]

Usability Quality attributed to an application system that describes its effectiveness and ease of use as determined by its users.[8]

Usability testing A testing event that determines how well the user will be able to use and understand the application.[6]

USB **Universal serial bus. 1.** A plug-and-play interface between a computer and add-on devices, such as media players, keyboards, etc. **2.** A commercial desktop standard input/output (I/O) bus that provides a single peripheral connection and vastly increases bus speed. It simplifies peripheral connections via a 'daisy chaining' scheme whereby the desktop system has only one I/O port to which all peripherals are connected in a series. Up to 120 peripherals can be connected to a single system.[42,47]

Use Sharing, employment, application, utilization, examination, or analysis of information within the entity that maintains such information.[48]

Use case Describes a set of activities of a system from the point of view of its actors, which lead to a perceptible outcome for the actors. A use case is always initiated by an actor. In all other respects, a use case is a complete, indivisible description.[8]

User A person, device, program, or computer system that uses a system for the purpose of data processing and information exchange.[8]

User access A person or a group/organization in need of data for legitimate service function, teaching, or research, authorized to have access.[1]

User authentication **1.** The provision of assurance of the claimed identity of an individual or entity. **2.** A means of identifying the user and verifying that the user is allowed access a restricted service.[1,2]

User datagram protocol *See* **UDP.**

User-defined keys *See* **UDK.**

User ID The string of characters that identifies a computer/system user. The user name by which the user is known to the network.[1] Also known as *username*.

User interface *See* **UI.**

User profile A description of a user, typically used for access control. A user profile may include data such as user ID, user name, password, access rights, and other attributes. It is a pattern of a user's activity that can be used to detect changes in the activity.[3]

User-friendly Characteristics of a computer-human interface which contribute to its acceptance by users.[7]

USHIK United States Health Information Knowledgebase. A metadata registry of healthcare-related data elements from Standard Development Organizations supported by the Agency for Healthcare Research and Quality (AHRQ).[173]

Utility program System software consisting of programs for routine, repetitive tasks, which can be shared by many users.[1]

Utilization management *See* **UM**.

Utilization review *See* **UR**.

UTP Type of cabling in which the insulated wire conductors are twisted together in an unshielded voice-grade cable. Used to implement 10BaseT and 100BaseT networks.[1]

V

Validation Determination of the correct implementation in the completed IT system, with the security requirements and approach agreed-upon by the users and the acquisition authority.[97]

Validity The extent to which data correspond to the actual state of affairs, or an instrument that measures what it purports to measure.[1]

Value stream The specific activities within a supply chain required to design, order and provide a specific product or service.[47]

Value stream map Visual representation of a value stream.[47]

Value-added network *See* **VAN**.

VAN Value-added network. A vendor of electronic data interchange (EDI) data communications and translation services.[10]

Vanilla An adjective meaning plain or basic. The unfeatured version of a product.[42]

Vaporware Software that does not currently exist, but may be introduced sometime in the future.[1]

Variance analysis Data collection and aggregation techniques that are used to determine difference in care, outcomes, performance, budgets, and systems.[6]

Variant virus A type of virus generated by modifying a known virus. These modifications may add functionality, or ways to evade detection.[1]

Variation Differences in the output of a process resulting from the influences of people, equipment, materials, and /or methods.[123]

VAX Virtual address extension. An established line of mid-range server computers from the Digital Equipment Corporation (DEC, now a part of Hewlett-Packard).[1] *See* **VMS**.

Vendor A company/consortium that provides products and/or services.[8]

Verification Confirmation, through the provision of objective evidence, that specified requirements have been fulfilled.[68]

Veronica A title search and retrieval system for use with the Internet Gopher.[147]

Veterans Health Information Systems Technology Architecture *See* **VistA**.

VGA Video graphics array. Color display system providing high-resolution graphics displays of 16 colors at a 640x480 resolution, and 256 colors at a 320x200 resolution.[1]

Video graphics array *See* **VGA**.

Video RAM or video random access memory *See* **VRAM**.

Virtual address extension *See* **VAX**.

Virtual card The data elements contained in the data indices without regard for physical addresses.[1]

Virtual community A virtual community is a community of people sharing common interests, ideas, and feelings over the Internet of collaborative networks.[7]

Virtual machine *See* **VM**.

Virtual private network *See* **VPN**.

Virtual reality An emerging technology that attempts to fully immerse the user in an interactive computer-generated environment. The participant, in a virtual reality experience, interacts with the system via a series of sensors and sophisticated output devices.[1]

Virtual reality modeling language
See **VRML**.

Virtualization The abstraction of IT resources that masks the physical nature and boundaries of those resources from resource users. IT resources can be a server, client, storage, network, application, or operating system.[47]

Virtualization software The creation of a virtual (rather than actual) version of a hardware platform, operating system (OS), storage device, or network resources.[7]

Virus **1.** A type of programmed threat—a code fragment (not an independent program) that reproduces by attaching to another program. It may damage data directly, or it may degrade system performance by taking over system resources, which are then not available to authorized users. **2.** Code embedded within a program that causes a copy of itself to be inserted in one or more other programs; in addition to propagation, the virus usually performs some unwanted function.[118]

Virus scanner **1.** A computer program (anti-virus software) that detects a virus computer program or other kind of malware (e.g., worms and Trojans), warns of its presence, and attempts to prevent it from affecting the protected computer. Malware often results in undesired side effects generally unanticipated by the user. **2.** Software used to prevent, detect, and remove malware, including, but not limited to computer viruses, computer worms, Trojan horses, spyware, and adware.[45,2]

Visit **1.** An episode of care at a healthcare facility. **2.** A visit to an individual care provider ('encounter').[8]

VistA **Veterans Health Information Systems Technology Architecture.** An enterprise-wide system built around an electronic health record and used throughout the Veterans

Health Administration's 163 hospitals, 800+ clinics, and 135 nursing homes. Commonly considered to be one of the largest and most effective health IT systems in use today. Developed as the decentralized hospital computer system (DHCP), the name change to VistA signified deeper clinical content and increased GUI-zation.[99]

VISTA Microsoft's name for the 2007 version of its Windows operating system. Succeeded by Windows 7.[12]

VM **Virtual machine.** Completely isolated guest operating system installation within a normal host operating system.[7]

Vocabulary A set of terms used for a particular purpose.[4]

Voice over Internet protocol *See* **VoIP**.

Voice recognition A software program that converts the voice audio analog to a digital signal for dictation. For a computer to decipher the signal, it must have a digital database, or vocabulary, of words or syllables, and a speedy means of comparing this data with signals.[1]

Voice response system A unit that allows a customer to call in by telephone and give instructions to a computer by speaking or by pressing digits on the phone.[1]

Voice response unit *See* **VRU**.

VoIP **Voice over Internet protocol. 1.** A technology that allows telephone calls using a broadband Internet connection instead of a regular (or analog) phone line. Some services using VoIP may only allow you to call other people using the same service, but others may allow you to call anyone who has a telephone number—including local, long distance, mobile, and international numbers. Also, while some services work only over your computer or a special VoIP phone, other services allow you to use a traditional phone through an adaptor. **2.** Refers to the use of the Internet protocol (IP) to transfer voice communications in much the same way that web pages and e-mail are transferred. Each piece of voice data is digitized in to chunks and then sent across the Internet (in the case of public VoIP) to a destination server where the chunks are re-assembled. This process happens in real-time so that two or more people can carry on a conversation.[2,168]

Volume and stress testing A testing event that determines the ability of the application to function under maximum volumes of data and peak loads.[6]

VPN Virtual private network. **1.** Refers to a network in which some of the parts are connected using the public Internet, but the data sent across the Internet are encrypted, so the entire network is 'virtually' private. Secure and encrypted connection between two points across the Internet. **2.** VPNs transfer information by encrypting and encapsulating traffic in IP packets and sending the packets over the Internet. That practice is called 'tunneling.' Most VPNs are built and run by Internet service providers, and secure protocols like Point-to-Point Tunneling Protocol (PPTP) to ensure that data transmissions are not intercepted by unauthorized parties.[8] *See* **Tunneling**.

VRAM Video RAM or video random access memory. Refers to all forms of random access memory used to store image data for a computer display. VRAM is a type of buffer between the computer and the display.[1]

VRML Virtual reality modeling language. A standard for describing interactive 3-dimensional scenes delivered across the Internet.[1]

VRU Voice response unit. Same as interactive voice response (IVR).

Vulnerability A weakness in a system that can be exploited to violate the system's intended behavior. There may be security, integrity, availability, and other vulnerabilities.[1]

Vulnerability assessment 1. Systematic examination of an information system or product to determine the adequacy of security measures, identify security deficiencies, provide data from which to predict the effectiveness of proposed security measures, and confirm the adequacy of such measures after implementation. **2.** The process of identifying and quantifying vulnerabilities.[97,175]

Vulnerable user access level System users who need access to information only within their job responsibility.[1]

W

WAIS Wide-area information server. WAIS is best at searches for various sources of academic information that have been indexed based on content. Its indices consist of every word in a document, and each word carries the same weight in a search.[1]

Wall paper A graphical pattern displayed on the desktop computer.[1]

WAN Wide area network. A collection of long-distance telecommunication links and networks used to connect local area networks and end stations across regional, national, or international distances.[2] *See* **LAN, MAN, WLAN**.

WAP Wireless application protocol. A specification for a set of communication protocols to standardize the way that wireless devices, such as cellular telephones and radio transceivers, can be used for Internet access, including e-mail, the World Wide Web, newsgroups, and Internet Relay Chat.[1]

WASP Wireless application service provider. A part of a growing industry sector resulting from the convergence of two trends: wireless communications and the outsourcing of services.[1]

WAV or WAVE Waveform audio format (.wav). A proprietary format sponsored by Microsoft and IBM, the Resource Interchange File Format Waveform Audio Format (.wav) was introduced in MS Windows Version 3.1 and is most commonly used on Windows-based PCs.[1]

Waveform audio format (.wav) *See* **WAV** or **WAVE**.

Wavelet A software compression algorithm, such as that used with radiological studies.[1]

Web address An IP number or uniform resource locator (URL); a string of characters that represents the location or address of a resource on the Internet, and how that resource should be accessed.[1]

Web crawler A program that browses the web in a methodical, automated manner. Web crawlers are mainly used to create a copy of all the visited pages for later processing by a search engine, which will index the downloaded pages to provide fast searches.[7]

Web master A person who maintains and administers a web server; also a standard e-mail address at most web hosts where comments and questions can be sent to reach the responsible web engineer.[1]

Web page A document created with hypertext markup language (HTML) that is part of a group of hypertext documents or resources available on the Internet.[1] *See* **HTML, WWW**.

Web portal A web portal is a web site that provides a starting point, a gateway, or portal, to other resources on the Internet or an intranet.[7]

Web security A set of procedures, practices, and technologies for protecting web servers, web users, and their surrounding organizations.[1]

Web server **1.** More often refers to software than the physical hardware. A web server is a program that uses the client/server model and the WWW HTTP to serve the files that form web pages to web users (whose computers contain hypertext transfer protocol [HTTP] clients that forward their requests). **2.** Every computer on the Internet that contains a web site must have a web server program. References may be made to hardware, or the dedicated computers on which server software resides.[1] *See* **HTTP, S-HTTP**.

Web services description language *See* **WSDL**.

Web stack The collection of software required for web development. At a minimum, a web stack contains an operating system (OS), a programming language, database software and a web server.[42]

WEP **Wired equivalent privacy.** A security protocol, specified in the IEEE Wireless Fidelity (Wi-Fi) standard, 802.11b, that is designed to provide a wireless local area network (WLAN) with a level of security and privacy comparable to what is usually expected of a wired LAN.[2]

Wet signature Ink on paper signature.[56]

WG **Work group.** A collection of individuals working together on a task. Workgroup computing occurs when all the individuals have computers connected to a network that allows them to send e-mail to one another, share data files, and schedule meetings. Sophisticated workgroup systems allow users to define workflows

so that data are automatically forwarded to appropriate people at each stage of a process.[58]

What you see is what you get *See* **WYSIWYG**.

White board Display in which multiple computer users in different geographical locations can write or draw while others watch. They are often used in teleconferencing.[11]

Whois Search provides domain name registration information by domain names, IP addresses, and/or network information center handle.[147]

Wide area network *See* **WAN**.

Wide SCSI **Wide small computer system interface.** 20-40 Mbps high-speed interface for connecting devices to the computer bus.[1]

Wide small computer system interface *See* **Wide SCSI**.

Wide-area information server *See* **WAIS**.

Wi-Fi **Wireless fidelity.** Wireless network components that are based on one of the Wi-Fi Alliance's 802.11 standards. The Wi-Fi Alliance created the 802.11 standards so that manufacturers can make wireless products that work with other manufacturers' equipment.[2]

Wi-Fi protected access *See* **WPA**.

Wiki Piece of server software that allows users to freely create and edit web page content using any web browser.[32]

Wildcard Used when searching for files, a wildcard is a character (usually * or ?) that can stand for one or more unknown characters during a search, and cause the search results to yield all files within a general description or type of software.[1]

Window An object on the screen that presents information, such as a document or message.[12]

Wired equivalent privacy *See* **WEP**.

Wireless application protocol *See* **WAP**.

Wireless application service provider *See* **WASP**.

Wireless e-mail device A hand-held wireless device providing e-mail, telephone, text messaging, web browsing, and other wireless data access.[36]

Wireless fidelity *See* **Wi-Fi**.

Wireless local area network *See* **WLAN**.

Wireless technology Recent radio frequency architecture that transmits signals from remote, lightweight workstations to the wireless local area network (LAN) in such a way that health-related work processes can be re-engineered toward greater mobility with an improved focus on the patient, such as bedside patient registration.[1] *See* **LAN, MAN, WAN**.

WLAN **Wireless local area network.** A communication system that transmits and receives data using wireless technology and implemented as an extension to or as an alternative for a hard-wired LAN.[2]

Workflow **1.** A process description of how tasks are done, by whom, in what order, and how quickly. Workflow can be used in the context of electronic systems or people (i.e., an electronic workflow system can help automate a physician's personal workflow). **2.** A graphic representation of the flow of work in a process and its related subprocesses, including specific activities, information dependencies, and the sequence of decisions and activities.[2,1]

Workflow management An approach that allows for the definition and control of business processes that span applications.[47]

Workflow services The workflow service is responsible for maintaining lists of active components and the workflow schedules/process. It assembles the components and uses an executable engine to execute the workflow.[8]

Work group *See* **WG**.

Workstation Node, terminal, or computer, attached to a network that runs local applications, or connects to servers to access shared server resources. Usually a microcomputer.[1] *See* **Terminal**.

Workstation on wheels *See* **WOW**.

World Wide Web *See* **WWW**.

World Wide Web Consortium (W3C) An international organization that develops programming and interoperability standards for the web. Among its many projects, W3C is involved in initiatives for digital signatures, XML, and Dynamic Hypertext Mark-up Language (DHTML).[7]

WORM **Write once, read many times.** Process used for applications where permanent data storage is required.[1]

Worm A self-replicating program that hides its existence and spreads copies of itself within a computer system or through networks. Worms do not integrate their code into host programs.[1]

WOW **Workstation on wheels.** Carts with mounted computer monitors (typically laptops or other computer systems) that connect to a network in a wireless manner and are wheeled so easily moved from room to room.[2]

WPA **Wi-Fi protected access.** A security standard for users of computers equipped with Wi-Fi wireless connection. It is an improvement on, and is expected to replace, the original Wi-Fi security standard. Wired Equivalent Privacy (WEP), WPA provides more sophisticated data encryption than WEP and also provides user authentication.[2]

Write back A storage method in which data are written into the cache every time a change occurs, but is written into the corresponding location in main memory only at specified intervals or under certain conditions.[42]

Write once, read many times *See* **WORM**.

WSDL **Web services description language.** Provides a model and an XML format for describing web services. WSDL enables one to separate the description of the abstract functionality offered by a service from concrete details of a service description, such as 'how' and 'where' that functionality is offered.[8]

WWW **World Wide Web. 1.** Global network of networks offering various services to users with browsing software (web browsers). A project originated at the European Organization for Nuclear Research (CERN), aimed at providing hypertext-style access to information from a wide range of sources. **2.** The graphical interface with which millions of users access Internet files that conform to the hypertext protocol (HTTP). The web is the most accessible and widely used branch of the Internet.[8]

WYSIWYG What you see is what you get. Some early systems yielded a screen image that was unlike a printed document or file. This term is used to confirm that the system presents a screen image that matches what prints on paper. Pronounced 'wizzy-wig.'[1]

X

X.25 1. Standard protocol suite for packet switched wide area network (WAN) communication developed by the International Telecommunication Union-Telecommunication (ITU-T) Standard Sector. **2.** A packet-switching network protocol with extensive error checking and accounting capability. Employs the use of permanent virtual circuits (PVC), switched virtual circuits (SVC), and packet assemblers and dissemblers.[7,1]

X12 standard Used to describe any American National Standards Institute Accredited Standards Committee (ASC X12) standard that has been balloted and approved.[1]

XDS Cross enterprise document sharing. Focused on providing a standards-based specification for managing the sharing of documents that healthcare enterprises (anywhere from a private physician, to a clinic, to an acute care inpatient facility) have decided to explicitly share. This contributes to the foundation of a shared electronic health record.[56] *See* **Profile.** NOTE: XDS is an Integrating the Healthcare Enterprise (IHE) Profile.

XML Extensible markup language. 1. General-purpose markup language for creating special-purpose markup languages. It is a simplified subset of standard generalized markup language, capable of describing many different kinds of data. Its primary purpose is to facilitate the sharing of data across different systems, particularly systems connected via the Internet. **2.** Describes a class of data objects, called XML documents, and partially describes the behavior of computer programs that process them. XML is an application profile or restricted form of SGML, the Standard Generalized Markup Language (ISO 8879). By construction, XML documents are conforming SGML documents.[7]

XSL Extensible Stylesheet Language. A family of languages which allows one to describe how files encoded in the XML standard are to be formatted or transformed. XSL Transformation (XSLT) is used to transform the XML document and XSL Formatting Objects (XSL-FO) is used to render the transformed document.[8] Also known as *eXtensible Style Language (ESL).*

Y

Yahoo Internet search engine.[32]

Z

Zero Latency The immediate exchange of information across geographical, technical and organizational boundaries so that all departments, customers, and related parties can work together in real time.[47]

Zigbee A specification for a suite of high-level communication protocols using small, low-power digital radios based on an IEEE 802 standard for personal area networks.[2]

Zip drive A small, portable disk drive used primarily for backing up and archiving personal computer files. The trademarked 'Zip' drive was developed and sold by Iomega Corporation.[1]

.zip The filename extension used by files compressed into the ZIP format common on PCs.[1]

Zip or zipping To package or compress a set of files into an archive file that is called a zip file. The compressed file takes up less space in storage, or takes less time to send to someone. Several popular tools exist for zipping.[1]

Zombie 1. UNIX process that does not terminate. Must be removed by the kill command.[1] **2.** A compromised web site that is used as an attack launch point to launch an overwhelming number of requests toward an attacked web site, which will soon be unable to service legitimate requests from its users.[1]

Appendix A
Acronym List

A

AA   Attribute authority. Authority that assigns privileges by issuing attribute certificates.[121]

ABC   Activity-based costing. An accounting technique that allows an organization to determine the actual cost associated with each product and service produced by the organization, without regard to the organizational structure.[1]

ACA   Affordable Care Act. On March 23, 2010, President Obama signed the Patient Protection and Affordable Care Act, which extends healthcare coverage to an estimated 32 million uninsured individuals and makes coverage more affordable for many others. Section 1561 request the Department of Health & Human Services, in consultation with the Health Information Technology Policy Committee and the HIT Standards Committee, to develop interoperable and secure standards and protocols that facilitate electronic enrollment of individuals in federal and state health and human services programs.[178]

ACDF   Access control decision function. Specialized function that makes access control decisions by applying access control policy rules to an access request, access control decision information (of initiators, targets, access requests, or that retained from prior decisions), and the context in which the access request is made.[125]

ACG   Ambulatory care group. Preventive, diagnostic, therapeutic, surgical, and/or rehabilitative outpatient care, for which the duration of treatment is less than 24 hours.[2] Also known as an *adjusted clinical group*.

ACI   Access control information. Information used for access control purposes, including contextual information.[125]

ACID   Atomicity, consistency, isolation, and durability. The basic properties of a database transaction: atomicity, consistency, isolation, and durability. Either all the steps in a transaction succeed, or the entire transaction is rolled back; partial completion should never be observed.[7]

**ACK   **General acknowledgment message.[16]

ACL   Access control lists. Table that tells a computer operating system which access rights each user has to a particular system object, such as a file directory or individual file. Each object has a security attribute that identifies its access control list. The list has an entry for each system user with access privileges. The most common privileges include the ability to read a file (or all the files in a directory), to write to the file or files, and to execute the file (if it is an executable file, or program).[42]

ACO   Accountable care organization. Groups of doctors, hospitals, and other healthcare providers, who come together voluntarily to give coordinated high quality care to the Medicare patients they serve. Coordinated care helps ensure that patients, especially the chronically ill, get the right care at the right time, with the goal of avoiding unnecessary duplication of services and preventing medical errors. When an ACO succeeds in both delivering high-quality care and spending healthcare dollars more wisely, it will share in the savings it achieves for the Medicare program.[102]

ACS   Access control service. Includes embedded security management capabilities (provided as precursor information to this construct) and all other user-side access control and decision-making capabilities (policy enforcement point, policy decision point, PIP, PAP, obligation service, etc.) needed to enforce user-side system-object security and privacy policy. The ACS is responsible for creating trustworthy credentials forwarded in cross-domain assertions regarding security information and attributes. Access control services may be hierarchical and nested, distributed, or local.[48]

AD Active directory. A Microsoft central directory service that manages user data, security, and other system related resources. It is part of Windows Server operating system to centrally provide network administration and security across a domain. [12]

AD Addendum. A portion added on to a document.[32]

ADE Adverse drug event. An injury resulting from the use of a drug. Under this definition, the term ADE includes harm caused by the drug (adverse drug reactions and overdose) and harm from the use of the drug (including dose reductions and discontinuations of drug therapy). Adverse drug events may result from medication errors, but most do not.[96]

ADLs Activities of daily living. Activities that are considered a normal part of everyday life. Some of these are bathing, dressing, eating, toileting, and transferring (e.g., moving from and into a chair). These activities are used to measure the degree of impairment and can effect the eligibility for certain types for insurance benefits.[102]

ADPAC Automated data processing application coordinator. The person assigned by a service to coordinate computer activities for that service.

ADR Adverse drug reaction. 1. Response to a drug that is characterized as a noxious and unintended response and that occurs at doses normally used in humans for prophylaxis, diagnosis, or therapy of disease; or for the modification of physiological function. **Note:** There is a causal link between a drug and an adverse drug reaction. In summary, an adverse drug reaction is harm directly caused by the drug at normal doses, during normal use. **2.** A complication caused by use of a drug in the usual (i.e., correct) manner and dosage.[96,18]

ADR ADT response message. Admission, discharge, and transfer response message.[16]

ADSL Asymmetric digital subscriber line. A high-speed line that allows voice and data to travel concurrently over a local copper loop (or pair), with speeds ranging from 2-8 Mbps downstream, and 640-960 kpbs upstream.[1]

ADT Admission, discharge, and transfer message for patients in a healthcare facility.[102]

AE Adverse event. 1. Untoward incidents, therapeutic misadventures, iatrogenic injuries, or other adverse occurrences directly associated with care or services provided within the jurisdiction of a medical center, outpatient clinic, or other medical facility. **2.** An injury caused by medical management rather than by the underlying condition of the patient.[97]

AE Title Application entity title. An identifier utilized by picture archiving and communication systems (PACS) to uniquely name devices that can send and/or receive information to the imaging/PACS system.[192]

AEF Access control enforcement function. Specialized function that is part of the access path between an initiator and a target on each access control request, and enforces the decision made by the access control decision function.[125]

AHLTA The US Department of Defense electronic health record. A clinical information system that generates, maintains, stores, and provides secure electronic access to comprehensive patient records.[18]

AHT Average handling time. The average duration of a call handled by a customer service associate.[15]

AIDC Automatic identification and data capture. The ability to use unique numbers, and other sets of standardised data, shown in bar codes or other data carriers to identify different items automatically, without any human intervention. Technologies typically considered part of AIDC include bar codes, radio frequency identification (RFID), biometrics, magnetic stripes, optical character recognition (OCR), smartcards, and voice recognition.[201,7] Also known as *automatic identification, auto-ID*, and *automatic data capture.*

AIS privileges Automated information system. Permissions to perform specified functions within a computer system.[1]

ALOS Average length of stay. The American Hospital Association computes the average length of hospital stay by dividing the number of inpatient days by the number of admissions.

ALU Arithmetic logic unit. Portion of the CPU that performs the following arithmetic operations: add, subtract, multiply, divide, and negate.[1]

AMR Ambulatory medical record. An electronic (or paper-based) medical record used in the outpatient or ambulatory care setting.[45]

AIMS Anesthesia information management system. An information system that allows integrated communication with other hospital and provider systems throughout the perioperative period (such as clinical information systems used by nurses, data clinical repositories used by hospitals, and professional billing systems).[2]

APACHE Acute Physiology and Chronic Health Evaluation. A severity-of-disease classification system scoring system widely used in the United States. APACHE II is the most widely studied version of this instrument (a more recent version, APACHE IV, is proprietary, whereas APACHE II is publicly available); it derives a severity score from such factors as underlying disease and chronic health status.[1,2] Other points are added for 12 physiologic variables (e.g., hematocrit, creatinine, Glasgow Coma Score, mean arterial pressure) measured within 24 hours of admission to the ICU. The APACHE II score has been validated in several studies involving tens of thousands of ICU patients.[14]

Apache A widely-used web server platform written by the Apache Software Foundation (ASF). The Apache web server browser had a key role in the initial growth of the World Wide Web.[186]

APC Ambulatory payment class. A payment type for outpatient PPS claims.[5]

API Application program interface. 1. A set of standard software interrupts, calls, functions, and data formats that can be used by an application program to access network services, devices, applications, or operating systems. **2.** A set of pre-made functions used to build programs. APIs ask the operating system or another application to perform specific tasks. There is an API for almost everything, including messaging APIs for e-mail, telephony APIs for calling systems, Java APIs, and graphics APIs, such as DirectX.[1,12] See **Socket, SSL**.

ARI Access to radiology information. Specifies a number of query transactions providing access to radiology information, including images and related reports, in a DICOM format, as they were acquired or created. Such access is useful, both to the radiology department and to other departments, such as pathology, surgery, and oncology.[56] See **Profile**.

ARP Address resolution protocol. Used in TCP/IP networks to provide the physical address (MAC address) or a device from the assigned Internet protocol address.[1]

ARPANET Advanced research projects agency network. 1. Developed by the Defense Advanced Research Projects Agency (DARPA), this distributed network grew into the Internet. **2.** The first operational packet switching network.[18,7]

ARRA American Recovery and Reinvestment Act of 2009. An economic stimulus bill enacted by the 111th US Congress that provides $30 billion for various health Information technology investments. Some of this funding was allocated by the Centers for Medicare & Medicaid Services (CMS) to promote physicians and hospital providers to adopt certified EHRs.[2]

ASA Average speed of answer. The average amount of time (measured in seconds) from when a caller calls customer service (enters the customer service queue) to when the caller begins speaking to a customer service associate.[140]

ASCII American standard code for information interchange. Extensively used bit standard information processing code that represents 128 possible standard characters used by PCs. In an ASCII file, each alphabetic, numeric, or special character is represented with a 7-bit number (a string of seven 0s or 1s), which yields the 128 possible characters.[1]

ASMOP A simple matter of programming. An expression used to convey the sense 'yes, it's possible, but it would require an unknown, and most likely large, expenditure of resources.'[7]

ASN Abstract syntax notation. A metadata standard to define standards, mainly used in the area of telecommunications.[119]

ASO Administrative services only. An arrangement whereby a self-insured entity contracts with a third-party administrator (TPA) to administer a health plan.[10]

ASP **Active server pages.** A protocol for creating and displaying web pages.[99]

ASP **Application service provider. 1.** An entity that provides some type of specialty automation service or access, under a service agreement for a customer, with the business model of being able to provide expertise and reliability at a desired lower cost than the customer could provide for itself within a local data center. **2.** Network administration includes the deployment, maintenance, and monitoring of active network gear: switches, routers, firewalls, etc.; network administration commonly includes activities such as network address assignment, assignment of routing protocols and routing table configuration, as well as configuration of authentication and authorization directory services. This function may be outsourced by the healthcare organization.[1,2]

ATA **Advanced technology attachment.** Specifies the power and data signal interfaces between the motherboard and the integrated disk controller and drive. A disk drive interface standard based on the IBM PC ISA 16-bit bus and also used on other personal computers.[7] Also known as *AT Attachment* or *Integrated Drive Electronics, IDE*.

ATCB **Authorized testing and certification body.** An entity that tests and certifies that certain types of electronic health record (EHR) technology (Base EHRs and EHR Modules) are compliant with the standards, implementation specifications, and certification criteria adopted by the US Department of Health & Human Services Secretary and meet the definition of 'certified EHR technology.'[178]

ATM **Asynchronous transfer mode.** A high-performance, cell-oriented switching and multiplexing technology that utilizes fixed-length packets to carry different types of traffic.[34] *See* **Frame relay, SONET.**

ATNA **Audit trail and node authentication.** Establishes the characteristics of a Basic Secure Note: **1.** Describes the security environment (user identification, authentication, authorization, access control, etc.). **2.** Defines basic security requirements for the communications of the node. **3.** Defines basic auditing requirements for the node. The profile also establishes the characteristics of the communication of audit messages between the Basic Secure Nodes and Audit Repository Nodes that collect audit information.[56] *See* **Profile. NOTE: ATNA is an IHE Profile.**

AUI **Attachment unit interface.** Connector port on network devices.[1]

AUP **Acceptable use policy.** Set of rules and guidelines that specify, in more or less detail, the expectations in regard to appropriate use of systems or networks.[48]

AVR **Analysis, visualization, and reporting.** Ability to analyze, display, report, and map accumulated data and share data and technologies for analysis and visualization with other public health partners.[46]

B

b/w **Between.**[32]

B/W **Black and white.** Indicates a print image is being formulated to be readable in pure black and white, without the use of color (and perhaps without the use of grayscale).[7]

B2B **Business-to-business.** Healthcare commerce applications that support online business enhancements to standardize previous processes that involved paper, fragmented interfaces, or delay. The electronic commerce is conducted between the business of the hospital (or other healthcare entity) and the business of the supplier.[1]

B2C **Business-to-consumer. 1.** The electronic commerce (eCommerce) conducted between the business of the hospital (or other healthcare entity) and the consumer or patient. **2.** eCommerce transactions conducted over the Internet. **3.** Healthcare eCommerce applications that support online business enhancements to standardize previous processes that involved paper, fragmented interfaces, or delay.[1]

BAN **Body area network.** A communication standard optimized for low power devices and operation on, in, or around the human body (but not limited to humans) to serve a variety of applications including medical, consumer electronics / personal entertainment and other.[155]

BASIC Beginner's all-purpose symbolic instruction code. A programming language. Originally devised as an easy-to-use programming language, it became widespread on home microcomputers in the 1980s and remains popular to this day in a handful of heavily evolved dialects.[33]

BAT Filename extension for a batch file.[1]

BBS Bulletin board service. A non-commercial dial-up service usually run by a user group or software company. One can exchange messages with other users and upload or download software.[1]

BCMA Bar code medication administration. Electronic system designed to prevent medication errors in healthcare settings and improve the quality and safety of medication administration. The overall goals of BCMA are to improve accuracy, prevent errors, and generate online records of medication administration.[7]

BDC Backup domain controller. **1.** Secondary Windows NT server that contains a copy of the security database. Authenticates users of the primary domain controller (PDC) when the PDC is unavailable. **2.** When changes are made to the master accounts database on the PDC, the PDC pushes the updates down to the BDCs (read-only copy).[1,7]

BGI Binary gateway interface. Provides a method of running a program from a web server. Uses a binary Dynamic Link Library (DLL), which is loaded into memory when the server starts.[1]

BGP Border gateway protocol. Used to advertise the networks that can be reached within an autonomous system. Newer than the exterior gateway protocol (EGP).[1]

BIOS Basic input output system. **1.** The first operating system code that executes the open computer boot-up. This is contained in flash memory or ROM firmware on the motherboard. **2.** Instructs the computer how to perform a number of basic functions such as booting and keyboard control.[7]

BPS Bits per second. The basic unit of speed associated with data transmission.[1]

BRFSS Behavioral risk factor surveillance system. A state-based system of health surveys

that collects information on health risk behaviors, preventive health practices, and healthcare access primarily related to chronic disease and injury.[46]

C

C, Programming language. A standardized imperative computer programming language, developed in the early 1970s by Dennis Ritchie, for use on the UNIX operating system. It has since spread to many other operating systems and is one of the most widely used programming languages. C is prized for its efficiency and is the most popular programming language for writing system software, though it is also used for writing applications. It is also commonly used in computer science education, despite not being designed for novices.[7]

CA Certification authority. The official responsible for performing the comprehensive evaluation of the technical and non-technical security features of an IT system and other safeguards, made in support of the accreditation process, to establish the extent that a particular design and implementation meet a set of specified security requirements.[97]

caBIG™ Cancer Biomedical Informatics Grid.[37] An open source, open access information network initiative for the cancer community developed by the National Cancer Institute and maintained by the Center for Biomedical Informatics and Information Technology (CBIIT).[7]

CAD Computer-aided design. The use of a wide range of computer-based tools that assist engineers and architects in their design activities. It involves both software and special-purpose hardware.[7]

CAD Computer-aided detection. Combining elements of artificial intelligence and digital image processing with radiological image processing to assist in the interpretation of medical images. Also known as *CADe* and *computer-aided diagnosis (CADx)*.

CAH Critical-access hospital. Rural community hospitals that receive cost-based reimbursement. To be designated a CAH, a rural hospital must meet defined criteria that were outlined in the Conditions of Participation 42 CFR 485 and subsequent legislative refinements to the program through the Balanced Budget Refinement Act of 1999 (BBRA), Benefits Improvement and Protection Act (BIPA, 2000), Medicare Modernization Act, Medicare Improvements for Patients and Providers Act (MIPPA, July 15, 2008), and the Patient Protection and Affordable Care Act (ACA, 2010).[171]

CAL Computer-assisted learning. Refers to a system of educational instruction performed almost entirely by computer. Such systems typically incorporate functions, such as assessing student capabilities with a pre-test; presenting educational materials in a navigable form; providing repetitive drills to improve the student's command of knowledge; possibly, providing game-based drills to increase learning enjoyment; assessing student progress with a post-test; routing students through a series of courseware instructional programs; and recording student scores and progress for later inspection by a courseware instructor.[7] See **CBL**.

CAP Capitation. Pre-established payment of a set dollar amount to a provider on a per member basis, for certain contracted services for a given period of time. Amount of money paid to provider depends on number of individuals registered to their patient list, not on volume or type of service provided.[15]

CAP Common alerting protocol. A general format for exchanging all-hazard emergency alerts and public warnings over all kinds of networks.[91]

CAS Computer-assisted surgery. Represents a surgical concept and set of methods that use computer technology for pre-surgical planning and for guiding or performing surgical interventions.[7] Also known as *computer-aided surgery.*

CASE Computer-assisted software engineering. A computer-assisted method to organize and control the development of software. CASE allows developers to share a common view, allow checkpoint process, and serves as a repository.[42]

CAT Computerized axial tomography. An x-ray procedure that combines many x-ray images with the aid of a computer to generate cross-sectional views and, if needed, 3-dimen-

sional images of the internal organs and structures of the body.[197]

CAT-1-5 Categories 1-5. Categories of unshielded twisted pair cable (UTP). Allows voice grade only transmission rates below 100 Mbps up to 100 meters, or 328 feet in length per segment.[1]

CATH Cardiac catheterization workflow. Establishes the continuity and integrity of basic patient data in the context of the cardiac catheterization procedure. This profile deals specifically with consistent handling of patient identifiers and demographic data, including that of emergency patient presentation where the actual patient identity may not be established until after the beginning of the procedure, or even a significant time after the completion of the procedure. It also specifies the scheduling and coordination of procedure data across a variety of imaging, measurement, and analysis systems, and its reliable storage in an archive form where it is available to support subsequent workflow steps, such as reporting. It also provides central coordination of the completion status of steps of a potentially multi-phase (diagnostic and interventional) procedure.[56] See **Profile**. Note: CATH is an IHE Profile.

CBL Computer-based learning. Refers to the use of computers as a key component of the educational environment. While this can refer to the use of computers in a classroom, the term more broadly refers to a structured environment in which computers are used for teaching purposes. The concept is generally seen as being distinct from the use of computers in ways where learning is at least a peripheral element of the experience (e.g., computer games and web browsing).[7]

CBSA Core-based statistical area. Defined by the Census Bureau as a geographic area with an urbanized population of at least 50,000, or an urban cluster with a population of at least 10,000, plus the adjacent counties that have a high degree of social and economic integration with the core as measured through commuting ties.[2]

CCC Clinical Care Classification System. A concept-oriented nursing terminology framework and coding structure for the electronic documentation and classification of the nursing practice and process. The nomenclature is discrete atomic-level data elements about the nursing process, encompassing nursing assessment, diagnosis, intervention, actions, and actual and expected outcomes to measure patient outcomes over time, across population groups and geographic locations. Recognized by American Nurses Association. (Formerly known as the Home Health Care Classification, HHCC).[27]

CCD   Continuity of care document. A specification that is an XML-based markup standard (developed between HL7 and ASTM) intended to specify the encoding, structure, and semantics of a patient summary clinical document for exchange.[16]

CCO   Chief compliance officer. Responsible for legal processes and procedures, maintaining industry standards, and ensuring compliance with healthcare regulations.[2]

CCoM   Clinical context management. Coordinates different healthcare applications on a desktop, creating a user-driven, patient-centered information workspace.[7]

CCOW   Clinical context object workgroup. Using a technique called 'context management,' CCOW provides the clinician with a unified view on the information held in separate and disparate healthcare applications referring to the same patient, encounter, or user. This means that when a clinician signs onto one application within the group of disparate applications tied together by the CCOW environment, that same sign-on is simultaneously executed on all other applications within the group. Similarly, when the clinician selects a patient, the same patient is selected in all the applications. CCOW then builds a combined view of the patient on one screen. CCOW works for both client-server and web-based applications. The acronym CCOW is a reference to the standards committee within the HL7 group that developed the standard.[16]

CCR   Continuity of care record. 1. A standard specification developed jointly by ASTM International, the Massachusetts Medical Society (MMS), the Healthcare Information and Management Systems Society (HIMSS), the American Academy of Family Physicians (AAFP), and the American Academy of Pediatrics (AAP). It is intended to foster and improve continuity of patient care, reduce medical errors, and assure at least a minimum standard

of health information transportability when a patient is referred or transferred to, or is otherwise seen by another provider. **2.** A new XML document standard for a summary of personal health information that clinicians can send when a patient is referred and that patients can carry with them to promote continuity, quality, and safety of care.[39]

CD   Committee draft. The second internal technical committee balloting stage for international standards from the International Organization for Standardization (ISO).[3]

CD   Compact disc. Optical disk used to store digital data, originally developed for storing digital audio files.[7]

CDA   Clinical document architecture. 1. An XML-based document markup standard that specifies the structure and semantics of clinical documents for the purpose of exchange. **2.** Known previously as the patient record architecture, CDA provides an exchange model for clinical documents, such as discharge summaries and progress notes, and brings the healthcare industry closer to the realization of an electronic medical record. By leveraging the use of XML, the HL7 Reference Information Model (RIM), and coded vocabularies, the CDA makes documents both machine-readable (so documents are easily parsed and processed electronically) and human-readable so documents can be easily retrieved and used by the people who need them.[2,16]

CDFS   CD-ROM file system. 32-bit file system used in conjunction with CD-ROMs on Windows 95 and Windows NT machines.[1]

CDMA   Code division multiple access. A wireless technology that includes digital voice service with 9.6 Kpbs to 14.4 Kpbs data services and includes enhanced calling features, such as caller ID, but lacks an 'always-on' data connection feature.[1]

CDPD   Cellular digital packet data. A TCP/IP-based industry standard for data, which is compatible with nearly all TCP/IP applications. Data packets can follow the user from cell to cell of calling regions, keeping an 'always-on' data connection alive while the user is in motion.[1]

CDR   Clinical data repository. 1. A structured, systematically collected storehouse of patient-specific clinical data. **2.** A centralized database that allows organizations to collect, store, access, and report on clinical, administrative, and financial information collected from various applications within or across the healthcare organization that provides an open environment for accessing/viewing, managing, and reporting enterprise information.[12]

CD-ROM Compact disk read-only memory. Read-only optical disk storage used for imaging, reference, and database application with massive amounts of data and for multimedia.[1]

CDS Clinical decision support. The use of automated rules based on clinical evidence to provide alerts, reminders, clinical guidelines, and other knowledge to assist in healthcare delivery.[151]

CDT Current Dental Terminology. Official coding system for dentists to report professional dental services and procedures to third parties for payment produced by the American Dental Association.[151]

CDW Clinical data warehouse. Grouping of data accessible by a single data management system, possibly of diverse sources, pertaining to a health system or sub-system; and enabling secondary data analysis for questions relevant to understanding the functioning of that health system, and hence can support proper maintenance and improvement of that health system.[94]

CE Coded element. A data type that transmits codes and the text associated with the code.[16]

CEN European Committee for Standardization. Major provider of European standards and technical specifications CEN is the only recognized European organization for the planning, drafting and adoption of European standards in all areas of economic activity with the exception of electrotechnology (CENELEC) and telecommunication (ETSI).[86]

CERT Computer emergency response team. A team of system specialists and other professionals, such as lawyers, who investigate computer break-ins and attacks.[1]

CERT Community emergency response team. Federal Emergency Management Agency (FEMA) disaster preparedness program that educates the communities about hazards that may impact areas and trains communities in basic disaster response skills, such as fire safety, light search and rescue, team organization, and disaster medical operations.[225]

CF Conditional formatting/coded formatted element. 1. A tool that allows a user to apply formats to a cell or range of cells and have that formatting change, depending on the value of the cell or the value of a formula. **2.** Coded element with formatted values data type. This data type transmits codes and the formatted text associated with the code.[41,16]

CGI Common gateway interface. A standard or protocol for external gateway programs to interface with information servers, such as HTTP servers. Part of the overall HTTP protocol.[1]

CHAP Challenge handshake authentication protocol. An authentication protocol used to logon a user to an Internet access provider.[1]

CHG Charge posting. Specifies the exchange of information from the department system scheduler/order filler actor to the charge processor actor regarding charges associated with particular procedures, as well as communication between the ADT/patient registration and charge processor actors about patient demographics, accounts, insurance, and guarantors. The charge-posted transaction contains all of the required procedure data to generate a claim. Currently, these interfaces contain fixed field formatted, or HL7-style data. The goal of including this transaction in the IHE Technical Framework is to standardize the charge-posted transaction to a charge processor, thus reducing system interface installation time between clinical systems and charge processors. Additionally, the charge-posted transaction reduces the need of the billing system to have knowledge of the radiology internals. The result is that the charge processor will receive more complete, timely, and accurate data.[56] *See* **Profile. NOTE: CHG is an IHE Profile.**

CHIN Community health information network. The service model for delivery of medical information across a local community, shared between providers, that was promulgated in the early 1990s. The movement failed to take hold due to concerns about aligning costs with benefits, with confidentiality of patient and propriety information, and for other factors.[99] *See* **RHIO**.[1]

C-HOBIC **Canadian health outcomes for better information and care.** Joint project between the Canadian Nurses Association (CNA) and Canada Health Infoway to begin the process of collecting standardized clinical outcomes reflective of nursing practice for inclusion in electronic health records.[200]

CHV **Consumer health vocabulary initiative.** Open access, collaborative initiative that links everyday words and phrases about health to technical terms or jargon used by healthcare professionals.[199]

CIA **Confidentiality / integrity / availability.** The CIA triad is one of the core principles of information security.[7]

CIO **Chief information officer.** Responsible for the overall planning and management of the information technology department, including establishing strategic long-term goals and determining long-term systems needs and hardware acquisitions to accomplish business objectives.[2]

CIO **Chief informatics officer.** Healthcare executive generally responsible for the health informatics platform required to work with clinical IT staff to support the efficient design, implementation, and use of health technology within a healthcare organization.[7]

CIS **Clinical information system.** A system dedicated to collecting, storing, manipulating, and making available clinical information important to the delivery of healthcare. Clinical information systems may be limited in scope to a single area (e.g., lab system, ECG management system) or they may be comprehensive and cover virtually all facets of clinical information (e.g., electronic patient; the original discharge summary residing in the chart, with a copy of the report sent to the admitting physician, another copy existing on the transcriptionist's machine).[8]

CISC **Complex instruction set computer processor.** CISC computers use microprocessors with a large number of execution steps and many clock cycles to operate. Intel computers are CISC computers.[1]

CM **Composite message/composite data type.** A field that is a combination of other meaningful data fields. Each portion is called a component.[16]

CMD **Command.** File type: External Command Menu. Dot (.)CMD is similar to a DOS .bat (batch file) or an .exe (executable file). A way of giving command line (like DOS) prompts to the computer (e.g., to map the drive).[7]

CMET **Common message element type.** Reusable data types, which can be included in any number of messages without repeating the common internal structure.[16]

CMIO **Chief medical information officer.** Provides overall leadership in the ongoing development, implementation, advancement, and optimization of electronic information systems that impact patient care. Works in partnership with the organization's IT leadership to translate clinician requirements into specifications for new clinical and research systems.[2]

CMIO **Chief medical informatics officer.** Responsible for the health informatics platform required to work with clinical information technology staff to support the efficient design, implementation, and use of health technology within a healthcare organization.[7]

CMYK **Cyan, magenta, yellow, and black.** **1.** Printing processes, such as offset lithography, use CMYK inks; digital art must be converted to CMYK color for print. **2.** The 'K' in CMYK stands for Key, since in four-color printing, cyan, magenta, and yellow printing plates are carefully keyed or aligned with the key of the black key plate.[57,7]

CNCL **Cancelled.**

CNIO **Chief nursing information officer.** Leads the strategy, development and implementation of information technology to support, nursing, nursing practice and clinical applications, collaborating with the Chief Nursing Officer on the clinical and administration decision-making process.[2]

CNIO **Chief nursing informatics officer.** Provides visionary leadership and establishes direction for a comprehensive nursing informatics program, with a primary focus on nursing practice, administration, research and academic partnership in support of interdisciplinary patient-driven care. Serves as the principal for developing strategic nursing informatics plans, data analysis, creation of policies and procedures and services as a champion for complex nursing projects and systems that support efficiency and effectiveness with the primary goal of advancing nursing evidence-based practice.[2]

COA Compliance-oriented architecture. The virtues of service-oriented architectures (SOAs) applied to the specific business challenge of compliance; the result is a flexible architecture that can meet compliance challenges now and in the future. Compliance requirements can be expressed as a set of core services.[88]

COAS Clinical observations access service. Standardizes access to clinical observations in multiple formats, including numerical data stored by instruments, or entered from observations.[88]

COB Close of business.[99]

COB Coordination of benefits. 1. The process by which a payer handles claims that may involve other insurance companies (i.e., situations where an insured individual is covered by more than one insurance plan). **2.** Process of determining which health plan or insurance policy will pay first and/or determining the payment obligations of each health plan, medical insurance policy, or third-party resource when two or more health plans, insurance policies, or third-party resources cover the same benefits.[184]

COMSEC Communications security. Measures and controls taken to deny unauthorized persons information derived from telecommunications and ensure the authenticity of such telecommunications. Communications security includes cryptosecurity, transmission security, emission security, and physical security of COMSEC material.[97]

CORBA Common object request broker architecture. A language-independent object model and specification for a distributed applications development environment.[1]

COW Computer-on-wheels.[16]

CP Certificate policy. Named set of rules that indicates the applicability of a certificate to a particular community and/or class of application with common security requirements.[121]

CPI Consistent presentation of images. Specifies a number of transactions that maintain the consistency of presentation for grayscale images and their presentation state information (including user annotations, shutters, flip/rotate, display area, and zoom). It also defines a standard contrast curve, the Grayscale Standard Display function, against which different types of display and hardcopy output devices can be calibrated. It thus supports hardcopy, softcopy, and mixed environments.[56] *See* **Profile. NOTE: CPI is an IHE Profile.**

CPM Control program for microcomputers. Introduced in the late 1970s, this was the first standard microcomputer operating system, and generally used by the first generation of microcomputers. It relied on an 8-bit architecture and was configured to run on a variety of microprocessors. Usage decreased after the advent of MS-DOS and the Apple operating system.[99]

CPOE Computerized practitioner order entry. 1. An order entry application specifically designed to assist practitioners in creating and managing medical orders for patient services and medications. This application has special electronic signature, workflow, and rules engine functions that reduce or eliminate medical errors associated with practitioner ordering processes. **2.** A computer application that accepts the provider's orders for diagnostic and treatment services electronically, instead of the clinician recording them on an orders sheet or prescription pad.[2] Also known as *computerized physician order entry, computerized patient order entry,* and *computerized provider order entry.*

CPR Computer-based patient record. *See* **EHR.**

CPRS Computer-based patient record system. *See* **EHR.**[1]

CPS Certification practices statement. Statement of the practices that a certification authority employs in issuing certificates.[121]

CPT Current Procedural Terminology. 1. The official coding system for physicians to report professional services and procedures to third parties for payment. It is produced by the American Medical Association (AMA). **2.** A medical code set, maintained and copyrighted by the AMA, that has been selected for use under HIPAA for non-institutional and non-dental professional transactions.[151,9]

CPU   Central processing unit. 1. The component in a digital computer that interprets and executes the instructions and data contained in software. Microprocessors are CPUs that are manufactured on integrated circuits, often as a single-chip package. **2.** Brain of the computer. Main system board (motherboard) integrated chip that directs computer operations. Performs the arithmetic, logic, and controls operations in the computer.[1]

CQM   Clinical quality measures. Tools that measure and track the quality of healthcare services provided by eligible professionals (EPs), eligible hospitals, and critical access hospitals (CAHs) within the US healthcare system.[102]

CRA   Countermeasure response administration. Systems that manage and track measures taken to contain an outbreak or event, and to provide protection against a possible outbreak or event. This public health information network (PHIN) functional area also includes multiple dose delivery of countermeasures: anthrax vaccine and antibiotics; adverse events monitoring; follow-up of patients; isolation and quarantine; and links to distribution vehicles (such as the Strategic National Stockpile).[46]

CRM   Customer relationship management. The approach of establishing relationships with customers on an individual basis, then using collected information about the customer and their buying habits to treat different customers differently.[1]

CRUD   Create, read, update, and delete.[18]

CSMA/CD   Carrier sense multiple access with collision detection. A network control protocol in which: a.) carrier-sensing scheme is used; and b.) a transmitting data station that detects another signal while transmitting a frame, stops transmitting that frame, transmits a jam signal, and then waits for a random time interval (known as 'backoff delay' and determined using the truncated binary exponential backoff algorithm) before trying to send that frame again. Ethernet is the classic CSMA/CD protocol.[7]

CSO   Chief security officer. The person with the responsibility for the security of the paper-based and electronic health information, as well as the physical and electronic means of managing and storing that information.[1]

CSU/DSU   Channel sharing unit/data service unit. A unit that shapes digital signals for transmission. The CSU is a device that performs protective and diagnostic functions for a telecommunications line.[1]

CT   Computed tomography. Specialized x-ray imaging technique.[7] Also known as *computerized tomography*.

CT   Consistent time. Mechanisms to synchronize the time base between multiple actors and computers. Various infrastructure, security, and acquisition profiles require use of a consistent time base on multiple computers. The consistent time profile provides a median synchronization error of less than one second.[56] *See* **Profile**. **NOTE: CT is an IHE Profile.**

CTI   Computer telephony integration. Systems that enable a computer to act as a call center, accepting incoming calls and routing them to the appropriate device or person.[1]

CTO   Chief technology officer. 1. Has overall responsibility for managing technical vendor relationships and performance, as well as the physical and personnel technology infrastructure, including technology deployment, network and systems management, integration testing, and developing technical operations personnel. **2.** Develops technical standards and ensures compatibility for the enterprise-wide computer environment.[1,2]

CTS   Common terminology services. Specification developed as an alternative to a common data structure.[16]

CU   Control unit. Portion of the CPU that coordinates all computer operations through the machine cycle: fetch, decode, execute, and store.[1]

CUI   Concept unique identifier. The class of names that uniquely identify an instance of entity. Some examples of unique identifiers are the keys of tables in database applications and the ISBN.[1]

CVE   Common vulnerabilities and exposures. A list of standardized names for vulnerabilities and other information security exposures. CVE aims to standardize the names for all publicly known vulnerabilities and secure exposures.[125]

CVS Concurrent versions system. Keeps track of all work and all changes in a set of files.[7]

CWE Coded with exceptions. A data type coded with exceptions.[16]

CWE Common weakness enumeration. A community-developed formal list of software weaknesses, idiosyncrasies, faults, and flaws.[125]

CxO Corporate executives or C-level. A short way to refer to, collectively, corporate executives at what is sometimes called the C-level, whose job titles typically start with 'Chief' and end with 'Officer.'[42]

D

DAT Digital audio tape. A magnetic tape that stores audio data converted to digital form. [47]

DBMS Database management system. 1. A program that lets one or more computer users create and access data in a database. On personal computers, Microsoft Access is a popular example of a single or small group user DBMS. Microsoft's SQL server is an example of a DBMS that serves database requests from multiple users. **2.** A set of programs used to define, administer, store, modify, process, and extract information from a database.[2,1]

DCE Data circuit-terminating equipment. Typically a modem or other type of communication device.[90]

DDL Data definition language. A syntax similar to a computer programming language for defining data structures, especially database schemas.[7] Also known as *data decription language.*

DEA Data encryption algorithm. A method for encrypting information.[7] *See* **DES**.

DEEDS Data elements for emergency department systems. The recommended data set for use in emergency departments; it is published by the Centers for Disease Control and Prevention (CDC).[46]

DELOS WP5 Network on Excellence on Digital Libraries (EURO), Knowledge Extraction & Semantic Interoperability.[142]

DES Data encryption standard. An algorithm implemented in electronic hardware devices, and used to protect computer data through cryptography.[1]

DHCP Dynamic host configuration protocol. Standard protocol that allows a network device to obtain all network IP configuration information automatically from host-based pooled IP addresses. Alleviates manual static IP address assignment.[1]

DI Diagnostic imaging. The use of digital images and textual reports prepared as a result of performing diagnostic studies, such as x-rays, CT scans, MRIs, etc.[8]

DICOM Digital imaging and communications in medicine. 1. DICOM is a standard for the electronic communication of medical images and associated information. DICOM relies on explicit and detailed models of how the patients, images, and reports involved in radiology operations are described and how the above are related. The DICOM standards contain information object definitions, data structure, data dictionary, media storage, file format, communications formats, and print formats. **2.** An ANSI-accredited standards development organization that has created a standard protocol for exchanging medical images among computer systems.[151]

DIP switch Dual in-line package switch. A grouping of small on (1)/off (0) switches used in computers and associated devices to configure hardware options. DIP switches commonly allow a user to change the configuration of a circuit board to suit a particular computer.[1]

DIS Draft international standard. The fourth balloting stage for a draft international standard document. This most important phase of balloting lasts five months.[3]

DLC Dynamic link control. Protocol used for networked-enabled HP printers, and for connectivity to IBM mainframe machines from Windows NT.[1]

DLL Dynamic link library. A file of code containing functions that can be called from other executable code (either an application or another DLL). Programmers use DLLs to provide code that they can reuse and to parcel out distinct jobs. Unlike an executable file, a DLL cannot be directly run. DLLs must be called from other code that is already executing.[1]

DMA Direct memory access. Rapid data movement between computer subsystems. Accomplished through the use of the DMA controller without the use of the CPU.[1]

DML Data manipulation language. A family of computer languages including commands permitting users to manipulate data in a database. This manipulation involves inserting data into database tables, retrieving existing data, deleting data from existing tables and modifying existing data. DML is most often incorporated in SQL databases.[156]

DNS Domain name server. An online database that resolves human readable names to IP addresses. The DNS is a distributed database used by TCP/IP applications to map between host names and IP addresses, and to provide electronic mail routing information. The DNS provides the protocol to allow clients and servers to communicate with each other.[1]

DNSSEC Domain name system security extension. 1. Secure Domain Name System for authentication and integrity. **2.** A suite of Internet Engineering Task Force (IETF) specifications for securing certain kinds of information provided by the DNS as used on Internet protocol (IP) networks.[1,7] DNSSEC is a set of extensions to DNS which provide to DNS clients (resolvers) origin authentication of DNS data, authenticated denial of existence, and data integrity; not availability or confidentiality.

DOS Disk operating system. The first widely installed operating system for personal computers.[42]

DPI Dots per square inch. A measure of the resolution of a printer, scanner, or monitor. It refers to the number of dots per inch. The more dots per inch, the higher the resolution.[1]

DRAM Dynamic random-access memory. RAM that must be continuously refreshed to maintain the current RAM value. Most RAM in microcomputers is dynamic RAM, although there is a trend toward synchronous dynamic random access memory (SDRAM).[1]

DRG Diagnosis related group. Group of International Classification of Diseases (ICD) coded diagnoses, procedures, and other information used to group patients for reimbursement by Medicare.[102]

DS-2-3 Digital signal. Digital Signal 2. 6.312-3.45 Mbps synchronous digital 1 transmission.[1]

DSA Digital signature algorithm. *See* **Digital signature**.

DSG Document digital signature. *See* **Digital signature**.

DSL Digital subscriber line. 1. DSL technologies use sophisticated modulation schemes to pack data onto copper wires. **2.** A family of technologies that provides digital data transmission over the wires of a local telephone network.[1,2] Also known as *digital subscriber loop*.

DSLAM Digital subscriber line access multiplexer. A mechanism at a phone company's central location that links many customer digital subscriber line (DSL) connections to a single high-speed asynchronous transfer mode (ATM) line. When the phone company receives a DSL signal, an asymmetric digital subscriber line (ADSL) modem with a plain old telephone system (POTS) splitter detects voice calls and data.[1]

DSM Diagnostic and Statistical Manual of Mental Disorders. Manual produced by the American Psychiatric Association to facilitate communication among mental health clinicians, researchers, and administrators; improve patient care by facilitating reliable and valid diagnoses and differential diagnoses; facilitate education and training in psychopathology; and facilitate collection of statistical data about mental disorders.[151]

DSML Directory services markup language. Combines the directory services technology Lightweight Directory Access Protocol (LDAP) with XML syntax to provide an easy way to share and use personalized data across company and technology boundaries.[7]

DSMO Designated standard maintenance organization. Designed to maintain ongoing updates to International Organization for Standardization (ISO) standards. Responsible to ISO Central Secretariat and the Technical Committee Secretariat.[3]

DSM Daily response message. Request and response messages may be exchanged between a client and server.[12]

DSR Data set ready. Modem control that indicates that the modem is attached to a communications line.[1]

DSS Decision support system. Computer tools or applications to assist in clinical decisions by providing evidence-based knowledge in the context of patient-specific data. Examples include drug interaction alerts at the time medication is prescribed and reminders for specific guideline-based interventions during the care of patients with chronic disease. Information should be presented in a patient-centric view of individual care and also in a population or aggregate view to support population management and quality improvement.[178]

DSTU Draft standard for trial use. An archaic term for any standard that has been approved.[10]

DSU Data service unit. Provides digital-to-digital communication.[1]

DSU/CSU Data service unit/channel service unit. Digital-interface device used to connect a Data Terminal Equipment (DTE) device, such as a router to a digital circuit, such as a T1 line. The DSU/CSU implements two different functions. The CSU is responsible for the connection to the telecom network while the DSU is responsible for handling the interface with the DTE. A DSU/CSU is the equivalent of the modem for an entire local area network.[7]

DT Date data type (YYYYMMDD). 1. International method of writing the date. **2.** International format defined by the International Organization for Standardization (ISO 8601) to define a numerical date system as follows: YYYY-MM-DD where YYYY is the year [all the digits, i.e. 2012], MM is the month [01 (January) to 12 (December)], DD is the day [01 to 31].[33]

DTD Document type definition. Defines the legal building blocks of an XML document. It defines the document structure with a list of legal elements.[1]

DTE Data terminal equipment. An end instrument that converts information into signals or reconverts received signals.[7]

DTR Data terminal ready. Modem control that indicates that a terminal is ready for transmission.[1]

DTR Draft technical report. A standards document containing only informative information ready for ballot.[3]

DVD Digital video disk or digital versatile disk. Backwardly compatible with CD-ROMs (i.e., DVDs can read CD-ROMs). The DVD specification can support a disk with capacities from 4.7 gigabytes to 17 gigabytes.[11]

E

e-[text] or e-text Electronic. Short for 'electronic,' 'e' or 'e-' is used as a prefix to indicate that something is Internet-based, not just electronic. The trend began with e-mail in the 1990s and now includes eCommerce, eHealth, e-GOV, etc.[32]

E-1-3 European digital signal. 2.048-3.139.254 Mbps digital transmission that is similar to Integrated Service Digital Network (ISDN).[1]

EAI Enterprise application integration. 1. The use of software and architectural principles to bring together (integrate) a set of enterprise computer applications. It is an area of computer systems architecture that gained wide recognition from about 2004 onwards. EAI is related to middleware technologies, such as message-oriented middleware (MOM), and data representation technologies, such as eXtensible markup language (HTML, XML). Newer EAI technologies involve using web services as part of service-oriented architecture as a means of integration. **2.** A presentation-level integration technology that provides a single point of access to conduct business transactions that utilize data from multiple disparate applications.[1,7] *See* **System integration**.

EAP Extensible authentication protocol. A general protocol for authentication that also supports multiple authentication methods, such as token cards, one-time passwords, certificate, public key authentication, and smartcards.[2]

EBB Eligibility-based billing. Process in which a payer bills a customer based on their eligibility. Clients are responsible for their own eligibility and data accuracy.

EBCDIC Extended binary coded decimal interchange code. A character set coding scheme that represents 256 standard characters. IBM mainframes use EBCDIC coding, while personal computers use ASCII coding. Networks that link personal computers to IBM mainframes must include a translating device to mediate between the two systems.[157]

EC Electronic commerce. Consists of the buying and selling of products or services over electronic systems such as the Internet and other computer networks.[158] Also known as *eCommerce*.

ECG Retrieve ECG for display. Specifies a mechanism for broad access throughout the enterprise to electrocardiogram (ECG) documents for review purposes. The ECG documents may include 'diagnostic quality' waveforms, measurements, and interpretations. This integration profile allows the display of this information without requiring specialized cardiology software or workstations, but with general purpose computer applications, such as a web browser. This integration profile is intended primarily for retrieving resting 12-lead ECGs, but may also retrieve ECG waveforms gathered during stress, Holter, and other diagnostic tests. This integration profile only addresses ECGs that are already stored in an information system. It does not address the process of ordering, acquiring, storing, or interpreting the ECGs.[56] See **Profile. NOTE: ECG is an IHE Profile.**

ECHO Describes the workflow associated with digital echocardiography (diagnostic test that uses ultrasound waves to create an image), specifically transthoracic echo, transesophageal echo, and stress echo. As with the Cath Workflow integration profile, this profile deals with patient identifiers, orders, scheduling, status reporting, multi-stage exams (especially stress echo), and data storage. It also specifically addresses the issues of acquisition modality devices that are only intermittently connected

to the network, such as portable echo machines, and addresses echo-specific data requirements.[56] *See* **Profile. NOTE: ECHO is an IHE Profile.**

ECN Explicit congestion notifier. A 2-bit IP packet header field that allows reduction of the number of Transmission Control Protocol (TCP) retransmissions in the Internet.[1]

eCommerce Commonly known as *e-commerce* or *electronic commerce*, consists of the buying, selling, marketing and servicing of products or services over electronic systems such as the Internet and other computer networks.[158] *See* **EC.**

ED Encapsulated data. The coupling or encapsulation of the data with a select group of functions that defines everything that can be done with the data.[7]

ED Evidence documents. Defines interoperable ways for observations, measurements, results, and other procedure details recorded in the course of carrying out a procedure step to be output by devices, such as acquisition systems and other workstations; to be stored and managed by archival systems; and to be retrieved and presented by display and reporting systems. This allows detailed non-image information, such as measurements, CAD results, procedure logs, etc., to be made available as input to the process of generating a diagnostic report. The evidence documents may be used either as additional evidence for the reporting physician, or in some cases, for selected items in the evidence document to be included in the diagnostic report.[56] See **Profile. NOTE: ED is an IHE Profile.**

EDC Electronic data capture system. A computerized system designed for the collection of clinical data in electronic format for use mainly in human clinical trials.[7]

EDDS Electronic document digital storage. Document management systems available online.[32] *See* **Decision support clinical and analytic** and **Decision support system.**

EDI Electronic data interchange. 1. Even before HIPAA, the American National Standards Institute (ANSI) approved the process for developing a set of EDI standards known as the X12. EDI is a collection of standard message formats that allows businesses to exchange data via any electronic messaging service. **2.** The electronic transfer of data between companies using networks, to include the Internet. Secure communications are needed in healthcare to exchange eligibility information, referrals, authorization, claims, encounter, and other payment data needed to manage contracts and remittance.[43]

EDI Electronic data interchange gateway. An electronic process to send data (claims, membership, and benefits) back and forth between providers and insurance companies.[5]

EDIT In CMS, the logic within the Standard Claims Processing System (or PSC Supplemental Edit Software) that selects certain claims, evaluates or compares information on the selected claims or other accessible source, and, depending on the evaluation, takes action on the claims, such as pay in full, pay in part, or suspend for manual review.[118]

EED Early event detection. This component of PHIN preparedness uses case and suspect case reporting, along with statistical surveillance of health-related data, to support the earliest possible detection of events that may signal a public health emergency.[46]

EDXL Emergency data exchange language. A standard message distribution framework for data sharing among emergency information systems.

EDXL–HAVE Emergency data exchange language - hospital availability exchange. The Hospital AVailability Exchange (HAVE) describes a standard message for data sharing among emergency information systems using the XML-based Emergency Data Exchange Language (EDXL).[91]

EEPROM Electronically erasable programmable read only memory. A reprogrammable memory chip that can be electronically erased and reprogrammed via a reader/writer device.[1]

EGA Enhanced graphics adapter. Color display system providing 16 to 64 colors at a resolution of 640x480.[1]

E-GOV The 'E-Government Act of 2002' was signed into law by President George W. Bush in July 2002: 'This legislation builds upon the Administration's expanding E-Government initiative by ensuring strong leadership of the

information technology activities of Federal agencies, a comprehensive framework for information security standards and programs, and uniform safeguards to protect the confidentiality of information provided by the public for statistical purposes. The Act also assists in expanding the use of the Internet and computer resources in order to deliver Government services, consistent with the reform principles I outlined on July 10, 2002, for a citizen-centered, results-oriented, and market-based Government.'[44]

EGP Exterior gateway protocol. An old protocol that advertises the networks that can be reached within an autonomous system by advertising its IP addresses to a router in another autonomous system.[1]

EHR Electronic health record. 1. A longitudinal electronic record of patient health information generated by one or more encounters in any care delivery setting. Included in this information are patient demographics, progress notes, problems, medications, vital signs, past medical history, immunizations, laboratory data, and radiology reports and images. The EHR automates and streamlines the clinician's workflow. The EHR has the ability to generate a complete record of a clinical patient encounter, as well as supporting other care-related activities directly or indirectly via interface; including evidence-based decision support, quality management, and outcomes reporting. **2.** Health-related information on an individual that conforms to nationally recognized interoperability standards and that can be created, managed, and consulted by authorized clinicians and staff across more than one healthcare organization.[45,84] *See* **CPR, EMR,** and the **EHR Appendix**.

EHRS Electronic health record system.

EIDE Enhanced or extended integrated drive electronics. A standard interface for high-speed disk drives that operate at speeds faster than the standard Integrated Drive Electronics (IDE) interface. It allows the connection of four IDE devices.[1]

EIN Employer identification number. 1. Employers, as sponsors of health insurance for their employees, often need to be identified in healthcare transactions, and a standard identifier for employers would be beneficial for electronically exchanged transactions. Healthcare providers may need to identify the employer of the participant on claims submitted electronically to health plans. **2.** The HIPAA standard is the EIN, the taxpayer identifying number for employers that is assigned by the Internal Revenue Service. This identifier has nine digits with the first two digits separated by a hyphen, as follows: 00-000000.[1,10]

EIP **Enterprise information portal. 1.** A framework for integrating information, people and processes across organization boundaries. Provides a secure unified access point.[176] **2.** An Internet-based approach to consolidate and present an organization's business intelligence and information resources through a single access point via an intranet.[7,1] Also known as *Internet portal* and *enterprise portal*.

EIS **Enterprise information system.** A class of decision support systems that provide predefined and easy-to-use data presentation, and exploration functionality to top-level executives.[1]

EIS **Executive information system.** A class of decision-support systems that provide predefined data presentation and exploration functionality to top-level executives. The system is intended to facilitate and support the information and decision-making needs of senior executives by providing ready access to both internal and external information relevant to meeting the strategic goals of the organization. Commonly considered a specialized form of decision-support systems (DSS). The emphasis of EIS is on graphical displays with reporting and drill-down capabilities. In general, EIS are an enterprise-wide DSS that allows executives to analyze, compare, and highlight trends and important variables, as well as monitor performance and identify opportunities and problems.[2]

EISA **Extended industry standard architecture.** 32-bit internal bus. Introduced in 1988 to compete with the PS/2 (Micro Channel) line of computers.[1]

eMAR **Electronic medication administration record.** An electronic record keeping system that documents when medications are given to a patient during a hospital stay. This application supports the five rights of medication administration (right patient, right medication, right dose, right time, and right route of administration) and can be used with bar coding functionality, although bar coding is not required. eMAR functionality is normally found within a nursing documentation application.[2]

EMC **Electronic media claims.** This term usually refers to a flat file format used to transmit or transport claims.[10]

EMI **Electromagnetic interference.** Any disruption caused by electromagnetic waves.[1]

EMPI **Enterprise master person index.** A system that maintains online listings of patients and medical records across multiple facilities and/or hospitals. It includes admission, registration, and discharge dates, as well as all data pertinent for re-registration. It provides for quick access to previous records and the ability to send new patient information to them.[2]

EMR **Electronic medical record. 1.** An application environment that is composed of the clinical data repository, clinical decision support, controlled medical vocabulary, order entry, computerized practitioner order entry, and clinical documentation applications. This environment supports the patient's electronic medical record across inpatient and outpatient environments, and is used by healthcare practitioners to document, monitor, and manage healthcare delivery. **2.** Health-related information on an individual that can be created, gathered, managed, and consulted by authorized clinicians and staff within one healthcare organization.[2,84]

EMRAM **Electronic medical record adoption model.** A tool developed by HIMSS Analytics guiding hospitals to improved clinical outcomes.[2]

EMSEC **Emanations security.** Measures taken to deny unauthorized persons information derived from intercept and analysis of compromising emanations from crypto-equipment of an IT system.[97]

EN **European standard.** Developed by the European Committee for Standardization (CEN). CEN is a major provider of European standards and technical specification.[7]

ENP **European nursing care pathways.** Provides nursing knowledge for nursing professionals in terms of a nursing language implemented in a classification system for the illustration of the nursing process. The nursing classification ENP® consists of the vertical level of the classes: nursing diagnoses, characteristics, resources, nursing objectives and nursing interventions, and intervention guiding specifications. Within the individual classes, the organizing principle is either hierarchical or coordinate. In the ENP® system, every single ENP® nursing diagnosis, supported by nursing literature, relates horizontally and class-spanning to other objects (characteristics, etiologies, resources, nursing objectives, and nursing interventions). According to the ENP® developers, these nursing diagnosis-related pathways represent up-to-date nursing knowledge and can be understood as a knowledge management system for nursing due to semantic networks. ENP® is among the pre-combined nursing classifications and is conceived for front-end use.[113]

EOB Explanation of benefits. A document detailing how a claim was processed according to the insured's benefits.[15]

EOP Explanation of payment. Generated to the provider in reply to a claim submission.[15]

EP Eligible professional. According to the Centers for Medicare & Medicaid Services (CMS), Eligible Professionals (EPs) under the Medicare EHR Incentive Program include: Doctors of medicine or osteopathy, doctors of dental surgery or dental medicine, doctors of podiatry, doctors of optometry and chiropractors. Medicaid Eligible professionals include: Physicians (primarily doctors of medicine and doctors of osteopathy), nurse practitioners, certified nurse-midwives, dentists, and physician assistants who furnish services in a Federally Qualified Health Center or Rural Health Clinic that is led by a physician assistant.[130]

EPHI Electronic protected health information. Any protected health information (PHI) that is created, stored, transmitted, or received electronically.[48]

ePHR Electronic personal health record. A universally accessible, layperson comprehensible, lifelong tool for managing relevant health information, promoting health maintenance, and assisting with chronic disease management via an interactive, common data set of electronic health information and eHealth tools. The ePHR is owned, managed, and shared by the individual or his or her legal proxy(s), and must be secure to protect the privacy and confi-

dentiality of the health information it contains. It is not a legal record unless so defined, and is subject to various legal limitations.[45] *See* **PHR**.

EPROM Erasable programmable memory. Reusable firmware that can be programmed. Previous contents are erased by applying ultraviolet light through the window in the chip.[1]

ERA Electronic remittance advice. Any of several electronic formats for explaining the payments of healthcare claims.[10]

ERD Emergency repair disk. Disk that contains machine-specific repair process information on registry (system, software, security, SAM) and system files for use when failures occur.[1]

ERD Entity relationship diagram. 1. A diagram showing entities and their relationships. Relates to business data analysis and database design. **2.** An entity relationship (ER) model shows how the sets of information contained in architectures are related to each other.[18,7]

ERISA Employee Retirement Income and Security Act of 1975. Most group health plans covered by ERISA are also health plans under Health Insurance Portability and Accountability Act (HIPAA).[48]

ERP Enterprise resource planning. Management information systems that integrate and automate many of the business functions associated with the operations or production aspects of an enterprise, such as general ledger, budgeting, materials management, purchasing, payroll, and human resources.[7,1]

ESDI Enhanced small device interface. Short-lived hard disk drive interface standard introduced by Compaq. Step in technology after MFM, and before Integrated Device Electronics (IDE).[1]

ESL eXtensible style sheet Language. A family of languages that allows one to describe how files encoded in the XML standard are to be formatted or transformed. XSL Transformation (XSLT) is used to transform the XML document, and XSL Formatting Objects (XSL-FO) is used to render the transformed document.[8]

ETL Extraction transformation loading. A data warehousing term. The collection of methods, processes, and technology that perform the acquisition, cleansing, transformation, integration, and loading of raw data sources into a data warehouse.[1]

EUA Enterprise user authentication. A means to establish one name per user that can then be used on all of the devices and software that participate in this integration profile, greatly facilitating centralized user authentication management and providing users with the convenience and speed of a single sign-on. This profile leverages Kerberos (RFC 1510) and the HL7 clinical context object workgroup standard (user subject).[56]

F

FAQ Frequently asked questions. A collection of information on any subject for which questions are typically asked. FAQ postings provide quick answers without the need or expense of a staff person answering the question on the phone or in writing, and are viewed as a time-saving feature of web sites that provides a return on investment.[1]

FAR False acceptance rate. Refers to the rate at which an unauthorized individual is accepted by the system as a valid user.[114]

FAT File allocation table. 16-bit file cluster system technique used by MS-DOS and Windows operating systems to manage disk space. Can also be used with Windows NT.[1]

FCOE Fiber channel over Ethernet. An encapsulation of fiber channel frames over Ethernet networks. This allows a fiber channel to use 10-gigabit Ethernet networks (or higher speeds) while preserving the fiber channel protocol.[2]

FDDI Fiber distributed data interface. Fiber optic dual token ring network within the 802.8 standard.

FFS Fee for service. Contract method to pay a contracted fee for services performed by providers.[32]

FHA Federal health architecture. An E-government Line of Business initiative managed by the Office of the National Coordinator of Health IT. Formed to coordinate health IT activities among the more than 20 federal agencies that provide health and healthcare services to citizens, including the Department of Health & Human Services (HHS), Department of Defense (DoD), Department of Veterans Affairs (VA), Department of Homeland Security (DHS), Environmental Protection Agency (EPA), Department of Agriculture (USDA), and Department of Energy (DOE). FHA provides a framework for linking health business processes to technology solutions and standards and for demonstrating how these solutions achieve improved health performance outcomes.[178]

FHIR Fast healthcare interoperability resources. Defines a set of resources for health. These resources represent granular clinical concepts that can be exchanged in order to quickly and effectively solve problems in healthcare and related processes. The resources cover the basic elements of healthcare—patients, admissions, diagnostic reports, medications, and problem lists—with their typical participants, and also support a range of richer and more complex clinical models. The simple direct definitions of the resources are based on thorough requirements gathering, formal analysis and extensive cross-mapping to other relevant standards.[16]

FIFO First in, first out. An abstraction related to way of organizing and manipulating data relative to time and prioritization.

FIPS Federal information processing standard. A standard for adoption and use by federal departments and agencies that has been developed within the Information Technology Laboratory and published by NIST, a part of the US Department of Commerce. A FIPS covers some topics in information technology to achieve a common level of quality or some level of interoperability.[114]

FSA Flexible spending account. A method of setting aside pre-tax dollars for healthcare reimbursement.[15]

FTF Face to face.

FTP File transfer protocol. 1. A standard high-level protocol for transferring files of different types between computers over a TCP/IP network. FTP can be used with a command line interface or graphical user interface. **2.** The name of a utility program available on several operating systems, which makes use of this protocol to access and transfer files on remote computers.[1]

G

GB **Gigabyte.**[1]

GBps **Gigabytes per second.** Transmission of a billion bits per second.[1]

GELLO **Guideline Expression Language, Object Oriented.**[30] An object-oriented query and expression language for clinical decision support.[92]

GIF **Graphics interchange format.** Standard for encoding, transmitting, decoding, and providing photo quality images. Introduced by CompuServe in 1987 to allow network transmission of photo-quality graphics images.[1]

GIG **Global information grid.** A globally interconnected, end-to-end set of information capabilities, associated processes, and personnel for collecting, processing, storing, disseminating, and managing information on demand.[23]

GIGO **Garbage in, garbage out.** Synonymous with the entry of inaccurate or useless data and processed output of worthless/useless information.[1]

GSM **Global system for mobile communications. 1.** A worldwide digital standard used in nearly all countries in the world except Japan and the United States GSM is a pure digital service that can transmit IP packets to the Internet, and uses an array of fixed antennas in geographical cells that connect various mobile devices to the network. **2.** GSM uses 1,900 MHz in the United States, and 800 to 900 MHz in Europe and Asia. GSM providers also offer wireless application protocol (WAP) services, such as connection of a GSM phone to a laptop with a PC card or cable at a data rate of 9.6 Kbps.[1]

GSNW **Gateway services for NetWare.** Provides the ability to connect to and make NetWare server resources available to a Windows NT server.[1]

GUDID **Global unique device identification database.** A proposed Food and Drug Administration (FDA) publicly accessible database that would hold information about each medical device marketed in the United States.

GUI **Graphical user interface. 1.** User interface that employs graphical images for the execution of resources, as opposed to command line entry. Employs windows, icons, and menus in lieu of text to run programs and give commands to the computer. It is usually a window system accessed through a pointing device, such as a mouse. **2.** Options on how the mouse interacts with the objects on the screen allows a point-and-click interface to identify or activate an icon, or a drag-and-drop interface to move an item to another location. **3.** A type of display format that enables user to choose commands, initiate programs, and other options by selecting pictorial representation (icons) via a mouse or a keyboard.[1]

H

HAN **Health alert network.** To ensure that each community has rapid and timely access to emergent health information; a cadre of highly-trained professional personnel; and evidence-based practices and procedures for effective public health preparedness, response, and service on a 24/7 basis.[46]

HCO **Healthcare organization.** Coordinates the delivery of healthcare. The organization should equip healthcare personnel with the knowledge, tools, and expertise that they need to deliver care and act as a link to community resources. One approach to addressing healthcare systems is to divide them into the micro level (patient interaction), meso level (healthcare organization and community), and the macro level (policy).[25]

HCPCS **Healthcare common system coding system. 1.** A set of healthcare procedure codes based on the American Medical Association Current Procedural Terminology. **2.** Currently incorporates CPT-4, national coach reporting certain healthcare supplies, durable medical equipment and other services not listed in CPT-4, and local codes for Medicaid reporting.[102,151]

hData A specification for exchanging electronic health data.[16]

HDSL **High bit-rate digital subscriber line.** One of the earliest forms of DSL, used for wideband digital transmission within a corporate site and between the telephone company and a customer. The main characteristic of HDSL is that it is symmetrical: an equal amount of bandwidth is available in both directions.[1]

HEDIS   Health plan employer data and information set. Set of standards for employers to use as a guide to compare health plans.[1] Also known as *Healthcare effectiveness data and information set. See* **MPI**.

HGC   Hercules graphics card. Monochrome graphics display at a resolution of 720x348. Display type used before CGA and EGA.[1]

HIE   Health information exchange.[1]. The sharing action between any two or more organizations with an executed business/legal arrangement that have deployed commonly agreed-upon technology with applied standards, for the purpose of electronically exchanging health-related data between the organizations. **2.** A catch-all phrase for all health information exchanges, including RHIOs, QIOs, AHRQ-funded communities, and private exchanges. **3.** A concept evolved from the Community Health Information Exchanges of the mid-1990s. HIE provides the capability to electronically move clinical information among disparate healthcare information systems and maintain the meaning of the information being exchanged. The goal of HIE is to facilitate access to and retrieval of clinical data to provide safer, more timely, efficient, effective, equitable, patient-centered care. HIE is also used by public health authorities to assist in the analysis of the health of populations.[45,15,84]

HIEx   Health insurance exchange. A set of state-regulated and standardized healthcare plans in the United States from which individuals may purchase health insurance eligible for federal subsidies. All exchanges must be fully certified and operational by January 1, 2014, under federal law.[7]

HIO   Health information organization. An organization that oversees and governs the exchange of health-related information among organizations according to nationally recognized standards. The purpose of an HIO is to perform oversight and governance functions for health information exchanges (HIEs).[84]

HIPAA   Health Insurance Portability and Accountability Act of 1996. According to the Centers for Medicare & Medicaid Services (CMS) web site, Title I of HIPAA protects health insurance coverage for workers and their families when they change or lose their jobs. Title II of HIPAA, the Administrative Simplification (AS) provisions, requires the establishment of national standards for electronic healthcare transactions and national identifiers for providers, health insurance plans, and employers. The AS provisions also address the security and privacy of health data. The standards are meant to improve the efficiency and effectiveness of the nation's healthcare system by encouraging the widespread use of electronic data interchange in healthcare.[7] Also known as the *Kennedy-Kassebaum Bill, K2*, or *Public Law 104-191*.

HIS   Health information system. The National Committee on Vital and Health Statistics (NCVHS) describes HIS as a comprehensive, knowledge-based system, capable of providing information to all who need it to make sound decisions about health.[103]

HIT   Health information technology. A 'marriage' between the clinical healthcare activities and computer science for the benefit of patients and those who provide healthcare services.[138]

HITECH Act   Health Information Technology for Economic and Clinical Health Act. Part of the ARRA that addresses privacy and security concerns related to the transmission of electronic health information. The HITECH Act broadened the scope of privacy and security measures for personal health records under Health Insurance Portability and Accountability Act, and also increased certain legal liabilities for noncompliance.[130]

HITEP   Health Information Technology Expert Panel. Expert panel charged with recommending a standardized quality data model for data representation to enable quality measurement through improved data flows within and across care settings.[208]

HITPC   Health information technology policy committee. A federal advisory committee charged with making recommendations to the National Coordinator for Health IT for the development and adoption of a nationwide health information infrastructure, including standards for the exchange of patient medical information.

HITSC   Health IT Standards Committee. A federal advisory committee charged with making recommendations to the National Coordinator for Health IT on standards, implementation specifications, and certification criteria for the electronic exchange and use of health information.[130]

HITSP   Healthcare Information Technology Standards Panel. A multi-stakeholder coordinating body, based on a contract by the Department of Health & Human Services, Office of National Coordinator for Health Information Technology, and the American National Standards Institute designed to provide the process within which affected parties can identify, select, and harmonize standards for communicating healthcare information throughout a National Nationwide Healthcare Information Network.[48]

HMO   Health maintenance organization. An entity that provides, offers, or arranges for coverage of designated health services needed by plan members for a fixed, prepaid premium.[15]

HPID   (Unique) Health plan identifier. HHS proposed a 2012 rule to establish a unique health plan identifier under the HIPAA standards for electronic healthcare transactions. The adoption of HPID and other entity identifier (OEID) would increase standardization within HIPAA standard transactions and would eliminate problems that several hospitals and healthcare providers experience frequently, such as improper routing of transactions, rejected transactions due to insurance identification errors, difficulty in determining patient eligibility and other claims processing challenges.[209]

HTML   Hypertext markup language. 1. ASCII-based language used for creating files to display documents or web pages to web browsers. **2.** Hypertext markup language is the standard provided by W3G used for web pages on the Internet.[1,4]

HTTP   Hypertext transfer protocol. 1. Communication link protocol used by World Wide Web servers and browsers to transfer/exchange HTML documents or files (text, graphic images, sound, video, and other multimedia files) over the Internet. **2.** Protocol with lightness and speed necessary for a distributed collaborative hypermedia information system. It is a generic, stateless, object-oriented protocol, which may be used for many similar tasks, such as name servers; and distributed object-oriented systems, by extending the commands or 'methods' used.[1,16] *See* **S-HTTP**.

Hz   Hertz. One cycle per second. Processing speeds for CPUs are measured in MHz.[1]

I

I/O   Input/output device. Allows computer to communicate with external devices, such as printers.[4]

IAM   Identity access management. Set of services to include authentication, user provisioning (UP), password management, role matrix management, enterprise single sign-on, enterprise access management, federation, virtual and meta-directory services, and auditing.[48]

IAP   Internet access provider. Company that provides basic Internet connection access. No additional services are provided, such as e-mail hosting.[1]

ICC   Integrated circuit chip. Another name for a chip, an integrated circuit is a small electronic device made out of a semiconductor material. Integrated circuits are used for a variety of devices, including microprocessors, audio and video equipment, and automobiles. Integrated circuits are often classified by the number of transistors and other electronic components they contain.[1]

ICD   The International Classification of Diseases. ICD is the standard diagnostic tool for epidemiology, health management and clinical purposes including the analysis of the general health situation of population groups. Also used to monitor the incidence and prevalence of diseases and other health program and to classify diseases and other health problems records on the many types of health and vital records include death certificates and health records. And, used for reimbursement and resource allocation decision-making by countries.[25]

ICIDH   International Classification of Impairments, Disability and Health. Classification system issued by the World Health Organization, for common language for clinical use, data collection and research.[151]

Icon A picture or symbol that graphically represents an object or a concept.[32]

ICON The ICON is an informational tool to describe nursing practice and provides data representing nursing practice in comprehensive health information systems. A combinatorial terminology for nursing practice that includes nursing phenomena, nursing actions, and nursing outcomes, and facilitates cross-mapping of local terms and existing vocabularies and classifications.[49]

ICR Intelligent call routing. Capability that automatically routes each call, based on caller profile, to the best available agent to handle the need, anywhere in the network.[1] See **PING**.

ICR Intelligent character recognition. The computer translation of manually entered text characters into machine-readable characters.[1]

ICR Internet relay chat. A program that allows 'live' conversations between people all over the world by typing messages back and forth across the Internet.[1]

ICU Intensive care unit. A specialized section of a hospital containing the equipment, medical and nursing staff, and monitoring devices necessary to provide intensive care. Also known as *critical care unit*, or may have a specialty name, such as *cardiac care unit*.[32]

IDE Integrated device electronics. A standard ISA 16-bit bus interface for high-speed disk drives that operates a 5 Mbps with two attached devices (master and slave). Invented in 1986 and introduced in microcomputers in 1989/1990.[1]

IDM Identity digital management. Comprised of the set of business processes, and a supporting infrastructure, for the creation, maintenance, and use of digital identities within a legal and policy context.[48]

IDMS Identity management system. 1. Comprised of one or more systems or applications that manages identity verification, validation, and issuance process. **2.** Software that is used to automate administrative tasks such as resetting user passwords. It enables users to reset their own passwords. There is also iden-

tity management 'password synchronization' software that enables users to access resources across the system with a single password, or single sign-on. In an enterprise setting, identity management is used to increase security and productivity, while decreasing cost and redundant effort.[114,2]

IDN Integrated delivery network. Commonly used to refer to an integrated delivery system, but may also be used when referring more to the network of providers vs. the system as a whole.[1]

IDR Intelligent document recognition. 1. Based on intelligent character recognition, the IT system automatically identifies structural features of a document to allow for a more rapid creation of the document text. **2.** Provides the ability to make sense of and help manage the unstructured, untagged information that is coming into the corporation or organization. It can provide the front-end understanding needed to feed business process management (BPM) and business intelligence (BI) applications, as well as traditional accounting and document or records management systems.[17,226]

IDS Integrated delivery system. A healthcare organization (HCO) that owns at least two hospitals.[2]

IGP Interior gateway protocol. Used to advertise routing information within an autonomous system.[1]

IHE Integrating the Healthcare Enterprise. An initiative by healthcare professionals and industry to improve the way computer systems in healthcare share information. IHE promotes the coordinated use of established standards such as DICOM and HL7 to address specific clinical need in support of optimal patient care. Systems developed in accordance with IHE communicate with one another better, are easier to implement, and enable care providers to use information more effectively.[56] See **Appendix B**.

IIF Information in identifiable form. Any representation of information that permits the identity of an individual to whom the information applies to be reasonably inferred by either direct or indirect means.[114]

IIS Internet information server. Server that provides HTTP and FTP services to web browsers.[1]

IKE   Internet key exchange. A key management protocol standard that is used in conjunction with the IPSec standard. IPSec is an IP security feature that provides robust authentication and encryption of IP packets.[1]

ILD   Injection laser diode. Laser diode that provides the light pulses used with single-mode fiber to convey data transmission information.[1]

IMP   Internet control message protocol. An extension to the Internet protocol, or IP, that supports packets containing error, control, and information messages. The PING command uses IMP to test an Internet connection.[1]

InterNIC   Internet Network Information Center. Agency that provides and coordinates Internet services, such as IP addresses. In addition, the center also handles registration of IP addresses and domain names.[1] Also known as *NIC.*

iOS   (originally) iPhone operating system. Mobile operating system developed and distributed by Apple. Apple does not license iOS for installation on non-Apple hardware.

IP   Internet protocol. Basic Internet transmission protocol based on a connectionless best-effort packet.[1]

IPA   Individual practice association. HMO model that contracts with an entity, which in turn contracts with physicians to provide healthcare services in return for a negotiated fee. Physicians continue in their existing individual or group practices and are compensated on a per capita, fee schedule, or fee-for-service basis.[15]

IRB   Institutional review board. A specially constituted review body established or designated by an entity, in accordance with 45 CFR Part 46, to protect the welfare of human subjects recruited to participate in biomedical or behavioral research.[118]

IRD   Information resource department. Department within a facility that provides data automation, hardware, software, and user support. Usually associated with US Army facilities.[1]

IrDA   Infrared Data Association. A group of device manufacturers that worked on the development of a standard for transmitting data via infrared light waves, the IrDA port.[143]

IRM   Information resource management. Department within a facility that provides data automation, hardware, software, and user support. Usually associated with US Air Force and Marine Corps facilities.[1]

IRQ   Interrupt request. Standard interrupt assignment for the system timer.[1]

ISA   Industry standard architecture. Eight- and 16-bit internal busused to identify an Internet server application.[1]

ISDN   Integrated service digital network. A data transfer technology that can transfer data significantly faster than a dial-up modem. ISDN enables wide-bandwidth digital transmission over the public telephone network, which means more data can be sent at one time. A typical ISDN connection can support transfer rates of 64K or 128K of data per second.[2]

ISO/TC 215   International Organization for Standardization (ISO) Technical Committee for Health Informatics. Standardization in the field of information for health, and Health Information and Communications Technology (ICT). Promotes interoperability between independent systems, to enable compatibility and consistency for health information and data, as well as to reduce duplication of effort and redundancies.[3]

ISP   Internet service provider. Company that provides Internet connectivity and Internet-related services, online computer access, web site hosting, and domain name registration for an added fee beyond their costs with the InterNIC or other registration retailers.[1]

ITMRA   Information Technology Management Reform Act of 1996. Former name of the Clinger-Cohen Act of 1996.[1]

ITSEC   Information Technology Security. Protection of information technology against unauthorized access to or modification of information, whether in storage, processing, or transit, and against the denial of service to authorized users, including those measures necessary to detect, document, and counter such threats. Protection and maintenance of confidentiality, integrity, availability, and accountability.[97]

IVD   Interactive video disk. A combination of computer and laser disk technology, which can be rapidly accessed through instructions on the computer disk to hold still and motion pictures; useful for providing simulation experiences.[6]

IVR Interactive voice response. Ability to access information over the phone (claim payments, claim status, and a patient's eligibility).[15]

J

JAD Joint application development. A development methodology that involves continuous interaction with users and designers of the system in development. JAD centers on workshop sessions that are structured and focused to improve the quality of the final product by focusing on the up-front portion of the development lifecycle, thus reducing the likelihood of errors that are expensive to correct later.[58]

JPEG Joint photographic experts group. Standard for encoding, transmitting, and decoding full-color and gray-scale still images. JPEG is a graphic file format that has a sophisticated technique for compressing full-color bitmapped graphics, such as photographs.[1]

JTC Joint technical committee. A standards body straddling the International Organization for Standardization (ISO) and International Electrotechnical Commission (IEC).[220]

JWG Joint working group. A harmonization initiative of Health Informatics Standards organizations: CEN/TC251, ISO/TC215 and HL7 formed at an inaugural Joint Working Group meeting in Brisbane hosted by ISO/TC215 and Standards Australia.[16]

K

KB Kilobyte. Equal to 1,024 bytes of digital data.[1]

Kbps Kilobits per second. Transmission of a thousand bits per second.[1]

KHz Kilohertz. One thousand cycles per second.[1]

KIN Key image notes. Specifies transactions that allow a user to mark one or more images in a study as significant by attaching to them a note managed together with the study. This note includes a title stating the purpose of marking the images and a user comment field. Physicians may attach key image notes to images for a variety of purposes: referring physician access, teaching files selection, consultation with other departments, and image quality issues, etc.[56] *See* **Profile. NOTE: KIN is an IHE Profile.**

L

LIS Laboratory information system. An application to streamline the process management of the laboratory for basic clinical services, such as hematology and chemistry. This application may provide general functional support for microbiology reporting, but does not generally support blood bank functions. Provides an automatic interface to laboratory analytical instruments to transfer verified results to nurse stations, chart carts, and remote physician offices. The module allows the user to receive orders from any designated location, process the order, and report results, and maintain technical, statistical, and account information. It eliminates tedious paperwork, calculations, and written documentation, while allowing for easy retrieval of data and statistics.[2] Also known as *LIS, laboratory information management system (LIMS)*, and *laboratory management systems (LMS)*.

LAN Local area network. A single network of physically interconnected computers that is localized within a small geographical area. Operates in a span of short distances (office, building, or complex of buildings).[1,2] *See* **MAN, WAN, WLAN.**

LAT Local-area transport. Non-routable and bridgeable protocol used by DEC to support terminal servers.[1]

LCD Liquid crystal display. The display screen of an electronic device.[1]

LEAP Lightweight and efficient application protocol. One of several protocols used with the International Electrical and Electronics Engineers (IEEE) 802.1 standard for local area network (LAN) port access control. In the IEEE framework, a LAN station cannot pass traffic through an Ethernet hub or wide local area network (WLAN) access point until it successfully authenticates itself. The station must identify itself and prove that it is an authorized user before it is actually allowed to use the LAN.[2]

LIFO   Last in, first out. A queue that executes last-in requests before previously queued requests.[1] Also called a *stack.*

LIMS   Laboratory information management systems. *See* **LIMS.**

LLC   Logical link control. Upper part of the second layer of the OSI model. Oversees and controls the exchange of data between two network nodes.[1]

LMHOSTS   LAN manager hosts. Text file that maps IP addresses to Windows computer names (NetBIOS names) to network computers outside the local subnet. Acts as a local WINS equivalent to provide a static type of WINS service.[1]

LOINC   Logical observation identifiers names and codes. Universal identifiers for laboratory and clinical observations, including such things as vital signs, hemodynamic measures, intake/output, EKG, obstetric ultrasound, cardiac echo, urologic imaging, gastro endoscopic procedures, pulmonary ventilator management, selected survey instruments, and other clinical observations.[50]

LQS   Lexicon query service. Standardizes a set of read-only interfaces able to access medical terminology system definitions, ranging from sets of codes, to complex hierarchial classification and categorization schemes.[124]

LSWF   Laboratory scheduled workflow. Establishes the continuity and integrity of clinical laboratory testing and observation data throughout the healthcare enterprise. It involves a set of transactions to maintain the consistency of ordering and patient information, to control the conformity of specimens, and to deliver the results at various steps of validation.[56] *See* **Profile. NOTE: LSWF is an IHE Profile.**

LTC   Long-term care. The segment of the healthcare continuum that consists of maintenance, custodial, and health services for the chronically ill or disabled; may be provided on an inpatient (rehabilitation facility, nursing home, mental hospital) or outpatient basis, or at home.[1]

LU   Logical unit. Portion of the ALU within the CPU that coordinates logical operations.[1]

M

MAC   Mandatory access control. A system of access control that assigns security labels or classifications to system resources and allows access only to entities (people, processes, devices) with distinct levels of authorization or clearance.[1]

MAC   Media access control. Lower portion of the second layer of the OSI model. Identifies the actual physical link between two nodes.[1]

MAC   Message authentication code. A digital code generated using a cryptographic algorithm, defined in an ISO standard that establishes that the contents of a message have not been altered or generated by an unauthorized party.[3]

MAN   Metropolitan-area network. 1. Provides high-speed data transfer regional connectivity through multiple physical networks. Operates over distances sufficient for a metropolitan area. An IEEE 802.6 standard. **2.** A backbone network that covers a metropolitan area and is regulated by state or local utility commissions. Suppliers that provide MAN services are telephone companies and cable services.[1,2] *See* **LAN, WAN. WLAN.**

MAP   Manufacturing automation protocol. A set of protocols developed by General Motors based on token bus (IEEE 802.4) and giving predictable real-time response.[220]

MAU   Media access unit. A token-ring network hub.[1]

Mb   Megabit. 1,048,576 bits or 1,024kb.[1]

MBDS   Minimum basic data set. A set of data that is the minimum required for a healthcare record to conform to a given standard.[4]

Mbps   Megabits per second. Transmission of a million bits per second.[1]

MDA   Model-driven architecture. A platform independent model providing for separate business and application functionality from the technology-specific code, while enabling interoperability within and across platform boundaries.[111]

MDM Medical document management message.

MDS Minimum data set. A core of elements to use in performing comprehensive assessments in long-term care facilities.[102]

MedDRA Medical Dictionary for Regulatory Activities. 1. Used by regulatory agencies and drug manufacturers. 2. A terminology developed under the auspices of the International Conference on Harmonization of Technical Requirements for Registration of Pharmaceuticals for Human Use. MedDRA is a standard international terminology for regulatory communication in the registration, documentation, and safety monitoring of medical products throughout all phases of their regulatory cycle. As a standard, MedDRA is expected to promote the harmonization of regulatory requirements and documentation for medical products in the US, Japan, and European Union.[14,151]

MEDS Minimum emergency data set. A standardized view of the critical components of a patient's past medical history.[1]

MeSH Medical subject heading. A thesaurus of concepts and terms used for the indexing of biomedical literature.[4]

mHealth Mobile health. A term used for the practice of medicine and public health, supported by mobile devices.[7]

MHz Megahertz. One million times, cycles, occurrences, alterations, or pulses per second. Used to describe a measurement of CPU or processor speed.[1]

MIB Medical information BUS. 1. A hardware and software standard (IEEE P1073) that enables standardized connections between medical monitoring devices and clinical information systems. 2. Institute of Electrical and Electronics Engineers P1073 (standard designation) standard for data exchange in a medical environment.[51]

MID Management information department. Department within a facility that provides data automation, hardware, software, and user support.[1]

MIME Multi-purpose Internet mail extensions. A format originally developed for attaching sounds, images, and other media files to electronic mail, but now also used with World Wide Web applications.[1]

MIPS Millions of instructions per second. Rate that a processor executes instructions. Used as a measurement of processing power and computer speed.[1]

MIS Management information system (services). A class of software that provides managers with tools for organizing and evaluating their department, or the staff that supports information systems.[1]

MITA Medicaid information technology architecture. A national framework to support improved systems development and healthcare management for the Medicaid enterprise.[102]

MLM Medical logic model. Arden Syntax for Medical Logic Systems Version 1.0 was adopted by ASTM in 1992.[39]

MMIS Medicaid Management Information System. An integrated group of procedures and computer processing operations (subsystems) developed at the general design level to meet the principal objectives of the Medicaid program.[102]

MOLAP Multidimensional online analytical processing (OLAP). A technical OLAP approach in which data are pre-summarized using specialized multi-dimensional DBMS technology in a very structured manner within pre-determined dimensions, allowing for very high performance.[1]

MOU Memorandum of understanding. 1. A document providing a general description of the responsibilities that are to be assumed by two or more parties in their pursuit of some goals. More specific information may be provided in an associated statement of work (SOW). 2. A document describing an agreement between parties that expresses a convergence of will and indicates an intended common line of action. Often used when parties do not wish to imply a legal commitment or in situations where the parties cannot create a legally enforceable agreement.[7]

MOV **QuickTime Video.** A file extension that denotes the file is a movie or video in Quick-Time format.[1]

MPEG **Motion picture expert group.** Standard for digital encoding, transmitting, decoding, and presentation of video recorder quality motion video.[1]

MPI **Master patient index. 1.** The unique numerical index identity of a patient that may contain the patient's Social Security number or any other locally derived or system-generated unique number. **2.** The MPI is important because it serves as the centerpiece for all subsequent functionality and software applications, such as links to the patient clinical record, the patient schedule for appointments, reporting results of lab, x-ray, pharmacy, patient-related images, etc. **3.** As part of HIPAA's unique identifier codes, a mandated standard considered controversial due to patient concern about these numbers being accidentally made available providing potential means for, and thereby identifying, the confidential records to other persons.[1]

MPP **Massively parallel processing.** A computing platform technology that clusters multiple independent servers, each managed by its own operating system.[1]

MRI **Magnetic resonance imaging.** Magnetic fields and radio waves to construct 2-D images or 3-D models of internal body structures.[2]

MS-DOS **Microsoft disk operating system.** Set of 16-bit software programs that direct system-level computer operation. Developed by Microsoft in the early 1980s for the 8086 CPU.[1]

MTBF **Mean time between failure.** The average device operating time, as measured between the last failure until the next failure occurs.[1]

MTTD **Mean time to diagnose.** The time taken to diagnose a problem.[1]

MTTR **Mean time to repair.** The time it takes to restore a device to service from a failure.[1]

MU **Meaningful Use.** The set of standard defined by the Centers for Medicare & Medicaid Services (CMS) Incentive Programs that governs the use of electronic health records and allows eligible providers and hospitals to earn incentive payments by meeting specific criteria.[178]

MUMPS **Massachusetts General Hospital Utility Multi-Programming System.** A procedural, interpreted general-purpose programming language oriented toward database applications, with built-in multi-user/multi-tasking support.[1]

MUX **Multiplexer, multipleXer, or multipleXor.** A network device in which multiple streams of information are combined from different sources onto a common medium for transmission.[1]

N

NAHDO **National Association of Health Data Organizations.** A group that promotes the development and improvement of state and national health information systems.[9]

NAS **Network attached storage.** A hard disk storage system that has its own network address rather than being attached to the department computer that is serving applications to a network's workstation users. By removing storage access and its management from the department server, both application programming and files can be served faster because they are not competing for the same processor resources.[2]

NAT **Network address translation.** Involves rewriting the source and/or destination addresses of IP packets as they pass through a router or firewall. Most systems using NAT do so in order to enable multiple hosts on a private network to access the Internet using a single public IP address. According to specifications, routers should not act in this way, but many network administrators find NAT a convenient technique and use it widely. Nonetheless, NAT can introduce complications in communication between hosts.[7] Also known as *network masquerading* or *IP-masquerading*.

NAV **Notification of document availability.** A mechanism allowing notifications to be sent point-to-point to systems and users within an affinity domain, eliminating the need for manual steps or polling mechanisms.[56] **NOTE: NAV is an IHE Profile.**

NCPDP **National Council for Prescription Drug Programs.** Develops business solutions, including ANSI-accredited standards, and guidance for promoting information exchanges related to medications, supplies, and services within the healthcare system.[54]

NDC **National Drug Code.** The Drug Listing Act of 1972 requires registered drug establishments to provide the Food and Drug Administration (FDA) with a current list of all drugs manufactured, prepared, propagated, compounded, or processed by it for commercial distribution. (*See* Section 510 of the Federal Food, Drug, and Cosmetic Act [Act] [21 U.S.C. § 360]). Drug products are identified and reported using a unique, three-segment number, called the National Drug Code (NDC), which is a universal product identifier for human drugs.[1]

NDIS **Network driver interface specification.** For writing device drivers for network interface cards. Using the NDIS specification, multiple protocols can be bound to a single network adapter.[1]

NEDSS **National Electronic Disease Surveillance System.** An initiative that promotes the use of data and information system standards to advance the development of efficient, integrated, and interoperable surveillance systems at federal, state, and local levels. It is a major component of the Public Health Information Network (PHIN).[48]

NEMSIS **National Emergency Medical System Information System.** Framework for collecting, storing, and sharing standardized emergency medical system (EMS) data from states nationwide.[211]

NetBEUI **NetBIOS extended user interface.** Fast, easy to install, non-configurable, non-routable network protocol for use with up to 200 network nodes. Resides at the open systems interconnection (OSI) transport layer.[1]

NetBIOS **Network basic input output system.** Standard interface to networks employing IBM and compatible PCs. Implemented at the application layer. NetBIOS names cannot exceed 15 characters.[1]

NFS **Network file system.** A protocol developed by Sun Microsystems that allows a computer system to access files over a network as if they were on its local disks.[1]

NHII **Nationwide Health Information Infrastructure.** A healthcare standardization initiative for the development of an interoperable health information technology system. First proposed under President George W. Bush, the goal of NHII was to build an interoperable system of clinical, public health and health information technology (HIT) that encouraged public-private collaboration with the federal government in a leadership role. The NHII has evolved to become the Nationwide Health Information Network.[42]

NwHIN **Nationwide Health Information Network. 1.** A secure, nationwide, interoperable health information infrastructure to connect providers, consumers, and others involved in supporting health and healthcare. **2.** A web-services series of specifications designed to securely exchange healthcare-related data. The Nationwide Health Information Network, often abbreviated as NHIN or NwHIN. **3.** Provides for the exchange of health information across the nation, between and among various organization and constituents, and is facilitated by nationally established standards for this exchange. NwHIN components include authentication, delivery protocols, security, directories, and vocabulary/documents/message standards.[178,7,2]

NHRIC **National Health Related Items Code.** A system for identification and numbering of marketed device packages that is compatible with other numbering systems such as the National Drug Code (NDC) or Universal Product Code (UPC). In the early 1970s, the Drug Listing Branch of FDA set aside a block of numbers that could be assigned to medical device manufacturers and distributors. Those manufacturers who desire to use the NHRIC number for unique product identification may apply to FDA for a labeler code.[207]

NIC **Network information center. 1.** An organization that provides information, assistance, and services to network users. **2.** A computer circuit board or card that is installed in a computer so that it can be connected to a network.[1]

NIC **Network interface card.** A card that allows one to access a network. *See* **LAN adapter**.

NIC **Nursing intervention classification.** A comprehensive, research-based, standardized classification of interventions that nurses perform. NIC is useful for clinical documentation, communication of care across settings, integration of data across systems and settings, effectiveness research, productivity measurement, competency evaluation, reimbursement, and curricular design.[25]

NLP **Natural language processing.** A subfield of artificial intelligence and linguistics. It studies the problems inherent in the processing and manipulation of natural language, and natural language understanding devoted to making computers 'understand' statements written in human languages.[7]

NM **Nuclear medicine image integration.** Specifies how nuclear medicine images should be stored by acquisition modalities and workstations and how image displays should retrieve and make use of them. It defines the basic display capabilities that image displays are expected to provide and also how result screens, both static and dynamic, such as those created by NM cardiac processing packages, should be stored using DICOM objects that can be displayed on general purpose image display systems.[56] *See* **Profile. NOTE: NM is an IHE Profile.**

NMB **National member body.** The standards institute in each country that is a member of International Organization for Standardization (ISO).[3]

NMDS **Nursing minimum data set. 1.** The foundation for nursing languages development that identified nursing diagnosis, nursing intervention, nursing outcomes, and intensity of nursing care as unique nursing components of the Uniform Hospital Discharge Data Set (UHDDS). **2.** Essential set of information items that has uniform definitions and categories concerned with nursing. It is designed to be an abstraction tool or system for collecting uniform, standard, compatible, minimum nursing data.[52,6]

NMMDS **Nursing management minimum data set.** A data set used to describe environment at unit level of service related to nursing delivery (unit/service, patient/client population, care delivery method), as well as nursing care resources and financial resources.[52]

NOC **Nursing outcome classification.** A comprehensive, standardized classification of patient/client outcomes developed to evaluate the effects of nursing interventions. Standardized outcomes are necessary for documentation in electronic records, for use in clinical information systems, for the development of nursing knowledge, and for the education of professional nurses.[26]

NOC **Network operation center.** A location from which the operation of a network or Internet is monitored. Additionally, this center usually serves as a clearinghouse for connectivity problems and efforts to resolve those problems.[1]

NOI **Notice of intent.** A document that describes a subject area for which the federal government is considering developing regulations. It may describe the presumably relevant considerations and invite comments from interested parties. These comments can then be used in developing a notice of proposed rulemaking (NPRM) or a final regulation.[10]

NOS **Network operating system.** Operating system that includes special functions for connecting computers and devices into a local-area network (LAN). The term *network operating system*, however, is generally reserved for software that enhances a basic operating system by adding networking features. Novell Netware, Artisoft's LANtastic, Microsoft Windows Server, and Windows NT are examples of an NOS.[58]

NPF **National provider file.** The database envisioned for use in maintaining a national provider registry.[10]

NPI **National provider identifier. 1.** A system for uniquely identifying all providers of healthcare services, supplies, and equipment. **2.** A Health Insurance Portability and Accountability Act (HIPAA) Administrative Simplification Standard. The NPI is a unique identification number for covered healthcare providers. Covered healthcare providers, and all health plans and healthcare clearinghouses must use the NPIs in the administrative and financial transactions adopted under HIPAA. The NPI is a 10-position, intelligence-free numeric identifier (10-digit number). This means that the numbers do not carry other information about healthcare providers, such as the state in which they live or their medical specialty. The NPI must be used in lieu of legacy provider identifiers in the HIPAA standards transactions.[10,102]

NPRM   Notice of proposed rulemaking. A document that describes and explains regulations that the federal government proposes to adopt at some future date and invites interested parties to submit comments related to them. These comments can then be used in developing a final regulation.[10]

NSF   National standard format. Generically, this applies to any nationally standardized data format, but it is often used in a more limited way to designate the professional flat file record format used to submit professional claims.[10]

NSP   Network service provider. A company providing consolidated service for some combination of e-mail, voice mail, phone, and fax configurations on broadband or wireless handheld devices.[1] Also known as *unified messaging solutions* or *universal messaging*.

NSSN   National standards system network. A National Resource for Global Standards is a search engine that provides users with standards-related information from a wide range of developers, including organizations accredited by the American National Standards Institute (ANSI), other US private sector standards bodies, government agencies, and international organizations.[43]

NUMA   Non-uniform memory architecture. A computing platform technology that clusters multiple symmetrical multi-processing (SMP) nodes together, similar to massively parallel processing (MPP) technology.[1] *See* **SMP, MPP**.

NWIP   New work item proposal. First balloting phase for draft standards and draft technical specifications. During this phase, at least five experts from five participating ISO/TC 215 countries are chosen to work on the document.[3]

O

OASIS   Outcome and assessment information set. A group of data elements that represent core items of a comprehensive assessment for an adult home care patient, and form the basis for measuring patient outcomes for purposes of outcome-based quality improvement.

This assessment is performed on every patient receiving services of home health agencies that are approved to participate in the Medicare and/or Medicaid programs.[102]

OC   Optical carrier. Used to specify the speed of fiber optic networks conforming to the Synchronous Optical Networking (SONET) standard.[2]

OCR   Optical character recognition. A technology that scans a printed page and converts it into an electronic document that can be edited on a computer.[1]

OCSP   Online certificate status protocol. An Internet protocol used for obtaining the revocation status of an X.509 digital certificate.[7]

ODA   Open document architecture. A standard document file format created by the International Telecommunications Union-Telecommunication Standardization (ITU-T) to replace all proprietary document file formats. It should not be confused with the OASIS Open Document Format for Office Applications.[7] Also known as *open document*.

ODS   Operational data store. A subject-oriented, integrated, real-time, volatile store of detailed data, in support of operational and tactical decision making.[1]

OEID   Other entity identifier. Proposed data element for entities needing to be identified in standard transactions that are not health plans, healthcare providers or individuals.[103]

OEM   Original equipment manufacturer.[1]

OID   Object identifier. An identifier used to name an object, usually strings of numbers. In computer programming, an object identifier generally takes the form of an implementation-specific integer or pointer that uniquely identifies an object.[7]

OLAP   Online analytical processing. A high-level concept that describes a category of tools that aid in the analysis of multi-dimensional queries.[156]

OLE   Object linking and embedding. 1. A document standard developed by Microsoft that allows for the creation of objects within one application, and linking them into a second application. **2.** OLE is used for compound document management, as well as application data transfer via drag-and-drop and clipboard operations.[1,156]

OLTP Online transaction processing. A class of systems that supports or facilitates high transaction-oriented applications. OLTP's primary system features are immediate client feedback and high individual transaction volume.[156]

OM Outbreak management. The capture and management of information associated with the investigation and containment of a disease outbreak or public health emergencies are primary functions of public health.[46]

OOA Out of area. Not within the market geographic bounds.[15]

OON Out of network. In the geographic bounds, but not contracted.[7]

OOP Out of pocket. An amount patient pays at time of service.[8]

OOP Object-oriented programming. 1. An approach to software development that combines data and procedures into a single object. **2.** A computer program composed of a collection of individual units or objects, as opposed to a traditional view in which a program is a list of instructions to the computer. Each object is capable of receiving messages, processing data, and sending messages to other objects. **3.** Software programming model constructed around objects. This model compartmentalizes data into objects (data fields) and describes object contents and behavior through the declaration of classes (methods).[1,156] *See* **SOA.**

OpArc Operational architecture. *See* **Architecture.**[20]

OS Operating system. Software that manages basic computer operations, and supervises and controls tasks, such as Windows 95, 98, NT, Windows 2000, Me, CE, Linus, Palm OS, MAC OS X, OS/2, and UNIX.[1]

OS/2 Operating system/2. IBM's 32-bit GUI multi-tasking operating system with the ability to run DOS, Win16, Win 32, OS/2 16, and OS/2 32 applications, for 80286 and 80386 computers.[1]

OSI Open systems interconnection. A reference model to the protocols in the seven-layer data communications networking standards

model and services performed at each level. The OSI standard is defined by the International Organization for Standardization (ISO). The seven layers from the bottom are physical, data link, network, transport, session, presentation, and application.[1]

OWL Web ontology language. Designed for use by applications that need to process the content of information instead of just presenting information to humans. OWL facilitates greater machine interpretability of web content that that support by extensible markup language (XML), resource description framework (RDF) and RDF Schema (RDF-S) by providing additional vocabulary along with a formal semantics.[33]

P

P2P Peer-to-peer. 1. A network structure in which the computers share processing and storage tasks as equivalent members of the network. Different from a client/server network, in which computers are assigned specific roles. **2.** A general term for popular file-sharing systems like Gnutella, in which there is no central repository of files. Instead, files can be stored on, and retrieved from, any user's computer.[107]

P4P Pay for performance. Refers to the general strategy of promoting quality improvement by rewarding providers (meaning individual clinicians or, more commonly, clinics or hospitals) who meet certain performance expectations with respect to healthcare quality or efficiency. Performance can be defined in terms of patient outcomes but is more commonly defined in terms of processes of care (e.g., the percentage of eligible diabetics who have been referred for annual retinal examinations, the percentage of children who have received immunizations appropriate for their age, patients admitted to the hospital with pneumonia who receive antibiotics within six hours).[14]

PACS Picture archiving and communication systems. A system that begins by converting the standard storage of x-ray films into digitized electronic media that can later be retrieved by radiologists, clinicians, and other staff to view exam data and medical images. Computers or networks dedicated to the storage, retrieval, distribution, and presentation of images. Full PACS handle images from various modalities, such as ultrasonography, magnetic resonance imaging, positron emission tomography, computed tomography, and radiography (plain x-rays). Small-scale systems that handle images from a single modality (usually connected to a single acquisition device) are also known as *mini-PACS*.[1]

PAN   Personal-area network. Personal wireless devices, such as mobile phones, headsets and notebook PCs, connected together wirelessly via protocol such as Bluetooth.[47]

PAP   Password authentication protocol. Allows the use of clear text passwords at its lowest level. [1]

PAS   Publicly available specification. Standards from the International Organization for Standardization (ISO) freely available for standardization purposes. PAS are protected by ISO copyright.[3]

PBM   Pharmacy benefit manager. A company that administers drug benefit programs for employers and health insurance carriers.[47]

PC   Personal computer. A computer designed for use by one person at a time. PC is also commonly used to describe an IBM-compatible personal computer in contrast to an Apple Macintosh computer.[1]

PCB   Printed circuit board. Used to mechanically support and electrically connect electronic components using conductive pathways, tracks, or signal traces etched from copper sheets laminated onto a non-conductive substrate. Printed circuit boards are used in virtually all but the simplest commercially produced electronic devices.[7] Also known as a *printed wiring board* or *etched wiring board.*

PCDS   Patient care data set. A compilation of pre-coordinated terms used in patient records to record patients' problems, therapeutic goals, and care actions.[151]

PCI   Peripheral component interconnect. Standard CPU to I/O device interface with 32-, 64-, and 128-bit data paths. PCI motherboards automatically configure interrupts. Introduced in 1993.[1]

PCM   Patient care management. A system that enrolls or assigns patients to interventions

across the continuum of health and illness. It includes wellness exams and routine screenings, utilization reviews, event focus, short-term case management, and the management of long-term chronic conditions.[47]

PCMCIA   Personal computer memory card international. Association that has worked to standardize and promote PC card technology.[1]

PCMH   Patient-centered medical home. 1. A healthcare setting that facilitates partnerships between individual patients, and their personal physicians, and when appropriate, the patient's family. Care is facilitated by registries, information technology, health information exchange and other means to assure that patients get the indicated care when and where they need and want it in a culturally and linguistically appropriate manner. **2.** A model for transforming the organization and delivery of primary care.[191,14] Also known as a *primary care medical home.*

PCO   Physician contracting organization. A legal entity representing multiple physicians, practices, and clinics that contracts with other entities to provide healthcare services.[47]

PCP   Primary care provider. 1. PCPs specialize in internal medicine, pediatrics, family practice, or obstetrics/gynecology. They provide primary care to members and make referrals to specialty care providers. **2.** A nurse practitioner or a licensed physician's assistant can also provide this basic level of healthcare.[15,102]

PDA   Personal digital assistant. A hand-held computing device capable of containing streamlined versions of healthcare software that is compatible with other major systems, and capable of communicating through a direct serial connection, modem, or wireless interface.[2]

PDC   Primary domain controller. First operational computer in a Windows NT domain, and only PDC in a domain. Authenticates all users and maintains the master security accounts database.[1]

PDF   Portable document format. A PDF file is an electronic facsimile of a printed document; the filename extension for a packed data file.[1]

PDF 417   A two-dimensional bar code symbology, enabling error-free transmission of larger blocks of data than is feasible with a one-dimensional bar code.[99]

PDI Portable data for imaging. Specifies actors and transactions that provide the distribution of diagnostic and therapeutic imaging information on interchange media. The goal of this profile is to provide reliable interchange of evidence objects and diagnostic reports for import, display, or print by a receiving actor.[56] *See* **Profile**. **NOTE: PDI is an IHE Profile.**

PDP Policy decision point. The system entity that evaluates applicable policy and renders an authorization decision.[125] *See* **ACS**.

PDQ Patient demographic query. Provides ways for multiple distributed applications to query a central patient information server for a list of patients, based on user-defined search criteria. Patient demographics data can be entered directly into the application from which the user is querying by picking the appropriate record from a list of possible matches called a patient pick list.[56] *See* **Profile**. **NOTE: PDQ is an Integrating the Healthcare Enterprise (IHE) Profile.**

PEP Policy enforcement point. The system entity that performs access control, by making decision requests and enforcing authorization decisions.[125] *See* **ACS**.

Perl Practical extraction and report language. An interpreted procedural programming language designed by Larry Wall. Perl has a unique set of features, some borrowed from imperative computer programming language (C), and from others.[1] *See* **CGI**.

PET scan Positron emission tomography scan. A digital imaging modality capable of detecting subtle differences in temperature.[36]

PGP Presentation of grouped procedures. Addresses what is sometimes referred to as the linked studies problem: viewing image subsets resulting from a single acquisition with each image subset related to a different requested procedure (e.g., CT chest, abdomen, and pelvis). It provides a mechanism for facilitating workflow when viewing images and reporting on individual requested procedures that an operator has grouped (often for the sake of acquisition efficiency and patient comfort). A single acquired image set is produced, but the combined use of the scheduled workflow transactions and the consistent presentation of images allow separate viewing and interpretation of the image subsets related to each of the requested procedures.[56] *See* **Profile**. **NOTE: PGP is an IHE Profile.**

PGP Pretty good privacy. A public key encryption program used to encrypt and decrypt e-mail over the Internet. Also, PGP may be used for digital signatures to let the receiver know the sender's identity and that the transmission was not changed en route.[1]

PHI Protected/personal health information. Any individually identifiable health information, whether oral or recorded in any form or medium that is created or received by a healthcare provider, health plan, public health authority, employer, life insurer, school or university, or healthcare clearinghouse; and relates to the past, present, or future physical or mental health or condition of an individual; the provision of healthcare to an individual; or the past, present, or future payment for the provision of healthcare to an individual. Any data transmitted or maintained in any other form or medium by covered entities, including paper records, fax documents and all oral communications, or any other form (i.e., screen prints of eligibility information, printed e-mails that have identified an individual's health information, claim, or billing information, hard copy birth or death certificate). Protected health information excludes school records that are subject to the Family Educational Rights and Privacy Act and employment records held in Department of Homeland Security's role as an employer.[118]

PHIN Public health information network. Centers for Disease Control and Prevention vision for advancing fully capable and interoperable information systems in the many organizations that participate in public health. PHIN is a national initiative to implement a multi-organizational business and technical architecture for public health information systems.[46] *See* **CDC**.

PHIN-MS Public health information network-messaging system. A protocol for secure transmission of data, based on the ebXML model. Developed and supported by Centers for Disease Control and Prevention (CDC). The protocol allows for rapid and secure messages to send sensitive health information over the

Internet to other local, state, and federal organizations, as well as the CDC.[46]

PHMT   Personal health management tool. A set of functions that assist a consumer in managing his or her health status or healthcare.[47]

PHO   Physician hospital organization. A management service organization in which the partners are physicians and hospitals.[220]

PHR   Personal health record. 1. An electronic personal health record (ePHR) is a universally accessible, layperson comprehensible, lifelong tool for managing relevant health information, promoting health maintenance, and assisting with chronic disease management via an interactive, common data set of electronic health information and e-health tools. The ePHR is owned, managed, and shared by the individual or his or her legal proxy(s) and must be secure to protect the privacy and confidentiality of the health information it contains. It is not a legal record unless so defined and is subject to various legal limitations. **2.** Usually used when referring to the version of the health/medical record owned by the consumer/patient. **3.** An electronic record of health-related information on an individual that conforms to nationally recognized interoperability standards and that can be drawn from multiple sources while being managed, shared, and controlled by the individual.[45,15,84] *See* **Appendix E**.

PIDS   Person identification service. Defines a set of interfaces to an interchangeable set of services that provides a best match or ordered list of best matches to possibly incomplete or conflicting data about a person.[124]

PIM   Platform independent model. A model of a software or business system that is independent of the specific technological platform used to implement it. For example, HTML defines a model for hypertext that includes concepts such as title, headings, paragraphs, etc. This model is not linked to a specific operating system or web browser and is, therefore, being successfully implemented on a variety of different computing systems. The term *platform-independent model* is most frequently used in the context of model-driven architectures.[144]

PIN   Personal identification number. Used to authenticate or identify a user.[1]

PING   Packet INternet groper. Utility used to test destination reachability. Sends an Internet control message protocol (ICMP) echo request to the destination and waits for a reply.[1]

PIP   Policy information point. Point that can provide external information to a policy decision point.[125] *See* **ACS**.

PIR   Patient information reconciliation. Extends the scheduled workflow integration profile by offering the means to match images, diagnostic reports, and other evidence objects acquired for a misidentified or unidentified patient (e.g., during a trauma case) with the patient's record.[56] *See* **Profile**. **NOTE: PIR is an IHE Profile.**

PIV   Personal identification verification.

PIX   Patient identifier cross-referencing. Provides cross-referencing of patient identifiers from multiple patient identifier domains. These patient identifiers can then be used by identity consumer systems to correlate information about a single patient from sources that know the patient by different identifiers.[56] *See* **Profile**. **NOTE: PIX is an IHE Profile.**

PKC   Public key certificate. X.509 public key certificates (PKCs), which bind an identity and a public key; the identity may be used to support identity-based access control decisions after the client proves that it has access to the private key that corresponds to the public key contained in the PKC.[121]

PKI   Public key infrastructure. 1. Technology, facilities, people, operational procedures, and policy to support public key-based security mechanisms. It is an enabler for these encryption and digital signatures. **2.** Infrastructure used in the relation between a key holder and a relying party that allows a relying party to use a certificate relating to the key holder for at least one application using a public key dependent security service, and that includes a certification authority, a certificate data structure, means for the relying party to obtain current information on the revocation status of the certificate, a certification policy, and methods to validate the certification practice.[1,121]

PNDS   Perioperative nursing data set. A standardized nursing vocabulary of nursing diagnoses, nursing interventions, and nurse-sensitive patient outcomes that addresses the perioperative patient experience from pre-admission to discharge.[52]

PNG Portable network graphics. A bit-mapped image format that employs lossless data compression. PNG was created to improve upon and replace graphics interchange format (GIF) as an image-file format not requiring a patent license.[7]

POP Post office protocol. A server using this protocol to hold users' incoming e-mail until they read or download it.[1]

POP server Point of presence server. A description for a server supporting POP, serving as a dial-up modem for an Internet service provider (ISP) or e-mail service provider.[1] See **ISP**.

PORT Patient outcomes research teams.

POSIX Portable open systems interface. IEEE standard for UNIX-like program implementation. Capable of case-sensitive file naming, last-access time stamping, and hard links. A standard, not an operating system. Windows NT supports POSIX.[1]

POTS Plain old telephone system.[1] See **PSTN**.

PPACA Patient Protection and Affordable Care Act (Public Law 111-148). Focuses on provisions to expand healthcare coverage, control healthcare costs, and improve healthcare delivery system.[228]

PPO Preferred provider organization. A list of preferred providers that members utilize at a discounted fee.[1]

PPP Point-to-point protocol. Protocol that links two networks for serial data transfer. Supports multiple network protocols (TCP/IP, IPX/SPX, and NetBEUI) compression and encryption.[1]

PPS Prospective payment system. A system for paying for services that is not based on costs or charges, but on clinical characteristics of a case. DRGs are an example.[15]

PPTP Point-to-point tunneling protocol. Protocol for data transfer over the Internet supporting secure communication through encryption.[1]

PRAM Parameter RAM. A small portion of the RAM set aside to hold basic information,

such as the date and time, speaker volume, desktop pattern, and keyboard and mouse settings.[1]

PRG Procedure-related group.[9]

PRO Professional review organization, or Peer review organization. A group that provides utilization review and quality oversight to provider organizations.[32]

PROM Programmable read-only memory. Subclass of ROM, non-volatile memory chip used in control devices because it can be programmed once.[1]

PSA Patient synchronized applications. A means for viewing data for a single patient using independent and unlinked applications on a user's workstation, reducing the repetitive tasks of selecting the same patient in multiple applications. Data can be viewed from different identifier domains when used with the Patient Identifier Cross-referencing Integration profile to resolve multiple identifications for the same patient. This profile leverages the HL7 CCOW standard specifically for patient subject context management.[56] See **Profile**. NOTE: PSA is an IHE Profile.

PSTN Packet-switched telephone network. Regular dial-up telephone lines. Also known as *plain old telephone system (POTS)*. The international telephone system, based on copper wires carrying analog voice data, in contrast to newer telephone networks, based on digital technologies.[1]

PVC Permanent virtual circuit. A fixed circuit between two users in a packet-switched network. PVCs are more efficient for connections between hosts that communicate frequently.[7] See **SVC**.

PWF Post-processing workflow. Addresses the need to schedule, distribute, and track the status of typical post-processing workflow steps, such as computer-aided detection or image processing. Work lists for each of these tasks are generated and can be queried, work items can be selected, and the status returned from the system performing the work to the system managing the work.[56] See **Profile**. NOTE: PWF is an IHE Profile.

PWP Personnel white pages. Provides access to basic human workforce user directory information. This information has broad use among many clinical and non-clinical applications across the healthcare enterprise. The information can be used to enhance the clinical workflow (contact information), enhance the user interface (user friendly names and titles), and ensure identity (digital certificates). This Personnel White Pages directory will be related to the user identity provided by the Enterprise User Authentication (EUA) Integration Profile previously defined by IHE.[56] *See* **Profile**. **NOTE: PWP is an IHE Profile.**

Q

QDM   Quality data model. An information model that defines concepts used in quality measure and clinical care and is intended to enable automation of EHR use.

QMF   Query management facility. Ad hoc query tool to extract data from some mainframe systems.[15]

QMR   Quick medical reference. Search system for the National Library of Medicine.[141]

QoS   Quality of service. A negotiated contract between a user and a network provider that renders some degree of reliable capacity in the shared network.[47]

QR Codes   Quick response codes. High-density, two-dimensional bar codes that are readable by mobile phones and computer cameras with the correct software.[47]

R

R&C   Reasonable & customary. An amount charged by a provider for services or supplies that is not in excess of the charge made by most providers in the same locality.[15]

RA   Registration authority. 1. Body responsible for assigning healthcare coding scheme designators and for maintaining the Register of Health Care Coding Schemes, as described in a standard. **2.** Entity that is responsible for identification and authentication of certificate subjects, but that does not sign or issue certificates (i.e., an RA is delegated certain tasks on behalf of a CA).[4,121]

RAD   Rapid application development. An application development approach that includes small teams, typically two to six people using joint application development (JAD) and iterative-prototyping techniques to construct interactive systems of low to medium complexity within a timeframe of 60 to 120 days.[47]

RAID   Redundant array of independent disks. A method of storing data on multiple hard disks. When disks are arranged in a RAID configuration, the computer sees them all as one large disk. However, they operate much more efficiently than a single hard drive. Since the data are spread out over multiple disks, the reading and writing operations can take place on multiple disks at once, which can speed up hard drive access time significantly.[2]

RAM   Random access memory. 1. Primary storage of data or program instructions that can directly access any randomly chosen location in the same amount of time. **2.** The data in RAM stays there only as long as the computer is running. When the computer is turned off, RAM loses its data.[1]

RARP   Reverse address resolution protocol. Discovers the IP address of a device by broadcasting a request on a network. Hardware address to IP address resolution.[1]

RAS   Remote access server. Dial-in capability of Windows NT providing remote access to the server or the entire network from a remote location. Allows the use of modems, ISDN, and X.25 adapters for connectivity.[1]

RBAC   Role-based access control. An approach to restricting system access to authorized users.[7]

RDBMS   Relational database management system. A type of Database Management System (DBMS) that stores data in the form of related tables. Relational databases are powerful because they require few assumptions about how data are related or how they will be extracted from the database. As a result, the same database can be viewed in many different ways.[1] *See* **DBMS**.

RDF   Resource description framework. A family of World Wide Web Consortium (W3C) specifications originally designed as a metadata model. Used as a general method for conceptual description or modeling of information that is implemented in web resources, using a variety of syntax formats.[7]

RDISK   Repair disk utility. Windows NT command to initiate the creation or updating of an emergency repair (rescue) disk (ERD).[1]

REC   Recommendation.

RFI   Request for information. A standard business process, the purpose of which is to collect written information about the capabilities of various suppliers. Normally it follows a format that can be used for comparative purposes.[7]

RFID   Radio frequency identification. The RFID tag is attached to the patient, medications, or supplies. The tag consists of a microchip with an antenna, and an interrogator or reader with an antenna. The reader sends out electromagnetic waves. The tag antenna is tuned to receive these waves. A passive RFID tag draws power from the field created by the reader and uses it to power the microchip's circuits. The chip then modulates the waves that the tag sends back to the reader, and the reader converts the new waves into digital data.[2]

RFP   Request for proposal. An RFP typically asks for more than a price, including basic corporate information and history, financial information, and product information, such as stock availability and estimated completion period. The bidder returns a quote or proposal by a set date and time, known as a tender closing. The proposals are used to evaluate the suitability as a supplier, vendor, or institutional partner.[7]

RGB   Red, green, blue color model. A device-dependent color model. Different devices detect or reproduce a given RGB value differently since the color elements (such as phosphors or dyes) and response to the individual R, G, and B levels vary from manufacturer to manufacturer, or even in the same device over time. The name of the model comes from the initials of the three additive primary colors, red, green, and blue. The RGB color model is used in color image-producing technology for sensing, representation, and display of images in electronic systems, such as televisions and computers.[7]

RHIN   Regional health information network. *See* **RHIO**.[1]

RHIO   Regional health information organization. 1. A network of stakeholders within a defined region who are committed to improving the quality, safety, access, and efficiency of healthcare through use of health IT. No two RHIOs look alike, and each reflects the unique nature and interests of its region and resources. **2.** A group of organizations with a business stake in improving the quality, safety, and efficiency of healthcare. **3.** A health information organization that brings together healthcare stakeholders within a defined geographic area and governance health information exchange among them for the purpose of improving health and care in that community.[45,84]

RID   Retrieve information for display. A simple and rapid read-only access to patient information necessary for provision of better care. It supports access to existing persistent documents in well-known presentation formats, such as CDA, PDF, JPEG, etc. It also supports access to specific key patient-centric information, such as allergies, current medications, summary of reports, etc., for presentation to a clinician.[56] *See* **Profile**. **NOTE: RID is an IHE Profile.**

RIM   Reference information model. A static model of health and healthcare information as viewed within the scope of HL7 standards development activities. It is the combined consensus view of information from the perspective of the HL7 working group and the HL7 international affiliates. The RIM is the ultimate source from which all HL7 Version 3.0 protocol specification standards draw their information-related content.[16]

RIP   Routing information protocol. Used to advertise and exchange information between routers within an autonomous system.[1]

RIS   Radiology information system. 1. The components of radiology software, hardware, and network infrastructure to support patient documentation, retrieval, and analysis. **2.** An automated RIS manages the operations and services of the radiology department. The functionality includes scheduling, patient and image tracking and rapid retrieval of diagnostic reports.[1,2] *See* **PACS**.

RISC   Reduced instruction set computer. Non-microcode computer that uses a simplified set of instructions in internal firmware to speed operation. Digital Equipment Corporation (DEC, now a part of Compaq), Alpha, IBM, Power PC, and MIPS are RISC computers.[1]

RM   Records management. Technologies that enable organizations to enforce policies and rules for the retention and disposition of required business transaction content. RM strategies and policies are an essential part of the organization-wide lifecycle management of records. RM principles and technologies apply to both physical and electronic content. The US National Archives and Records Administration (NARA) is the nation's RM agency for RM training to Federal employees and contractors on RM topics from archive schedules to emergency preparedness.[47]

RMI   Remote method invocation. An adaptation of the remote procedure call paradigm for object-oriented environments.[32]

RM-ODP   Reference model for open distributed processing. The RM-ODP efforts began in 1987 as part of the International Standards Organization for Standardization (ISO) Object Management Group (OMG) to enable the inter-working of applications and sharing of data across computer networks spanning organizational and national boundaries. As it relates to the healthcare domain, the uppermost two of five layers deal with the information viewpoint (such as HL7, X12, DICOM, CPT) and the enterprise viewpoint (such as patient registration, order communications, results retrieval).[1]

RMON   Remote network monitor. Device that collects network traffic information for use by remote monitoring stations.[1]

ROI   Return on investment. A calculation used to determine whether a proposed investment is wise and how well it will repay the investor. It is calculated as the ratio of the amount gained (taken as positive) or lost (taken as negative), relative to the basis.[7]

ROI   Release of information. Formal process to request to release health information to other healthcare providers and authorized users, ensuring that the information is timely, accurate, complete, and confidential.[62]

ROLAP   Relational online analytical processing (OLAP). A technical OLAP approach where data are presented dimensionally, but stored and accessed using traditional two-di-

mensional relational database management system technology allowing for very high flexibility.[1] *See* **OLAP**.

ROM   Read-only memory. Non-volatile permanent memory written in firmware. Contents usually cannot be changed.[1]

RSA   A public key crypto-system, invented and patented by Ronald Rivest, Ade Shamir, and Leonard Adelman, based on large prime numbers. RSA is the best-known asymmetric algorithm.[1]

RTF   Rich text format. A minimum file format for text files that includes formatting instructions, the text itself, and very little additional information.[1] Also known as *interchange format.*

RTLS   Real-time location service. Provides actionable information regarding the location, status and movement of equipment and people. Advanced RTLS search capabilities allow searching by specific location (floor, area, room) or unique asset identifiers (department owner, type, manufacturer, model number, asset control number or EIN). The detailed asset information and reporting capabilities of RTLS allow further analysis to support a variety of uses including equipment utilization data to identify inefficiencies that have required excess equipment inventory purchases.[2]

RTM   Reference terminology model. Integration of a reference terminology model for nursing is an essential first step in creating comparable nursing data across settings and countries. Without such data, it is impossible to identify and implement 'best nursing practices' (i.e., those most likely to result in positive health outcomes for patients, families, and communities, or to determine how scarce nursing resources should be spent).[3]

RTO   Recovery time objective. Time goal for the restoration and recovery of functions or resources based on the acceptable downtime and acceptable level of performance in case of a disruption of operations.[175]

RTS   Request to send. Modem control operation from DTE requesting clearance to transmit.[1]

RVU   Relative value unit. A comparable service measure used by hospitals to permit comparison of the amounts of resources required to perform various services within a single department or between departments. It is determined by assigning weight to such factors as personnel time, level of skill, and sophistication of equipment required to render patient services. RVUs are a common method of physician bonus plans based partially on productivity.[139]

RWF Reporting workflow. Addresses the need to schedule, distribute, and track the status of the reporting workflow tasks, such as interpretation, transcription, and verification. Work lists for each of these tasks are generated and can be queried; work items can be selected, and the resulting status returned from the system performing the work to the system managing the work.[56] *See* **Profile. NOTE: RWF is an IHE Profile.**

S

S/MIME Secure MIME. Extends the Multipurpose Internet Mail Extensions (MIME) standard to allow for encrypted e-mail.[1]

SaaS Software as a service. 1. A software delivery model in which software and associated data are centrally hosted on the cloud. Typically accessed using a thin client via a web browser. **2.** Software that is owned, delivered, and managed remotely by one or more providers. The provider delivers software based on one set of common code and data definitions, which are consumed in a one-to-many model by all contracted customers at any time on a pay-for-use basis or a subscription based on metrics.[7,47] Also known as *on-demand software.*

SAML Security assertion markup language. An XML standard for exchanging authentication and authorization data between security domains; that is, between an identity provider and a service provider.[91]

SAN Storage area network. A high-speed special purpose network (or sub-network) that interconnects different kinds of data storage devices with associated data servers on behalf of a larger network of users. Typically, a storage area network is part of the overall network of computing resources for an enterprise.[2]

SATA Serial Advanced Technology Application. De facto standard for internal PC storage, SATA is the evolutionary replacement for the Parallel ATA storage interface. A serial interface that can operate at speeds up to 6 Gb/s.[218]

SATAN Security administrator tool for analyzing networks. A testing and reporting toolbox that collects a variety of information about networked hosts.[1,157]

SBAR Situation-background-assessment-recommendation. Institute for Healthcare Improvement (IHI) technique that provides a framework for communication between members of the healthcare team about a patient's condition.[213]

SCOS Smartcard operating system. Organizes data on the integrated circuit chip into files, and protects them from unauthorized access.[1]

SCSI Small computer system interface. Set of standards for physically connecting and transferring data between computers and peripheral devices.[7]

SCUI Smartcard user interface. Provides a standard interface between applications and the data on the chip. Multiple applications can reside on the chip, and the SCUI allows an application to access its own data without affecting another application's data.[1]

SDLC System design lifecycle. The process used by a systems analyst to develop an information system, including requirements, validation, training, and user ownership through investigation, analysis, design, implementation, and maintenance. An SDLC should result in a high-quality system that meets or exceeds customer expectations, within time and cost estimates, works effectively and efficiently in the current and planned information technology infrastructure, and is inexpensive to maintain, and cost-effective to enhance.[7] Also known as *information systems development* or *application development.*

SDO Standard development organization. Standardization in the field of information for health, and health information and communications technology, to achieve compatibility and interoperability between independent systems. Also, to ensure compatibility of data for comparative statistical purposes (e.g., classifications) and to reduce duplication of effort and redundancies.[3]

SDXC Secure digital extended capacity. A flash memory card that resembles a Secure Digital (SD) card with greater storage capacity. SD and SDXC cards make storage portable among devices such as smartphones, eBooks, digital cameras, camcorders, music players, and computers.[42]

SEC Security. Establishes basic security measures that can, as part of an institution's overall security policies and procedures in the enterprise, help protect the confidentiality of patient information. It also provides institutions with a mechanism to consolidate audit trail events on user activity across several systems interconnected in a secure manner.[56] *See* **Profile**. NOTE: SEC is an IHE Profile.

SET Secure electronic transmission. A cryptographic protocol designed for sending encrypted credit card numbers over the Internet.[1]

sFTP Secure file transport protocol. Standard for secure transfer of packets of information from one computer system to another. Commonly used in the transport of files of information containing confidential information.[99]

SGML Standardized general markup language. A metalanguage in which one can define markup languages for documents. SGML is a descendant of IBM's Generalized Markup Language (GML), developed in the 1960s by Charles Goldfarb, Edward Mosher, and Raymond Lorie (whose surname initials also happen to be GML). SGML should not be confused with the Geography Markup Language (GML) developed by the Open Geographic Information System (Open GIS) Consortium, cf, or the Game Maker scripting language, GML. SGML provides a variety of markup syntaxes that can be used for many applications.[3]

SGMP Simple gateway monitoring protocol. Allows commands to be issued to application protocol entities to set or retrieve values (integer or octet string types), for use in monitoring the gateways on which the application protocol entities reside. SGMP was replaced by SNMP (simple network management protocol).[7]

S-HTTP Secure HTTP. A system for signing and encrypting information sent over the web's HTTP protocol.[1] *See* **HTTP**.

SIG Special interest group. Subset of professional computer organizations that concentrates on a specific technical computing area.[1]

SIMM Single in-line memory module. A type of RAM chip.[1]

SINR Simple image and numeric report. Facilitates the growing use of digital dictation, voice recognition, and specialized reporting packages by separating the functions of reporting into discrete actors for creation, management, storage, and viewing. Separating these functions while defining transactions to exchange the reports between them enables a vendor to include one or more of these functions in an actual system.[56] *See* **Profile**. NOTE: SINR is an IHE Profile.

SLIP Serial line Internet protocol. Minimal overhead protocol for TCP/IP-only data transfer over serial links, such as telephone circuits or RS-232 cables. Does not support multiple protocols, encryption, or compression. The precursor to PPP.[1]

SMAU Multiple station access unit. A token-ring network hub.[1]

SME Subject-matter expert. An individual who has expertise on a particular topic.

SMP Symmetrical multi-processing. A computing platform technology in which a single server uses multiple CPUs in a parallel fashion managed by a single operating system.[1]

SMS Short message service. 1. A mechanism of delivery of short messages over the mobile networks. **2.** Part of the Global System for Mobile Communications (GSM) standard developed by the European Telecommunications Standards Institute that enables a mobile device to send, receive, and display messages of up to 160 characters in Roman text and variations for non-Roman character sets. Messages received are stored in the network if the subscriber device is inactive and are relayed when it becomes active. SMS has become available increasingly in Code Division Multiple Access (CDMA) technology networks.[7,47]

SMTP Simple mail transfer protocol. Protocol used to transfer mail between systems and from one computer to another. SMTP specifies how two mail systems interact and the format of control messages they exchange to transfer mail.[1]

SNA System network architecture. Network architecture developed by IBM for mainframe networking. Does not interoperate with TCP/IP.[1]

SNMP Simple network monitoring protocol. Used to monitor hosts, routers, and networks. Enables a monitoring management station to configure, monitor, and receive alarms from network devices.[1]

SNMP System network management protocol. Forms part of the Internet protocol suite as defined by the Internet Engineering Task Force. The protocol can support monitoring of network-attached devices for any conditions that warrant administrative attention.[7]

SNOMED CT Systematized Nomenclature of Medicine Clinical Terms. A controlled healthcare terminology developed by the College of American Pathologists in collaboration with the United Kingdom's National Health Service. SNOMED CT includes comprehensive coverage of diseases, clinical findings, therapies, procedures, and outcomes.[19]

SOA Service-oriented architecture. 1. An infrastructure where many N-tier applications are deployed, sharing common software services that are accessible from any user interface. In this environment, any application can access any service, provided the application has the proper security permissions. **2.** A software architectural concept that defines the use of services to support the requirements of software users. In an SOA environment, nodes on a network make resources available to other participants in the network as independent services that the participants access in a standardized way.[7,8]

SOAP Simple object access protocol. A third-generation programmable web service built on top of standards-based Internet protocols that can be implemented on any platform, in any language.[1]

SOAP Subjective, objective, assessment, and plan. A method of documentation employed by healthcare providers to write notes in a patient's chart.[7]

SONET Synchronous optical network. American National Standard Institute (ANSI) standard for connecting high-speed, high-quality, digital fiber-optic transmission systems. The international equivalent of SONET is synchronous digital hierarchy.[1] *See* **ATM, Frame relay**.

SOP Standard operating procedure. Formalized way of uniformly carrying out a process.[15]

SOW Statement of work. A document describing the specific tasks and methodologies that will be followed to satisfy the requirements of an associated contract or memorandum of understanding (MOU).[10]

SP Subportal. A subportal provides highly targeted aggregate content and interactive capabilities that focus on a specific vertical healthcare market segment, as opposed to overall portals, such as Yahoo or Microsoft Network.[1]

Spam The practice of blindly or intentionally posting commercial messages or advertisements to a large number of unrelated and uninterested newsgroups.[1]

SPD Summary plan description. Document that explains the product and services a subscriber purchased.[15]

SPIN Standard prescriber identification number. National Council for Prescription Drug Programs sponsored the Standard Prescriber Identification Number from the early to mid-1990s in an effort to address the need for a unique prescriber identifier for the retail pharmacy industry. However, the Health Insurance Portability and Accountability Act of 1996 (HIPAA) contained a provision for a National Provider Identifier (NPI). Years passed with no NPI. Unfortunately, the need that NCPDP and others had identified in the early to mid-1990s did not diminish but steadily grew over these years. By early 2001, NCPDP launched the HCIdea™ project. On January 23, 2004, HHS published the Final Rule for the HIPAA NPI in the Federal Register.[54]

SPOOL **Simultaneous peripheral operation online.** It refers to putting jobs in a buffer, a special area in memory, or on a disk where a device can access them when it is ready. This is similar to a sewing machine spool, which a person puts thread onto, and a machine pulls at its convenience. Spooling is useful because devices access data at different rates. The buffer provides a waiting station where data can reside while the slower device catches up. Material is only added and deleted at the ends of the area; there is no random access or editing. This also allows the CPU to work on other tasks, while waiting for the slower device to do its task.[7]

SQL **Structured query language.** A syntax used by many database programs to retrieve and modify information (pronounced either *see-kwell* or as separate letters). SQL is a standardized query language for requesting information from a database.[1]

SRAM **Static random access memory.** A type of memory that is faster and more reliable than the more common dynamic RAM or DRAM. The term *static* is derived from the fact that it does not need to be refreshed like dynamic RAM.[1]

SSH **Secure shell.** Encrypted remote terminal that provides confidentiality and authentication.[1]

SSL **Secure socket layer.** Secure method and protocol for managing the secure transfer of data between a web browser and a web server.[1] *See* **Socket, API**.

SSO **Single sign-on.** A specialized form of software authentication that enables a user to authenticate once and gain access to the resources of multiple software systems.[2]

STP **Shielded twisted pair.** Type of cabling 1.5 inches in diameter, in which the wire pairs are twisted together in a shielded protective jacket to reduce the effects of EMI. Used to implement 10BaseT - 100BaseT networks.[1]

SVC **Switched virtual circuit.** A temporary virtual circuit that is set up and used only as long as data are being transmitted. Once the communication between the two hosts is complete, the SVC disappears. In contrast, a permanent virtual circuit (PVC) remains available at all times.[1]

SVGA **Super video graphics array.** Color display system providing high-resolution graphics of multiple colors at various resolutions.[1]

SWF **Scheduled workflow.** Establishes the continuity and integrity of basic departmental imaging data acquired in an environment where examinations are generally being ordered. It specifies a number of transactions that maintain the consistency of patient and ordering information, as well as defining the scheduling and imaging acquisition procedure steps. This profile also makes it possible to determine whether images and other evidence objects associated with a particular performed procedure step have been stored (archived) and are available to enable subsequent workflow steps, such as reporting. It may also provide central coordination of the completion of processing and reporting steps.[56] *See* **Profile**. **NOTE: SWF is an IHE Profile.**

T

TAG **Technical advisory group.** A group of topic experts working in a particular area and building consensus among the group for specific positions. Used mainly in consensus standards work.[3,48]

TC **Technical committee.** A term, often used by consensus standards organizations, including Health Level Seven (HL7), European Committee for Standardization (CEN), and International Organization for Standardization (ISO) to describe a formal group of subject matter experts who work together in a committee structure to solve problems.[3,48]

TCO **Total cost of ownership.** A document that describes the cost of a project or initiative that usually includes hardware, software, development, and ongoing expenses.[15]

TCP **Transmission control protocol.** Connection-oriented data transmission mode portion of TCP/IP.[1]

TCP/IP **Transmission control protocol/Internet protocol. 1.** Routable protocol required for Internet access. TCP portion is associated with data. IP is associated with source to destination packet delivery. **2.** A set of communication protocols encompassing media access, packet transport, session communications, file transfer, electronic mail, and terminal emulation. It is supported by a large number of hardware and software vendors and is the basis for Internet transactions.[1,2]

TDR Time-domain reflectometer. Testing device that sends sound waves along cabling to detect shorts or breaks in the cable.[1]

TELNET TELecommunications NETwork. Protocol for remote terminal service connectivity. Connectivity from one site to interact with a remote system. A method of logging one computer onto another. A program that allows users to remotely use computers across networks.[1]

TFTP Trivial file transfer protocol. Minimal overhead file transfer used to upload or download bootstrap files to diskless workstations through the use of user datagram protocol (UDP).[1]

TIFF Tag image file format. A common format for exchanging raster graphics (bitmap) images between application programs, including those used for scanner images.[57]

TKIP Temporal key integrity protocol. Security protocol used in the IEEE 802.11 wireless networking standard.[2]

TLAlgia Term composed of 'TLA' for three-letter acronym and '-algia' meaning 'pain'; thus, pain induced by excessive use of three-letter acronyms.[99]

TPA Third-party administrator. A company that provides claim processing and administrative services for hospital or physicians groups.[15]

TPV Third-party vendor. A company designated to support specific services for healthcare.[15]

TQM Total quality management. An approach to quality assurance that emphasizes to all members of a production unit of the needs and desires of the ultimate service recipients in the chain of service, and acknowledges how to use specific data-related techniques to assess and improve the quality of their own and the team's outputs.[123]

TTL Time to live. Length of active Internet time technique used to avoid endless loop packets. Every packet is assigned a decrementing TTL. Packets with expired TTLs are discarded by routers.[1]

TTP Trusted third party. Third party that is considered trusted for purposes of a security protocol.[121] (ENV 13608-1). **Note:** This term is used in many ISO/IEC International Standards and other documents describing mainly the services of a certification authority (CA). The concept is, however, broader, and includes services such as time-stamping and possibly escrowing.

U

UART Universal asynchronous receiver transmitter. The microchip with programming that controls a computer's interface to its attached serial devices.[42]

UCC Uniform Code Council. In 2005, the organization changed its name to GS1. An administrative and educational organization whose mission is to promote multi-industry standards for product identification and related electronic communications. The Universal Product Code (UPC) is a bar code symbol used by companies in North America to uniquely identify themselves and their products worldwide.[7]

UDDI Universal description, discover, and integration. An XML-based registry for businesses worldwide to list themselves on the Internet. Its ultimate goal is to streamline online transactions by enabling companies to find one another on the web and make their systems interoperable for eCommerce. UDDI is often compared to a telephone book's White, Yellow, and Green pages. The project allows businesses to list themselves by name, product, location, or the web services they offer.[8]

UDI Unique device identifier. A method of knowing a specific object apart from other objects like itself.[109]

UDK User-defined keys. Used to store frequently used commands through the F6 to F20 keys on a video terminal keyboard.[1]

UDP User datagram protocol. A connectionless protocol that resides at the same level on the OSI model as TCP. Since it is connectionless, there is no handshaking or authentication.[1]

UI   User interface. 1. The part of the application that allows the user to access the application and manipulate its functionality. It can include menus, forms, command buttons, etc. **2.** The part of the information system through which the end user interacts with the system; type of hardware and the series of on-screen commands and responses required for a user to work with the system.[107,1]

UM   Utilization management. The evaluation of the necessity, appropriateness, and efficiency of the use of healthcare services, procedures, and facilities.[15]

UMDNS   Universal medical device nomenclature system. The purpose of UMDNS is to facilitate identifying, processing, filing, storing, retrieving, transferring, and communicating data about medical devices. The nomenclature is used in applications ranging from hospital inventory and work order controls to national agency medical device regulatory systems, and from eCommerce and procurement to medical device databases.[55]

UML   Unified Modeling Language. A language for specifying, visualizing, constructing, and documenting the artifacts of software systems. UML is a standard notation for the modeling of real-world objects.[47]

UMLS   The Unified Medical Language System. A large project sponsored by the United States National Library of Medicine (NLM) to produce a unified thesaurus and cross reference linking various medical nomenclatures, including the MeSH headings, ICD-9-CM, SNOMED, and the Terminology of DXPlain and QMR.[4]

UMS   Unified messaging system. The handling of voice, fax, and regular text messages as objects in a single mailbox that a user can access either with a regular e-mail client, or by telephone.[1]

UNC   Universal naming convention. Text-based method to identify the path to a remote device, server, directory, or file. Implemented as: \\computername\sharename\directoryname\filename.[1]

UPC   Universal product code. A unique 12-digit number assigned to retail merchandise that identifies both the product and the vendor that sells the product. The UPC on a product typically appears adjacent to its bar code, the machine-readable representation of the UPC. The first six digits of the UPC are the vendor's unique identification number. All of the products that one vendor sells will have the same first six digits in their UPCs. The next five digits are the product's unique reference number that identifies the product within any one vendor's line of products. The last number is called the check digit that is used to verify that the UPC for that specific product is correct.[58]

UPI   Unique patient identifier. 1. The identity of an individual consists of a set of personal characters by which that individual can be recognized. Identification is the proof of one's identity. Identifier verifies the sameness of one's identity. Patient identifier is the value assigned to an individual to facilitate positive identification of that individual for healthcare purposes. Unique patient identifier is the value permanently assigned to an individual for identification purposes and is unique across the entire national healthcare system. Unique patient identifier is not shared with any other individual. **2.** A form of identification and access control that identifies humans by their characteristics or traits. Biometric identifiers (or biometric authentication) are the distinctive, measurable characteristics used to label and describe individuals. Two categories of biometric identifiers include physiological and behavioral characteristics.[1,7]

UPN   Universal product number. *See* **UPC**.

UPS   Uninterruptible power supply. Device that keeps a computer running by protecting against power outages and power sags by maintaining constant power via battery. Provides the opportunity for a graceful shutdown in a commercial power-out condition.[1]

UR   Utilization review. An organized procedure carried out through committees to review admissions, duration of stay, professional services furnished, and to evaluate the medical necessity of those services and promote their most efficient use.[5]

URI   Uniform resource identifiers. Provides a simple and extensible means for identifying a resource. A URI can be further classified as a locator, a name, or both.[8]

URL Uniform resource locator. Provides the unique location information by using a naming convention of protocol type, followed by a specific service.[1]

URL Universal resource locator. A standardized address name layout for resources, such as documents or images, on the Internet or elsewhere.[7]

USB Universal serial bus. 1. A plug-and-play interface between a computer and add-on devices, such as media players, keyboards, etc. **2.** A commercial desktop standard input/output (I/O) bus that provides a single peripheral connection and vastly increases bus speed. It simplifies peripheral connections via a 'daisy chaining' scheme whereby the desktop system has only one I/O port to which all peripherals are connected in a series. Up to 120 peripherals can be connected to a single system.[42,47]

USHIK United States Health Information Knowledgebase. A metadata registry of healthcare-related data elements from Standard Development Organizations supported by the Agency for Healthcare Research and Quality (AHRQ).[173]

UTP Type of cabling in which the insulated wire conductors are twisted together in an unshielded voice-grade cable. Used to implement 10BaseT and 100BaseT networks.[1]

V

VAN Value-added network. A vendor of electronic data interchange (EDI) data communications and translation services.[10]

VAX Virtual address extension. An established line of mid-range server computers from the Digital Equipment Corporation (DEC, now a part of Hewlett-Packard.)[1]

VGA Video graphics array. Color display system providing high-resolution graphics displays of 16 colors at a 640x480 resolution, and 256 colors at a 320x200 resolution.[1]

VistA Veterans Health Information Systems Technology Architecture. An enterprise-wide system built around an electronic health record and used throughout the Veterans Health Administration's 163 hospitals, 800+ clinics, and 135 nursing homes. Commonly considered to be one of the largest and most effective health IT systems in use today. Developed as the decentralized hospital computer system (DHCP), the name change to VistA signified deeper clinical content and increased GUI-zation (Graphic User Interface).[99]

VM Virtual machine. Completely isolated guest operating system installation within a normal host operating system.[7]

VoIP Voice over Internet protocol. 1. A technology that allows telephone calls using a broadband Internet connection instead of a regular (or analog) phone line. Some services using VoIP may only allow you to call other people using the same service, but others may allow you to call anyone who has a telephone number—including local, long distance, mobile, and international numbers. Also, while some services work only over your computer or a special VoIP phone, other services allow you to use a traditional phone through an adaptor. **2.** Refers to the use of the Internet protocol to transfer voice communications in much the same way that web pages and e-mail are transferred. Each piece of voice data is digitized in to chunks and then sent across the Internet (in the case of public VoIP) to a destination server where the chunks are reassembled. This process happens in real-time so that two or more people can carry on a conversation.[2,168]

VPN Virtual private network. 1. Refers to a network in which some of the parts are connected using the public Internet, but the data sent across the Internet is encrypted, so the entire network is 'virtually' private. Secure and encrypted connection between two points across the Internet. **2.** VPNs transfer information by encrypting and encapsulating traffic in IP packets and sending the packets over the Internet. That practice is called 'tunneling.' Most VPNs are built and run by Internet service providers, and secure protocols like Point-to-Point Tunneling Protocol (PPTP) to ensure that data transmissions are not intercepted by unauthorized parties.[8] *See* **Tunneling.**

VRAM Video RAM or video random access memory. Refers to all forms of random access memory used to store image data for a computer display. VRAM is a type of buffer between the computer and the display.[1]

VRML Virtual reality modeling language. A standard for describing interactive three-dimensional scenes delivered across the Internet.[1]

VRU Voice response unit. Same as interactive voice response (IVR).

W

WAIS Wide-area information server. WAIS is best at searches for various sources of academic information that have been indexed based on content. Its indices consist of every word in a document, and each word carries the same weight in a search.[1]

WAN Wide area network. A collection of long-distance telecommunication links and networks used to connect local area networks and end stations across regional, national, or international distances.[2] *See* **LAN, MAN, WLAN.**

WAP Wireless application protocol. A specification for a set of communication protocols to standardize the way that wireless devices, such as cellular telephones and radio transceivers, can be used for Internet access, including e-mail, the World Wide Web, newsgroups, and Internet Relay Chat.[1]

WASP Wireless application service provider. A part of a growing industry sector resulting from the convergence of two trends: wireless communications and the outsourcing of services.[1]

WAV or WAVE Waveform audio format (.wav). A proprietary format sponsored by Microsoft and IBM, the Resource Interchange File Format Waveform Audio Format (.wav) was introduced in MS Windows Version 3.1 and is most commonly used on Windows-based PCs.[1]

WEP Wired equivalent privacy. A security protocol, specified in the IEEE Wireless Fidelity (Wi-Fi) standard, 802.11b, that is designed to provide a wireless local area network (WLAN) with a level of security and privacy comparable to what is usually expected of a wired LAN.[2]

WG Work group. A collection of individuals working together on a task. Workgroup computing occurs when all the individuals have computers connected to a network that allows them to send e-mail to one another, share data files,

and schedule meetings. Sophisticated workgroup systems allow users to define workflows so that data are automatically forwarded to appropriate people at each stage of a process.[58]

Wi-Fi Wireless fidelity. Wireless network components that are based on one of the Wi-Fi Alliance's 802.11 standards. The Wi-Fi Alliance created the 802.11 standards so that manufacturers can make wireless products that work with other manufacturers' equipment.[2]

WLAN Wireless local area network. A communication system that transmits and receives data using wireless technology and implemented as an extension to or as an alternative for a hard-wired LAN.[2]

WORM Write once, read many times. Process used for applications where permanent data storage is required.[1]

WOW Workstation on wheels. Carts with mounted computer monitors (typically laptops or other computer systems) that connect to a network in a wireless manner and are wheeled so easily moved from room to room.[2]

WPA Wi-Fi protected access. A security standard for users of computers equipped with Wi-Fi wireless connection. It is an improvement on, and is expected to replace, the original Wi-Fi security standard. Wired Equivalent Privacy (WEP), WPA provides more sophisticated data encryption than WEP and also provides user authentication.[2]

WSDL Web services description language. Provides a model and an XML format for describing web services. WSDL enables one to separate the description of the abstract functionality offered by a service from concrete details of a service description, such as 'how' and 'where' that functionality is offered.[8]

WWW World Wide Web. 1. Global network of networks offering various services to users with browsing software (web browsers). A project originated at the European Organization for Nuclear Research (CERN), aimed at providing hypertext-style access to information from a wide range of sources. **2.** The graphical interface with which millions of users access Internet files that conform to the hypertext protocol (HTTP). The web is the most accessible and widely used branch of the Internet.[8]

WYSIWYG **What you see is what you get.** Some early systems yielded a screen image that was unlike a printed document or file. This term is used to confirm that the system presents a screen image that matches what prints on paper. Pronounced 'wizzy-wig.'[1]

X

X.25 **1.** Standard protocol suite for packet switched wide area network (WAN) communication developed by the International Telecommunication Union-Telecommunication (ITU-T) Standard Sector. **2.** A packet-switching network protocol with extensive error checking and accounting capability. Employs the use of permanent virtual circuits (PVC), switched virtual circuits (SVC), and packet assemblers and dissemblers.[7,1]

XDS **Cross-enterprise document sharing.** Focused on providing a standards-based specification for managing the sharing of documents that healthcare enterprises (anywhere from a private physician, to a clinic, to an acute care inpatient facility) have decided to explicitly share. This contributes to the foundation of a shared electronic health record.[56] *See* **Profile**. **NOTE: XDS is an IHE Profile.**

XML **Extensible markup language. 1.** General-purpose markup language for creating special-purpose markup languages. It is a simplified subset of standard generalized markup language (SGML), capable of describing many different kinds of data. Its primary purpose is to facilitate the sharing of data across different systems, particularly systems connected via the Internet. **2.** Describes a class of data objects, called XML documents, and partially describes the behavior of computer programs which process them. XML is an application profile or restricted form of SGML, the Standard Generalized Markup Language (ISO 8879). By construction, XML documents are conforming SGML documents.[7]

XSL **Extensible Stylesheet Language.** A family of languages which allows one to describe how files encoded in the XML standard are to be formatted or transformed. XSL Transformation (XSLT) is used to transform the XML document, and XSL Formatting Objects (XSL-FO) is used to render the transformed document.[8] Also known as *eXtensible Style Language (XSL)*.

Appendix B
Healthcare Organizations that
Have a Focus on Health IT

AAAAI American Academy of Allergy, Asthma & Immunology
Physician membership organization focused on advancing the knowledge and practice of allergies, asthma and immunology.

555 East Wells Street
Suite 1100
Milwaukee, WI 53202-3823
Tel: 414-272-6071
www.aaaai.org

AAACN American Association of Ambulatory Care Nurses
The association of professional nurses and associates who identify ambulatory care practice as essential to the continuum of high-quality, cost-effective healthcare.

East Holly Avenue
Box 56
Pitman, NJ 08071-0056
Tel: 800-262-6877
www.aaacn.org

AACN American Association of Critical-Care Nurses
Acute and critical care nurses rely on AACN for expert knowledge and the influence to fulfill their promise to patients and their families.

101 Columbia
Aliso Viejo, CA 92656-4109
Tel: 949-362-2000
Toll free: 800-899-2226
Fax: 949-362-2020
www.aacn.org

AACN American Association of Colleges of Nursing
The national voice for America's baccalaureate and higher-degree nursing education programs.

One Dupont Circle, NW
Suite 530
Washington, DC 20036
Tel: 202-463-6930
Fax: 202-785-8320
www.aacn.nche.edu

AAD American Academy of Dermatology
Physician membership organization for dermatologists inside or outside the United States.

PO Box 4014
Schaumburg, IL 60168
Toll free: 866-503-SKIN (7546)
International: 847-240-1280
Fax: 847-240-1859
www.aad.org

AADE American Association of Diabetic Educators
A professional association dedicated to promoting the expertise of the diabetes educator.

200 W. Madison Street
Suite 800
Chicago, IL 60603
Toll free: 800-338-3633
www.diabeteseducator.org

AAFP American Academy of Family Physicians
Membership organization for physicians and physicians in training engaged in Family Medicine, the teaching of family medicine, or medical administration inside or outside the United States.

PO Box 11210
Shawnee Mission, KS 66207-1210
Tel: 913-906-6000
Toll free: 800-274-2237
Fax: 913-906-6075
www.aafp.org

AAHAM American Association of Healthcare Administrative Management
National membership association that represents a broad-based constituency of healthcare professionals.

> *11240 Waples Mill Road*
> *Suite 200*
> *Fairfax, VA 22030*
> *Tel: 703-281-4043*
> *Fax: 703-359-7562*
> *www.aaham.org*

AAHC American Association of Healthcare Consultants
Membership association for healthcare consultants.

> *1205 Johnson Ferry Road*
> *Suite 136-420*
> *Marietta, GA 30068*
> *Tel: 404-661-1710*
> *Fax: 770-874-4401*
> *www.aahc.net*

AAHC American Association for Homecare
Membership association of companies in the homecare community.

> *1707 L Street, NW*
> *Suite 350*
> *Washington, DC 20036*
> *Tel: 202-372-0107*
> *Fax: 202-835-8306*
> *www.aahomecare.org*

AAHC Association of Academic Health Centers
Non-profit organization to improve the healthcare system by mobilizing and enhancing the strengths and resources of the academic health centers.

> *1400 Sixteenth Street, NW*
> *Suite 720*
> *Washington, DC 20036*
> *Tel: 202-265-9600*
> *Fax: 202-265-7514*
> *www.aahcdc.org*

AAHN American Association for the History of Nursing
Membership network to advance historical scholarship in nursing and healthcare.

> *10200 W. 44th Avenue*
> *Suite 304*
> *Wheat Ridge, Co 80033*
> *Tel: 303-422-2685*
> *www.aahn.org*

AAHP American Association of Health Plans
See **AHIP** (AAHP is now AHIP.)

AAIHDS American Association of Integrated Healthcare Delivery Systems
A non-profit dedicated to the educational advancement of provider-based managed care professionals involved in integrated healthcare delivery.

> *4435 Waterfront Drive*
> *Suite 101*
> *Glen Allen, VA 23060*
> *Tel: 804-747-5823*
> *Fax: 804-747-5316*
> *www.aaihds.org*

AALNA American Assisted Living Nurses Association
Nationwide network of assisted living nurses.

> *P.O. Box 10469*
> *Napa, CA 94581*
> *Tel: 707-253-7299*
> *Fax: 707-253-8228*
> *www.alnursing.org*

AALNC American Association Legal Nurse Consultants
A not-for-profit membership organization dedicated to the professional enhancement and growth of registered nurses practicing in the specialty area of legal nurse consulting and to advancing this nursing specialty.

> *330 N. Wabash Ave.*
> *Chicago, IL 60611*
> *Tel: 877-402-2562*
> *Fax: 312-673-6655*
> *www.aalnc.org*

AAMA American Academy of Medical Administrators
Membership association of multi-specialty healthcare administrators in federal and public and private sectors.

> *701 Lee Street*
> *Suite 600*
> *Des Plaines, IL 60016*
> *Tel: 847-759-8601*
> *Fax: 847-759-8602*
> *www.aameda.org*

AAMA American Association of Medical Assistants
Membership organization for medical assistants.

> *20 N. Wacker Drive*
> *Suite 1575*
> *Chicago, IL 60606*
> *Tel: 312-899-1500*
> *Fax: 312-899-1259*
> *www.aama-ntl.org*

AAMC Association of American Medical Colleges
Membership association of medical schools accredited by the Liaison Committee on Medical Education (LCME), Not-for-profit teaching hospitals and academic society 501(c)3 organizations with primary missions that include advancing medical education and/or biomedical research in the United States and Canada.

> *2450 N Street, NW*
> *Washington, DC 20037-1126*
> *Tel: 202-828-0400*
> *Fax: 202-828-1125*
> *www.aamc.org*

AAMCN American Association of Managed Care Nurses
Membership community of nurses working in managed care throughout the country.

> *4435 Waterfront Drive*
> *Suite 101*
> *Glen Allen, VA 23060*
> *Tel: 804-527-1905*
> *Fax: 804-747-5316*
> *www.aamcn.org*

AAMI Association for Advancement of Medical Instrumentation
A unique alliance of over 6,000 members united by the common goal of increasing the understanding and beneficial use of medical instrumentation.

> *4301 N. Fairfax Drive*
> *Suite 301*
> *Arlington, VA 22203-1633*
> *Tel: 703-525-4890*
> *Fax: 703-276-0793*
> *www.aami.org*

AAN American Academy of Neurology
Membership academy for physicians, medical students and non-physician neurology professionals.

> *201 Chicago Avenue South*
> *Minneapolis, MN 55415*
> *Tel: 612-928-6000*
> *Toll free: 800-879-1960*
> *Fax: 612-454-2746*
> *www.aan.com*

AANA American Association of Nurse Anesthetists
Membership association of national and international nurse anesthetists.

> *222 S. Prospect Avenue*
> *Park Ridge, IL 60068-4037*
> *Tel: 847-692-7050*
> *Fax: 847-692-6968*
> *www.aana.com*

AANN American Association of Neuroscience Nurses
Membership organization of nurses passionate about neuroscience.

> *4700 W. Lake Avenue*
> *Glenview, IL 60025*
> *Tel: 847-375-4733*
> *Toll free: 888-557-2266 (US only)*
> *Fax: 847-375-6430*
> *International fax: 732-460-7313*
> *www.aann.org*

AANP American Academy of Nurse Practitioners
Membership-focused organization for nurse practitioners and others interested fostering the objectives of the NP profession.

National Administrative Office
P.O. Box 12846
Austin, TX 78711
Tel: 512-442-4262
Fax: 512-442-6469
www.aanp.org

AAOHN American Association of Occupational Health Nurses
Membership association of nurses engaged in occupational and environmental health nursing.

National Office
7794 Grow Drive
Pensacola, FL 32514
Tel: 850-474-6963
Toll free: 800-241-8014
Fax: 850-484-8762
www.aaohn.org

AAOS American Academy of Orthopaedic Surgeons
Physician membership organization for physicians in the exclusive practice of orthopaedic surgery in the United States and physicians enrolled in approved orthopaedic residency programs inside and outside the United States.

6300 North River Road
Rosemont, IL 60018-4262
Tel: 847-823-7186
Fax: 847-823-8125
www.aaos.org

AAP American Academy of Pediatrics
Physician membership organization for pediatricians, pediatric medical subspecialists, pediatric surgical specialists, and physicians in approved pediatric residency programs inside or outside the United States.

141 Northwest Point Boulevard
Elk Grove Village, IL 60007-1098
Tel: 847-434-4000
Toll free: 800-433-9016
Fax: 847-434-8000
www.aap.org

AAPA American Academy of Physicians Assistants
Membership organization for ARC-PA or NCCPA-certified physician assistants, PA affiliates, physicians, and related businesses.

2318 Mill Road
Suite 1300
Alexandria, VA 22314
Tel: 703-836-2272
Fax: 703-684-1924
www.aapa.org

AAPM&R American Academy of Physical Medicine and Rehabilitation
Physician membership organization for Diplomates of the American Board of Physical Medicine and Rehabilitation and physicians in an approved PM&R residency program inside or outside the United States.

9700 W. Bryn Mawr Avenue
Suite 200
Rosemont, IL 60018
Tel: 847-737-6000
Fax: 847-737-6001
www.aapmr.org

AAPPO American Association of Preferred Provider Organizations
Membership association of preferred provider organizations, including specialty networks, pharmaceutical manufacturers, provider organizations, consultants, benefit administrators, hospitals, and others.

222 S. First Street
Suite 303
Louisville, KY 40202
Tel: 502-403-1122
Fax: 502-403-1129
www.aappo.org

AARC American Association for Respiratory Care
Membership association for credentialed respiratory care professionals, individuals with a position related to respiratory care and students in a respiratory care program.

9425 N. MacArthur Boulevard
Suite 100
Irving, TX 75063-4706
Tel: 972-243-2272
Fax: 972-484-2720
www.aarc.org

AASCIN   American Association of Spinal Cord Injury Nurses
See **ASCIP** (AASCIN is now ASCIP.)

ABA   American Board of Anesthesiology
Physician certification organization to quality and examine anesthesiology candidates who have successfully completed an accredited program of anesthesiology training in the United States.

4208 Six Forks Road
Suite 900
Raleigh, NC 27609-5735
Tel: 866-999-7501
Fax: 866-999-7503
www.theABA.org

ABAI   American Board of Allergy and Immunology
Physician certification organization to qualify and examine allergists/immunologists who have successfully completed an accredited educational program.

111 S. Independence Mall East
Suite 701
Philadelphia, PA 19106
Tel: 215-592-9466
Toll free: 866-264-5568
Fax: 215-592-9411
www.abai.org

ABCGN   American Board of Certification for Gastroenterology Nurses
A volunteer non-profit organization to maintain and improve the knowledge, understanding, and skill of nurses in the fields of gastroenterology and gastroenterology endoscopy by developing and administering a certification program.

330 N. Wabash Avenue
Suite 2000
Chicago, IL 60611
Tel: 855-25-ABCGN and 855-252-2246
Fax: 312-673-6723
www.abcgn.org

ABCRS   American Board of Colon and Rectal Surgery
Physician certification organization to qualify and examine colon and rectal surgery candidates who have successfully completed an accredited educational program.

20600 Eureka Road
Suite 600
Taylor, MI 48180
Tel: 734-282-9400
Fax: 734-282-9402
www.abcrs.org

ABD   American Board of Dermatology
Physician certification organization to qualify and examine dermatologist and dermatology subspecialist candidates who have successfully completed an accredited educational program.

Henry Ford Health System
1 Ford Place
Detroit, MI 48202-3450
Tel: 313-874-1088
Fax: 313-872-3221
www.abderm.org

ABEM   American Board of Emergency Medicine
Physician certification organization to qualify and examine emergency medicine and seven subspecialty candidates who successfully meet certification requirements.

3000 Coolidge Road
East Lansing, MI 48823-6319
Tel: 517-332-4800
Fax: 517-332-2234
www.abem.org

ABFM   American Board of Family Medicine
Physician certification organization to qualify and examine family medicine and subspecialty candidates who have successfully completed an accredited program and meet certification requirements.

1648 McGrathiana Parkway
Suite 550
Lexington, KY 40511-1247
Tel: 859-269-5626
Toll free: 888-995-5700
Fax: 859-335-7501 and 859-335-7509
www.theabfm.org

ABIM   American Board of Internal Medicine
A non-profit independent evaluation organization for physicians in internal medicine and its 19 subspecialties.

510 Walnut Street
Suite 1700
Philadelphia, PA 19106-3699
Toll free: 800-441-2246
Fax: 215-446-3590
www.abim.org

ABMG   American Board Medical Genetics
Physician/Ph.D certification organization to qualify and examine medical genetic and subspecialty candidates who successfully meet certification requirements.

9650 Rockville Pike
Bethesda, MD 20814-3998
Tel: 301-634-7315
Fax: 301-634-7320
www.abmg.org

ABNM   American Board of Nuclear Medicine
The primary certifying organization for nuclear medicine physicians in the United States.

4555 Forest Park Boulevard
Suite 119
St. Louis, MO 63108-2173
Tel: 314-367-2225
www.abnm.org

ABNS   American Board of Neurological Surgery
Physician certification organization to qualify and examine neurological surgery candidates who have successfully completed an accredited educational program.

245 Amity Road
Woodbridge, CT 06525
Tel: 203-397-2267
Fax: 203-392-0400
www.abns.org

ABOG   American Board Obstetrics and Gynecology
Independent, non-profit organization that certifies obstetricians and gynecologists in the United States.

2915 Vine Street
Dallas, TX 75204
Tel: 214-871-1619
Fax: 214-871-1943
www.abog.org

ABOHN   American Board for Occupational Health Nurses
Nursing certification organization to qualify and examine occupational health and subspecialty candidates who successfully meet certification requirements.

201 East Ogden Avenue
Suite 114
Hinsdale, IL 60521-3652
Tel: 630-789-5799
Toll free: 888-842-2646
Fax: 630-789-8901
www.abohn.org

ABOP   American Board of Ophthalmology
Physician certification organization to qualify and examine ophthalmologist candidates who have successfully completed an accredited educational program and meet certification requirements.

111 Presidential Boulevard
Suite 241
Bala Cynwyd, PA 19004-1075
Tel: 610-664-1175
Fax: 610-664-6503
www.abop.org

ABOS   American Board of Orthopaedic Surgery
Physician certification organization to qualify and examine orthopaedic surgery candidates who have successfully completed an accredited educational program and meet certification requirements.

400 Silver Cedar Court
Chapel Hill, NC 27514
Tel: 919-929-7103
Fax: 919-942-8988
www.abos.org

ABPto   American Board of Otolaryngology
Physician certification organization to qualify and examine otolaryngology candidates who have successfully completed an accredited educational program and meet certification requirements.

5615 Kirby Drive
Suite 600
Houston, TX 77005
Tel: 713-850-0399
Fax: 713-850-1104
www.aboto.org

ABP   American Board of Pathology
Physician certification organization to qualify and examine anatomic pathology, clinical pathology, anatomic pathology, clinical pathology, and subspecialties candidates who have successfully completed an accredited educational program and meet certification requirements.

P.O. Box 25915
Tampa, FL 33622-5915
Tel: 813-286-2444
Fax: 813-289-5279
www.abpath.org

ABP   American Board of Pediatrics
Physician certification organization to qualify and examine pediatric and pediatric subspecialty candidates who have successfully completed an accredited educational program and meet certification requirements.

111 Silver Cedar Court
Chapel Hill, NC 27514
Tel: 919-929-0461
Fax: 919-929-9255
www.abp.org

ABPM   American Board of Preventive Medicine
Physician certification organization to qualify and examine physicians in aerospace medicine, occupational medicine, public health and general preventive medicine to candidates who have successfully completed an accredited program and meet certification requirements.

Tel: 312-939-2276
www.theabpm.org

ABPMR   American Board of Physical Medicine and Rehabilitation
Physician certification organization to qualify and examine physical medicine and rehabilitation candidates who have successfully completed an accredited educational program and meet certification requirements.

3015 Allegro Park Lane, SW
Rochester, MN 55902-4139
Tel: 507-282-1776
Fax: 507-282-9242
www.abpmr.org

ABPN   American Board of Psychiatry and Neurology
Physician certification organization to qualify and examine psychiatry and neurology candidates who have successfully completed an accredited program and meet certification requirements.

2150 E. Lake Cook Road
Suite 900
Buffalo Grove, IL 60089
Tel: 847-229-6500
Fax: 847-229-6600
www.abpn.com

ABPS   American Board of Plastic Surgery
Physician certification organization to qualify and examine plastic surgery specialist and subspecialty candidates who have successfully completed an accredited program and meet certification requirements.

Seven Penn Center
Suite 400
1635 Market Street
Philadelphia, PA 19103-2204
Tel: 215-587-9322
www.abplsurg.org

ABR   American Board of Radiology
Physician certification organization to qualify and examine diagnostic radiology, radiation oncology, and medical physics candidates who have successfully completed an accredited program and meet certification requirements.

5441 E. Williams Boulevard
Tucson, AZ 85711-7412
Tel: 520-790-2900
www.theabr.org

ABS   American Board of Surgery
An independent, non-profit organization certifying surgeons who have met a defined standard
of education, training, and knowledge.

1617 John F. Kennedy Boulevard
Suite 860
Philadelphia, PA 19103
Tel: 215-568-4000
Fax: 215-563-5718
www.absurgery.org

ABTS   American Board of Thoracic Surgery
Physician certification organization to qualify
and examine thoracic candidates who have successfully met certification requirements.

633 North St. Clair Street
Suite 2320
Chicago, IL 60611
Tel: 312-202-5900
Fax: 312-202-5960
www.abts.org

ABU   American Board of Urology
Physician certification organization to examine urology candidates who meet certification
requirements.

600 Peter Jefferson Parkway
Suite 150
Charlottesville, VA 22911
Tel: 434-979-0059
Fax: 434-979-0266
www.abu.org

ACAAI   American College of Allergy, Asthma
& Immunology
Membership organization for allergists /immu-
nologists and allied health professionals inside
or outside the United States who meet eligibility requirements.

85 West Algonquin Road
Suite 550
Arlington Heights, IL 60005
Tel: 847-427-1200
Fax: 847-427-1294
www.acaai.org

ACAHO   Association of Canadian Academic
Healthcare Organizations
Voluntary, member-based Canadian national
health association of teaching hospitals, academic regional health authorities (RHAs), and
their research institutes.

780 Echo Drive
Ottawa, Ontario KIS 5R7
Canada
Tel: 613-730-5818
Fax: 613-730-4314
www.acaho.org

ACAP   Alliance of Claims Assistance
Professionals
A national, non-profit organization dedicated to
the growth and development of the claims assistance industry.

1127 High Ridge Road, #216
Stamford, Connecticut 06905
Tel: 203-569-7610
Toll free: 888-394-5163
www.claims.org

ACC   American College of Cardiology
Membership organization for physicians,
nurses, nurse practitioners, physician assistants,
pharmacists and practice managers inside and
outside the United States.

Heart House
2400 N Street, NW
Washington, DC 20037
Tel: 202-375-6000, ext. 5603
Toll free: 800-253-4636, ext. 5603
Fax: 202-375-7000
www.acc.org

ACEP   American College of Emergency
Physicians
Physician membership organization for emer-
gency physician specialists.

1125 Executive Circle
Irving, Texas 75038-2522
Tel: 972-550-0911
Toll free: 800-798-1822
Fax: 972-580-2816
www.acep.org

ACM   Association for Computing Machinery
Professional organization of computing professionals. The special interest group (SIGHIT) emphasizes the computing and information science-related aspects of health informatics.

2 Penn Plaza
Suite 701
New York, NY 10121-0701
Tel: 212-626-0500
Toll free: 800-342-6626
Fax: 212-944-1318
www.acm.org

ACCE   American College of Clinical Engineering
Membership organization for engineers in a clinical environment.

5200 Butler Pike
Plymouth Meeting, PA 19462-1298
Tel: 610-825-6067
Fax: 480-247-5040
www.accenet.org

ACCP   American College of Chest Physicians
Physician education and board review organization for chest physicians and subspecialty candidates.

3300 Dundee Road
Northbrook, IL 60062-2348
Tel: 847-498-1400
Toll free: 800-343-2227
Fax: 847-498-5460
www.chestnet.org

ACEHSA   Accrediting Commission on Education for Health Services Administration
See **CAHME**. (ACEHSA is now CAHME.)

ACGME   Accreditation Council for Graduate Medical Education
A private professional organization responsible for the accreditation of residency education programs.

515 North State Street
Suite 2000
Chicago, IL 60654
Tel: 312-755-5000
Fax: 312-755-7498
www.acgme.org

ACHA   American College of Healthcare Architects
Professional education and board review organization for architects in the field of healthcare architecture.

P.O. Box 14548
Lenexa, KS 66285-4548

18000 W. 105th Street
Olathe, KS 66061-7543
Tel: 913-895-4604
Fax: 913-895-4652
www.healtharchitects.org

ACHCA   American College of Health Care Administrators
Membership organization for administrators, those with substantial interest in health/residential care administration, allied health professionals, and individual providers of healthcare products/services.

1321 Duke Street
Suite 400
Alexandria, VA 22314
Tel: 202-536-5120
Fax: 866-874-1585
www.achca.org

ACHE   American College of Healthcare Executives
Membership organization for healthcare executive who lead hospitals, healthcare systems, and other healthcare organizations.

One N. Franklin St.
Suite 1700
Chicago, IL 60606-3529
Tel: 312-424-2800
Fax: 312-424-0023
www.ache.org

ACHP   Alliance of Community Health Plans
National membership advocacy organization for health plans and provider groups.

1825 Eye Street, NW
Suite 401
Washington, DC 20006
Tel: 202-785-2247
Fax: 202-785-4060
www.achp.org

ACMA American Case Management Association
Certification organization to qualify and examine hospital/health system case management professionals who successfully meet certification requirements.

> *11701 W. 36th St*
> *Little Rock, AR 72211*
> *Tel: 501-907-ACMA (2262)*
> *Fax: 501-227-4247*
> *www.acmaweb.org*

ACNM American College of Nurse-Midwives
Membership organization for certified nurse-midwives and certified midwives who meet eligibility requirements in the United States.

> *8403 Colesville Road*
> *Suite 1550*
> *Silver Spring, MD 20910*
> *Tel: 240-485-1800*
> *Fax: 240-485-1818*
> *www.midwife.org*

ACOG American Congress of Obstetricians and Gynecologists
Physician certification organization for obstetrics and/or gynecology candidates.

> *PO Box 70620*
> *Washington, DC 20024-9998*
>
> *409 12th Street, SW*
> *Washington, DC 20024-2188*
> *Tel: 202-638-5577*
> *Toll free: 800-673-8444*
> *www.acog.org*

ACP American College of Physicians
Physician membership organization for internists, internal medicine subspecialists, medical students, residents, and fellows and physicians in an approved pediatric residency program inside or outside the United States.

> *190 North Independence Mall West*
> *Philadelphia, PA 19106-1572*
> *Tel: 215-351-2400*
> *Toll free:800-523-1546*
> *www.acponline.org*

ACPE American College of Physician Executives
Physician membership organization for licensed allopathic (MD), osteopathic (DO), dentists (DDS, DMS), podiatrists (DPM) inside and outside the United States.

> *400 North Ashley Drive*
> *Suite 400*
> *Tampa, FL 33602*
> *Tel: 813-287-2000*
> *Toll free: 800-562-8088*
> *Fax: 813-287-8993*
> *www.acpe.org*

ACR American College of Radiology
Physician membership organization for radiologists, radiation specialists, and physicians in an approved residency program who meet eligibility requirements.

> *1891 Preston White Drive*
> *Reston, VA 20191*
> *Tel: 703-648-8900*
> *www.acr.org*

ACS American College of Surgeons
Physician membership organization for surgeons, subspecialists, physicians in approved residency programs and members of the surgical team inside or outside the United States who meet eligibility requirements.

> *633 North St. Clair Street*
> *Chicago, IL 60611-3211*
> *Tel: 312-202-5000*
> *Toll free: 800-621-4111*
> *Fax: 312-202-5001*
> *www.facs.org*

ACT Association for Competitive Technology
Advocacy organization for small and mid-size application developers and information technology firms.

> *1401 K Street NW*
> *Suite 502*
> *Washington, DC 20005*
> *Tel: 202-331-2130*
> *www.actonline.org*

ADA   American Dental Association
Membership organization for dentists, students, or charitable practitioners inside or outside the United States.

> *211 E. Chicago Avenue*
> *Chicago, IL 60611-2678*
> *Tel: 312-440-2500*
> *www.ada.org*

ADA   American Diabetes Association
General membership organization designed for people with diabetes, their families, friends, and caregivers.

> *1701 North Beauregard Street*
> *Alexandria, VA 22311*
> *Tel: 703-549-1500, ext. 5203*
> *Toll free: 800-342-2383*
> *www.diabetes.org*

AdvaMed   Advanced Medical Technology Association
Membership organization open to medical technology firms worldwide.

> *701 Pennsylvania Ave, NW*
> *Suite 800*
> *Washington, DC 20004-2654*
> *Tel: 202-783-8700*
> *Fax: 202-783-8750*
> *www.advamed.org*

AeA   Advancing the Business of Technology
(In 2008, AeA merged with the Information Technology Association of America (ITAA) to form TechAmerica.) *See* **TechAmerica**.

AEP   Association of Emergency Physicians
Physician membership organization for emergency physicians from across the United States.

> *911 Whitewater Drive*
> *Mars, PA 16046-4221*
> *Toll free: 866-772-1818*
> *Fax: 866-422-7794*
> *www.aep.org*

AFEHCT   Association for Electronic Health Care Transactions
(In 2006, AFEHCT merged with HIMSS). *See* **HIMSS**.

> *33 West Monroe Street*
> *Suite 1700*
> *Chicago, IL 60603-5616*
> *Tel: 312-664-4467*
> *Fax: 312-664-6143*
> *www.himss.org*

AfPP
Membership organization for all who work in or around the perioperative environment.

> *Daisy Ayris House*
> *42 Freemans Way*
> *Harrogate, North Yorkshire, HG3 1DH*
> *Tel: 01423 881300*
> *Fax: 01423 880997*
> *www.afpp.org.uk*

AHA   American Heart Association
Volunteer organization dedicated to building healthier lives free of cardiovascular (heart) diseases and stroke.

> *National Center*
> *7272 Greenville Avenue*
> *Dallas, TX 75231*
>
> *AHA:*
> *800-AHA-USA-1 and*
> *800-242-8721*
> *www.heart.org*

AHA   American Hospital Association
Membership organization for hospitals, health care systems, pre-acute/post-acute patient care facilities, and hospital-affiliated educational programs (e.g., hospital school of nursing, program in health administration).

> *155 N. Wacker Drive*
> *Chicago, Illinois 60606*
> *Tel: 312-422-3000*
> *www.aha.org*

AHCJ Association of Health Care Journalists
An independent, nonprofit organization dedicated to advancing public understanding of health care issues. Its mission is to improve the quality, accuracy, and visibility of health care reporting, writing and editing.

Missouri School of Journalism
10 Neff Hall
Columbia, MO 65211
Tel: 573-884-5606
Fax: 573-884-5609
www.healthjournalism.org

AHHE Association of Hispanic Healthcare Executives
Membership organization for individuals in healthcare administration or persons on a career path to healthcare management, including healthcare consultants and full-time academicians who support AHHE's mission and objectives.

PO Box 230832 Ansonia Station
New York, NY 10023
Tel.: 212-877-1615
Fax: 212-877-2406
www.ahhe.org

AHIMA American Health Information Management Association
Membership organization for health information management (HIM) professionals interested in the AHIMA purpose.

233 N. Michigan Avenue
21st Floor
Chicago, IL 60601-5809
Tel: 312-233-1100
Toll free: 800-335-5535
Fax: 312-233-1090
www.ahima.org

AHIP America's Health Insurance Plans
National trade association for the health insurance industry.

601 Pennsylvania Avenue, NW
South Building
Suite 500
Washington, DC 20004
Tel: 202-778-3200
Fax: 202-331-7487
www.ahip.org

AHNA American Holistic Nurses Association
Membership organization open to everyone (nurses, other healthcare professionals, and the public) interested in all aspects of holistic caring and healing.

100 SE 9th Street
Suite 3A
Topeka, KS 66612-1213
Tel: 785-234-1712
Toll free: 800-278-2462
Fax: 785-234-1713
www.ahna.org

AHQA American Health Quality Association
Membership organization of State Health Care Quality Associations.

1776 I Street, NW
9th Floor
Washington, DC 20006
Tel: 202-331-5790
www.ahqa.org

AHRMM Association for Healthcare Resource & Materials Management
Membership organization of supply chain provider and suppliers for professionals, students, and retirees.

155 N. Wacker Drive
Chicago, IL 60606
Tel: 312-422-3840
Fax: 312-422-4573
www.ahrmm.org

AHRQ Agency for Healthcare Research and Quality
Federal agency within the Department of Health and Human Services focused on the national mission to improve the quality, safety, efficiency, and effectiveness of healthcare for Americans.

540 Gaither Road
Suite 2000
Rockville, MD 20850
Tel: 301-427-1364
www.ahrq.gov

AIM   Association for Automatic Identification and Mobility
An international trade association representing automatic identification and mobility technology solution providers.

One Landmark North
20399 Route 19
Suite 203
Cranberry Township, PA 16066
Tel: 724-742-4470
Fax: 724-742-4476
www.aimglobal.org

ALA   American Lung Association
Volunteer organization to prevent lung disease and promote lung health.

1301 Pennsylvania Avenue, NW
Suite 800
Washington, DC 20004
Tel: 202-785-3355
Fax: 202-452-1805
www.lungusa.org

Alliance HPSR   Alliance for Health Policy and Systems Research
Academic organization to promote health policy and systems research in developing countries.

20 Avenue Appia
1211 Geneva
Switzerland
Tel: +41 22 791 2973
Fax: +41 22 791 4817
www.who.int/alliance-hpsr

AMA   American Medical Association
Physician association of physicians and physicians in training committed to ethics in medicine.

515 N. State Street
Chicago, IL 60654
Tel: 800-621-8335
www.ama-assn.org

AMCP   Academy of Managed Care Pharmacy
National professional association of pharmacists and other healthcare practitioners organizations.

100 North Pitt Street
Suite 400
Alexandria, VA 22314
Tel: 703-683-8416
Toll free: 800-827-2627
Fax: 703-683-8417
www.amcp.org

AMDA   American Medical Directors Association
Professional association of medical directors and physicians practicing in the long-term care continuum.

11000 Broken Land Parkway
Suite 400
Columbia, MD 21044
Tel: 410-740-9743
Toll free: 800-876-2632
Fax: 410-740-4572
www.amda.com

AMDIS   Association of Medical Directors of Information Systems
Membership organization for Medical Directors of information systems.

682 Peninsula Drive
Lake Almanor, CA 96137
Tel: 719-548-9360
Fax: 978-389-7729
www.amdis.org

AGMA   American Medical Group Association
Physician membership organization for group practices, independent practice associations, academic/faculty practices, integrated delivery systems and other organized systems of care including groups with three or more licensed physicians organized to deliver healthcare services.

One Prince Street
Alexandria, VA 22314-3318
Tel: 703-838-0033
Fax: 703-548-1890
www.amga.org

AHDI Association for Healthcare Documentation Integrity
Membership organization for individuals enrolled in a medical transcription program, individual professionals working or involved in healthcare documentation and data capture, healthcare delivery facilities, companies or manufacturers that employs healthcare documentation specialists or provides services or products to the profession and educational facilities that train medical transcriptionists.

4230 Kiernan Avenue
Suite 130
Modesto, CA 95356
Tel: 209-527-9620
Toll free: 800-982-2182
Fax: 209-527-9633
www.ahdionline.org

AMIA American Medical Informatics Association
Membership organization open to individuals interested in biomedical and health informatics.

4720 Montgomery Lane
Suite 500
Bethesda, MD 20814
Tel: 301-657-1291
Fax: 301-657-1296
www.amia.org

AMP Applied Measurement Professionals, Inc.
Certification organization for psychometric consultation, testing, and measurement services

18000 W. 105th Street
Olathe, KS 66061
Tel: 913-895-4600
Fax: 913-895-4650
www.goamp.com

AMSN Academy of Medical-Surgical Nurses
Membership organization for nurses and licensed healthcare professionals interested in the care of adults.

East Holly Avenue
Box 56
Pitman, NJ 08071-0056
Toll free: 866-877-2676
www.amsn.org

ANA American Nurses Association
Professional membership organization representing the interests of the Registered Nurses through its constituent and state nurses associations and organizational affiliates.

8515 Georgia Avenue
Suite 400
Silver Spring, MD 20910-3492
Tel: 301-628-5000
Toll Free: 800-274-4ANA (4262)
Fax: 301-628-5001
www.nursingworld.org

ANASA Association of Nursing Agencies for South Africa
Membership association representing nursing agencies in South Africa.

P.O. Box 12339
Club View Pretoria 0014
South Africa
Tel: +083-444-9227
Fax: +086-535-1794
e-mail (Enquiries): office@anasa.org.za
www.anasa.org.za

ANIA American Nursing Informatics Association
Membership organization to advance the field of Nursing Informatics.

200 East Holly Avenue
Sewell, NJ 08080
Toll free: 866-552-6404
www.ania.org

ANCC American Nurses Credentialing Center
Nursing certification organization to qualify and examine nurse candidates who have successfully completed an accredited program and meet certification requirements.

8515 Georgia Avenue
Suite 400
Silver Spring, MD 20910-3492
Toll free: 800-284-2378
www.nursecredentialing.org

ANI Alliance for Nursing Informatics
Membership organization of Nursing Informatics associations and groups.

33 West Monroe Street
Suite 1700
Chicago, IL 60603-5616
Tel: 312-664-4467
Fax: 312-664-6143
www.allianceni.org

ANNA American Nephrology Nurses
Association
Membership organization for nurses, allied health professionals and others inside and outside the United States involved in the care of nephrology patients.

East Holly Avenue
Box 56
Pitman, NJ 08071
Toll free: 888-600-2662
www.annanurse.org

ANSI American National Standards Institute
National voice of the US standards and conformity assessment system, the American National Standards Institute is a membership organization for government agencies, organizations, companies, academic and international bodies, and individuals.

25 West 43rd Street
4th Floor
New York, NY 10036
Tel: 212-642-4900
Fax: 212-398-0023
www.ansi.org

AOA American Osteopathic Association
Membership organization for osteopathic physicians, associates and allied healthcare providers inside and outside the United States.

142 E. Ontario Street
Chicago, IL 60611-2864
Tel: 312-202-8000
Toll free: 800-621-1773
Fax: 312-202-2000
www.osteopathic.org

AONE American Organization of Nurse
Executives
Membership organization for nurses in leadership positions, students, and individuals interested in supporting the AONE mission and vision.

Governance
325 Seventh Street, NW
Washington, DC 20004
Tel: 202-626-2240
Fax: 202-638-5499

Operations
155 N. Wabash Drive
Suite 400
Chicago, IL 60606
Tel: 312-422-2800
Fax: 312-278-0861
www.aone.org

AORN Association of periOperative Registered
Nurses
Membership organization of perioperative nurses, nursing students, and industry professionals who provide direct or indirect perioperative services.

2170 South Parker Road
Suite 400
Denver, CO 80231
Tel: 303-755-6300
Toll free: 800-755-2676
Fax: 800-847-0045
www.aorn.org

APhA American Pharmacists Association
Membership organization for pharmacists, students, spouses, technicians, and retirees inside or outside the United States.

2215 Constitution Avenue, NW
Washington, DC 20037
Tel: 202-628-4410
Fax: 202-783-2351
www.pharmacist.com

APHA American Public Health Association
Membership organization open to health professionals, other career workers in the health field, and persons interested in public health.

800 I Street, NW
Washington, DC 20001-3710
Tel: 202-777-2742
Fax: 202-448-8734
www.apha.org

API Association for Pathology Informatics
Membership organization for individuals, trainees (e.g. residents, fellows, students, and post-docs), teaching institutions, commercial entities, and other organizations interested in pathology informatics.

5607 Baum Boulevard
Room 522
Pittsburgh, PA 15206
Tel: 412-624-3340
Fax: 412-624-5100
www.pathologyinformatics.org

APNA American Psychiatric Nurses Association
Membership organization for nurses and affiliated mental health professionals inside and outside the United States who are committed to the specialty practice of psychiatric-mental health (PMH) nursing, wellness promotion, prevention of mental health problems, and the care and treatment of persons with psychiatric disorders.

3141 Fairview Park Drive
Suite 625
Falls Church, VA 22042
Tel: 571-533-1919
Toll free: 855-863-2762
Fax: 855-883-2762
www.apna.org

APTA American Physical Therapy Association
Membership organization for physical therapists (PT) and assistants (PTA) inside and outside the United States.

1111 North Fairfax Street
Alexandria, VA 22314-1488
Tel: 703-684-APTA (2782)
Toll free: 800-999-2782
TDD: 703-683-6748
Fax: 703-684-734
www.apta.org

ARN Association of Rehabilitation Nurses
To promote and advance professional rehabilitation nursing practice through education, advocacy, collaboration, and research to enhance the quality of life for those affected by disability and chronic illness.

4700 W. Lake Avenue
Glenview, IL 60025
Toll free: 800-229-7530
e-mail: info@rehabnurse.org
www.rehabnurse.org

ASAE American Society of Association Executives
Membership organization for professional staff, students, consultants, executives of a non-profit association or association management companies.

1575 I Street, NW
Washington, DC 20005
Tel: 202-371-0940
Toll free: 888-950-2723
Fax: 202-371-8315
www.asaecenter.org

ASCIP Academy of Spinal Cord Injury Professionals
Membership association of physicians, nurses, psychologists, social workers, counselors, therapists, and researchers engaged in education, research, advocacy, policy for spinal cord injuries inside and outside the United States.

206 South Sixth Street
Springfield, IL 62701
Tel: 217-753-1190
Fax: 217-525-1271
www.academyscipro.org

ASC   X12 The Accredited Standards Committee
Membership organization chartered by Accredited Standards Committee (ASC) under the American National Standards Institute (ANSI) to support business and technical professionals in a cross-industry forum to enhance business processes.

Tel: 703-970-4480
www.x12.org
e-mail: info@disa.org

ASCO   American Society of Clinical Oncology
Membership organization for oncology professionals.

2318 Mill Road
Suite 800
Alexandria, VA 22314
Tel: 571-483-1300
Toll free: 888-282-2552
www.asco.org

ASCP   American Society for Clinical Pathology
Membership organization for pathologists and laboratory professionals.

33 West Monroe
Suite 1600
Chicago, IL 60603
Tel: 312-541-4999
Fax: 312-541-4998
www.ascp.org

ASHE   American Society for Healthcare Engineering
Membership organization for individuals devoted to optimizing the healthcare physical environment in a healthcare facility, company or organization other than health care, educators and students.

155 N. Wacker Drive
Suite 400
Chicago, Illinois 60606
Tel: 312-422-3800
Fax: 312-422-4571
www.ashe.org

ASHP   American Society of Health-System Pharmacists
Membership organization for pharmacists, students, spouses, technicians, and retirees inside or outside the United States.

7272 Wisconsin Avenue
Bethesda, MD 20814
Toll free: 866-279-0681
International Tel: 0-01-301-664-8700
www.ashp.org

ASHRM   American Society for Healthcare Risk Management
Membership organization for anyone who is actively involved or interested in healthcare risk management or whose primary job responsibility includes healthcare risk management.

155 N. Wacker Drive
Suite 400
Chicago, Illinois 60606
Tel: 312-422-3980
Fax: 312-422-4580
www.ashrm.org

ASNC   American Society of Nuclear Cardiology
Membership organization for physicians, scientists, technologists, biomedical engineers, computer specialists, and other healthcare personnel involved in nuclear cardiology as well as industry representatives who actively work in this field of medicine.

4340 East-West Highway
Suite 1120
Bethesda, MD 20814
Tel: 301-215-7575
Fax: 301-215-7113
www.asnc.org

ASPAN   American Society of PeriAnesthesia
Nurses
Membership organization for nurses involved in
all phases of preanesthesia and postanesthesia
care, ambulatory surgery, and pain management
or in the management, teaching, or research of
the same, students, licensed healthcare professionals interested in perianesthesia inside or
outside the United States.

90 Frontage Road
Cherry Hill, NJ 08034-1424
Tel: 856-616-9600
Toll free: 877-737-9696
Fax: 856-616-9601
www.aspan.org

ASQ   American Society for Quality
Global membership community of people passionate about quality.

P.O. Box 3005
Milwaukee, WI 53201-3005

600 North Plankinton Avenue
Milwaukee, WI 53203
Tel: 800-248-1946
Mexico: 001-800-514-1564
All other locations: +1-414-272-8575
Fax: 414-272-1734
www.asq.org

ASSE   American Society of Safety Engineers
Membership organization for the safety, health,
and environmental (SH&E) profession with an
interest in the Healthcare Practice Specialty.

1800 E. Oakton Street
Des Plaines, IL 60018
Tel: 847-699-2929
www.asse.org

ASTHO   Association of State and Territorial
Health Officials
All state and territorial health agency staff mem-
bers are eligible to participate in open meetings.

2231 Crystal Drive
Suite 450
Arlington, VA 22202
Tel: 202-371-9090
Fax: 571-527-3189
www.astho.org

ASTM   ASTM International
Membership organization chartered by ASTM
under the American National Standards Institute (ANSI) to support the development of test
methods, specifications, guides, and practice
standards that support industries and governments worldwide.

100 Barr Harbor Drive
P.O. Box C700
West Conshohocken, PA 19428-2959
Toll free: 877-909-ASTM
www.astm.org

ATA   American Telemedicine Association
Membership is open to all individuals and
organizations interested in providing distance
healthcare through technology.

1100 Connecticut Avenue, NW
Suite 540
Washington, DC 20036
Tel: 202-223-3333
Fax: 202-223-2787
www.americantelemed.org

AUPHA   Association of University Programs in
Health Administration
Membership organization of healthcare man-
agement/administration education programs in
North America includes non-academic insti-
tutions and individuals inside and outside the
United States.

2000 N. 14th Street
Suite 780
Arlington, VA 22201
Tel: 703-894-0940
Fax: 703-894-0941
www.aupha.org

AWHONN   Association of Women's Health,
Obstetric and Neonatal Nurses
Membership organization for nurses and other
healthcare professionals interested in improving the health of women and newborns.

2000 L Street, NW
Suite 740
Washington, DC 20036
Tel: 202-261-2400
Toll free US: 800-673-8499
Toll free Canada: 800-245-0231
Fax: 202-728-0575
www.awhonn.org

BACCN   British Association of Critical Care Nurses
Membership organization open to any professional with an interest in critical care.

c/o Benchmark Communications
14 Blandford Square
Newcastle Upon Tyne
NE1 4HZ
www.baccn.org.uk

BCI   Business Continuity Institute
Membership organization open to business continuity management practitioners at all levels of experience worldwide.

1964 Gallows Road
Suite 330
Vienna, VA 22182
Tel: 703-637-4424
International Tel: +44 118 918 7935
www.thebci.org

CAC   Citizen Advocacy Center
Membership organization for state health professional licensing boards and other interested organizations and individuals.

1400 16th Street, NW
Suite 101
Washington, DC 20036
Tel: 202-462-1174
Fax: 202-354-5372
www.cacenter.org

CACCN   Canadian Association of Critical Care Nurses
Canadian nursing membership organization for any registered nurse with an interest in critical care who possesses a current and valid license or certificate.

P.O. Box 25322
London, Ontario
N6B 6B1Canada
Tel: 519-649-5284
Toll free: 866-477-9077
Fax: 519-649-1458
www.caccn.ca

CADTH   Canadian Agency for Drugs and Technologies
An independent, not-for-profit agency funded by Canadian federal, provincial, and territorial governments to provide credible, impartial advice and evidence-based information about the effectiveness of drugs and other health technologies to Canadian healthcare decision makers.

865 Carling Avenue
Suite 600
Ottawa, Ontario
K1S 5S8 Canada
Tel: 613-226-2553
Toll free: 866-988-1444
Fax: 613-226-5392
www.cadth.ca

CAHME   Commission on Accreditation of Healthcare Management Education
Any interested healthcare organization or corporation may become a corporate member.

2111 Wilson Boulevard
Suite 700
Arlington, VA 22201
Tel: 703-351-5010
Fax: 703-991-5989
www.cahme.org

CAHTA   Catalan Agency for Health Technology Assessment and Research
See **HEN**. (CAHTA is now HEN.)

CAP   College of American Pathologists
Membership organization exclusively for pathology residents.

325 Waukegan Road
Northfield, IL 60093-2750
Toll free: 800-323-4040
Fax: 847-832-8000
International fax: 001-847-832-7000
www.cap.org

CAQH Council for Affordable Quality Healthcare
Membership alliance of nonprofit health plans and trade associations.

> *601 Pennsylvania Avenue, NW*
> *South Building*
> *Suite 500*
> *Washington, DC 20004*
> *Tel: 202-861-1492*
> *Fax: 202-861-1454*
> *www.caqh.org*

CARING Capital Area Roundtable on Informatics in Nursing
(In 2011, CARING merged with ANIA.)
See **ANIA**.

CCA Care Continuum Alliance
Membership organization of corporate and individual members from health plans and disease management organizations; health information technology innovators and manufacturers; pharmaceutical manufacturers and pharmacy benefit managers; employers and other purchasers, physicians, researchers and nurses.

> *701 Pennsylvania Avenue, NW*
> *Suite 700*
> *Washington, DC 20004-2694*
> *Tel: 202-737-5980*
> *Fax: 202-478-5113*
> *www.carecontinuumalliance.org*

CCC Computing Community Consortium
Cooperative consortium formed by the Computing Research Association (CRA) and the US National Science Foundation, CCC is broadly inclusive, and any computing researcher who wishes to become involved.

> *1828 L Street, NW*
> *Suite 800*
> *Washington, DC 20036-4632*
> *Tel: 202-234-2111*
> *Fax: 202-667-1066*
> *www.cra.org/ccc*

CCHIT Certification Commission for Healthcare Information Technology
An independent 501(c)3 nonprofit organization. Volunteers serve on work groups and advisory panels to develop interoperable health information technology certification and test scripts.

> *200 S. Wacker Drive*
> *Suite 3100*
> *Chicago, IL 60606*
> *Tel: 312-674-4930*
> *Fax: 312-896-1466*
> *www.cchit.org*

CDC Centers for Disease Control and Prevention
Federal agency within the Department of Health and Human Services focused on the national mission to improve the quality, safety, efficiency, and effectiveness of healthcare for Americans.

> *1600 Clifton Road*
> *Atlanta, GA 30333*
> *Toll free: 800-CDC-INFO (800-232-4636)*
> *www.cdc.gov*

CDISC Clinical Data Interchange Standards Consortium
Membership organization open to any organization of any size interested in information system interoperability to improve medical research and related areas of healthcare.

> *P.O. Box 2068*
> *Round Rock, TX 78680*
> *www.cdisc.org*

CEN European Committee for Standardization
Membership is the 27 European Union National Standards Bodies (NSBs), Croatia, The Former Yugoslav Republic of Macedonia, Turkey, and three countries of the European Free Trade Association (Iceland, Norway, and Switzerland).

> *CEN-CENELEC Management Centre*
> *Avenue Marnix 17*
> *B-1000 Brussels*
> *Tel: + 32 2 550 08 11*
> *Fax: + 32 2 550 08 19*
> *www.cen.eu*

CHCA   Child Health Corporation of America
Private alliance of non-competing children's hospitals owned and governed by North America's leading children's hospitals offering collaborative services and projects that enhance healthcare and operational processes.

> *6803 West 64th Street*
> *Shawnee Mission, KS 66202*
> *Tel: 913-262-1436*
> *Fax: 913-262-1575*
> *www.chca.com*

CHI   Canada Health Infoway
Organization accountable to Canada's 14 federal, provincial, and territorial governments represented by their Deputy Ministers of Health to foster development and adoption of information technology to transform healthcare in Canada.

> *www.infoway-inforoute.ca*

CHI   Consolidated Health Informatics
One of the Office of Management and Budget's (OMB) eGov initiatives. CHI is a collaborative effort to adopt health information interoperability standards, particularly health vocabulary and messaging standards, for implementation in federal government systems.

CHIME   College of Healthcare Information Management Executives
Membership open to CIOs and senior IT leaders at healthcare-related organizations.

> *3300 Washtenaw Avenue*
> *Suite 225*
> *Ann Arbor, MI 48104-4250*
> *Tel: 734-665-0000*
> *Fax: 734-665-4922*
> *www.cio-chime.org*

CHT   Center for Health and Technology
Private, academic research organization.

> *University of California Davis*
> *Center for Health and Technology*
> *2315 Stockton Boulevard*
> *Sacramento, CA 95817*
> *Tel: 916-734-5675*
> *Fax: 916-734-3580*
> *www.ucdmc.ucdavis.edu/cht*

CIHI   Canadian Institute for Health Information
An independent, not-for-profit organization that provides essential data and analysis on Canada's health system and the health of Canadians.

> *495 Richmond Road*
> *Suite 600*
> *Ottawa, Ontario*
> *K2A 4H6 Canada*
> *Fax: 613-241-8120*
> *www.cihi.ca*

CIHR   Canadian Institutes of Health Research
Agency responsible for funding health research in Canada.

> *160 Elgin Street*
> *9th Floor*
> *Address Locator 4809A*
> *Ottawa, Ontario*
> *K19 0W9 Canada*
> *Tel: 613-941-2672*
> *Toll free: 888-603-4178*
> *Fax: 613-954-1800*
> *www.cihr-irsc.gc.ca*

CITL   Center for Information Technology Leadership
Independent information technology and health technologies research organization.

> *www.citl.org*

CITPH   Center for Innovation and Technology in Public Health
A research group engaged in public policy development, public health (PH) practices, and the direct provision of services related to enabling technologies. *See* **Public Health Institute.**

> *www.citph.org*

CLMA   Clinical Laboratory Management Association
Membership organization for individuals who hold, have held, or aspire to hold an administrative, managerial, or supervisory position in the clinical laboratory or whose administrative responsibilities include diagnostic services.

> *330 N. Wabash Avenue*
> *Suite 2000*
> *Chicago, IL 60611*
> *Tel: 312-321-5111*
> *www.clma.org*

CLSI   Clinical and Laboratory Standards Institute
Membership organization for IVD manufacturers and suppliers, LIS/HIS companies, pharmaceutical and biotechnology companies, consulting firms, professional societies, trade associations, government agencies.

950 West Valley Road
Suite 2500
Wayne, PA 19087 USA
Tel: 610-688-0100
Fax: 610-688-0700
www.clsi.org

CMS   Centers for Medicare & Medicaid Services
Federal agency within the Department of Health and Human Services focused on the national mission to improve the quality, safety, efficiency and effectiveness of healthcare for Americans.

7500 Security Boulevard
Baltimore, MD 21244
Tel: 410-786-3000
Toll free: 877-267-2323
TTY: 410-786-0727
TTY: 866-226-1819
www.cms.gov

CMSA   Case Management Society of America
Membership organization for individuals engaged in the field of case management inside and outside the United States.

6301 Ranch Drive
Little Rock, AR 72223
Tel: 501-225-2229
Fax: 501-221-9068
www.cmsa.org

CNA   Canadian Nurses Association
National professional membership organization for registered nurses in Canada.

50 Driveway
Ottawa, Ontario
K2P 1E2 Canada
Tel: 613-237-2133
Toll free: 800-361-8404
Fax: 613-237-3520
www.cna-nurses.ca

CNC   Center for Nursing Classification and Clinical Effectiveness
Academia research center at the University of Iowa School of Nursing.

University of Iowa College of Nursing
101 College of Nursing Building
50 Newton Road
Iowa City, IA 52242-1121
Tel: 319-335-7018
Fax: 319-335-9990
www.nursing.uiowa.edu/cnc

COACH   Canada's Health Informatics Association
Open to all individuals with an interest in health informatics, health information management, or related healthcare issues and practices.

250 Consumers Road
Suite 301
Toronto, Ontario
M2J 4V6 Canada
Tel: 416-494-9324
Toll free: 888-253-8554
Fax: 416-495-8723
www.coachorg.com

COC   AHIMA's Commission on Certification
Certification organization for the AHIMA mission of quality healthcare through quality information.

233 N. Michigan Avenue
21st Floor
Chicago, IL 60601-5800
Tel: 312-233-1100
Fax: 312-233-1090
www.ahima.org/certification

CompTIA   The Computing Technology Industry Association Trade association
Non-profit trade association for IT professionals and companies inside and outside the United States.

3500 Lacey Road
Suite 100
Downers Grove, IL 60515
Tel: 630-678-8300
Fax: 630-678-8384
www.comptia.org

CVAA Canadian Vascular Access Association
Membership organization open to corporations
and all nurses registered with their provincial
governing body, extended to the United States
and Bermuda, engaged in the field of intrave-
nous or vascular access therapy.

> 753 Main Street East
> P.O. Box 68030
> Hamilton, Ontario
> L8M 3M7 Canada
> Tel: 289-396-8824
> Fax: 289-396-1624
> www.cvaa.info

DAHTA German Agency for Health Technology
Assessment
German Institute of Medical Documentation
and Information (DIMDI) agency responsible for granting research assignments for the
assessment of procedures and technology relevant to health in the form of Health Technology
Assessment (HTA) reports and for the maintenance of a database-supported information system for the assessment of the effectiveness and
cost of medical procedures and technologies.

> Tel: +49 221 4724-1
> Fax: +49 221 4724-444
> www.dimdi.de

DAMA Data Management Association
International
Chapter-based, as well as global, membership
organization for those who engage in information and data management.

> 1685 Ansonborough Drive
> Chesterfield, MO 63017
> Tel: 813-778-5495
> Fax: 1-813-464-7864
> www.dama.org

Danish Health and Medicines Authority
Government agency for the regulation of health
and medicines in Denmark.

> Axel Heides Gade 1
> 2300 Copenhagen S
> Denmark
> Tel: +45 72 22 74 00
> www.sst.dk

DARPA Defense Advanced Research Projects
Agency
US Military research agency.

> 675 North Randolph Street
> Arlington, VA 22203-2114
> Tel: 703-526-6630
> www.darpa.mil

DHHS Department of Health and Human
Services
The US government's principal agency for
protecting the health of all Americans and providing essential human services, especially for
those who are least able to help themselves.

> 200 Independence Avenue, SW
> Washington, DC 20201
> Tel: 202-619-0257
> Toll free: 877-696-6775
> www.hhs.gov

HHS Department of Health and Human
Services
See **DHHS**.

DICOM Digital Imaging and Communications
in Medicine
Membership organization chartered by Digital Imaging and Communications in Medicine
(DICOM) under the American National Standards Institute (ANSI) to develop health information standards.

> NEMA
> 1300 N. 17th Street
> Suite 1752
> Rosslyn, VA 22209
> Tel:703-841-3281
> medical.nema.org

DIHTA Danish Institute for Health Technology
Assessment
See **Danish Health and Medicines Authority**.
(DIHTA is now Danish Health and Medicines
Authority.)

DIMDI German Institute of Medical Documentation and Information
Institute within the German Federal Ministry of Health providing information in all fields of the life science to the interested public.

Tel: +49 221 4724-1
Fax: +49 221 4724-444
www.dimdi.de

DISA Data Interchange Standards Association
Organization providing administrative and technical support to ASCX12.

7600 Leesburg Pike
Suite 430
Falls Church, VA 22043
Tel: 703-970-4480
Fax: 703-970-4488
www.disa.org

DMAA Disease Management Association of America
See **CCA**. (DMAA is now the Care Continuum Alliance.)

DNA Dermatology Nurses' Association
Professional membership organization for nurses, individuals in related healthcare fields, and corporation interested in or involved in the care of dermatology patients.

15000 Commerce Parkway
Suite C
Mt. Laurel, NJ 08054
Tel: 800-454-4362
Fax: 856-439-0525
www.dnanurse.org

DoD Department of Defense (Health Affairs)
US Military department responsible for the health benefits and healthcare operations of those entrusted to our care.

http://prhome.defense.gov/HA

ECRI Emergency Care Research Institute
Independent, nonprofit organization that offers membership programs to improve the safety, quality, and cost-effectiveness of patient care.

Tel: 610-825-6000
www.ecri.org

eHI eHealth Initiative
Membership is open to all organizations in the healthcare industry.

818 Connecticut Avenue, NW
Suite 500
Washington, DC 20006
Tel: 202-624-3270
Fax: 202-429-5553
www.ehealthinitiative.org

EHRA Electronic Health Vendors Association
A trade association of Electronic Health Record (EHR) companies addressing national efforts to create interoperable EHRs in hospital and ambulatory care settings. The EHR Association operates on the premise that the rapid, widespread adoption of EHRs will help improve the quality of patient care, as well as the productivity and sustainability of the healthcare system.

33 West Monroe Street
Suite 1700
Chicago, IL 60603-5616
Tel: 312-664-4467
Fax: 312-664-6143
www.himssehrva.org

EMEA European Medicines Agency
Decentralized agency of the European Union responsible for the scientific evaluation of medicines developed by pharmaceutical companies for use in the European Union.

7 Westferry Circus
Canary Wharf
London E14 4HB
United Kingdom
Tel: +44 (0) 20 74 18 84 00
Fax: +44 (0) 20 7418 8416
www.ema.europa.eu/ema

ENA Emergency Nurses Association
Membership organization for nurses in emergency nursing practice.

915 Lee Street
Des Plaines, IL 60016-6569
Tel: 800-900-9659
www.ena.org

ESQH   European Society for Quality in Healthcare
A not-for-profit organisation dedicated to the improvement of quality in European healthcare.

St. Camillus Hospital
Shelbourne Road
Limerick
Ireland
Tel: 00353 61 483315
e-mail: info@esqh.net
www.esqh.net

ETSI   European Telecommunications Standards Institute
Membership organization for individuals, non-profit associations, universities, public research bodies, governmental organizations and observers interested in globally applicable standards for Information and Communications Technologies (ICT), including fixed, mobile, radio, converged, broadcast, and Internet technologies.

650, Route des Lucioles
06921 Sophia-Antipolis Cedex
France
Tel: +33 (0)4 92 94 42 00
Fax: +33 (0)4 93 65 47 16
www.etsi.org

EUnetHTA   European Network for Health Technology Assessment
Organization supporting collaboration between European Health Technology Applications (HTA).

Hosted by Danish Health and
Medicines Authority
Axel Heides Gade 1
2300 Copenhagen S
Denmark
Tel: +45 7222 7727
Fax: +45 2075 9647
www.eunethta.net

FAH   Federation of American Hospitals
Membership organization for investor-owned community hospitals and health systems including institutions, associations (hospital associations, medical societies, law firms and foundations, suppliers of services and products to the healthcare industry, management companies) and individual student members enrolled in a course in hospital administration or other career study in the healthcare industry.

750 9th Street, NW
Suite 600
Washington, DC 20001-4524
Tel: 202-624-1500
Fax: 202-737-6462
www.fah.org

FCC   Federal Communications Commission
An independent US government agency directly responsible to Congress charged with regulating interstate and international communications by radio, television, wire, satellite and cable.

445 12th Street SW
Washington, DC 20554
Toll free: 888-225-5322
TTY: 888-835-5322
Fax: 866-418-0232
www.fcc.gov

FDA   US Food and Drug Administration
Federal agency responsible for protecting the public health by assuring the safety, efficacy, and security of human and veterinary drugs, biological products, medical devices, our nation's food supply, cosmetics, and products that emit radiation.

10903 New Hampshire Avenue
Silver Spring, MD 20993
Tel: 888-463-6332
www.fda.gov

George Institute for Global Health
Global research and health policy center.

Level 13, 321 Kent Street
NSW 2000 Sydney
Australia
Tel: +61 2 9657 0300
Fax: +61 2 9657 0301
www.thegeorgeinstitute.org

GS1 US Global Standards-1
Authorized provider of globally unique GS1 company prefixes for businesses and the design and implementation of supply chain standards and solutions.

> *Local GS1 offices by country: USA,*
> *Princeton Pike Corporate Center*
> *1009 Lenox Drive*
> *Suite 202*
> *Lawrenceville, NJ 08648*
> *Tel: 609-620-0200*
> *Fax: 609-620-1200*
> *www.gs1.org*

HCCA Health Care Compliance Association
Membership organization for all compliance professionals, corporations, and students.

> *6500 Barrie Road*
> *Suite 250*
> *Minneapolis, MN 55435*
> *Tel: 952-988-0141*
> *Toll free: 888-580-8373*
> *Fax: 952-988-0146*
> *www.hcca-info.org*

HCCA Health Care Conference Administrators, LLC
Organization that develops, organizes, and administers conferences, trade shows, courses, customized learning. and education, and Internet-based programming, alone, or in joint venture with or on behalf of sponsoring organizations.

> *37 Tatoosh Key*
> *Bellevue, WA 98006 US*
> *Tel: 206-757-8053*
> *Fax: 206-757-7053*
> *www.ehcca.com*

HCEA Healthcare Convention and Exhibitors Association
Trade association for healthcare organizations involved as exhibitors at healthcare conventions and exhibitions. Membership includes healthcare associations and companies that provide products and services to the healthcare convention and exhibition industry.

> *1100 Johnson Ferry Road*
> *Suite 300*
> *Atlanta, GA 30342*
> *Tel: 404-252-3663*
> *Fax: 404-252-0774*
> *www.hcea.org*

HDWA Healthcare Data Warehousing Association
Membership is open to employees of healthcare payor and provider organizations. Memberships are held by organizations, not members.

> *www.hdwa.org*

Health Tech Health Technology Center
(In 2009, Health Tech merged with the Public Health Institute and established the Center for Innovation and Technology in Public Health.)

HEN World Health Organization Health Evidence Network
Network of organizations and institutions promoting the use of evidence in health policy or health technology assessment.

> *WHO Regional Office for Europe*
> *Scherfigsvej 8*
> *DK-2100 Copenhagen Ø Denmark*
> *Tel: +45 39 17 17 17*
> *Fax: +45 39 17 18 18*
> *www.euro.who.int/en/what-*
> *we-do/data-and-evidence/*
> *health-evidence-network-hen*

HFMA Healthcare Financial Management Association
Membership organization for healthcare financial management executives and leaders.

> *2 Westbrook Corporate Center*
> *Suite 600*
> *Westchester, IL 60154*
> *Tel: 708-531-9600*
> *Toll free: 800-252-4362*
> *Fax: 708-531-0032*
> *www.hfma.org*

HIAA Health Insurance Association of America
See **AHIP**. (HIAA is now AHIP.)

HIBCC   Health Industry Business Communications Council

An industry-sponsored and supported non-profit organization. As an ANSI-accredited organization, our primary function is to facilitate electronic communications by developing appropriate standards for information exchange among all healthcare trading partners. Our broad mission has consistently expanded to meet industry requirements and has involved HIBCC in a number of critical areas, including electronic data interchange message formats, bar code labeling data standards, universal numbering systems, and the provision of databases, which assure common identifiers. HIBCC plays a major advocacy and educational role in the healthcare industry and serves as the forum through which consensus can be reached as it electronically transforms itself for 21st century commerce.

2525 E. Arizona Biltmore Circle
Suite 127
Phoenix, Arizona 85016
Tel: 602-381-1091
Fax: 602-381-1093
www.hibcc.org

HIMA   Health Industry Manufacturers Association
See **AdvaMed**.

HIMSS   Healthcare Information and Management Systems Society

Membership in HIMSS is available to all individuals and organizations that are active and/or interested in the fields of healthcare information and management systems.

33 West Monroe Street
Suite 1700
Chicago, IL 60603-5616
Tel: 312-664-4467
Fax: 312-664-6143
www.himss.org

HITSP   Healthcare Information Technology Standards Panel

(On April 30, 2010, the organization was dissolved by David Blumenthal, MD, the National Coordinator for Healthcare Information Technology.)

25 West 43rd Street
Fourth Floor
New York, NY 10036
Tel: 212-642-4900
Fax: 212-398-0023
www.hitsp.org

HL7   Health Level Seven

Membership is available to everyone interested in the development and/or use of a cost-effective approach to system connectivity.

3300 Washtenaw Avenue
Suite 227
Ann Arbor, MI 48104
Tel: +1 734-677-7777
Fax: +1 734-677-6622
www.hl7.org

HLC   Healthcare Leadership Council

A coalition of chief executives from all disciplines within the healthcare system.

750 9th Street, NW
Suite 500
Washington, DC 20001
Tel: 202-452-8700
Fax: 202-296-9561
www.hlc.org

HPNA   Hospice and Palliative Nurses Association

Membership organization for all members of the nursing team—nurses, nursing assistants, students, and non-nurses—engaged in hospice and palliative end-of-life care.

One Penn Center West
Suite 229
Pittsburgh, PA 15276
Tel: 412-787-9301
www.hpna.org

HSC Center for Studying Health System Change
Nonpartisan, nonprofit 501(c)(3) organization established by the International Union, UAW; Chrysler Group LLC; Ford Motor Company; and General Motors to inform policy makers and private decision makers about how local and national changes in the financing and delivery of healthcare affect people.

1100 1st Street, NE
12th Floor
Washington, DC 20002-4221
Tel: 202-484-5261
Fax: 202-863-1763
www.hschange.com

HTAi Health Technology Assessment International
Membership organization embracing all stakeholders, including researchers, agencies, policymakers, industry, academia, health service providers, and patients/consumers, interested in the field of scientific research to inform policy and clinical decision-making around the introduction and diffusion of health technologies.

HTAi Secretariat
1200, 10405 Jasper Avenue
Edmonton, Alberta
T5J 3N4 Canada
Tel: 780-448-4881
Fax: 780-448-0018
www.htai.org

IAPP International Association of Privacy Professionals
Membership organization for privacy professionals, corporations, government agencies, and non-profit groups from around the world.

Pease International Tradeport
75 Rochester Avenue
Suite 4
Portsmouth, NH 03801 USA
Tel: +1 603-427-9200
Toll free: 800-266-6501
Fax: +1 603-427-9249
www.privacyassociation.org

ICCBBA International Council for Commonality in Blood Bank Automation
Registration and licensing organization for the ISBT 128 global standard for the identification, labeling, and information processing of human blood, cell, tissue, and organ products across international borders and disparate healthcare systems.

California, USA Office
P.O. Box 11309
San Bernardino, CA 92423-1309
Tel: 909-793-6516
Fax: 909-793-6214
www.iccbba.org

ICE Institute for Credentialing Excellence
Developer of standards for certification and certificate programs. Organizations may join at any time whether or not the organization has any programs accredited by the National Commission for Certifying Agencies (NCCA).

2025 M Street, NW
Suite 800
Washington, DC 20036
Tel: 202-367-1165
Fax: 202-367-2165
www.credentialingexcellence.org

ICN International Council of Nurses
A federation of more than 130 national nurses associations representing more than 13 million nurses worldwide.

3, Place Jean Marteau
1201 - Geneva
Switzerland
Tel: +41-22-908-01-00
Fax: +41-22-908-01-01
www.icn.ch

ICOR International Consortium of Organizational Resilience
Membership organization for professionals from a wide variety of public and private sectors including international organizations, government, consultant, or vendor with demonstrated experience in organizational resilience.

P.O. Box 1171
Lombard, IL 60148
Tel: 630-705-0910
Toll free: 866-765-8321
www.theicor.org

IEC International Electrotechnical Commission
A not-for-profit, non-governmental organization. Members are National Committees and
their appointed experts and delegates coming
from industry, government bodies, associations,
and academia to participate in technical and
conformity assessments.

3, rue de Varembé
P.O. Box 131
CH - 1211 Geneva 20 Switzerland
Tel: +41 22 919 02 11
Fax: +41 22 919 03 00
www.iec.ch

IEEE Institute of Electrical & Electronics
Engineers, Inc.
Membership organization for individuals and
students who are contributing or working in a
technology or engineering field.

2001 L Street, NW
Suite 700
Washington, DC 20036-4910
Tel: 202-785-0017
Fax: 202-785-0835
www.ieee.org

IEFT Internet Engineering Task Force
An open international community of network
designers, operators, vendors, and researchers
concerned with the evolution of the Internet
architecture and the smooth operation of the
Internet. Membership is open to any interested
individual.

48377 Fremont Blvd
Suite 117
Fremont, California 94538
Tel: 510-492-4080
Fax: 510-492-4001
www.ietf.org

IHE Integrating the Healthcare Enterprise
Membership organization composed of Member Organizations interested in improving
the interoperability of healthcare information
systems.

HIMSS
33 West Monroe Street
Suite 1700
Chicago, IL 60603-5616
Tel: 312-664-4467
Fax: 312-664-6143

RSNA
820 Jorie Boulevard
Oak Brook, IL 60523-2251
Tel: 630-571-2670
Toll free: 800-381-6660
www.ihe.net

IHF International Hospital Federation
Global association of healthcare organizations,
which includes in particular, but not exclusively,
hospital associations and representative bodies,
as well as their members and other healthcare
related organizations.

P.A. Hôpital de Loëx
Route de Loëx 151
1233 Bernex
Switzerland
Tel: +41 (0) 22 850 94 20
Fax: +41 (0) 22 757 10 16
www.ihf-fih.org

IHTSDO International Health Terminology
Standards Development Organization
Members of IHTSDO can be either an agency of
a national government or other bodies (such as
corporations or regional government agencies)
endorsed by an appropriate national government authority within the country it represents.
The IHTSDO welcomes new members.

Gammeltory 4, 1
1457 Copenhagen K
Denmark
Tel: +45 36 44 87 36
Fax: +45 44 44 87 36
www.ihtsdo.org

IIE   International Institute of Education
An international education and training organization providing global fellowships and scholarships in applied research and policy analysis

Midwest Office:
25 E. Washington Street
Suite 1735
Chicago, IL 60602
Tel: 312-346-0026
Fax: 312-346-2574
e-mail: midwest@iie.org
www.iie.org

IIR   Institute for International Research
Providers of trade conferences and expositions, seminars, training events, and specialized business information and networking experiences in America.

708 3rd Avenue
4th Floor
New York, NY 10017
Toll free: 800-345-8016
Fax: 212-599-2192
www.iirusa.com

IMIA   International Medical Informatics Association
Membership is limited to organizations, societies, and corporations interested in promoting informatics in healthcare.

c/o Health On the Net
Chemin du Petit-Bel-Air 2
CH-1225 Chêne-Bourg, Geneva
Switzerland
Tel: +41-22-3727249
www.imia.org

INAHTA   International Network of Agencies for Health Technology Assessment
An organization of non-profit making organizations producing health technology assessments (HTA) and linked to regional or national governments.

INAHTA Secretariat
c/o DIMDI
Waisenhausgasse 36-38a
50676 Cologne
Germany
Tel: +49 221 4724 550
Fax: +49 221 4724 444
www.inahta.net

INS   International Neuropsychological Society
Membership organization for persons with a significant proportion of activities devoted to neuropsychology or related fields.

700 Ackerman Road
Suite 625
Columbus, OH 43202
Tel: 614-263-4200
www.the-ins.org

INS   Infusion Nurses Society
Membership is open to healthcare professionals from all practice settings who are involved in or interested in the specialty practice of infusion therapy.

315 Norwood Park South
Norwood, MA 02062
Tel: 781-440-9408
Fax 781-440-9409
www.ins1.org/

INCITS   InterNational Committee for Information Technology Standards
Membership is open to organizations directly and materially affected by standardization in the field of Information and Communications Technologies (ICT), encompassing storage, processing, transfer, display, management, organization, and retrieval of information.

1101 K Street, NW
Suite 610
Washington, DC 20005
Tel: 202-737-8888
www.incits.org

IOM   Institute of Medicine of the National Academies
An honorific organization. The full membership annually elects up to 70 new members and 10 foreign associates for their excellence and professional achievement in a field relevant to the IOM's mission. These individuals represent the healthcare professions as well as the natural, social, and behavioral sciences.

500 Fifth Street, NW
Washington, DC 20001
Tel: 202-334-2352
Fax: 202-334-1412
www.iom.edu

IOMSN   International Organization for Multiple Sclerosis Nurses

Membership organization for licensed nursing professional whose professional interest and activities are devoted to the care of patients with multiple sclerosis either through direct practice, research, or education who reside throughout the world.

359 Main Street
Suite A
Hackensack, NJ 07601
Tel: 201-487-1050
Fax: 201-678-2291
www.iomsn.org

ISNCC   International Society of Nurses in Cancer Care

Membership is open to cancer nursing associations, institutions, and individual cancer nursing professionals worldwide.

375 West 5th Avenue
Suite 201
Vancouver, British Columbia
V5Y 1J6 Canada
Tel: +1-604-630-5516
Fax: +1-604-874-4378
www.isncc.org

ISO   International Organization for Standardization

A network of national standards bodies that develop and publish International Standards. The national standards bodies represent ISO in their country.

1, ch. De la Voie Creuse
Case Postale 56
CH-1211
Switzerland
Tel: +41 22 749 01 11
Fax: +41 22 733 34 30
www.iso.org

ISPN   International Society of Psychiatric-Mental Health Nurses

An international membership organization for all advanced practice psychiatric nurses.

2424 American Lane
Madison, WI 53704-3102
Tel: 608-443-2463
Toll free: 866-330-7227
Fax: 608-443-2474 or 2478
www.ispn-psych.org

ISQUA   International Society for Quality in Health Care

Membership organization with individual, institutional, and affiliated categories for those engaged in quality improvement.

www.isqua.org

ISSA   Information Systems Security Association

Volunteer organization for information security professionals and practitioners.

9220 SW Barbur Boulevard
#119-333
Portland, OR 97219
Tel: 206-388-4584
Toll free: 866-349-5818
Fax: 206-299-3366
www.issa.org

ITAC   Information Technology Association of Canada

A membership organization of for-profit companies with a presence in Canada, for whom the provision of information technology products or services is a significant component of revenue and of strategic importance, or one which increases the efficiency of electronic markets by facilitating the meeting and interaction of buyers and sellers over the Internet.

5090 Explorer Drive
Suite 801
Mississauga, Ontario
L4W 4T9 Canada
Tel: 905-602-8345
www.itac.ca

ITU   International Telecommunication Union

Membership organization representing a cross-section of the global Information and Communication Technologies (ICT) sector along with leading research and development (R&D) institutions and academia. ITU is the United Nations specialized agency for Information and Communication Technologies (ICT).

Place des Nations
1211 Geneva 20
Switzerland
Tel: +41 22 730 5111
Fax: +41 22 733 72 56
www.itu.int

JCAHO The Joint Commission on Accreditation of Healthcare Organizations
See **Joint Commission.** (JCAHO is now The Joint Commission.)

Joint Commission The Joint Commission
Accreditation organization to support performance improvement in healthcare organizations.

> *Tel: 630-792-5800*
> *www.jointcommission.org*

JCR Joint Commission Resources
Publication subsidiary of The Joint Commission offering products, publications, educational conferences, consulting, and distance learning services.

> *1515 W. 22nd Street*
> *Suite 1300W*
> *Oak Brook, IL 60523*
> *Tel: 630-792-5900*
> *International Tel: +1-770-238-0454*
> *www.jcrinc.com*

Leapfrog Group The Leapfrog Group
Voluntary program aimed at mobilizing employer purchasing power to alert America's health industry that big leaps in healthcare safety, quality, and customer value will be recognized and rewarded.

> *1660 L Street, NW*
> *Suite 308*
> *Washington, DC 20036*
> *Tel: 202-292-6713*
> *Fax: 202-292-6813*
> *www.leapfroggroup.org*

LOINC Logical Observation Identifiers Names and Codes
LOINC is a database and universal standard for identifying medical laboratory observations developed and maintained by the Regenstrief Institute, an international non-profit medical research organization, associated with Indiana University. The scope of the LOINC effort includes laboratory and other clinical observations.

> *410 W. 10th Street*
> *Suite 2000*
> *Indianapolis, IN 46202-3012*
> *Tel: 317-423-5558*
> *Fax: 317-423-5695*
> *www.loinc.org*

MGMA Medical Group Management Association
Membership organization for individuals, teaching faculty, students, and uniformed services interested in practice management.

> *104 Inverness Terrace East*
> *Englewood, CO 80112-5306*
> *Tel: 303-799-1111*
> *Toll free: 877-275-6462*
> *www.mgma.com*

mHealth Initiative mHealth Initiative
US Department of Health & Human Services (HHS) initiative to provide citizens with an unprecedented level of access to health resources to achieve the goal of a healthier and more secure nation by leveraging the expansion of mobile health (mHealth) technologies, including health text messaging, mobile phone apps, remote monitoring, and portable sensors.

> *200 Independence Avenue, SW*
> *Washington, DC 20201*
> *Tel: 202-619-0257*
> *Toll free: 877-696-6775*
> *www.hhs.gov/open/initiatives/mhealth/*
> *index.html*

MITA Medical Imaging and Technology Alliance
The leading organization and collective voice of medical imaging equipment manufacturers, innovators, and product developers, a division of the National Electrical Manufacturers Association (NEMA).

> *1300 North 17th Street*
> *Suite 1752*
> *Arlington, VA 22209*
> *Tel: 703-841-3200*
> *Fax: 703-841-3392*
> *www.medicalimaging.org*

MLA Medical Library Association
Membership organization for individuals with an interest in the health sciences information field.

> *65 East Wacker Place*
> *Suite 1900*
> *Chicago, IL 60601-7246*
> *Tel: 312-419-9094*
> *Fax: 312-419-8950*
> *www.mlanet.org*

MS-HUG Microsoft Healthcare Users Group
Membership organization for members in the global community with healthcare IT expertise.

www.mshug.org

MTPPI Medical Technology & Practice Patterns Institute
A non-profit organization conducting research on the clinical and economic implications of health care technologies. MTPPI research is directed toward the formulation and implementation of local and national health care policies.

5272 River Road
Suite 500
Bethesda, MD 20816
Tel: 301-652-4005
Fax: 301-652-8335
www.mtppi.org

NAFAC National Association for Ambulatory Care
A national membership association of urgent and ambulatory care providers for mutual education, networking, and representing our concerns and needs to insurers and state and federal governments.

www.urgentcare.org - or - www.nafac.com

NAHC National Association for Home Care & Hospice
A membership organization for agencies delivering hands-on care to patients at home, corporate (multi-entity) providers delivering care at home, businesses that provide products or services to home care agencies, State home care and hospice associations that are organized into the National Association for Home Care's Forum of State Associations, and nonprofit groups, universities, libraries, schools of nursing, and international groups with an interest in home care and/or hospice.

228 Seventh Street, SE
Washington, DC 20003
Tel: 202-547-7424
Fax: 202-547-3540
www.nahc.org

NAHDO National Association of Health Data Organizations
A national, not-for-profit membership organization dedicated to improving healthcare through the collection, analysis, dissemination, public availability, and use of health data.

448 East 400 South
Suite 301
Salt Lake City, UT 84111
Tel: 801-532-2299
Fax: 801-532-2228
www.nahdo.org

NAHIT National Alliance for Health Information Technology
Organization dissolved in September 2009.

NAHQ National Association for Healthcare Quality
Membership organization open to anyone involved in the healthcare quality field and any healthcare organization with four or more individuals is eligible for membership.

4700 West Lake Avenue
Glenview, IL 60025
Tel: 847-375-4720
Toll free: 800-966-9392
Fax: 847-375-6320
www.nahq.org

NANDA North American Nursing Diagnosis Association - International
Membership organization open to those who meet their country's requirements for professional nursing licensure and to matriculating undergraduate students.

PO Box 157
Kaukauna, WI 54130-0157
www.nanda.org

NAPHSIS National Association for Public Health Statistics and Information Systems
Membership association of state vital records and public health statistics offices in the United States.

962 Wayne Avenue
Suite 701
Silver Spring, MD 20910
Tel: 301-563-6001
Fax: 301-563-6012
e-mail: hq@naphsis.org
www.naphsis.org

NASCIO   National Association of State Chief Information Officers
Membership organization of state chief information and information technology executives from the states, territories, and the District of Columbia. Leading advocate for technology policy at all levels of government. Other public sector and non-profit organizations may join.

c/o AMR Management Services
201 East Main Street
Suite 1405
Lexington, KY 40507
Tel: 859-514-9156
Fax: 859-514-9166
www.nascio.org

NASEMSO   National Association of State EMS Officials
Membership organization for individuals in state Emergency Medical Service (EMS) office, federal agencies, and individuals with an interest in emergency care, education, professional standards, trauma systems, and data systems.

201 Park Washington Court
Falls Church, VA 22046-4527
Tel: 703-538-1799
Fax: 703-241-5603
www.nasemso.org

NASN   National Association of School Nurses
Membership organization for registered professional nurses having as their primary assignment, the administration, education, or the provision of school health services.

8484 Georgia Avenue
Suite 420
Silver Spring, MD 20910
Tel: 240-821-1130
www.nasn.org

NBDHMT   National Board of Diving & Hyperbaric Medical Technology
Certification organization for hyperbaric technologists, nurses, and diving medical technicians to ensure that the fields of hyperbaric medicine, hyperbaric chamber operation, and diving medicine are filled with highly qualified personnel.

9 Medical Park
Suite 330
Columbia, SC 29203
Tel: 803-434-7802
Fax: 866-451-7231
www.nbdhmt.org

NCCA   National Commission for Certifying Agencies.
(NCCA merged with NOCA.) *See* **Institute for Credentialing Excellence**.

NCCLS   National Committee for Clinical Laboratory Standards. (See **CLSI**.)

NCEMI   National Center for Emergency Medicine Informatics
Website designed for qualified physicians and other medical professionals.

www.ncemi.org

NCHS   National Center for Health Statistics
Centers for Disease Control and Prevention (CDC) center for statistical information.

1600 Clifton Road
Atlanta, GA 30333
Toll free: 800-232-4636
www.cdc.gov/nchs

NCPDP   National Council for Prescription Drug Program
Membership organization producers/providers, payers/processors, and general vendors interested in ANSI-accredited standards, and guidance for promoting information exchanges related to medications, supplies, and services within the healthcare system.

9240 East Raintree Drive
Scottsdale, AZ 85260-7518
Tel: 480-477-1000
Fax: 480-222-7555
www.ncpdp.org

NCQA National Committee for Quality Assurance
Certification organization to improve the quality of healthcare.

1100 13th Street, NW
Suite 1000
Washington, DC 20005
Tel: 202-955-3500
Fax: 202-955-3599
www.ncqa.org

NCSBN National Council of State Boards of Nursing
Nursing examination organization to qualify and examine nurses who have successfully completed an accredited program and meet examination requirements for the National Council Licensure Examination for Registered Nurses (NCLEX-RN) and the National Council Licensure Examination for Practical Nurses (NCLEX-PN) that are used by boards of nursing to assist in making state licensure decisions.

111 East Wacker Drive
Suite 2900
Chicago, IL 60601-4277
Tel: 312-525-3600
Fax: 312-279-1032
International Tel: 001 1 312 525 3600
www.ncsbn.org

NCVHS National Committee on Vital and Health Statistics
Established by Congress to serve as an advisory body to the Department of Health and Human Services on health data, statistics, and national health information policy.

www.ncvhs.dhhs.gov

NeHC National eHealth Collaborative
A public-private partnership established through a grant from the Office of the National Coordinator for Health IT (ONC) to build on the accomplishments of the American Health Information Community (AHIC), a federal advisory committee to the US Department of Health and Human Services (HHS) until 2008.

1250 24th Street, NW
Suite 300
Washington, DC 20037
Tel: 877-835-6506
www.nationalehealth.org

NEHTA National E-Health Transition Authority
Established by the Australian State and Territory governments to develop better ways of electronically collecting and securely exchanging health information.

Level 25, 56 Pitt Street
Sydney NSW 2000
Australia
Tel: (02) 8298 2600
Fax: (02) 8298 2666
www.nehta.gov.au

NHCAA National Health Care Anti-Fraud Association
Member organization open to private for-profit and not-for-profit health care reimbursement organizations (health insurers, managed care organizations, self-insured/self-administered organizations, third-party administrators, Medicare Program Safeguard Contractors [PSC]) interested in fighting against healthcare fraud.

1201 New York Avenue, NW
Suite 1120
Washington, DC 20005
Tel: 202-659-5955
Fax: 202-785-6764
www.nhcaa.org

NHIC National Health Information Center
A health information referral service sponsored by the Office of Disease Prevention and Health Promotion, Office of Public Health and Science, Office of the Secretary, US Department of Health and Human Services (HHS). NHIC links people to organizations that provide reliable health information.

Tel: 240-453-8280
Fax: 240-453-8282
www.health.gov/nhic

NHII National Health Information Infrastructure
An initiative set forth to improve the effectiveness, efficiency, and overall quality of health and healthcare in the US

US Dept. of Health & Human Services
200 Independence Avenue, SW
Washington, DC 20201
www.aspe.hhs.gov/sp/NHII

NHLBI   National Heart, Lung, and Blood Institute
The Institute, part of the National Institutes of Health, promotes the prevention and treatment of diseases of the heart, lung, and blood.

Building 31, Room 5A52
31 Center Drive MSC 2486
Bethesda, MD 20892
Tel: 301-592-8573
Fax: 240-629-3246
www.nhlbi.nih.gov

NIH   National Institutes of Health
A part of the US Department of Health & Human Services, NIH is the nation's medical research agency.

9000 Rockville Pike
Bethesda, MD 20892
www.nih.gov

NIHR   National Institute of Health Research
An independent research center producing information about the effectiveness, costs, and broader impact of healthcare treatments and tests for those who plan, provide, or receive care in the National Health Service, U.K.

National Institute for Health Research
Room 132
Richmond House
79 Whitehall
London SW1A 2NS
www.nihr.ac.uk

NINR   National Institute of Nursing Research
Institute, part of the National Institutes of Health, supports and conducts nursing and clinical research and research training on health and illness across the lifespan.

31 Center Drive
Room 5B10
Bethesda, MD 20892-2178
Tel: 301-496-0207
Fax: 301-480-8845
www.ninr.nih.gov

NIST   National Institute of Standards and Technology
Federal agency responsible for advancing measurement science, standards, and technology to improve quality of life. Manages the Malcolm Baldrige National Quality Award.

100 Bureau Drive
Stop 1070
Gaithersburg, MD 20899-1070
Tel: 301-975-6478
TTY: 800-877-8339
www.nist.gov

NITRD   The Networking and Information Technology Research and Development Program
National program that provides a framework in which many federal agencies coordinate networking and information technology (IT) research and development (R&D) efforts. Operates under the aegis of the NITRD Subcommittee of the National Science and Technology Council's (NSTC) Committee on Technology.

4201 Wilson Boulevard
Suite II-405
Arlington, VA 22230
Tel: 703-292-4873
Fax: 703-292-9097
www.nitrd.gov

NKCHS   Norwegian Knowledge Centre for Health Services
See **NOKC.** (NKCHS is now NOKC.)

NKF   National Kidney Foundation
A major health organization. NKF seeks to prevent kidney and urinary tract diseases, improve the health and well-being of individuals and families affected by these diseases, and increase the availability of all organs for transplantation.

30 East 33rd Street
New York, NY 10016
Toll free: 800-622-9010
www.kidney.org

NLM   National Library of Medicine
NLM is the world's largest medical library. The Library collects materials in all areas of biomedicine and healthcare, as well as works on biomedical aspects of technology, the humanities, and the physical, life, and social sciences. The collections stand at more than 9 million items—books, journals, technical reports, manuscripts, microfilms, photographs and images. NLM is a national resource for all US health science libraries through a National Network of Libraries of Medicine®.

8600 Rockville Pike
Bethesda, MD 20894
Tel: 301-594-5983
TTD: 800-735-2258
Fax: 301-402-1384
www.nlm.nih.gov

NLN   National League for Nursing
A membership organization for nurse faculty and leaders in nursing education dedicated to excellence in nursing. Members include nurse educators, health care agencies, and interested members of the public.

61 Broadway
33rd Floor
New York, NY 10006
Tel: 212-363-5555
Fax: 212-812-0391
www.nln.org

NOA   Nursing Organizations Alliance
Membership is open to any nursing organization whose focus is to address current and emerging nursing and health care issues. Structural nursing components of a multidisciplinary organization are also welcome.

201 East Main Street
Suite 1405
Lexington, KY 40507
Tel: 859-514-9157
Fax: 859-514-9166
www.nursing-alliance.org

NOCA   National Organization for Competency Assurance
See **ICE.** (NOCA is now the Institute for Credentialing Excellence [ICE].)

NOKC   Norwegian Knowledge Centre for Health Services
Organized under the Norwegian Directorate of Health, product and services include systematic reviews, health economic evaluations, patient and user experience surveys and other quality measurements to support the development of quality in the health services by summarizing research, promoting the use of research results, measuring the quality of health services and working to improve patient safety.

P.O. Box 7004
St. Olavs plass
N-0130 Oslo, Norway
Tel: +47 23 25 50 00
Fax: +47 23 25 50 10
www.kunnskapssenteret.no

NQF   National Quality Forum
Private sector standard-setting organization whose efforts center on the evaluation and endorsement of standardized performance measurement.

1030 15th Street, NW
Suite 800
Washington, DC 20005
Tel: 202-783-1300
Fax: 202-783-3434
www.qualityforum.org

NSF   National Science Foundation
An independent federal agency funding approximately 20 percent of all federally supported basic research conducted by America's colleges and universities. In many fields, such as mathematics, computer science, and the social sciences, NSF is the major source of federal backing.

4201 Wilson Boulevard
Arlington, VA 22230
Tel: 703-292-5111
FIRS: 800-877-8339
TDD: 800-281-8749
www.nsf.gov

NUBC National Uniform Billing Committee
Membership includes national provider and payer organizations. Recently, the NUBC increased it membership to include public health sector as well as the electronic standard development organization. NUBC maintains the integrity of the UB-92 data set.

www.nubc.org

NUCC National Uniform Claim Committee
A voluntary organization comprised of key parties affected by health care electronic data interchange (EDI), generally payers and providers. Criteria for membership include a national scope and representation of a unique constituency affected by health care EDI, with an emphasis on maintaining or enhancing the provider/payer balance.

American Medical Association
515 N. State Street
Chicago, IL 60654
Tel: 800-621-8335
www.nucc.org

NZHTA New Zealand Health Technology Assessment
Clearinghouse for health outcomes and health technology assessment, operating from 1997 to June 2007. Publications can still be accessed.

University of Otago, Christchurch
2 Riccarton Avenue
Christchurch 8140
New Zealand
Tel: +64 3 364 0530
Fax: + 64 3 364 0525
www.otago.ac.nz/christchurch/research/
nzhta

OASIS Advancing Open Standards for the Information Society
Open membership to ensure that all those affected by open standards have a voice in their creation.

www.oasis-open.org

OMG Object Management Group
An international, open membership, not-for-profit computer industry consortium of government agencies, small and large information technology users, vendors and research institutions. Any organization may join OMG and participate in the standards-setting process. OMG Task Forces develop enterprise integration standards for a wide range of technologies.

140 Kendrick Street
Building A
Suite 300
Needham, MA 02494
Tel: 781-444 0404
Fax: 781-444-0320
www.omg.org

ONC Office of the National Coordinator for Health Information Technology
The Office of the National Coordinator for Health Information Technology is the principal federal entity charged with coordination of nationwide efforts to implement and use the most advanced health information technology and the electronic exchange of health information. ONC is organizationally located within the Office of the Secretary for the US Department of Health & Human Services.

200 Independence Avenue, SW
Suite 729-D
Washington, DC 20201
Tel: 202-690-7151
Fax: 202-690-6079
e-mail: onc.request@hhs.gov

ONS Oncology Nursing Society
A professional membership organization for registered nurses and other healthcare providers dedicated to excellence in patient care, education, research, and administration in oncology nursing.

125 Enterprise Drive
Pittsburgh, PA 15275
Tel: 412-859-6100
Toll free: 866-257-4ONS
Fax: 412-859-6162
Toll free Fax: 877-369-5497
www.ons.org

OSHA   Occupational Safety & Health Administration

Part of the US Department of Labor with responsibility to assure the safety and health of America's workers by setting and enforcing standards; providing training, outreach, and education; establishing partnerships; and encouraging continual improvement in workplace safety and health.

200 Constitution Avenue, NW
Washington, DC 20210
Toll free: 800-321-6742
TTY: 877-889-5627
www.osha.gov

PCPCC   Patient-Centered Primary Care Collaborative

Organization dedicated to advancing primary care and the patient-centered medical home (PCMH) though activities to ensure innovations in care delivery, payment reform, benefit design and patient engagement. General public membership is free of charge.

The Homer Building
601 Thirteenth Street, NW
Suite 430 North
Washington, DC 20005
Tel: 202-417-2081
Fax: 202-417-2082
www.pcpcc.net

Perio   American Academy of Peridontology

Membership organization periodontists and general dentists inside the United States and around the world.

737 N. Michigan Avenue
Suite 800
Chicago, IL 60611-6660
Tel: 312-787-5518
Fax: 312-787-3670
www.perio.org

PHDSC   Public Health Data Standards Consortium

A non-profit membership-based organization representing stakeholders including federal, state, and local health agencies; professional associations; academia; public and private sector organizations; international members; and individuals with an interest in health information technology and population health.

111 South Calvert Street
Suite 2700
Baltimore MD 21202
Tel: 410-385-5272
Fax: 866-637-6526
www.phdsc.org

PHI   Public Health Institute

An independent, nonprofit organization that partners with foundations, federal and state agencies, and other non-profit organizations to support a diverse array of research products and public health interventions.

555 12th Street
10th Floor
Oakland, CA 946075
Tel: 510-285-5500
Fax: 510-285-5501
www.phi.org

PHII   Public Health Informatics Institute

A program of the Task Force for Global Health at the Centers for Disease Control and Prevention that works to improve health outcomes worldwide by transforming health practitioners' ability to apply information effectively. The Institute works with public health organizations, both domestically and internationally, through a variety of projects funded by government agencies and private foundations.

325 Swanton Way
Decatur, Georgia 30030
Toll free: 866-815-9704
Toll free fax: 800-765-7520
www.phii.org

PITAC President's Information Technology Advisory Committee

The President's Information Technology Advisory Committee (PITAC) was authorized by Congress under the High-Performance Computing Act of 1991 (P.L. 102-194) and the Next Generation Internet Act of 1998 (P.L. 105-305) as a Federal Advisory Committee. The Committee provides the President, Congress, and the Federal agencies involved in networking and information technology research and development with expert, independent advice on maintaining America's preeminence in advanced information technologies, including such critical elements of the national information technology infrastructure as high performance computing, large-scale networking, cyber security, and high assurance software and systems design.

4201 Wilson Boulevard
Suite ll-405
Arlington, VA 22230
Tel: 703-292-4873
Fax: 703-292-9097
www.itrd.gov/pitac/index.html

PMI Project Management Institute

Individual membership is open to anyone interested in project management.

14 Campus Boulevard
Newtown Square, PA 19073-3299
Tel: 610-356-4600
Toll free: 855-746-4849
Fax: 610-482-9971
www.pmi.org

RCN Royal College of Nursing

Professional nursing body and union for nurses in the United Kingdom (UK).

20 Cavendish Square
London W1G 0RN
United Kingdom
Tel: +020 7409 3333
www.rcn.org.uk

Regenstrief Institute Regenstrief Institute

An internationally recognized informatics and healthcare research organization. It is closely affiliated with the Indiana University School of Medicine, Roudebush VA Medical Center, and Wishard Health Services to improve health through research that enhances the quality and cost-effectiveness of healthcare.

1050 Wishard Boulevard
6th Floor
Indianapolis, IN 46202-2872
Tel: 317-630-6083
www.regenstrief.org

RSNA Radiological Society of North America

International physician membership organization of radiologists, medical physicists, and other medical professionals.

820 Jorie Boulevard
Oak Brook, IL 60523-2251
Tel: 630-571-2670
Toll free US and Canada: 1-800-381-6660
www.rsna.org

SBU Swedish Council on Technology Assessment in Health Care

Mandated by the Swedish Government to comprehensively assess healthcare technology from medical, economic, ethical, and social standpoints.

Visiting address: Olof Palmes Gata 17
Box 3657
103 59 Stockholm, Sweden
Tel: +46 8 412 32 00
Fax: +46 8 411 32 60
www.sbu.se/en

Scottsdale Institute
Not-for-profit organization facilitating collaboration, education, and networking on information topics including strategy, deployment, adoption, national direction and trends, benchmarking and benefits realization for executives in health systems who wish to share experiences in information technology management.

1660 Highway 100, South
Suite 306
Minneapolis, MN 55416
Tel: 952-545-5880
Fax: 952-545-6116
www.scottsdaleinstitute.org

SGNA   Society of Gastroenterology Nurses and Associates
A professional organization of nurses and associates dedicated to the safe and effective practice of gastroenterology and endoscopy nursing. SGNA carries out its mission by advancing the science and practice of gastroenterology and endoscopy nursing through education, research, advocacy, and collaboration, and by promoting the professional development of its members in an atmosphere of mutual support.

330 North Wabash Avenue
Suite 200
Chicago, IL 60611
Tel: 312-321-5165
Toll free: 800-245-7462
Fax: 312-673-6694
www.sgna.org

SHS   The Society for Health Systems
Membership association for productivity and efficiency professionals specializing in industrial engineering, healthcare, ergonomics and other related professions.

3577 Parkway Lane
Suite 200
Norcross, GA 30092
Tel: 770-449-0460
Toll free: 800-494-0460
Fax: 770-441-3295
www.iienet2.org

SIIM   The Society for Imaging Informatics in Medicine
Membership open to anyone with an interest in the vital and growing field of medical imaging informatics and image management.

19440 Golf Vista Plaza
Suite 330
Leesburg, VA 20176-8264
Tel: 703-723-0432
Fax: 703-723-0415
www.siimweb.org

SIR   Society of Interventional Radiology
Membership organization for individuals who have a special interest in interventional radiology inside and outside the United States.

3975 Fair Ridge Drive
Suite 400 North
Fairfax, VA 22033
Tel: 703-691-1805
Toll Free: 800-488-7284
Fax: 703-691-1855
www.sirweb.org

SNRS   Southern Nursing Research Society
Membership organization for registered professional nurses, non-nurses, corporations, and institutions interested in promoting nursing research.

10200 W. 44th Avenue
Suite 304
Wheat Ridge, CO 80033
Toll free: 877-314-SNRS
www.snrs.org

TAANA   The American Association of Nurse Attorneys
Membership association of nurse attorneys.

P.O. Box 14218
Lenexa, KS 66285-4218
Tel: 913-895-4625
Toll free: 877-538-2262
Fax: 913-895-4652
www.taana.org

TechAmerica

Membership organization open to companies that design, manufacturer, market or conduct research in technology products including, but not limited to, electronics components, software, telecommunications, Internet commerce or communications, information technology products, consulting or services, or other development of human capital for the technology industries with operations in the United States.

601 Pennsylvania Avenue, NW
North Building
Suite 600
Washington, DC 20004
Tel: 202-682-9110
Fax: 202-682-9111
www.techamerica.org

TIGER Initiative Foundation   Technology Informatics Guiding Education Reform (TIGER) Initiative Foundation

The Technology Informatics Guiding Educational Reform (TIGER) Initiative aims to enable practicing nurses and nursing students to fully engage in the unfolding digital electronic era in healthcare.

33 West Monroe Street
Suite 1700
Chicago, IL 60603-5616
Tel: 312-664-4467
www.thetigerinitiative.org

TNA   Transplant Nurses Association

Membership organization to advance the education of nurses and allied health professionals involved in the transplant process.

80 Missenden Road
Camperdown NSW 2050
Australia
Fax: 08 8204 6959
www.tna.asn.au

UCC   Uniform Code Council

(UCC is now GS1, 2006.) *See* **GS1 US**.

UNECE   United Nations Economic Commission for Europe

The United Nations Economic Commission for Europe (UNECE) internships are open to graduate or post-graduate students who have specialized in a field related to UNECE programmes of work, namely: environment, transport, statistics, sustainable energy, trade, timber and forests, housing and land management, population, economic cooperation and integration and gender.

Palais des Nations, Office 363
CH - 1211
Geneva 10
Switzerland
www.unece.net

VA   Department of Veterans Affairs; Veterans Health Administration

Comprehensive system of assistance to serve our Nation's veterans and their families.

810 Vermont Avenue, NW
Washington, DC 20420
Toll free: 800-827-1000
www.va.gov

VATAP   Veterans Affairs Technology Assessment Program

A national program within the Office of Patient Care Services dedicated to advancing evidence-based decision making in VA.

Boston VA Healthcare System
150 South Huntington Avenue
Boston, MA 02130
Tel: 857-364-5939
Fax: 857-364-6587
www.va.gov/vatap

VNAA   Visiting Nurse Associations of America

Membership organization for nonprofit, free-standing home health and/or hospice providers, organizations that provide or promote home healthcare and/or hospice-related services, and individuals who wish to stay connected and advance nonprofit home healthcare and hospice.

900 19th Street, NW
Suite 200
Washington, DC 20006
Tel: 202-384-1420
Tol free: 888-866-8773
www.vnaa.org

WEDI Workgroup for Electronic Data Interchange

Membership organization actively seeking membership of all key parties in healthcare to ensure broad representation from throughout the healthcare community including individuals, providers, healthplans, hybrid organizations (formerly mixed provider/healthplan), government organizations, standards organizations, vendors, not-for-profit, and affiliates/regional entities.

1984 Isaac Newton Square
Suite 304
Reston, VA 20190
Tel: 202-688-2488
Fax: 202-318-4812
www.wedi.org

WHO World Health Organization

The directing and coordinating authority for health within the United Nations system. It is responsible for providing leadership on global health matters, shaping the health research agenda, setting norms and standards, articulating evidence-based policy options, providing technical support to countries and monitoring and assessing health trends.

Avenue Appia 20
1211 Geneva 27
Switzerland
Tel: +41 22 791 21 11
Fax: + 41 22 791 31 11
www.who.int

Appendix C
Healthcare Credentials

I. Certifications

Credential	Full Name	Organization Acronym	Organization Full Name
ACNP	Acute Care Nurse Practitioner	ANCC	American Nurses Credentialing Center
ACNS	Adult Health Clinical Nurse Specialist	ANCC	American Nurses Credentialing Center
ACRN	AIDS Certified Registered Nurse	HANCB	HIV/AIDS Nursing Certification Board
AGACNP	Adult-Gerontology Acute Care Nurse Practitioner	ANCC	American Nurses Credentialing Center
AGPCNP	Adult-Gerontology Primary Care Nurse Practitioner	ANCC	American Nurses Credentialing Center
ANP	Adult Nurse Practitioner	ANCC	American Nurses Credentialing Center
AOCN	Advanced Oncology Certified Nurse	ONCC	Oncology Nursing Certification Corporation
AOCNP	Advanced Oncology Certified Nurse Practitioner	ONCC	Oncology Nursing Certification Corporation
APHN	Advanced Public Health Nurse	ANCC	American Nurses Credentialing Center
APRN	Advanced Practice Registered Nurse	ANCC	American Nurses Credentialing Center
BC	Board Certified	ANCC	American Nurses Credentialing Center
CAAMA	Credentialed Member of the American Academy of Medical Administrators	AAMA	American Academy of Medical Administrators
CAP	Certification and Accreditation Professional	$(ISC)^2$	International Information Systems Security Certification Consortium
CCA	Certified Coding Associate	AHIMA	American Health Information Management Association
CCM	Certified Case Manager	CCMC	Commission for Case Manager Certification
CCNS	Critical Care Nurse Specialist	AACN	American Association of Critical-Care Nurses Certification Corporation
CCRN	Critical Care Registered Nurse	AACN	American Association of Critical-Care Nurses

Credential	Full Name	Organization Acronym	Organization Full Name
CCRN-E	Adult Tele-ICU Acute/Critical Care Nursing	AACN	American Association of Critical-Care Nurses Certification Corporation
CCS	Certified Coding Specialist	AHIMA	American Health Information Management Association
CCS-P	Certified Coding Specialist – Physician-based	AHIMA	American Health Information Management Association
CDE	Certified Diabetes Educator	NCBDE	National Certification Board for Diabetes Educators
CDIP	Certified Documentation Improvement Practitioner	AHIMA	American Health Information Management Association
CDMS	Certified Disability Management Specialist	CDMSC	Certification of Disability Management Specialists Commission
CDN	Certified Dialysis Nurse	NNCC	Nephrology Nursing Certification Commission
CEN	Certified Emergency Nurse	BCEN	Board of Certification for Emergency Nursing
CERT	Community Emergency Response Team	FEMA	Federal Emergency Management Agency
CHCIO	Certified Healthcare CIO	CHIME	College of Healthcare Information Management Executives
CHDA	Certified Health Data Analyst	AHIMA	American Health Information Management Association
CHE	Certified Healthcare Executive	ACHE	American College of Healthcare Executives
CHESP	Certified Healthcare Environmental Services Professional	AHA-CC	American Hospital Association Credentialing Center
CHFM	Certified Healthcare Facility Manager	AHA-CC	American Hospital Association Credentialing Center
CHFP	Certified Healthcare Financial Professional	HFMA	Healthcare Financial Management Association
CHPS	Certified in Healthcare Privacy and Security	AHIMA	American Health Information Management Association
CISA	Certified Information Systems Auditor	ISACA	Information Systems Audit and Control Association
CISM	Certified Information Security Manager	ISACA	Information Systems Audit and Control Association
CISSP	Certified Information Systems Security Professional	$(ISC)^2$	International Information Systems Security Certification Consortium
CLSSBB	Certified Lean Six Sigma Black Belt	ASQ	American Society for Quality or other certified credentialing body

Credential	Full Name	Organization Acronym	Organization Full Name
CLSSGB	Certified Lean Six Sigma Green Belt	ASQ	American Society for Quality or other certified credentialing body
CMA	Certified Management Accountant	IMA	Institute of Management Accountants
CMRP	Certified Materials and Resource Professional	AHA-CC	American Hospital Association Credentialing Center
CMSRN	Certified Medical-Surgical Registered Nurse	AMSN	Academy of Medical-Surgical Nurses
CNM	Certified Nurse Midwife	AMCB	American Midwifery Certification Board
CNML	Certified Nurse Manager and Leader	AONE / AACN	American Organization of Nurse Executives Credentialing Center / American Association of Critical-Care Nurses Certification Corporation
CNN	Certified Nephrology Nurse	NNCC	Nephrology Nursing Certification Commission
CNS	Clinical Nurse Specialist	AACN	American Association of Critical-Care Nurses Certification Corporation
CNOR	Certified in Operating Room Nursing	CCI	Competency and Credentialing Institute of the Association of Perioperative Nurses
COHN	Certified Occupational Health Nurse	ABOHN	American Board for Occupational Health Nurses, Inc.
CPA	Certified Public Accountant	AICPA	American Institute of Certified Public Accountants
CPC	Certified Professional Coder	AAPC	American Academy of Professional Coders
CPE	Certified Physician Executive	CCMM	Certifying Commission in Medical Management
CPEHR	Certified Professional in Electronic Health Records	HITC	Health IT Certification
CPEN	Certified Pediatric Emergency Nurse	PNCB / BCEN	Pediatric Nurse Certification Board / Board of Certification for Emergency Nursing
CPHIE	Certified Professional in Health Information Exchange	HITC	Health IT Certification
CPHIMS	Certified Professional in Healthcare Information and Management Systems	HIMSS	Healthcare Information and Management Systems Society
CPHIT	Certified Professional in Health Information Technology	HITC	Health IT Certification

Credential	Full Name	Organization Acronym	Organization Full Name
CPHON	Certified Pediatric Hematology Oncology Nurse	ONCC	Oncology Nursing Certification Corporation
CPHQ	Certified Professional in Healthcare Quality	HQCB	Healthcare Quality Certification Board
CPHRM	Certified Professional in Healthcare Risk Management	AHA-CC	American Hospital Association Credentialing Center
CPN	Certified Pediatric Nurse	PNCB	Pediatric Nurse Certification Board
CPNP	Certified Pediatric Nurse Practitioner	PNCB	Pediatric Nurse Certification Board
CPORA	Certified Professional in Operating Rules Administration	HITC	Health IT Certification
CPSN	Certified Plastic Surgical Nurse	PSNCB	Plastic Surgical Nursing Certification Board
CRNA	Certified Registered Nurse Anesthetist	AANA	American Association of Nurse Anesthetists
CRNFA	Certified Registered Nurse First Assistant	CCI	Competency and Credentialing Institute of the Association of Perioperative Nurses
CRNI	Certified Registered Nurse Infusion	INCC	Infusion Nurses Certification Corporation
CRRN	Certified Rehabilitation Registered Nurse	RNCB	Rehabilitation Nursing Certification Board
FNP	Family Nurse Practitioner	ANCC	American Nurses Credentialing Center
GCNS	Gerontological Nurse Practitioner	ANCC	American Nurses Credentialing Center
GNP	Gerontological Clinical Nurse Specialist	ANCC	American Nurses Credentialing Center
HCQM	Health Care Quality Management	ABQAURP	American Board of Quality Assurance and Utilization Review Physicians
IIP	Imaging Informatics Professional	SIMM	Society for Imaging Informatics in Medicine
ISSAP	Information Systems Security Architecture Professional	(ISC)^2	International Information Systems Security Certification Consortium
ISSEP	Information Systems Security Engineering Professional	(ISC)^2	International Information Systems Security Certification Consortium
ISSMP	Information Systems Security Management Professional	(ISC)^2	International Information Systems Security Certification Consortium
MCDBA	Microsoft Certified Database Administrator		Microsoft

Credential	Full Name	Organization Acronym	Organization Full Name
MCITP	Microsoft Certified IT Professional		Microsoft
MCP	Microsoft Certified Professional		Microsoft
MCPD	Microsoft Certified Professional Developer		Microsoft
MCSA	Microsoft Certified Solutions Associate		Microsoft
MCSD	Microsoft Certified Solutions Developer		Microsoft
MCSE	Microsoft Certified Systems Engineer		Microsoft
MCSM	Microsoft Certified Solutions Master		Microsoft
MCTS	Microsoft Certified Technology Specialist		Microsoft
MOS	Microsoft Office Specialist		Microsoft
MT (ASCP)	Certified Medical Technologist	ASCP	American Society for Clinical Pathology
MTA	Microsoft Technology Associate		Microsoft
NEA	Nurse Executive, Advanced	ANCC	American Nurses Credentialing Center
NP-C	Nurse Practitioner-Certified	AANPCP	American Academy of Nurse Practitioners Certification Program
OCN	Oncology Certified Nurse	ONCC	Oncology Nursing Certification Corporation
ONC	Orthopaedic Nurse Certified	ONCB	Orthopaedic Nurses Certification Board
PA-C	Physician Assistant-Certified	NCCPA	National Commission on the Certification of Physician Assistants
PCNS	Pediatric Clinical Nurse Specialist	ANCC	American Nurses Credentialing Center
PMHCNS	Adult Psychiatric-Mental Health Clinical Nurse Specialist	ANCC	American Nurses Credentialing Center
PMHNP	Psychiatric–Mental Health Nurse Practitioner	ANCC	American Nurses Credentialing Center
PMHS	Pediatric Mental Health Specialist	PNCB	Pediatric Nurse Certification Board
PMP	Project Management Professional	PMI	Project Management Institute
PNP	Pediatric Nurse Practitioner	ANCC	American Nurses Credentialing Center
RHIA	Registered Health Information Administrator	AHIMA	American Health Information Management Association
RHIT	Registered Health Information Technician	AHIMA	American Health Information Management Association

Credential	Full Name	Organization Acronym	Organization Full Name
RN, BC / RN-BC	Registered Nurse-Board Certified	ANCC	American Nurses Credentialing Center
RNC	Registered Nurse, Certified	NCC	National Certification Corporation
SSCP	Systems Security Certified Practitioner	(ISC)^2	International Information Systems Security Certification Consortium

II. Healthcare and Related Degrees

Designation	Full Name
AAS / ADN	Associate of Applied Science / Associate Degree Nursing
B.Comm	Bachelor of Commerce
BA	Bachelor of Arts
BS or BSc	Bachelor of Science
BScN or BSN	Bachelor of Science in Nursing
BSCS	Bachelor of Science in Computer Science
DBA	Doctor of Business Administration
DO	Doctor of Optometry or Doctor of Osteopathy
DNP	Doctor of Nursing Practice
DNS/DNSc / DSN / DScN	Doctor of Nursing Science
DPH/DrPH	Doctor of Public Health
EdD	Doctor of Education
JD	Doctor of Law
MA	Master of Arts
MBA	Master of Business Administration
MD	Doctor of Medicine
MEd	Master of Education
MHA	Master of Health Administration
MHSA	Master of Health Services Administration
MPH	Master of Public Health
MPharm	Master of Pharmacy
MS / MSc	Master of Science
MSCIS	Master of Science in Computer Information Systems
MSIS	Master of Science in Information Systems
MSN	Master of Science in Nursing
MSHI	Master of Science in Health Informatics
MSW	Master of Social Work
PharmD	Doctor of Pharmacy
PhD	Doctor of Philosophy

III. Professional Fellowships

Designation	Full Name
FAAFP	Fellow of the American Academy of Family Physicians
FACC	Fellow of the American College of Cardiology
FACEP	Fellow of the American College of Emergency Physicians
FACHE	Fellow of the American College of Healthcare Executives
FACMPE	Fellow of the American College of Medical Practice Executives
FACP	Fellow of the American College of Physicians
FASCP	Fellow, American Society of Clinical Pathologists
FCAP	Fellow, College of American Pathologists
FHFMA	Fellow of the Healthcare Financial Management Association
FHIMSS	Fellow of the Healthcare Information and Management Systems Society
FIEEE	Fellow of the Institute of Electrical and Electronics Engineers
FNLM	Friends of the National Library of Medicine
LHIMSS	Life Member of the Healthcare Information and Management Systems Society
LFHIMSS	Life Member and Fellow of the Healthcare Information and Management Systems Society
SMIEEE	Senior Member of the Institute of Electrical and Electronics Engineers

IV. Honors Designations

ACMI	American College of Medical Informatics
FAAN	Fellow of the American Academy of Nursing
FAAFP	Fellow of the American Academy of Family Physicians
FACC	Fellow of the American College of Cardiology
FACEP	Fellow of the American College of Emergency Physicians
FACHE	Fellow of the American College of Healthcare Executives
FACMI	Fellow, American College of Medical Informatics
FACMPE	Fellow of the American College of Medical Practice Executives
FACP	Fellow of the American College of Physicians
FHAPI	Honorary Fellow, Association for Pathology Informatics

Appendix D
Evolution of Health Information
Technology Terms

1. National Alliance for Health Information Technology's (NAHIT) Key Health Information Technology Terms
http://healthit.hhs.gov

The ambiguity of meaning created by not having a shared understanding of key health IT terms (listed hereafter) could become an obstacle to progress in health IT adoption when questions about a term's definition and application complicate important policy expectations or directives, contractual matters, and product features. Differences in how a term is used can cause confusion and misunderstanding about what is being purchased, considered in proposed legislation, or included in current applicable policies and regulations.

To address these issues and to provide support for increased adoption of health IT, the Office of the National Coordinator for Health Information Technology (ONC) issued a contract to the National Alliance for Health Information Technology (NAHIT, also known as 'The Alliance') to reach consensus on definitions for the terms EMR, EHR, PHR, HIE, and RHIO. As discussions and public comments took place around the meanings of these terms, it was noted that dual interpretations of HIE existed, as both a process and an entity. As such, there arose a need to clarify the difference between the process of information exchange and the oversight and accountability functions necessary to support that process. To address this need, a sixth term, health information organization (HIO), was added and defined.

*(**Editor's note:** The consensus-based definitions below were developed by two NAHIT-led work groups, two public forums, two online public comment periods and are excerpted from Defining Key Health Information Technology Terms.)*

1.1. Electronic Medical Record (EMR)
An electronic record of health-related information on an individual that can be created, gathered, managed, and consulted by authorized clinicians and staff within one healthcare organization.

The EMR's structure as a store of electronic information capable of being searched, categorized, and analyzed makes it superior to the traditional paper chart for informing the care process. Nevertheless, proceeding from its historical basis as the digital version of a patient's chart, the EMR is a provider-focused view of the patient's health history. It comprises health-related information that is created by clinicians or that results from clinician orders and activity on behalf of a patient, such as diagnostic tests or prescriptions for medications. A main objective of an EMR is to improve the ability of a clinician to document observations and findings and to provide more informed treatment of persons in his or her care.

1.2. Electronic Health Record (EHR)

An electronic record of health-related information on an individual that conforms to nationally recognized interoperability standards and that can be created, managed, and consulted by authorized clinicians and staff across more than one healthcare organization.

An EHR is patient-focused in that it is not limited by what a single provider organization is able to accumulate on behalf of a patient under its care. Through the capabilities of interoperability, an EHR becomes an authorized means to access information from whatever sources have chronicled the healthcare experience of a patient over time. The boundaries of an EHR are built not around the organization documenting the information, but around the patient and his or her health-related information. Though it is patient-focused, it is managed and used primarily by authorized care providers, as well as by members of their staff who have a need to access the EHR to support the process of care.

1.3. Personal Health Record (PHR)

An electronic record of health-related information on an individual that conforms to nationally recognized interoperability standards and that can be drawn from multiple sources while being managed, shared, and controlled by the individual.

The most salient feature of the PHR, and the one that distinguishes it from the EMR and EHR, is that the information it contains is under the control of the individual. The concise definition above names the individual as the source of control, but that leaves room for others acting in the individual's interest—their agent or agents—to have control over access to the PHR. An agent may be expressly designated by the individual but not in all cases; examples of an agent acting for an individual include parents acting for children, or, in the later stages of life, children acting for parents.

1.4. Health Information Exchange (HIE)

The electronic movement of health-related information among organizations according to nationally recognized standards.

To act as the medium of interoperable exchange between electronic records and organizations, HIE must itself meet nationally recognized interoperability standards. In addition, other classes of standards enabling the flow of information safely, consistently, accurately and securely must be part of the requirements for HIE. Interoperability, security and other standards required for HIE are in various stages of being developed and recognized by the US Department of Health & Human Services. The definition of HIE includes readiness to use these developing information exchange standards; these standards for interoperability and information exchange, used consistently in HIE, will contribute to the foundation of what will become a Nationwide Health Information Network (NHIN).

1.5. Health Information Organization (HIO)
An organization that oversees and governs the exchange of health-related information among organizations according to nationally recognized standards.

The purpose of an HIO is to perform oversight and governance functions for HIE. Oversight functions of an HIO may include, but are not limited to:

- Facilitation of operations associated with the movement of information—assuring that hardware, software, protocols, standards, stakeholders and services supporting the interoperable exchange of health-related information are available and engaged.

- Fiduciary responsibility for the assets, accountability for abiding by regulatory requirements for handling personal health information, and adherence to standards enabling interoperable information exchange.

- Maintenance of information-sharing agreements, business associate agreements, or other such contracts.

- Adoption and maintenance of standards ensuring interoperability while protecting the confidentiality and security of the information.

- Making decisions regarding certain types of information for which no nationally recognized interoperability standard is available.

- Developing and sharing best practices among organizations.

1.6. Regional Health Information Organization (RHIO)
A health information organization that brings together healthcare stakeholders within a defined geographic area and governs health information exchange among them for the purpose of improving health and care in that community.

To be designated a RHIO, an entity needs to have certain core features. These attributes distinguish it from other organizations that do not or cannot execute the distinct purpose and responsibilities of a RHIO. An organization designated as a RHIO:

- Must involve data-sharing participants that are separate and distinct legal entities operating within a defined geographic area whose collaboration through the RHIO will cross organizational boundaries.

- Must intend to benefit the population in the community. This requires that stakeholders come from the defined geographic area and that the RHIO provides well-defined and transparent processes to facilitate the interoperable exchange of health information across the range of participating stakeholders.

- Must be inclusive and convene various types of stakeholders in the delineated geographic area who are vested in improving the health of the community.

- Can arrange for the provision of additional technical and operational services supporting its primary purpose. Such services may vary based on stakeholder needs and a range of environmental factors.

1. AAMSI
   American Association for Medical Systems and Informatics

   In 1989, AAMSI merged with the Symposium on Computer Applications in Medical Care (SCAMC) and the American College of Medical Informatics (ACMI) to form the American Medical Informatics Association (AMIA).[7]

2. AHCPR
   Agency for Health Care Policy Research
   (Now the Agency for Healthcare Research and Quality)

3. AHIC
   American Health Information Community
   (Dissolved in 2008)

   A federal advisory body chartered in 2005 to make recommendations to the Secretary of the US Department of Health & Human Services on how to accelerate the development and adoption of health information technology. AHIC was formed by the Secretary to help advance efforts to achieve President George W. Bush's goal for most Americans to have access to secure electronic health records by 2014. The final AHIC meeting was November 2008.[130]

5. Banyan VINES
   Virtual Integrated NEtwork Service

   A networking operating system that allows users of PC desktop operating systems, such as OS/2, Windows, DOS, and Macintosh, to share information and resources with each other and with host computing systems.[1]

6. Canon Group (The)

   A group of leading health informaticists who convened in the early 1990s and defined the need for a concept-oriented (ontology based) medical terminology.[38]

7. CHIM
   Center for Healthcare Information Management
   (Merged with HIMSS in 2001)

   To positively impact the industry through the promotion of healthcare information technology. By disseminating information, convening educational programming, and fostering a collaborative environment, CHIM members seek to bring a greater awareness and understanding among professionals on how information technology can be harnessed to improve the quality and cost effectiveness of healthcare.

8. CINAHL
   Cumulative Index to Nursing and Allied Health Literature

   Complete coverage of English-language nursing journals and publications from the National League for Nursing and the American Nurses' Association since

1937. The database covers nursing, biomedicine, health sciences librarianship, alternative/complementary medicine, consumer health and 17 allied health disciplines. Since 2006, EBSCO Publishing has owned and published CINAHL®.[223]

9. Clipper chip

   A data encryption chip used by the federal government in data communications equipment, such as computers, modems, fax machines, and phones for protection from hackers, intruders, and criminals.[1]

10. Clone

    A computer, software product, or device that works the same as another or better known product.[2]

11. Commission on Systemic Interoperability

    Authorized by the Medicare Modernization Act, the Commission held its first meeting on January 10, 2005. The Commission was formed to develop a strategy to make healthcare information instantly accessible at all times by consumers and their healthcare providers. It released its report and disbanded in October 2005.[7]

12. CoSTART
    Coding Symbols for a Thesaurus of Adverse Reaction Terms

    Developed by the US Food and Drug Administration (FDA) for the coding, filing and retrieving of post-marketing adverse reaction reports. CoSTART provides a method to deal with the variation in vocabulary used by those who submit adverse event reports to the FDA. Use of the dictionary allowed for standardization of adverse reaction reporting towards the FDA in a consistent way.[7]

13. CPRI
    Computer-based Patient Record Institute (CPRI)
    (Merged with HIMSS in 2002)

    A non-profit organization composed of members of groups such as nursing, medical records, dentistry, patients, and third-party payers whose goal is the development of the computerized patient record.[11]

14. CRT monitors
    Cathode ray tube monitors

    CRT is a technology used in traditional computer monitors and televisions. The image on a CRT display is created by firing electrons from the back to the phosphors located toward the front of the display. Once the electrons hit the phosphors, the electrons light up the screen. The color seen on the screen is produced by a blend of red, green, and blue light, often referred to as RGB.[151]

15. Cut

    To save information by highlighting the desired text or object from the page and placing it onto the clipboard.[1]

16. Data category

    A significant attribute of a data element or data set that may be used by a trust engine to determine what type of element is under discussion, such as physical contact information.[57]

17. DHCP
    Decentralized Hospital Computer System

    The earlier name of the Veterans Administration (VA) Clinical Information System, developed in the late 1970s and early 1980s by staff in local VA hospitals, over the objection of some of the Veterans Hospital Central (Washington, DC) administrators. Eventually, the DHCP system was ported into the Indian Health System and Department of Defense. In the late 1990s, the DHCP development was renamed the VistA system, as it acquired more graphical user interface (GUI) characteristics and deeper clinical content.[99]

18. Document imaging

    The process by which print and film documents are fed into a scanner and converted into electronic documents.[2]

19. DSSS

    Direct sequence spread spectrum. Also known as *direct sequence code division multiple access*. Allows a digital signal to resist interference, and also enables the original data to be recovered if data bits are damaged during transmission.[2]

20. Enterprise Electronic Health Record

    An application environment that is composed of the clinical data repository, clinical decision support, controlled medical vocabulary, order entry, computerized physician order entry, and clinical documentation applications. This environment supports the patient's electronic medical record across the continuum of care (e.g., across inpatient and outpatient environments) and is used by healthcare professionals to document, monitor, and manage healthcare delivery.[2] *See* **EHR**.

21. Floppy disk

    A floppy disk, or diskette, is a disk storage medium composed of a disk of thin and flexible magnetic storage medium, sealed in a rectangular plastic carrier lined with fabric that removes dust particles. Floppy disks are read and written by a floppy disk drive (FDD). Floppy disks, initially as 8-inch (200 mm) media and later in 5.25-inch (133 mm) and 3.5-inch (89 mm) sizes, were a ubiquitous form of data storage and exchange from the mid-1970s well into the first decade of the 21st century. [7]

22. GCPR framework
Government Computer-based Patient Record

A government computer-based patient record framework project of the Department of Defense, Department of Veterans Affairs, and Indian Health Service to build the infrastructure and standards to allow the sharing of information among existing systems to achieve a comprehensive life-long medical record.[151]

23. HCFA
Health Care Financing Administration
(Now the Centers for Medicare & Medicaid Services)

24. HISB
Healthcare Informatics Standards Board

American National Standards Institute (ANSI) Healthcare Informatics Standards Board (HISB) was an open, public forum for the voluntary coordination of healthcare informatics standards among all United States Standard Development Organizations (SDOs). Every major developer of healthcare informatics standards in the United States participated, including professional societies, trade associations, private companies, federal agencies, and others. The HISB mission was to facilitate, coordinate, harmonize, and promote the development and use of national and international healthcare informatics standards.[43]

As an ANSI organization, HISB coordinated the development of standards for exchange of healthcare information. The organization dissolved in 2005 with creation of the Healthcare Information Technology Standards Panel (HITSP) by the Office of the National Coordinator for Health Information Technology (ONCHIT).[151]

25. IDCOP
Idealized Design of the Clinical Office Practice

A collaborative initiative, sponsored by the Institute for Healthcare Improvement, aimed at comprehensive redesign of the office system. IDCOP designs, tests, and deploys new models of office-based practices, including e-communication practices, to improve performance.[107]

26. Information highway
The Internet. *See* **Information superhighway**.

27. Information superhighway
The Internet.

The information highway was a term used, especially in the 1990s, to describe the Internet. The official project was dubbed the National Information Infrastructure (NII) and went beyond the interconnectivity of just computers; the scope broadened to include all types of data transmissions between a plethora of places, people, and devices.[7] *See* **Internet**.

28. Mainframe computer server

    Industry term for a large computer, typically manufactured for commercial applications and other large-scale computing purposes. Historically, a mainframe is associated with centralized, rather than distributed, computing.[2]

29. Mainframe computer system

    A computing environment in which the main processing is done by a mainframe, and information is accessed via terminals or personal computers (PCs) linked to the host mainframe.[2]

30. MFM
    Modified frequency modulation

    A line code used by most floppy disk formats, notably by most CPM machines, as well as PCs running DOS.[7]

31. Midrange

    A computer platform or system that typically has less processing power than mainframe systems, but more power than workstations or microcomputers. A midrange is sometimes referred to as a *minicomputer*.[2]

32. MSAU
    Multiple station access unit

    A device to attach multiple network stations in a star topology in a token ring network, internally wired to connect the stations into a logical ring. The MAU contains relays to short nonoperating stations. Multiple MAUs can be connected into a larger ring through their ring in/ring out connectors.[7] Also known as a *media access unit*.

    A hub or concentrator that connects a group of computers ('nodes' in network terminology) to a token ring local area network.[42]

33. MSO
    Management service organization.

    A corporation owned by the system or network, or a physician's system or network joint venture, which provides management services to one or more medical group practices. As part of a full-service management agreement, the MSO purchases the tangible assets of the practices and leases them back, employs all non-physician staff, and provides all supplies, IT services, and administrative services for a fee.[2]

34. Multitasking

    Ability of an operating system to run multiple tasks concurrently. Windows NT and OS/2 are multitasking operating systems.[1]

35. NAPCI
    National Alliance for Primary Care Informatics

    I. To promote the creation of a national health information infrastructure (NHII) that identifies and supports the unique needs of primary care practitioners and provides incentives to primary care practitioners to participate in the NHII; **II.** To document and report on the use of informatics and information technology in primary care, and to promote primary care clinical research through the NHII in the most care quality and cost-efficient manner possible; **III.** To educate primary care providers in the use of informatics and information technology in the practice of primary care; **IV.** To facilitate work within NAPCI and between NAPCI and other organizations to present a unified coalition representing the interests of primary care in the NHII and promoting the NHII; **V.** To take part in, and sponsor meetings, publications, and other forums for the purpose of advancing the mission of NAPCI and its member organizations.

36. Networking application

    Type of networking application (i.e., browser, database management system, interface engine, network operating systems, or Web development tools).[2]

37. NIDSEC
    Nursing Information and Data Set Evaluation Center

    Develops and disseminates standards pertaining to information systems that support the documentation of nursing practice, and evaluates voluntarily submitted information systems against these standards.

38. ONCHIT
    Office of the National Coordinator for Health Information Technology[130]

    Created by Executive Order in 2004 and charged with developing and implementing a strategic plan to guide the nationwide implementation of health information technology (HIT) in the public and private healthcare sectors. Abbreviated as ONC beginning with the legislative mandate in the Health Information Technology for Economic and Clinical Health Act of 2009.

39. Order communication

    The interface from order entry applications to departmental systems that communicates the service needs for the department.[2]

40. Order entry

    A legacy HIS application that allows for entry of orders from multiple sites including nursing stations, selected ancillary departments, and other service areas; allows viewing of single and composite results for each patient order. This function creates billing records as a by-product of the order entry function.[2]

41. Palm operating system
    See **Palm OS**.

42. Palm OS
    Palm operating system

    Hand-held computer operating system from Palm, Inc., which provides a basic set of calendar, address book, and wireless access functions. Typing is done by either a mini-keyboard and stylus, or a graffiti style of handwritten shorthand.[1]

43. Paste

    To insert information from the clipboard. Information can be pasted multiple times. Many software programs allow for a shortcut from the keyboard by pressing and holding the control button or key and the 'V' button at the same time.[1]
    See **Cut**.

44. Personal system
    See **PS/2**.

45. Physician dashboard

    An application that allows physicians to designate the type of data they want to see and where they want to see it on the graphical user interface they use for accessing their patients' information. It allows physicians to design the display and interaction of the data they use to diagnose and treat patients. It is extremely flexible and can be modified by each individual doctor to suit his or her needs.[2]

46. Physician online directory

    A type of physician referral service that can be accessed from a computer, through a variety of online services.[1]

47. Plain text

    The original communication form, also called *clear text*, or *readable text*.[1]

48. Portland Pattern Repository

    Understood to be the first wiki (1995) and referred to as *Wiki* (with a capital 'W') or *WikiWikiWeb*.[154]

49. PS/2

Personal System 2.

Second generation series of IBM computers that used Micro Channel architecture.[1]

50. SCAMC

Symposium on Computer Applications in Medical Care

In 1989, SCAMC dissolved its separate corporate status to merge with the American Medical Informatics Association.[183]

51. SCAR

Society for Computer Applications in Radiology

In 2006, SCAR announced a name change to the Society for Imaging Informatics in Medicine (SIIM).[224]

52. Shared Environment

A computing environment in which a midrange or mainframe computer at a remote location provides the main information systems processing for several clients. Terminals are linked to the shared host computer.[2]

53. Shared service

An approach to computerization provided by service organizations that offer remote computer services with supporting software functions for the full range of hospital business and clinical applications.[2]

54. Stark plans

Hospital plans for providing ambulatory applications to affiliated physicians and/or clinics that comply with the new Stark relaxation laws. The physicians/clinics must still pay at least 15 percent of the cost of these application services.[2]

55. Thumb Drive

A thumb drive, also called a 'flash drive' or 'jump drive,' is a portable solid-state data-storage device. It is re-writeable and preserves information without a power supply. Thumb drives will fit into any USB port on a computer. They can also be 'hot swapped,' which means a user can plug the drive into a computer and will not have to restart it to access the thumb drive. The drives are quite small, about the size of a human thumb—hence, their name—and can safely be tossed into a pocket or purse without fear of damage.[170]

56. UHDDS

Uniform Hospital Discharge Data Set

Data collection to obtain uniform comparable discharge data on all inpatients.[151]

57. VMS

Virtual memory system. An operating system from Digital Equipment Corporation (DEC) that runs on its computers. VMS originated in 1979 as a new operating system for DEC's new VAX computer, the successor to DEC's PDP-11.[1]

58. XOR

A logic function, eXclusive that simulates the function of the logical operator XOR.

OR, in which the output is triggered when only A or B is true, but not if both are true.[7]

Appendix E
Electronic Health Record (EHR) Definitions

Editor's note: A number of definitions are currently in use for computerized auto-mated health/medical/personal records. This appendix includes the most commonly used definitions.

1. **Electronic health record.** A longitudinal electronic record of patient health information produced by encounters in one or more care settings. Included in this information are patient demographics, progress notes, problems, medications, vital signs, past medical history, immunizations, laboratory data, and radiology reports. The EHR automates and streamlines the clinician's workflow. The EHR has the ability to generate a complete record of a clinical patient encounter and support other care-related activities such as decision support, quality manage-ment, and outcomes reporting.[45]

2. **Electronic health record.** Electronically maintained information about an indi-vidual's lifetime health status and healthcare (across multiple episodes of care), in all pertinent clinical environments; replacing the paper medical record as the pri-mary record of care, meeting all clinical, legal and administrative requirements; and providing added value in supporting decisions about patient management.[1]

3. **Electronic health record.** A newer concept of an automated health record. The EHR concept begins by highlighting the comparative difficulty of ever achieving a true, longitudinal, completely paperless, interoperable complete patient record from birth to death. Components include clinical workstation systems, data entry systems, templates or forms, communication (wireless, hardwired, or Inter-net-enabled), speech recognition, transcription, security, Master Patient Index (MPI), order entry, results reporting, and decision support.[1]

4. **Electronic health record.** A medical record or any other information relating to the past, present, or future physical and mental health, or condition of a patient which resides in computers that capture, transmit, receive, store, retrieve, link, and manipulate multimedia data for the primary purpose of providing healthcare and health-related services. EHRs include patient demographics, progress notes, SOAP notes, problems, medications, vital signs, past medical history, immuniza-tions, laboratory data and radiology reports.[7]

5. **Electronic health record.** The current term used to refer to computerization of health record content and associated processes.[62]

6. **Electronic health record.** A term that may be treated synonymously with computer-based patient record and/or EHR; often used in the U.S. to refer to an EHR in a physician office setting or a computerized system of files (often scanned via a document imaging system) rather than individual data elements.[62]

7. **Electronic health record.** The ASTM workgroup concluded that E1384 offers the best definition for clinical encounter and adopted that definition to define the

scope for their effort. EHR is the primary repository for information from various sources; the structure of the EHR is receptive to the data that flow from other systems.[63]

8. **Electronic health record.** Also known as computerized patient records (CPR). EHRs allow for entry and storage of a wide variety of patient information in electronic format, and subsequent access to this information, by healthcare providers, patients, and other authorized users. In its fullest form, an EHR replaces the paper record, eliminating the need for filing and storage, as well as the risk and inconvenience of misplaced or otherwise inaccessible charts. Lesser versions of an EHR may require some paper to be retained (such as outside consults or hospital reports), but still allow for most clinical transactions to take place online, speeding transmission of information and reducing the risk of errors.[64]

9. **Electronic health record.** Literally defined, it is the accumulation of medical information concerning the patient.[65]

10. **Electronic medical record.** A computer-based patient medical record. An EMR facilitates access of patient data by clinical staff at any given location; accurate and complete claims processing by insurance companies; building automated checks for drug and allergy interactions; clinical notes; prescriptions; scheduling; and sending and viewing labs. The term has become expanded to include systems that keep track of other relevant medical information. The practice management system is the collected medical office functions that support and surround the EMR and relevant medical information.[63]

11. **Electronic medical record.** A generic term used to describe computer-based patient medical records. The term has become expanded to include systems that keep track of other relevant medical information.[64]

12. **Electronic health record.** A general term describing computer-based patient record systems. It is sometimes extended to include other functions such as computerized practitioner order entry (CPOE).[65]

13. **Electronic health record.** A repository of electronically maintained information about an individual's lifetime health status and healthcare, stored such that it can serve the multiple legitimate users of the record.[69]

14. **Electronic healthcare record.** Five levels of an electronic healthcare record can be distinguished:
    - The automated medical record is a paper-based record with some computer-generated documents.
    - The computerized medical record (CMR) makes the documents of level 1 electronically available.
    - The electronic medical record (EMR) restructures and optimizes the documents of the previous levels ensuring interoperability of all documentation systems.
    - The electronic patient record (EPR) is a patient-centered record with information from multiple institutions.

- The electronic health record (EHR) adds general health and disease-related information to the EPR.[70]

15. **Electronic medical record.** An electronic medical record encompasses:
    - A longitudinal collection of electronic health information for and about persons.
    - Immediate electronic access to person- and population-level information by authorized users.
    - Provision of knowledge and decision-support systems that enhance the quality, safety, and efficiency of patient care.
    - Support for efficient processes for healthcare delivery.[71]

16. **Electronic health record.** Provides each individual in Canada with a secure and private lifetime record of their key health history and care within the health system. The record is available electronically to authorized healthcare providers and the individual anywhere, anytime in support of high-quality care. The EHR is the central component that stores, maintains, and manages clinical information about patients/persons. The extent of the clinical information sustained by the EHR component may vary based namely on the presence or absence of domain repositories in any given jurisdiction.[74]

17. **Electronic patient record.** Electronic set of information about a single patient/person. An EPR system is a system specifically designed to provide patient/person records electronically. This is not necessarily restricted to a single clinical information system.[72]

18. **Patient care record.** A patient care record that is fully computerized. Also may be called an electronic patient record (EPR) or a computerized patient record (CPR). As envisioned by the CPRI-host this would be a lifetime healthcare record for an individual that would be accessible by authorized users including the patient anywhere in the country. It would also include decision support, contain clinical reminders and alerts, and provide links to factual knowledge bases.[11]

19. **Medical record.** Data source; data obtained from the records or documentation maintained on a patient in any healthcare setting (for example, hospital, home care, long-term care, practitioner office). Includes automated and paper medical record systems.[31]

20. **Computer-based patient record healthcare record.** Stored in an electronic format. This framework representing the main healthcare subsystems, their connections, rules, etc., is the basis for the development of information and communication systems.[73]

21. **Continuity of care record.** A patient health summary standard; a way to create flexible documents that contain the most relevant and timely core health information about a patient, and to send these electronically from one caregiver to another. The CCR contains various sections—such as patient demographics, insurance information, diagnosis and problem list, medications, allergies, and care plan—that represent a 'snapshot' of a patient's health data that can be useful, even lifesaving, if available when patients have their next clinical encounter.

CCR is designed to permit easy creation by a physician using an electronic health record (EHR) software program or electronic medical record (EMR) system at the end of an encounter.[61]

22. **Continuity of care record.** The continuity of care record (CCR) is an emerging standard for communicating patient information electronically among providers. The CCR is intended to provide a snapshot of essential patient information, rather than a complete patient record, that will enable a physician to understand a patient context and provide appropriate care. The format of the CCR allows it to be used universally to help bridge the gaps between EHR systems and improve portability of patient information.[74]

23. **Electronic health record for integrated care.** Repository of information regarding the health status of a subject of care, in computer processable form, stored and transmitted securely and accessible by multiple authorized users, having a standardized or commonly agreed logical information model that is independent of EHR systems and whose primary purpose is the support of continuing, efficient and quality integrated healthcare.[75]

24. **Electronic health record.** Basic generic form repository of information regarding the health status of a subject of care in computer processable form.[75]

25. **EHR system.** Set of components that form the mechanism by which electronic health records are created, used, stored and retrieved including people, data rules and procedures, processing and storage devices, and communication and support facilities.[75]

26. **Electronic health record.** An electronic longitudinal collection of personal health information, usually based on the individual, entered or accepted by healthcare providers, which can be distributed over a number of sites or aggregated at a particular source. The information is organized primarily to support continuing, efficient, and quality healthcare. The record is under control of the consumer and is stored and transmitted securely [ISO/TS 18308:2005].[76]

27. **Electronic health record system.** A system for recording, retrieving, and manipulating information in electronic health records [ISO/TC 215:2005]. Note: the EHR system provides functions only that directly relate to the health record. Other functions required to support clinical care delivery, such as order entry, e-prescribing, and scheduling, are provided by additional, complimentary systems collectively called *clinical information systems*.[76]

28. **Personal health record.** An electronic personal health record (ePHR) is a universally accessible, layperson comprehensible, lifelong tool for managing relevant health information, promoting health maintenance, and assisting with chronic disease management via an interactive, common data set of electronic health information and e-health tools. The e-PHR is owned, managed, and shared by the individual or his or her legal proxy(s) and must be secure to protect the privacy and confidentiality of the health information it contains. It is not a legal record unless so defined and is subject to various legal limitations.[45]

29. **The electronic health record.** A longitudinal electronic record of patient health information produced by encounters in one or more care settings. Included in this information are patient demographics, progress notes, problems, medications, vital signs, past medical history, immunizations, laboratory data, and radiology reports. The EHR automates and streamlines the clinician's workflow. The EHR has the ability to independently generate a complete record of a clinical patient encounter, as well as supporting other care-related activities such as decision support, quality management, and clinical reporting.[45]

30. **Personal health record.** Electronic application(s) through which individuals can maintain and manage their health information (and that of others for whom they are authorized) in a private, secure, and confidential environment.[130]

31. **Electronic medical record.** An electronic medical record is a medical record in digital format. Most EMR solutions also offer the opportunity to receive critical information—such as formulary or drug interaction checks—at the point of care. Using an EMR typically facilitates (1) access of patient data by clinical staff at any given location, (2) accurate and complete claims processing by insurance companies, (3) clinical note composition, (4) prescribing, (5) scheduling, and (6) sending orders to laboratories and receiving and viewing labs.[131]

32. **Personal health record.** A personal health record is the documentation of any form of patient information—including medical history, medicines, allergies, visit history, or vaccinations—that patients themselves may view, carry, amend, annotate, or maintain.[131]

References

1. Rognehaugh A, Rognehaugh R. (2001). *Healthcare IT Terms*. Chicago: HIMSS 2001.

2. HIMSS Analytics. 33 West Monroe, Suite 1700, Chicago, IL 60603. Available at: www.himssanalytics.com. Last accessed October 2012.

3. International Organization for Standardization (ISO).1, ch. de la Voie-Creuse CP 56 CH-1211 Geneva 20, Switzerland. Available at: www.iso.org.

4. RACGP: Royal Australian College of General Practitioners (RACGP) RACGP College House, 1 Palmerston Crescent South Melbourne Vic 3205.

5. University of Victoria (UVIC). Available at: www.uvic.ca. Last accessed October 2012.

6. *Guide to Nursing Informatics*. Chicago: HIMSS; 1996.

7. Wikipedia. www.wikipedia.org.

8. Infoway. Available at: www.infoway-inforoute.ca. Last accessed October 2012.

9. Behavioral Health Care Services (BHCS). Available online at: www.co.alameda.ca.us/board/mentalhealth/glossary.htm. Last accessed October 2012.

10. HIPAA Glossary. Available at: www.wedi.org. Last accessed October 2012.

11. Informatics & Nursing: Opportunities & Challenges. Web supplement; 2003. Available at: http://dlthede.net/Informatics/Informatics.html. Last accessed October 2012.

12. Microsoft. Available at: www.microsoft.com. Last accessed October 2012.

13. Coiera E. (2003). *Guide to Health Informatics, 2nd Ed.* Arnold, London. www.coiera.com/glossary.htm

14. Agency for Healthcare Research and Quality (AHRQ). Office of Communications and Knowledge Transfer. 540 Gaither Road, Suite 2000, Rockville, MD 20850. Available at: www.ahrq.gov. Last accessed October 2012.

15. CIGNA. Available at: www.cigna.com. Last accessed October 2012.

16. Health Level 7 (HL7). 3300 Washtenaw Avenue, Suite 227, Ann Arbor, MI 48104. Available at: www.hl7.org. Last accessed October 2012.

17. Global Information Grid. Available at: www.cnss.gov. Last accessed October 2012.

18. Department of Defense (DoD). Discovery Metadata Standard (DDMS), Version 1.2. June 2, 2003.

19. SNOMED. International Health Terminology Standards Development Organization (IHTSDO). Gammeltory 4, 1. 1457 Copenhagen K, Denmark. Available at: www.ihtsdo.org. Last accessed October 2012.

20. Military Health System Enterprise Architecture. Available at:www.tricare.osd. mil/Architecture.

21. US Government Accountability Office. Available at:http://www.gao.gov/ special.pubs/bprag/bprgloss.htm. Last accessed October 2012.

22. Oracle. Available at: www.orafaq.com. Last accessed October 2012.

23. Clinger-Cohen Act of 1996. Available at: www.cio.gov. Last accessed October 2012.

24. 2005 International Council of Nurses (ICN). Available at:www.icn.ch. Last accessed October 2012.

25. World Health Organization (WHO). Available at: www.who.org. Last accessed October 2012.

26. University of Iowa College for Nursing Centers. Available at: www.nursing. uiowa.edu; http://www.nursing.uiowa.edu/cncce/nursing-interventions-classification-overview. Last accessed October 2012.

27. Virginia Saba, EdD, Honorary PhD, RN, FAAN, FACMI, LL, Distinguished Scholar, Georgetown University. Available at: www.clinicalcareclassification. com; www.sabacare.com. Last accessed October 2012.

28. Christopher Chute, MD, DrPH, Professor and Chair Medical Informatics, Mayo Clinic College of Medicine. www.mayo.edu

29. The OMAHA System. Available at: www.omahasystem.org/systemo.htm. Last accessed October 2012.

30. Institute of Medicine (IOM). 500 Fifth Street NW, Washington, DC 20001. Available at: www.medterms.com. Last accessed October 2012.

31. Joint Commission (formerly Joint Commission on Accreditation of Healthcare Organizations). Available at: www.jointcommission.org. Last accessed October 2012.

32. Available at: www.merriam-webster.com. Last accessed October 2012.

33. World Wide Web Consortium (W3C) Portal to Glossaries. Available at: www.w3.org/Glossary. Last accessed October 2012.

34. International Engineering Consortium. Available at: www.iec.org. Last accessed October 2012.

35. Available at: www.answers.com. Last accessed October 2012.

36. Available at: www.bitpipe.com. Last accessed October 2012.

37. National Cancer Institute—*Cancer Biomedical Informatics Grid.* Available at: https://cabig.nci.nih.gov. Last accessed October 2012.

38. Canon Group. Available at: www.pubmedcentral.nih.gov/articlerender.fcgi?artid=116200. Last accessed October 2012.

39. ASTM. Available at: www.astm.org. Last accessed October 2012.

40. American Dental Association (ADA). Available at: www.ada.org. Last accessed October 2012.

41. Pearson Software Consulting. Available at: http://www.cpearson.com/excel/search.htm. Last accessed October 2012.

42. Available at: whatis.techtarget.com. Last accessed October 2012.

43. ANSI. American National Standards Institute. Available at: www.ansi.org. Last accessed October 2012.

44. United States Congress. Available at: www.house.gov. Last accessed October 2012.

45. Healthcare Information and Management Systems Society (HIMSS). Available at: www.himss.org. Last accessed October 2012.

46. CDC Centers for Disease Control. Available at: www.cdc.gov. Last accessed October 2012.

47. Gartner Group. www.gartner.com/it-glossary. Last accessed October 2012.

48. Healthcare Information Technology Standards Panel (HITSP). Available at: www.ansi.org; http://hitsp.org. Last accessed October 2012.

49. International Council of Nurses (ICN). Available at: www.icn.ch. Last accessed October 2012.

50. Logical Observation Identifiers Names and Codes (LOINC). Last accessed October 2012.

51. Lundy, K.S., & Bergamini, A. (2003). *Essentials of Nursing Informatics.* Jones & Bartlett Publishers: Sudbury, MA

52. American Nursing Association (ANA). Available at: www.nursingworld.org. Last accessed October 2012.

53. Mayo Clinic College of Medicine. Available at: www.mayo.edu. Last accessed October 2012.

54. National Council on Prescription Drug Programs (NCPDP). Available at: www.ncpdp.org. Last accessed October 2012.

55. ECRI (formerly Emergency Research Care Institute). Available at: www.ecri.org. Last accessed October 2012.

56. Integrating the Healthcare Enterprise. Available at: www.ihe.net. Last accessed October 2012.

57. National Institute for Standards Technology (NIST). Available at: www.nist.gov/healthcare/index.cfm. Last accessed October 2012.

58. Available at: www.webopedia.com. Last accessed October 2012.

59. Public Health Data Standards Consortium. Available at: www.phdsc.org. Last accessed October 2012.

60. National Security Council. Available at: www.whitehouse.gov/nsc. Last accessed October 2012.

61. Developed jointly by ASTM, the Massachusetts Medical Society (MMS), the Healthcare Information and Management Systems Society (HIMSS), the American Academy of Family Physicians (AAFP), the American Academy of Pediatrics (AAP), along with multiple healthcare IT vendors.

62. American Health Information Management Association (AHIMA). Available at: www.ahima.org. Last accessed October 2012.

63. The ASTM definition from E1384-02a Practice for Content and Structure of the Electronic Health Record (EHR) was adopted by the President's e-Government Consolidated Health Informatics Initiative (CHI).

64. Indian Health Service. Available at: www.ihs.gov. Last accessed October 2012.

65. Available at: www.hipaadvisory.com/action/patientconf.htm Last accessed October 2012.

68. ISO 14971:2007 Medical devices. Application of risk management to medical devices (terms only). Available at: www.iso.org. Last accessed October 2012.

69. Available at: www.cordis.lu/ist/ka1/administrations/publications/glossary.htm Last accessed October 2012.

70. Medical Records Institute.

71. Institutes of Medicine; 2003.

72. Available at: www.infoway-inforoute.ca. EHRS-Blueprint. Last accessed October 2012.

73. Available at: http://www.connectingforhealth.nhs.uk. Last accessed October 2012.

74. Available at: http://www.ehealthinfo.gov.au/glossary. Last accessed October 2012.

75. ISO/TR 20514 EHR Definition, Scope and Context (terms only). Available at: www.iso.org. Last accessed October 2012.

76. Available at: www.nehta.gov.au. Last accessed October 2012.

77. Available at: www.centerforhit.org/x174.xml. Last accessed October 2012.

78. H.R. 2458: the E-Government Act of 2002. Available at: http://www.ssa.gov/legislation/legis_bulletin_112202a.html Last accessed October 2012.

79. Available at: www.cchit.org. Last accessed October 2012.

80. Available at: www.ehealthinitiative.org. Last accessed October 2012.

81. Available at: www.himssehra.org. Last accessed October 2012.

82. Available at: www.ibm.com. Last accessed October 2012.

83. Available at: www.IEC.org. Last accessed October 2012.

84. Available at: http://healthit.hhs.gov/portal. Last accessed October 2012.

85. Available at: www.wedi.org. Last accessed October 2012.

86. CEN/ISSS e-Health Standardization Focus Group. Available at: www.who.int/classifications/terminology/prerequisites.pdf. Last accessed October 2012.

87. Miller, 2000; Hewlett-Packard, 2003. Available at: www.cancore.ca/semantic_and_syntactic_interoperability.html. Last accessed October 2012.

88. Object Management Group. Available at: www.omg.org. Last accessed October 2012.

89. Available at: www.cve.mitre.org/cwe. Last accessed October 2012.

90. Available at: www.linktionary.com. Last accessed October 2012.

91. Available at: www.oasis-open.org. Last accessed October 2012.

92. Available at:www.openclinical.org/docs/int/docs/gello.pdf. Last accessed October 2012.

93. ISO/TR 28380-1. IHE Global Standards Adoption - Part 1 The Process (terms only). Available at: www.iso.org. Last accessed October 2012.

94. ISO/TR 22221. Good Principles and practices for a clinical data warehouse (terms only). Available at: www.iso.org. Last accessed October 2012.

95. ISO/TS 22220. Identification of Subjects of Health Care (terms only). Available at: www.iso.org. Last accessed October 2012.

96. National Center for Patient Safety (NCPS). Available at: www.patientsafety.gov. Last accessed October 2012.

97. Department of Defense (DoD). Information Technology Security Certification and Accreditation Process (DITSCAP) definitions. Available at: www.csrc.nist.gov. Last accessed October 2012.

98. ISO/TS 17117 (revision). Criteria for the Categorization and Evaluation of Terminological Systems (terms only). Available at: www.iso.org. Last accessed October 2012.

99. Los Angeles County, Department of Public Health, Los Angeles, California.

100. Arnold S. (editor). (2008). *Guide to the Wireless Medical Practice: Finding the Right Connections for Healthcare.* Chicago: HIMSS

101. The Care Continuum Alliance. Available at: www.carecontinuumalliance.org. Last accessed October 2012.

102. Centers for Medicare & Medicaid Services (CMS). Available at: www.cms.gov. Last accessed October 2012.

103. National Committee on Vital and Health Statistics (NCVHS). Available at: www.ncvhs.hhs.gov. Last accessed October 2012.

104. The City University of New York. Available at: www.cuny.edu. Last accessed October 2012.

105. Kwantlen University College. Available at: www.kwantlen.bc.ca/home.html. Last accessed October 2012.

106. American College of Physicians. Available at: www.acponline.org. Last accessed October 2012.

107. iHealthBeat. Available at: www.ihealthbeat.org. Last accessed October 2012.

108. Rosenbloom ST, Miller RA, Johnson KB et al. (2008). A model for evaluating interface terminologies. *JAMIA.*15:1; 65-76.

109. Auto ID and Bar Code Task Force, HIMSS. 2007.

110. Richesson RL, Krischer J. (2007). Data standards in clinical research: Gaps, overlaps, challenges and future directions. *JAMIA.* 14:6;687-696.

111. Mulyar N, Van der Aalst, WMP, Peleg, M. (2007). A pattern-based analysis of clinical computer–interpretable guideline modeling languages. *JAMIA.*14:6; 781-797.

112. Van der Aalst WMP, Hofstede AHM, Russell N et al. Control Flow Patterns 2003, 2006. Available at: http://www.workflowpatterns.com/patterns/control. Last accessed October 2012.

113. Wieteck P. Available at: DOI: 10-111/j.1466-7657.2008.00639x. International Nursing Review, Vol. 55, Issue 3, September 2008. Last accessed October 2012.

114. Federal Identity Management. Available at: www.cio.gov/ficc/documents. Last accessed October 2012.

115. Available at: www.privacy.gov.au/materials. Last accessed October 2012.

116. ISO/IS #13606-1. Electronic health record communication - Part 1: Reference model (terms only). Available at: www.iso.org. Last accessed October 2012.

117. ISO/IS #21549-7. Patient Health Card Data Part 7 E-Prescription to Med Data (terms only). Available at: www.iso.org. Last accessed October 2012.

118. Available at: www.dhs.gov/index.shtm. Last accessed October 2012.

119. Beolchi L, Facchinetti S. (2003). *Telemedicine Glossary.* 5th Ed.

120. Tufts Health Care Institute. Available at: www.thci.org. Last accessed October 2012.

121. ISO/IS #17090-1. Public Key Infrastructure-1 Framework and Overview (terms only). Available at: www.iso.org. Last accessed October 2012.

122. ISO/TS #21298. Functional and Structural Roles (terms only). Available at: www.iso.org. Last accessed October 2012.

123. Health Care Improvement Project (HCI); US Agency for International Development (USAID). Available at: www.hciproject.org. Last accessed October 2012.

124. Information Security Management Guidelines for Telecommunications, based on ISO/IEC 27002. ITU-T Study Gp 17 TD 2318.

125. ISO/TS 22600-3. HealthCare Information Privilege Management & Access Control P-3 (terms only). Available at: www.iso.org. Last accessed October 2012.

126. ISO/IS #17115. Vocabulary for Terminological Systems (terms only). Available at: www.iso.org. Last accessed October 2012.

127. ISO/IS #22307. Financial services—Privacy impact assessment (under development) (terms only). Available at: www.iso.org. Last accessed October 2012.

128. Lumetra.

129. Available at: www.himssehra.org/ASP/index.asp. Last accessed October 2012.

130. US Health and Human Services. Available at: www.hhs.gov. Last accessed October 2012.

131. Available at: www.medicalrecords.com/mrcbase/emr/propractica-inc-streamline-md. Last accessed October 2012.

132. Care Coordination Work Group: MA Consortium for CSHCN - June 2, 2005; revised October 6, 2005.Available at: neserve.org. Last accessed October 2012.

133. Available at: www.treatment-now.com/resources/definitions. Last accessed October 2012.

134. American Academy of Pediatrics. Available at: www.medicalhomeinfo.org. Last accessed October 2012.

135. Deloitte LLP. Available at: www.deloitte.com. Last accessed October 2012.

136. European Telecommunications Standards Institute (ETSI). Available at: www.etsi.org. Last accessed October 2012.

137. Available at: www.txtgroup.com/newsletter/attachment/Athena_Paper.pdf. Last accessed October 2012.

138. Robert Wood Johnson Foundation. Available at: www.rwjf.org. Last accessed October 2012.

139. *Mosby's Medical Dictionary,* 8th Ed. (2009) St. Louis: Elsevier.

140. Available at: www.creativyst.com/Prod/Glossary. Last accessed October 2012.

141. Available at: www.ncbi.nlm.nih.gov/gquery/?term=glossary. Last accessed October 2012.

142. Available at: www.delos.info/files/pdf/events/2004_Sett_17/Patel.pdf. Last accessed October 2012.

143. Available at: www.mathsisfun.com/definitions/discrete-data.html. Last accessed October 2012.

144. Federal Health Architecture. Available at: www.healthit.hhs.gov/portal/server.pt?open=512&mode=2& cached=true&objID=1181. Last accessed October 2012.

145. Organization for Economic Co-operation and Development. Available at: www.oecd.org. Last accessed October 2012.

146. Available at: www.dbmi.columbia.edu. Last accessed October 2012.

147. Available at: www.techterms.com. Last accessed October 2012.

148. Microsoft Lexicon. Available at: www.cinepad.com/borg.htm. Last accessed October 2012.

149. Available at: www.cms.gov/Medicare/Quality-Initiatives-Patient-Assessment-Instruments/QualityImprovementOrgs/index.html?redirect=/QualityImprovementOrgs/03_HowtoBecomeaQIO.asp. Last accessed October 2012.

150. Available at: www.hqda.army.mil/acsim_ca/FAQS.ASPX. Last accessed October 2012.

151. Report on Uniform Data Standards for Patient Medical Record Information (2000). National Committee on Vital and Health Statistics (NCVHS). Available at: www.ncvhs.hhs.gov/hipaa000706.pdf. Last accessed October 2012.

152. Rosenberg W, Donald A (1995). Evidence-based medicine: An approach to clinical problem-solving. *BMJ.* 1995:310: 1122-26.

153. Huff SM, Carter JS. (2000). A characterization of healthcare terminology models, clinical templates, message models, and other kinds of clinical information models. AMIA Symp. 2000. Last accessed October 2012.

154. Academic Kids. Available at: academickids.com/encyclopedia. Last accessed October 2012.

155. Institute of Electrical and Electronics Engineers (IEEE). Available at: www.ieee.org. Last accessed October 2012.

156. Available at: www.techopedia.com. Last accessed October 2012.

157. Available at: www.linux.about.com. Last accessed October 2012.

158. Available at: www.newworldencyclopedia.org. Last accessed October 2012.

159. Data Management Association International (DAMA). *Dictionary of Data Management* 1st Ed. (2008).

160. ISO 18308:2011 Health informatics—Requirements for an electronic health record architecture. Available at: www.iso.org. Last accessed October 2012.

161. ISO/IEC 11179-1: 2004. Available at: www.iso.org. Last accessed October 2012.

162. ISO/IEC 11179-6:2005. Available at: www.iso.org. Last accessed October 2012.

163. PC Magazine Encyclopedia. Available at: www.pcmag.com. Last accessed October 2012.

164. Data Quality Department, Canadian Institute for Health Information. Available at: http://www.cihi.ca/CIHI-ext-portal/internet/EN/TabbedContent/ standards+and+data+submission/data+quality/cihi021513. Last accessed October 2012.

165. Canadian Institute for Health Information (CIHI). Available at: www.cihi.ca. Last accessed October 2012.

166. ISO 21667 (Health Indicator Framework). Available at: www.iso.org.

167. Information Technology Infrastructure Library (ITIL). Available at: www.itil-officialsite.com. Last accessed October 2012.

168. Infolific. Available at: infolific.com/search/VoIP. Last accessed October 2012.

169. MITRE. Available at: www.mitre.org. Last accessed October 2012.

170. Available at: www.wisegeek.com. Last accessed October 2012.

171. American Hospital Association. Available at: www.aha.org. Last accessed October 2012.

173. United States Health Information Knowledgebase. Available at: www.ushik. org. Last accessed October 2012.

174. ISO/PAS 22399:2007- Societal security - Guideline for incident preparedness and operational continuity management. Available at: www.iso.org.

175. ANSI/ASIS SPC.1-2009 Organizational Resilience: Security preparedness, and continuity management systems. Available at: www.ansi.org.

176. American Academy of Family Physicians. Available at: www.aafp.org. Last accessed October 2012.

177. Microstrategy Glossary of Terms Available at: http://www.microstrategy.com/ News/Glossary/Letter_d.htm er_d.htm. Last accessed October 2012.

178. Office of the National Coordinator for Health Information Technology. Available at: www.healthit.hhs.gov/portal/server.pt/community/healthit_hhs_gov_ onc/1200. Last accessed October 2012.

179. Available at: ori.dhhs.gov/education. Last accessed October 2012.

180. Available at: www.olympusconfocal.com/theory/resolutionintro.html. Last accessed October 2012.

181. Available at: www.isixsigma.com. Last accessed October 2012.

182. Available at: www.wiki.answers.com. Last accessed October 2012.

183. Available at: www.amia.org/applications-informatics/clinical-informatics. Last accessed October 2012.

184. Ohio Administrative Code: 5101:3 Division of Medical Assistance, Chapter 5101:3-1 General Provisions, 2007.

185. Special Libraries Associations. Available at: www.sla.org. Last accessed October 2012.

186. History of APACHE. Available at: www.salon.com. Last accessed October 2012.

187. Available at: www.technet.microsoft.com/en-us/library. Last accessed October 2012.

188. Available at: http://definitions.uslegal.com/a/ancillary-services. Last accessed October 2012.

189. Available at: http://medconditions.net/ancillary-information-system.html. Last accessed October 2012.

190. Available at: www.openehr.org. Last accessed October 2012.

191. National Committee for Quality Assurance. Available at: http://www.ncqa.org/tabid/631/Default.aspx. Last accessed October 2012.

192. TermWiki. Available at: www.termwiki.com/EN:application_entity_title_%28AE_title%29. Last accessed October 2012.

193. Encyclopedia.com Available at: www.encyclopedia.com. Last accessed October 2012.

194. Association for Automatic Identification and Mobility. Available at: www.aimglobal.org/technologies/card/optic al_cards.asp. Last accessed October 2012.

195. Google. Available at: www.google.com. Last accessed October 2012.

196. Success EHS. Available at: http://ehsmed.com/stimulus/body.cfm?id=158. Last accessed October 2012.

197. Medicine Net. Available at: www.medicinenet.com. Last accessed October 2012.

198. Providence Saint Joseph Medical Center. Available at: http://nursesl.me.associationcareernetwork.com. Last accessed October 2012.

199. University of Utah Available at: http://consumerhealthvocab.org. Last accessed October 2012.

200. Canadian. Health Outcomes for Better Information and Care. Available at: www2.cna-aiic.ca/c-hobic/about/default_e.aspx. Last accessed October 2012.

201. Intel Corporation. Available at: ftp://download.intel.com/museum/Moores_Law/Video-Transcripts/Excepts_A_Conversation_with_Gordon_Moore.pdf. Last accessed October 2012.

202. eHOW. Available at: www.ehow.com. Last accessed October 2012.

203. McGonigle D, Mastrain K. (2012). Nursing Informatics and the Foundation of Knowledge. *Jones and Bartlett Publishing: Boston, MA.*

204. American Nurses Association Nursing Informatics: *Scope and Standards of Practice* (2007). Silver Spring, MD, American Nurses Association.

205. Business Dictionary. Available at: www.businessdictionary.com. Last accessed October 2012.

206. Encyclopædia Britannica. Available at: www.britannica.com/EBchecked/topic/152168/data-compression. Last accessed October 2012.

207. Food and Drug Administration. Available at: http://www.fda.gov. Last accessed October 2012.

208. National Quality Forum. Available at: www.qualityforum.org. Last accessed October 2012.

209. Hospital Review. Available at: www.beckershospitalreview.com/cms-hhs/hhs-attempts-to-establish-unique-health-plan-identifiers-under-hipaa.html. Last accessed October 2012.

210. GS1. Available at: www.gs1ph.org/wcmqs/barcodes/AIDC. Last accessed October 2012.

211. National Highway Traffic Safety Administration. Available at: www.nhtsa.gov; http://www.nemsis.org/documents/NEMSISSurveillancePresentation_draft01312012.pdf. Last accessed October 2012.

212. ISO 14001:2004- Environmental Management. Available at: www.iso.org. Last accessed October 2012.

213. Institute for Healthcare Improvement. Available at: www.ihi.org/knowledge/Pages/Tools/SBARTechniqueforCommunicationASituationalBriefingModel.aspx. Last accessed October 2012.

214. Available at: http://dpc.senate.gov/healthreformbill/healthbill52.pdf. Last accessed October 2012.

215. How Stuff Works. Available at: http://computer.howstuffworks.com/question525.htm. Last accessed October 2012.

216. State of Tennessee Office of eHealth. Available at: http://tn.gov/ehealth. Last accessed October 2012.

217. Geisser S (1993). *Predictive Inference: An Introduction.* New York: Chapman & Hall.

218. The Serial ATA International Organization. Available at: http://www.serialata. org/technology/why_sata.asp. Last accessed October 2012.

219. Savenkov R (2008). *How to Become a Software Tester.* Roman Savenkov Consulting. P. 386. ISBN 978-0-615-23372-7. www.openisbn.com/download/ 615233724.pdf.

220. The Free Dictionary. Available at: http://encyclopedia2.thefreedictionary.com/ data+port. Last accessed October 2012.

221. ISO 9000:2000 - Quality Principles. Available at: www.iso.org Last accessed October 2012.

222. American Society for Quality. Available at: http://asq.org Last accessed October 2012.

223. EBSCO Publishing. Available at: www.ebscohost.com Last accessed October 2012.

224. Society for Imaging Informatics in Medicine. Available at: //siimweb.org Last accessed October 2012.

225. Federal Emergency Management Agency. Available at: www.fema.gov/ Last accessed October 2012.

226. KMWorld. Available at: www.kmworld.com Last accessed October 2012.

227. IT Law Wiki. Available at: //itlaw.wikia.com/wiki/Medical_Information_Bus Last accessed October 2012.

228. Kaiser Family Foundation. Available at: www.kff.org Last accessed October 2012.

229. National Committee on Vital and Health Statistics (NCVHS) Report on Uniform Data Standards for Patient Medical Record Information, July 6, 2000, pp. 21-22.

230. Institute of Electrical and Electronics Engineers. *IEEE Standard Computer Dictionary: A Compilation of IEEE Standard Computer Glossaries.* New York, NY: 1990.